SMALL JUSTICE

THE TRAGIC MURDER OF STEPHEN SMALL AND THE SHAMEFUL CONVICTION OF AN INNOCENT WOMAN

JIM RIDINGS

SMALL JUSTICE

THE TRAGIC MURDER OF STEPHEN SMALL
AND THE SHAMEFUL CONVICTION
OF AN INNOCENT WOMAN

Copyright © 2014 by Jim Ridings

Published by Side Show Books, PO Box 464, Herscher, IL 60941

First edition, June 1, 2014

ISBN: 978-0-615-99601-1

I want to thank my wife Janet, and my daughters and sons-in-law, Stephanie and Brandon Ferguson, and Laura and Dan Keller.

"I may not have all in life that I want, but all my needs are fulfilled. For that, I am grateful. Give thanks to God for all the blessings of this day, and for our lives which are in His care, and our souls which are in His keeping."

$28.00
ISBN 978-0-615-99601-1
52800>

9 780615 996011

Acknowledgements

Sources include trial transcripts and appeals briefs of Danny Edwards and Nancy Rish, in the Kankakee County courthouse; Kankakee Police Department files; Illinois State Police files; newspaper articles in the Kankakee *Daily Journal,* Kankakee *City News, Chicago Tribune, Washington Post* and *New York Times;* the Kankakee Public Library, a great source of local research; and interviews with numerous people.

Thanks to State Police Lt. Steve Lyddon for access to Illinois State Police files; Herscher Police Chief Rick Gilbert, Kankakee Police Chief Larry Regnier and Kankakee Police Investigations Commander Robin Passwater for access to Kankakee Police Department files; Kankakee Circuit Court Clerk Sandra Cianci and Deputy Clerk Amy Martin for access to trial transcripts and appeals briefs; attorneys Joshua Sachs and Michael Costello for access to appeals briefs; the Kankakee Public Library for access to *Daily Journal* newspaper stories on microfilm, and other research material; James Taylor Sr. for access to *City News* newspaper stories; Stacey Solano and Tom Shaer of the Illinois Department of Corrections for access to interviews in prison with Nancy Rish and Danny Edwards.

Primary interviews were with Danny Edwards, Nancy Rish, Lori Guimond, Lori Brault, Randy Irps, Beth Irps, Jack Karalevicz, Rick Gilbert, Ralph McClellan, Sherri Carr, John Michela, Mitch Levitt, Jeff Westerhoff, Genevieve Woodrich and Benjamin Rish. Additional information came from Maxine Shores, Kelly Klein, Bill Stark, Jeff Oetter, Linda Willibey, Alexia Chambers Helm, Ken McCabe, Carol Sperry, Carl Irps, Renee Dorsett, Bob Crawford, Greg Deuschle, Bob Schneider, Pat Hickey, Sherry Pasquinelli, Sherry Parbs-Offermann Lockwood, R. Craig Nafziger, Fred Morrissette, Pamela Tutt Sinclair, Jacalyn (Aratri) Wojtowicz and several others.

Thanks to Daniel and Laura Keller for their assistance. Thanks to William Gaines, Steven Becker and Margaret Byrne for their fine work. I also want to thank the four Bourbonnais and Kankakee Walgreens stores, and Walgreens managers Jeff Thompson, Bill Shaub, Matt Woyner and Mike Murray, for their support of local history.

About the Author

Jim Ridings was born in Joliet, Illinois. He earned a Bachelor of Science degree in Journalism from Southern Illinois University at Carbondale in 1976.

He was a reporter for *The Daily Times* in Ottawa and *The Beacon-News* in Aurora. He won more than a dozen awards for investigative reporting at both newspapers, from the Associated Press, United Press International, Copley Press, Illinois Press Association, Northern Illinois Newspaper Association, Aurora Lions Club, SDX Society of Professional Journalists and other organizations.

Jim Ridings was presented a Studs Terkel Humanities Service Award from the Illinois Humanities Council in 2006.

Ridings has written and published more than 20 books of local Illinois history. Four of his books have won awards from the Illinois State Historical Society: *County West: A Sesquicentennial History of Western Kankakee County* in 2004, *Cardiff: Ghost Town On the Prairie* in 2007, *Cardiff 2* in 2009, and *Greetings From Starved Rock* in 2012.

He also is the author of *Len Small: Governors And Gangsters* (2009); *Chicago To Springfield: Crime and Politics in the 1920s* (2010); *Wild Kankakee* (2012); *Kankakee County Confidential* (coming in 2015).

Jim and Janet Ridings live in Herscher, Illinois (Kankakee County), and have two beautiful daughters, Stephanie and Laura.

Cover photo:
Kankakee County
courthouse
(with the George Ryan
bench in front)
by Jim Ridings

Photo inside dust
jacket: by Stephanie
Ferguson, 2012

Photo this page:
author with Robert
Jordan, (WGN-TV,
Channel 9-Chicago),
2011, by Laura Keller

"Len Small: Governors and Gangsters is truly a comprehensively great contribution to Illinois historical literature. Thanks to Jim Ridings, an investigative reporter, Small's whole career is meticulously documented. Ridings shows no mercy, but also is scrupulously fair. The subject is long, long overdue, and from now on, every Illinois historian who refers to governors will be indebted to Jim Ridings. He has written a book that covers the subject of Len Small so completely that nothing more needs be said."

Legendary Chicago political commentator and WLS radio host Tom Roeser, October 15, 2009

"Ridings' book is the first complete biography of Gov. Small, and you really should go buy it. It's an absolute must-read. I just can't say enough good things about this book"

Rich Miller, Capitol Fax, June 3, 2010

"Len Small: Governors and Gangsters, praised by critics, has situated Ridings as a trailblazer among Chicago crime authors."

Arcadia Publications, December 2010

"Too many writers treat Chicago and Cook County as anomalies rather than as being part of the same fabric as the larger state. Bribery and vote fraud are not limited to the City of Big Shoulders. Ridings provides valuable context to his narrative by examining neglected regional and state newspapers other than relying upon the often cited back issues of the *Chicago Tribune* alone. The author deflates the mythology maintained in Kankakee, where the Small family continues to operate a chain of newspapers that treats the former governor as a local hero and humanitarian rather than as con artist and a swindler."

Chicago political columnist Daniel J. Kelley, book review of *Len Small: Governors & Gangsters,* October 26, 2009

"Every Illinois citizen and voter ought to read the biography as a civics lesson!"

Chicago political columnist Daniel J. Kelley, book review of *Chicago To Springfield: Crime & Politics in the 1920s,* January 7, 2011

"Jim Ridings takes us through the inner workings of the Len Small machine and makes us understand what made this infamous governor tick. Rather than just chastise Small, I can sort of understand why he did some of the things he did. Simply because he could get away with it. The author did an excellent job on his subject and kept me interested throughout this fine read. I shook my head in disbelief many times while reading about Small's gall and antics, but then I realized that things haven't changed at all. Today it's just kept more hush hush. Highly recommended in understanding the connection between the gangster and the politician."

Mario Gomes, founder of myalcaponemuseum.com, Aug. 22, 2009

Chapters

Introduction

Stephen B. Small died in one of the most horrific ways a person can die -- being buried alive.

The crime shocked and appalled the city of Kankakee, Illinois, and the entire nation in 1987.

It was the story of a wealthy man with a beautiful family who was kidnapped and held for a million dollars ransom. He was buried alive while the kidnapper awaited the payoff. But the plan went horribly wrong, and the victim suffocated to death in his underground coffin.

Danny Edwards and Nancy Rish were arrested, convicted and put away.

But that is not the entire story.

And the story does not end there.

Information from official files and from various individuals, which was not publicized or known at the time, shows there was a lot more to it than what was told.

There is no doubt about Danny Edwards' guilt.

However, new information, along with a more thorough examination of existing information, shows that Nancy Rish, the woman who has spent more than a quarter of a century in prison, has been telling the truth all along about not being involved.

Nancy Rish is innocent.

This book contains the only interviews Danny Edwards and Nancy Rish have given in prison. A lot of information that came from these interviews was not known at the time, because Danny Edwards was not cooperating with the police, and because the state was more interested in convicting Nancy Rish than in finding the truth.

This is not only the story about a gruesome and shocking crime, it also is the story of how an innocent woman was railroaded to prison by powerful people and a corrupt local political system.

Most people do not know much more about this case than the basics of the kidnapping, burial, arrest and convictions. The local newspaper added details in its coverage, but those details only supported the basics. The national media didn't do anything more that repeat a synopsis from the local newspaper. Only a *Chicago Tribune* series in 1993 and a Kankakee *City News* series in 1998 questioned the tactics and verdict in Nancy Rish's trial.

1

This book provides a lot more details and information that shows Nancy Rish is innocent and that her trial was a travesty.

Before the victim's body was recovered and before the suspects were arrested, the top guns in the state were called in to prosecute a case that already was a slam dunk. A first-year law student could have won a conviction of Danny Edwards. But the state also decided to go after Edwards' girlfriend. Why? Because Danny Edwards killed one of Kankakee's elite, and the local powers decided she also had to pay for his crime.

Nancy Rish was convicted on circumstantial events, false allegations and the weak argument that "she had to know" what Danny Edwards was planning because she lived with him.

The state had no case against Nancy Rish. But she was presumed guilty from the start. Her possible innocence was never a consideration.

The prosecutor said Danny Edwards made the phone call that got Stephen Small out of his house that night. Six months later at Nancy Rish's trial, the same prosecutor said it was Nancy Rish who made that phone call.

No evidence supported this. In fact, the evidence and the testimony refuted this.

It was just one of the falsehoods the state presented at Nancy Rish's trial.

In another example, the prosecutors' closing arguments to the jury claimed the store clerks testified that Nancy Rish bought the jug of distilled water that was found in the victim's box. The store clerks did not testify to that. The water in the box was tap water in an old milk jug. And no water or jug was introduced as an exhibit at the trial.

That is what passed for facts in convicting Nancy Rish.

Danny Edwards' fingerprints were on the box and other items, and soil from the burial site was on his shoes. No fingerprints, soil or hair samples from the crime matched Nancy Rish.

All the forensic evidence at the time proved that Nancy Rish was innocent.

The prosecutors said Nancy Rish was involved in every step of this crime. They said she was with Danny Edwards when he bought the materials for the box. That was not true, and every witness testified it was not true.

The state's case was more than just an argument. It was a deliberate falsehood. Without these falsehoods, the prosecution never would have gotten a conviction of Nancy Rish.

The fabrications and the theatrics of the prosecutors convinced a jury to believe an argument rather than the evidence, and the prosecutors were allowed to get away with it by a judge who said he had his mind made up before Nancy's trial started.

The state's case falls apart under closer examination. Unfortunately, the jury did not examine the facts. Their quick verdict proved that. The jury was enthralled by the performance of a prosecutor who was a trained actor, and who put on a display of theatrics that mesmerized jurors into accepting everything he said, whether or not it matched the testimony or the evidence that had been presented. The jury was so captivated, it all but gave him a standing ovation for his performance.

This is not a he said/she said tale of conflicting stories. Both Danny Edwards and Nancy Rish have been consistent all these years about his guilt and her innocence.

Whatever pressures or influences that were brought in this case were not always direct. Such things are unspoken in the city of Kankakee, a city that has been run a raft of crooked politicians since the day it was founded. The political bosses do not have to give every order that is carried out in their names. That is why every public defender and other attorney in Kankakee declined to defend Danny Edwards and Nancy Rish until lawyers were appointed.

Nancy Rish was charged on a theory of "murder by accountability," but she really was convicted of "guilt by association."

Nancy Rish got small justice and she got Small justice. If Danny Edwards had picked any other victim, his girlfriend never would have been prosecuted.

Danny Edwards never talked about the details of his crime -- until now. Danny Edwards and Nancy Rish have given their only in-depth interviews for this book.

This book gives a lot of background into Danny Edwards and Nancy Rish that had never been told. For instance, Danny Edwards is not the same man today. Instead of cocaine and crime, his life now centers on spirituality and salvation. He not only studies the Bible, he teaches it in prison and he writes essays. A few of them are printed here for the reader to judge. Some people may take issue with Edwards' biblical theory on the death of Stephen Small, but it is presented here as an insight into what he is thinking.

I hope the narrative is not too confusing. Danny Edwards' girlfriend was named Nancy, and Stephen's Small's wife was named Nancy. Nancy Rish's sister is Lori and her friend is Lori. That is not something that would happen in a story unless it was true.

The author does not have a stake in the guilt or the innocence of Danny Edwards or Nancy Rish. Neither of them approached me. I contacted both of them and was turned down several times before I somehow persuaded them to talk to me. I spoke to them and I weighed their stories as I proceeded into my investigation, and I went where the facts took me.

There were two major victims from this crime. A young husband and father died, simply because he was a very rich man. A young woman was sent to prison for life, simply because she lived with the wrong man.

The list of secondary victims who were deeply affected by this monstrous crime has gone on and on, for years and years.

Nancy Rish was convicted, even though there was no evidence presented in court that proved she was guilty or that she had prior knowledge of Edwards' plan, and even though not one witness testified that she was guilty or had prior knowledge of Edwards' plan.

It wasn't just that the system let an innocent woman down. The system actually conspired against an innocent woman because of the company she kept.

This book tells the incredible true story in detail for the first time.

The B. Harley Bradley House, built by Frank Lloyd Wright,
pictured in September 1987, as it was being renovated.
Illinois State Police file photo

Chapter 1
The Kidnapping

"Mrs. Small? We have your husband."
Danny Edwards to Nancy Small, September 2, 1987

Stephen Small was asleep in bed with his wife Nancy when the phone rang at 12:30 a.m., on Wednesday, September 2, 1987. Their 15-year-old son Ramsey answered the call.

The man on the phone identified himself as a Kankakee police officer. There had been a break-in at the Bradley House and the police wanted Mr. Small to come over. The boy asked the caller if it was important. The caller said yes, it was important.

The Bradley House is a historic house built by Frank Lloyd Wright in 1901 for the family of David Bradley, the farm implement manufacturer. The house is along the Kankakee River in the exclusive Riverview neighborhood. Stephen Small lived at 917 Cobb Boulevard in the same neighborhood, about a block from the Bradley House. His next door neighbor was Illinois Lt. Gov. George H. Ryan.

Ramsey came into his parents' bedroom, woke up his father and told him about the call. Stephen picked up the receiver, remarking to his wife, "Didn't the answering service get it?"

The caller told Mr. Small he was a Kankakee police officer. There was a break-in at the Bradley House and three intruders had been caught. The police needed Stephen to come down and secure the building, the caller said.

Stephen told his wife he needed to go over to see the police.

Stephen put on a red t-shirt, blue jeans and leather loafers. A sleepy Ramsey Small saw his father walk past his bedroom door and go down the back stairs, and he heard the garage door open.

The caller was not a Kankakee police officer. The caller was Danny Edwards, a local cocaine dealer and thug.

Small opened his garage door with a button inside the garage. Edwards was waiting when the garage door opened. He had a gun. He got into the car and he forced Small to drive out of town, to a remote area.

Edwards forced Small to make a tape recording with ransom demands and instructions. Small knelt on the cold sandy ground, a gun to his head, as he looked into his open grave while speaking his last words.

Edwards then forced Small into the large wooden box in the ground. He put the lid on the box, covered the box with sand and left.

Edwards called the Small family, telling them he had kidnapped

5

Stephen. He wanted a million dollars ransom or they would never see him again. Edwards said Stephen was buried in a box, with enough air for two days. He said he would call back with directions for leaving the ransom money.

The situation unraveled quickly for Danny Edwards. By the end of the day, the police had identified him as the kidnapper, and they were watching him.

And, unknown to the police or the kidnapper at that time, Stephen Small already was dead.

Danny Edwards had been planning the kidnapping for months. His plan started after his arrest on cocaine charges on January 23, 1987.

KAMEG agents -- Kankakee Area Metropolitan Drug Enforcement Group -- raided his house on Sand Bar Road in Aroma Park with a search warrant and seized $10,490 in cash on the kitchen counter, $318 on the dining room table, and 222 grams of cocaine worth $20,000 from a bedroom closet. They also found records of drug deals, with names of people who bought cocaine and who owed money, plus drug paraphernalia.

The police got the information about Edwards from a local man who had been arrested for selling drugs. The police squeezed him to get Danny Edwards. Then they squeezed Edwards to try to get to a bigger dealer.

Edwards was facing as much as 30 years in prison on his cocaine bust. But the police knew Edwards was not the big fish they wanted. They wanted to use him to catch major suppliers from Chicago. Ernie Richardson, a Bradley police officer and KAMEG agent, met with Edwards, his lawyer Gus Regas, State's Attorney William Herzog, and KAMEG Director John Moraitis on January 26. A deal was made. Edwards would get probation if he cooperated on three points: arrange for his drug supplier from Chicago to deliver a half kilo or more of cocaine, give the names of local people who bought cocaine and the amounts they bought, and take a polygraph examination naming the courthouse employee who was leaking information about investigations.

Edwards gave the police 18 names of his local customers and he said his big supplier from Chicago was Mitch Levitt. He said Levitt delivered a half kilo of cocaine to his Sand Bar Road house in Aroma Park on December 25, 1986, and he made another purchase from Levitt on January 9, 1987 at The Snuggery Lounge in Mount Prospect.

Edwards agreed to wear a wire to set up a drug buy with Levitt. Richardson went along, as Edwards met Levitt on February 9, 1987, inside The Snuggery Lounge.

Edwards was wired and the conversation was recorded. He tried to arrange a purchase of a kilo of cocaine, but no sale was made.

The attempt to trap Mitch Levitt failed. The police accused Edwards of tipping off Levitt. Edwards said it was the police who blew the operation by having Richardson come along.

Edwards got his probation, even after failing to bring down Mitch Levitt. State's Attorney William Herzog kept his promise of probation, even though the authorities believed Edwards didn't fulfill his part of the bargain.

And so, on April 10, 1987, Danny Edwards pleaded guilty only to possession of a controlled substance, cocaine. He was sentenced to four years probation. The deal was approved by Judge John Michela.

That deal cost Stephen Small his life.

Edwards knew the police were watching him, and he was afraid of getting busted again. Another arrest would void his probation, and that could mean 30 years.

Edwards was making a lot of money selling cocaine in Kankakee County. With that gone, he hatched a get-rich-quick scheme: he would kidnap a wealthy Kankakee man and hold him for a million dollar ransom. He chose Stephen B. Small as his victim.

Danny Edwards then spent months on a plan that seemed to have absolutely no thought behind it.

With his money and his cocaine supply gone, Danny Edwards needed a place to stay. He had been dating Nancy Rish for more than a year. They lived together in his house on Sand Bar Road for awhile. But that house was his place of business, where cocaine buyers came and went, so he set up Nancy and her son in a townhouse at 756 Stratford Drive East in Bourbonnais. He signed a one-year lease at $400 a month on December 1, 1986.

Edwards remained in the house on Sand Bar Road where he could conduct business. But now, in March 1987, he needed Nancy to take him in.

She did.

Danny started working part time for Jeff Westerhoff. He was Nancy's cousin and had known Danny for 10 years. Nancy helped Danny get the job.

Westerhoff was a self-employed carpenter. He used Danny perhaps one day a week, between February and July 1987, and not always every week. Danny didn't do much more than hand tools to Jeff and fetch things for him. Almost from the start of going to work for Jeff in February 1987, Danny began asking Jeff to help him build a box.

The box was for storing items at his brother's pool in Florida, Danny said. Danny needed help and he mentioned it to Jeff numerous times over the next several months. Finally, on June 1, 1987, after working half a day, Danny insisted they get the wood for the box.

Westerhoff went to Security Lumber in Bradley and bought two sheets of ¾" plywood, six 2x4s, two drill bits and a hinge. The bill was

7

charged to the account of Westerhoff's father. It came to $75.

Westerhoff put the material in his truck and took it to his parents' house. Edwards wanted to start building that day. That didn't happen. The wood sat in Westerhoff's basement for a month. Edwards finally came and got the wood and took it to his garage on Stratford Drive East.

Danny Edwards spent several weeks in July and August building the box in his garage. It was in plain sight of the Bourbonnais Police Department, located a short distance away across a field.

In mid-August, Edwards borrowed a saw from Westerhoff to cut a round hole in the side of the box. Westerhoff came over in the last week of August to get his saw and to pay a visit.

Westerhoff went in the garage and saw a big plywood box standing on its end. He remarked to Edwards, "'Boy, you finally got it done." Edwards replied, "Yeah, that is it." Westerhoff could see how proud Edwards was of the job he did.

Danny Edwards decided to put his kidnapping plan into action in late August.

Edwards put the big wooden box in his van on Sunday afternoon, August 30. He took it to a desolate area known as the Wichert sand hills in Pembroke Township, in the eastern part of Kankakee County.

Unlike the rich farm soil in most of Kankakee County, a large part of Pembroke Township is sandy, wooded, hilly and not worth much. The population is mostly African-American. It is one of the poorest townships in the United States, with few paved roads, no natural gas lines for heating, and entire neighborhoods without indoor plumbing. Township roads are so bad that some children miss school because the buses can't get down the roads. A number of times over the past several decades, Pembroke has been featured in local and national media as a sad example of abject poverty in a land of plenty. A number of prominent people, from Jesse Jackson to Oprah Winfrey and Barack Obama, have come here with camera crews and the empty promises that they would help these poor people. They never did. From the 1920s to today, this remote area of Kankakee County has been used by white gangsters and politicians to set up whorehouses and gambling joints out of the reach of the law. The sheriff of Kankakee County was removed from office in 1962 for his complicity in these operations.

Edwards buried the empty wooden box in a sand hill on that Sunday afternoon. It was an ideal place to go, without being seen.

Earlier on Sunday, Nancy Rish took her son Benjamin to his midget football game. That afternoon, Danny's best friend, Tracy Storm, stopped by the house, and later they went to Tracy's house on Sand Bar Road. It was the same house Danny had vacated earlier in the year. Danny spent most of the evening drinking at the Dam Tap with Tracy.

The next day, Monday, August 31, was just another day. Nancy got her son off to school. She left at 1:30 p.m. to help her friend, Julie Enright, clean her house. She took a break to get some wine and ice to celebrate the new house. Nancy left Julie's place at 4:40 p.m., and later went with Benjamin to get a movie at the Video 102 store.

Nancy stayed home and cleaned her house on Tuesday, September 1. She had a hair appointment with Anita Hamilton at 2 p.m. but, at Danny's insistence, she rescheduled the appointment for later that afternoon. Danny told Nancy he wanted to take her to Pembroke Township to show her some railroad tracks that he wanted her to remember. He said he wanted her to pick him up at that spot the next morning at 3 a.m. A strange request, Nancy thought, but she had come to know that Danny's strange habits and strange hours made for anything but a normal life.

Before they went to Pembroke, Nancy and Danny stopped at Englewood Electric. She sat in the van while he went in to get something for his brother's electrical company. Danny then drove her to a remote area and showed her the railroad tracks. Then they went home. At 5 p.m., Nancy dropped her son off at the Bourbonnais football field on Bethel Road, and then went to Anita Hamilton's house at 19 Emery Street in Bourbonnais to get her hair done. This took an hour and a half. Then she went home, had supper and helped her son with his homework. Nancy talked to her mother and to Julie Nanos on the phone that evening.

Danny left at 8 p.m. and came back not long after. Nancy noticed he was nervous and tense, and he was in and out of the house all evening.

The kidnapping went down a few hours later, just after midnight, in the early moments of Wednesday, September 2, 1987.

Danny told Nancy he needed to go out, and that she had to follow his van in her car, and then drop him off somewhere.

He got in his white van and she got in her blue Buick.

"Let's go, let's hit it!" he shouted, as they left their house.

Danny drove the van and parked it on the 800 block of South Greenwood Avenue, near George Ryan's house and just around the corner from Stephen Small's house.

Nancy Rish stopped her car in the street next to the van. Danny got out of the van, carrying a duffle bag. He put the bag in the trunk of Nancy's car. He got in Nancy's car and told her to drive a few blocks to the Phillips 66 gas station on River Street, across from Janeicke's root beer and hot dog stand.

Danny got out of the car and made a call at the pay phone at the gas station. Nancy stayed in the car. It was 12:30 a.m.

This was the call where Danny Edwards posed as a Kankakee police officer to lure Stephen Small from his house.

9

Danny got back in the car and had Nancy drive him to Cobb Park. She let him out and he told her to go home and pick him up at the designated spot by the railroad tracks in Pembroke Township at 3 a.m.

Nancy went home and watched a video she had rented, *Crocodile Dundee.* She left her apartment at 2:30 a.m., and picked up Danny by the railroad tracks a half hour later. She drove him back to his van on Greenwood Avenue. She drove the car home and he followed in his van.

By that time, Danny Edwards had committed his foul deed of kidnapping Stephen Small.

Small had gone out the back door of his house and through the greenhouse into the garage where Edwards was waiting for him. Edwards had taken a red motorcycle helmet from his duffle bag and put it on to disguise his face. He also had a gun in his bag.

Edwards got in the passenger side of the maroon Mercedes, pointed his gun, and told Small to drive. When they got out of town, Edwards stopped the car at a set of railroad tracks on a rural road between Waldron and Lowe roads, and he put Small in the trunk of the Mercedes.

Edwards drove the rest of the way, to a lonely country road.

When he got to the Wichert sand hills, Edwards took Small at gunpoint from the trunk and handcuffed him.

Edwards marched his victim a few yards to a grave site. A plywood box buried a few feet below ground was waiting. Edwards made Small kneel by the box.

Edwards had a tape recorder and a script. Edwards forced Small at gunpoint to read the dialogue into a tape recorder.

The tape was to be played over the telephone to Small's wife, asking for ransom money. Stephen had a hard time reading the script because he didn't have his glasses. Edwards whispered in his ear, prompting him.

Stephen Small was looking into his own open grave as he recorded his last words to his wife, telling her he loved her. He most likely was dead by the time it was played over the phone to her.

Edwards told Small he was holding him for a million dollars ransom and that he would be all right as long as the money was paid.

The box had a gallon of water and six candy bars -- two Hershey Almond bars, one Baby Ruth, one Snickers, one Butterfinger, one Three Musketeers, and one pack of Teaberry gum. The box also was outfitted with a light connected to two car batteries. A plastic pipe ran from the box to above ground. Edwards told Small it would provide enough air for two days.

The box was made of 3/4" plywood with 2x4" supports. It was six feet and one inch long by three feet and four inches wide, and two feet and three inches deep. Edwards caulked the seams to make it watertight. The top of the box was two feet below ground level. The 1-1/2" PVC pipe was in three sections and it went from the bottom of the box upwards, and then 26 feet northwest underground before coming to the surface.

Small was forced into the box at the point of a gun. Edwards cut a link in the handcuffs with a bolt cutter.

Edwards placed a plywood lid over the top of the box, and he shoveled the sandy soil on top to cover it.

And then Edwards went to the railroad tracks to wait for Nancy Rish.

After Danny and Nancy got home, Danny left the apartment by himself within a few minutes.

He had another call to make.

Danny drove his van to a pay phone at a Convenient Food Mart on Route 102 in Bourbonnais, and he made a second call to the Small house.

Nancy Small had gone back to sleep after her husband left at 12:30 a.m. She woke up at 3 a.m. and noticed her husband hadn't returned. She went back to sleep.

She was still sleeping when the phone rang at 3:30 a.m.

"Mrs. Small?"

"Yes."

"We have your husband."

Then Mrs. Small heard another voice. It sounded muffled, as if the man was speaking through a tunnel.

She didn't know it at the time, but the caller was Danny Edwards and the muffled voice was her husband's voice. She didn't recognize Stephen's voice and she didn't realize she was listening to a tape recording.

Her husband already was buried, but she didn't know it.

Stephen: "(inaudible) I, uh."

Danny: "Your wife, I want her name."

Stephen: "Nancy, this is, this is, umm, this, I, that, I thought this was a joke or something, but it's no joke. This is not some party or something at Yurgine's. I'm, there's somebody, and I've got handcuffs on, and I'm inside some, I guess a box."

Danny: "Grave"

Stephen: "Grave, he says. And it, it, uhh shit, it looks like its -- it's under a couple of feet of sand or something, like underground, and uhh -- I want you to get a million dollars. God only knows how you're going to do that, and I don't know who you're going to call, umm…"

Danny: "Hundreds and fifties, no consecutive serial numbers."

Stephen: "Fifties and hundred dollar bills, not consecutive serial numbers. I don't know who you can call. I really don't know who you can call because you can't, that, we don't, that money is all invested. God, I wish…"

Danny: "You got 48 hours of air."

Stephen: "There's, he says there's 48 hours of air for me. Umm…"

11

Stephen told his wife to call Cordy -- Cordell Overgaard, the family lawyer -- and he told her to call their stockbroker.

Stephen concluded the tape by telling his wife, "I love you. I really do, and the kids. That's all I know. This hurts like hell."

Then Danny Edwards got back on the phone and his voice sounded normal, not like the other man's voice in a tunnel.

Edwards said, "We have your husband."

He told Mrs. Small he wanted a million dollars, and he warned her to not call the police. He told her to get the money quickly, and if she didn't, he had nothing to lose, and he would never tell her where her husband was buried. Mrs. Small told him it would take a while to get that much money, and she told him to call back in the afternoon. He agreed and hung up.

Nancy Small called Stephen's sister, Sue Bergeron, and Sue's husband Jerry. She also called neighbor Ed Mortell, a Kankakee lawyer. Ed Mortell and Jerry Bergeron got to the house within a few minutes.

The police were called. Since this was a kidnapping, it became a federal matter, and the FBI was notified. Oren Lucas, an FBI agent for 22 years, lived in Kankakee. The FBI office in Springfield called him early that morning and told him there was a kidnapping for ransom in Kankakee.

Lucas met with Nancy Small and Jerry Bergeron at the Hardee's hamburger restaurant, on South Schuyler Avenue at River Street, at 7:30 a.m. Lucas chose Hardee's because he did not want to go to the Small house, in case the kidnappers were watching it.

The three went to Bergeron's insurance office down the street and discussed the procedures to be taken.

Nancy Small went home. FBI agents Joe Weatherall and Carl Quattrocchi were chosen to go inside the Small house because they were from outside Kankakee and wouldn't be recognized.

Lucas contacted Cordell Overgaard in Chicago to arrange the ransom money. Lucas also called the Kankakee police to arrange for a trap on Small's phone. Kankakee Detective Sgt. Robert Anderson called Illinois Bell at 6:20 a.m., and the trap was in place 14 minutes later.

Weatherall and Quattrocchi got to Small's house at 7 a.m. and hooked up a tape recorder to Nancy Small's telephone. When the phone rings, she was told, push the recording button and then pick up the receiver and answer it.

They were joined by FBI agent Dave Cook a couple of hours later. Their job was to interview Mrs. Small and to monitor incoming calls.

Overgaard quickly got the million dollars from the Federal Reserve Bank in Chicago and brought it to Kankakee.

The phone at the house rang numerous times during the day, and no one but Nancy Small answered it each time.

Morning dawned on Wednesday, September 2. Nancy Small spent the day in anguish and worry about her husband. Danny Edwards and Nancy Rish spent the day running errands.

Nancy Rish got her son off to school. Danny Edwards slept late. Before noon, Nancy called Pat's Groom & Clean to make an appointment for their dog, Porsche. Danny left in his van about 11 a.m. and came back a half hour later.

They left the dog at the groomers in Aroma Park at noon, and then Danny drove to a nearby horse ranch. He got out of the car and told Nancy to pick him up in an hour.

She drove to her sister Lori Guimond's house. Nancy bought a jewelry box from items Lori was preparing for a garage sale. They visited for an hour, then Nancy picked up Danny outside the horse ranch and they went home.

Danny and Nancy left their home again at 4:30 p.m. to pick up the dog. They went through Aroma Park, and Danny stopped at the Phillips 66 gas station at Lowe Road. Nancy sat in the car while Danny got out to make a call at the pay phone. It was just after 5 p.m.

The ransom call Nancy Small was expecting came at 5:03 p.m.
Nancy Small answered the call. "Hello, hello, hello?"
Danny Edwards: "Who is this?"
Mrs. Small: "This is Nancy Small. Who is this? Hello? Say again? Hello?"
Edwards: "How much?"
Mrs. Small: "How much? I...I...we have the money together, and it is on its way here."
Edwards: "I will call you back about midnight."
Mrs. Small: "I want to talk to my husband."
Edwards: "I can't do that."
Mrs. Small: "I want to talk to my husband."
Edwards: "I will call you at midnight."
And then Edwards hung up.

Stephen Small wasn't the only one in the family who was restoring a classic historic house in Kankakee's Riverview neighborhood. His aunt, Jean Alice Small, publisher of the Kankakee *Daily Journal,* had crews working on the Magruder-Deselm House at 691 S. Chicago Avenue. The house was built in 1891 by Henry Magruder, a mayor, banker and one of the founders of the village of North Kankakee. Arthur Deselm, a lawyer and judge, purchased it in 1923. The Queen Anne-style house is one of the most beautiful in Kankakee.

Danny Dobberphul was in charge of the painting crew. He fell at

13

11:20 a.m., Tuesday, September 1, and was hospitalized in serious condition. He died the next day.

Jean Alice came to her office at 9:45 a.m. on Wednesday and asked Managing Editor Marx Gibson if he heard any news about Dobberphul. Gibson took her into his office and told her that her nephew had been kidnapped.

Jean Alice stayed at the newspaper until mid-afternoon and then went home to lie down. She got a phone call around 4 p.m. from a woman who asked about Dobberphul's condition. The caller said her husband once was a very close friend of Dobberphul. Jean Alice told her that Dobberphul's condition was very serious and she suggested the woman get in touch with Dobberphul's boss.

Police later wondered if the caller was Nancy Rish. They decided it was not, after interviewing three other people who got similar calls from a woman inquiring about Dobberphul's condition. All the other people who received calls were friends of Dobberphul.

Jean Alice dozed off, only to be awakened by another call at about 5:40 p.m.

The call was from Danny Edwards, from a pay phone outside the Checker gas station at Armour Road and Route 45 in Bourbonnais. Jean Alice's phone was not tapped, so the police did not know where the call originated, and the call was not recorded.

The caller asked Jean Alice if she was a member of the Len Small family. When she said yes, the unidentified caller -- Danny Edwards -- went into a "tirade." Edwards told her to tell Nancy Small that she was "f...ing* up, and if she doesn't quit f...ing up, there is going to be the worst shootout tonight she has ever seen."

"I have got her husband. If she doesn't quit f...ing up, her husband is buried and he has got a two-day supply of food and water, and if she doesn't quit f...ing up, she is never going to find him."

"I know her phone is being tapped, and I know she has got the police there," Edwards continued. "If she doesn't quit f...ing up, I can take my bag and get out of here. She will never find her husband. I make my living this way, going to small towns and going after you rich people, so you call Nancy and tell her to quit f...ing up and get her shit together."

Mrs. Small said she responded, "in as a calm a voice as possible, 'Is there anything at all I could do to help?' It seemed that made him more angry than ever. This seemed to enrage him," she told police.

Edwards yelled, "If you f... up, then I am coming after you. I will kill your husband, too."

(The actual expletive word was said, but it will not be printed here)

14

Jean Alice's husband, Len H. Small, had been killed in an automobile accident seven years earlier.

Mrs. Small described the caller as a white male, in his 30s, "pathological, enraged, frightened, hyper, terrified," and he spoke in a "staccato, fast voice."

Edwards hung up. Jean Alice immediately called Nancy Small, but when she started to give her the message, it was just too difficult. After a while, she asked if there was anyone else there from the family, and Nancy handed the phone to Jerry.

Nancy Small: "Hello?"

Jean Alice: "Nancy?"

Nancy Small: "Oh yes."

Jean Alice: "I just had a call."

Nancy Small: "You did?"

Jean Alice: "Yes, and he said -- I don't know, except that he said if you f.... up and that if -- he knows your phone is tapped and that if -- is anybody there?"

Nancy Small: "Yes."

Jean Alice: "Is there anybody I know?"

Nancy Small: "Yes. Jerry is here and Reva is here."

Jean Alice: "Is Cordy there?"

Nancy Small: "No. Cordy is at Sue's."

Jean Alice: "You want to hear this?"

Nancy Small: "Do you want to tell Jerry what he said?"

Jean Alice: "Yeah."

Nancy Small: "OK. Jerry, this is Jean Alice, and she just had a phone call."

Jerry Bergeron: "Hello?"

Jean Alice: "Jerry?"

Jerry Bergeron: "Yes."

Jean Alice: "I just had a phone call. He says he knows your phone is tapped."

Jerry Bergeron: "He knows what?"

Jean Alice: "That her phone is tapped and that if she f.... up and that if she sees -- if he sees the police there today, there is going to be a shoot out and she will never know where her husband is."

Jerry Bergeron: "OK."

Jean Alice: "And, oh shit, I don't want to tell you what he said."

Jerry Bergeron: "Jean Alice, tell us what he said."

Jean Alice: "He said -- I think he said he is buried in the ground. That he has air. Have you heard that?"

Jerry Bergeron: "Yes."

Jean Alice: "And that he does this for a living."

15

Jerry Bergeron: "That he -- the guy who called does this for a living?"

Jean Alice: "Yes. And that, that he -- we people who live in small towns and have a lot of money think we can just get away with it. But if she continues to f... up, that he is just going to pack up and go and she will never know where he is."

Jerry Bergeron: "All right. What time did he call?"

Jean Alice: "Just a second."

Jerry Bergeron: "I beg your pardon."

Jean Alice: "Just a second. Now."

Jerry Bergeron: "Do you know what time he called?"

Jean Alice: "Yes. Well, yeah. Yes. Just three minutes ago."

Jerry Bergeron: "About three minutes ago?"

Jean Alice: "Now, just a minute. I called you. I didn't know if I had the right number or not. I was too rattled and so, now, are you in touch with the police?"

Jerry Bergeron: "Yeah. Yes. A gentleman would like to talk to you."

Jean Alice: "What gentleman?"

Jerry Bergeron: "The gentleman would like to talk to you. Hang on, Jean Alice, just a minute."

Nancy Small: "Hello?"

Jean Alice: "Nancy?"

Nancy Small: "Yeah."

Jean Alice: "This is Jean Alice. I thought of something I forgot to tell him."

Nancy Small: "OK. I will let you talk to him. He is right here."

After making the 5:03 p.m. call, Danny and Nancy went home.

Danny told Nancy to get a babysitter for Benjamin. Tell the kid we're going to the movies, Danny said, because he will want to know why he's getting a babysitter on a school night. Nancy took Benjamin to his Grandma Rish's house at 8:30 p.m.

Instead of taking Nancy to the movies, Danny said he was going out. Danny's behavior had been exceptionally strange in recent weeks. He frequently was going out without telling Nancy where he was going. She suspected that he was seeing other women.

Danny didn't ease Nancy's suspicions at all. His explanations were vague and mysterious. He told her now, as he had told her several times during the previous several weeks, that she did not want to know any details of what he was doing. However, this time he added, "Don't worry, after tonight this will be it. You don't have to worry about nothing else. It's gonna be over."

At first, he told Nancy he wanted her to drop him off somewhere. Then he changed his mind.

16

"I've been thinking more about this," Danny said. "I think it'd be too dangerous."

"What do you mean, too dangerous?" Nancy asked.

"I don't want you there tonight. I think it'd be too dangerous."

Danny started to tell Nancy that he was going to take her bicycle to be repaired. She could drop him and the bicycle off somewhere and then she could go home.

Nancy said she wanted to go along. She wanted to see where he was going.

Danny said he was taking the bicycle to his friend Jack's repair shop, between St. Anne and Aroma Park. She could come along.

Danny put the bicycle in the trunk of Nancy's car at 10:30 p.m. They left a half hour later. Nancy drove to Aroma Park toward the Precision Repair shop Danny previously had pointed out.

At 11:28 p.m., they stopped in Aroma Park so Danny could make another phone call. Danny told her he was calling Jack to see if he was home.

The FBI had a trap on Nancy Small's home phone. A trap doesn't tape-record the conversation, it only tells the number where the call originated. There was no Caller-ID in those days. Anyone who wished to remain anonymous could make a call without being detected, unless the authorities placed a trap on incoming calls.

The FBI knew at once the 5:03 p.m. ransom call came from the Phillips 66 gas station in Aroma Park. FBI agents and Kankakee police went to Aroma Park in unmarked cars to stake out the area.

FBI agents Michael Evans and David Cook tried to remain inconspicuous, which was not easy, because Aroma Park was a tiny village of 690 people. It isn't much more than that today.

Today, pay phones have all but disappeared because most people carry cell phones. But in 1987, before the age of cell phones, pay phones were everywhere. Aroma Park was so small that there were just three pay phones in the town. Each one was being watched by the police -- the phone at the Phillips 66 gas station, the one at Convenient Food Mart and the one outside the B&G Sunoco gas station and bait shop.

It was at 11:28 p.m. when Danny Edwards made his next ransom call to the Small house.

The police radio dispatcher notified the police cars that a call was coming in to Small's house. "OK, we have a telephone call in progress."

Evans and Cook were parked in the Convenient Food Mart lot. They could observe the phones at Phillips 66 and at Convenient, but the phone at the gas station and bait shop wasn't in view. So they knew the call must be coming from outside the bait shop at Bridge and Front streets. They drove there and saw a white male standing at the phone. A car was parked nearby, with a white female with blonde hair inside. The blue Buick's license plate number was SZG 507.

The license plate number was registered to Nancy Rish.

One of the cops doing surveillance in Aroma Park was Ernie Richardson, and when the check on the license plate revealed the owner, he recognized the name from his previous encounter with Danny Edwards.

Evans and Cook drove past the bait shop, trying not to attract attention.

The man at the phone booth, Danny Edwards, got in the car. Nancy drove away, making a U-turn on Front Street. She turned north on Bridge Street, then east on Third Street and out of Aroma Park. Police followed the car until it was out of town.

FBI agent Oren Lucas was with Illinois State Police Sgt. David Buhrmester on surveillance on Lowe Road in Aroma Park on Wednesday night. They saw 32 cars that night. They also saw the blue Buick with license plate SZG 507. The car's trunk was partially open. They noticed a bicycle was sticking out of the trunk.

But the blue Buick was of no particular significance to them because they did not get the police radio message that a call was being made from Aroma Park to the Small residence at that moment.

Sgt. William Willis later said the police didn't move to make an arrest because they didn't know if there were more kidnappers involved, and they didn't want to risk the life of Stephen Small if he was still alive.

"We kept a loose surveillance on them at that time," Willis later said. "My instructions were, Don't burn it. Don't get them all hot. We've made an I.D. now. Our main objective is to get Stephen Small back alive."

The officers fell back to surveillance as Edwards and Rish drove out of town.

The 11:28 p.m. ransom call was a disaster for Danny Edwards. Nothing went right for him. Edwards played the message over the phone from a cheap tape recorder. It was the recorded voice of Stephen Small, giving directions where to drop the ransom money.

Stephen Small was buried underground at this point. Edwards used the tape he forced Small to make. It was Edwards' way to get Mrs. Small to hear her husband's voice and believe he was still alive.

But the machine did not work properly, and Edwards had to rewind and start over several times. The quality of the tape was so poor that Mrs. Small did not know it was her husband's voice giving the directions.

Mrs. Small: "Hello, hello?"

Stephen: "Take 17 east to Route 1."

Mrs. Small: "Wait. Wait. I can't hear. I can't hear."

Stephen: "Just past…"

Mrs. Small: "Wait. Wait. I have to talk to my husband."

Stephen: "Just past…"

Mrs. Small: "I have to talk to my husband."

Stephen: "Just past the -- drop off the ransom…"

Mrs. Small: "Just a minute. I have to talk to my husband."

Stephen: "Route 17 east to Route 1…"

Mrs. Small: "Wait a minute."

Stephen: "St. Anne. Just past."

Edwards: "DeVries."

Stephen: "DeVries vegetable farm."

Mrs. Small: "I can't hear."

Stephen: "Take a left, which is by one of those signs, those green signs south."

Mrs. Small: "Wait. Wait. Slow down. I am trying to write this."

Stephen: "There is a sign on the side of the road, and you take this road until you come to railroad tracks. Leave the money on the tracks and leave. Drop off the ransom money. She is going to take Route 17 east to Route 1, going toward St. Anne. Just past the DeVries vegetable farm, you are to take a left which is down -- there are those signs you know, like those green signs, south 300 east this says, you see by the side of the road, and you take this road until you come to railroad tracks. Leave the money on the tracks and leave. I will need three to four hours to check the money. I guess he needs some time to check out the money. If everything checks out OK then, mail you a map to find me."

Mrs. Small: "I did not get all of it. I can't follow these directions. I need -- I need -- I need clearer directions. It is -- it is something about -- wait. I take Route 17 east, is that correct?"

Edwards: "Umm-hmm."

Mrs. Small: "Route 17 east."

Edwards: "Umm-hmm."

Mrs. Small: "To Route 1."

Edwards: "Umm-hmm."

Mrs. Small: "To St. Anne."

Edwards: "Towards."

Mrs. Small: "To what?"

Edwards: "Towards."

Mrs. Small: "Cords?"

Edwards: "Towards St. Anne."

Mrs. Small: "Oh, towards. Towards St. Anne."

Edwards: "Hurry up."

Mrs. Small: "Wait. 17 east to Route 1 towards St. Anne. And then, just Dutchball Farm, and then something about a green sign. Is that correct?"

Edwards: "Umm-hmm."

Mrs. Small: "Wait a minute. A green sign, and at the green sign -- I have lost it. I don't know. Just past Dutchball Farms, and I turn at a green sign. Do I turn right or left?"

Mrs. Small later said she could hear another voice in the background, swearing. The tape began running more smoothly and only then did she realize it was Stephen's voice. "Until then, I'd been asking to speak to my husband, and I realized it was his voice," she later told police. But at that time she still did not know the voice was on tape.

Stephen: "You take this road (cough) -- ssh -- drop off the ransom money. She is to go take Route 17 east to Route 1, going to St. Anne, just past..."

Edwards: "DeVries."

Stephen: "DeVries Vegetable Farm. You're to take a left, which is, now there are those signs, you know, it's like green signs. South 300 east. There's a sign, you see, to railroad tracks. Leave the money on the tracks and leave. I'll need three to four hours to check out the money. I guess he's saying he needs time to check out the money. If everything checks out, OK, mail you a map to find me."

Stephen: "Want to hear the answer on this. I don't know. You know, I know there's no money there."

Edwards: "Tell her to find it."

Stephen: "He says find it."

Edwards: (inaudible).

Stephen: "I think he's, he's very serious."

Edwards: "(inaudible) done it. I ain't going this far for nothing."

Stephen: "Damn. OK, I don't know. It, it, it, God damn."

Edwards: "If she pays the money, you'll be set free. You didn't see my face. I got nothing against you."

Stephen: "OK."

Edwards: "But if she don't, you're dead. I want to get that through your head right now."

Stephen: "OK."

Edwards: "And I ain't coming back to dig you back up. You got two days of air and that's it. And it's going to get real stuffy in here."

If that call went badly for Danny Edwards, the next call went badly for the FBI.

Edwards spotted the unmarked police cars in Aroma Park while he was making his 11:28 p.m. call. He started to panic as he and Nancy Rish drove away.

Nancy thought she and Danny were headed home. Instead, Danny

20

had Nancy stop the car at a Marathon gas station in a K-Mart plaza at 2225 E. Court Street in Kankakee. He had her pull up near another pay phone.

She thought the call he just made in Aroma Park was to Jack. She asked, "Who do you need to call now?"

"Mind you own business," Danny snapped. "It has nothing to do with you."

At the same time, FBI agents at the Small house rewound the tape to play back the 11:28 p.m. call.

There were some words they could not make out, and they wanted to write down the confusing instructions.

While they were doing this, Danny Edwards made another call to the Small house, at 11:46 p.m.

The FBI could not record this conversation because they were listening to the tape of the previous call. To activate the tape recorder would mean putting the tape back in the recorder and erasing the previous call. They did not have a backup cassette tape.

And so, this call was not recorded.

Danny Edwards ranted at Nancy Small over the phone. He shouted, "You f....d up!" about ten times. "You called the police!"

Mrs. Small: "No, I didn't."

Edwards: "Yes, you did!"

Edwards kept saying, "You f....d up," over and over. Mrs. Small told him she had the money and she was going to leave right then.

"No, you're not," Edwards said.

Edwards said he wouldn't be there to get the money, and that they'd try again tomorrow night. He hung up.

Chapter 2
Stalking the Kidnapper

" I saw the cops staking out the place. I knew it was over."
Danny Edwards, August 8, 2013

The ransom call at 5:03 p.m. was traced to the Aroma Park pay phone. The police decided to stake out the public telephones in Aroma Park in case the kidnapper was stupid enough to make his next call from the same place.

He was that stupid. And the police were waiting when Danny Edwards returned to make another call at 11:28 p.m.

Edwards spotted the police when he made the 11:28 p.m. call.

He knew at that point that they had him.

As soon as the police ran a computer check on the license plate and knew the identities of Edwards and Rish, other police units were conducting surveillance of the house on Stratford Drive East before they even got home.

"He's driving out of town, and we already know who he is and where he lives," Sgt. William Willis later said.

As Nancy Rish drove the car from Aroma Park, Edwards panicked. He tossed the tape recorder and the cassette tape out the window along the way. Danny told Nancy to pull over. He took a duffle bag from the back seat and hid it among some evergreen trees. Then they drove to Kankakee and stopped at a Marathon gas station so Danny could make the 11:46 p.m. call from a pay phone.

Surveillance was set up outside the townhouse at 756 Stratford Drive East in Bourbonnais by 1 a.m., on Thursday, September 3. Ronald Tjarks, a special agent with the Illinois State Police Division of Criminal Investigation, and FBI Special Agent Thomas Bonness, were observing the townhouse in one unmarked car. State Trooper John Russell and Kankakee Police Sgt. Maurice Meitzner were in another unmarked car.

They saw Edwards' 1978 GMC white van, license number 563478B, parked there when they arrived.

At 1:20 a.m., the two-door blue 1983 Buick Skylark pulled up and Edwards and Rish got out. The car trunk was partially open. Edwards and Rish went inside. Edwards came out by himself ten minutes later. He took a bicycle from the trunk and put it in the garage.

Edwards then drove his van to the Kroger's supermarket a short distance away on Route 45. Tjarks and Bonness followed. Edwards was there for about two minutes, and then he got back in the van and drove to the Checker gas station at Route 45 and Armour Road. He briefly stopped at a pay phone there and then drove back.

Edwards later said he went to the gas station to pretend to make a call, just to see if police were following him. Edwards had seen the unmarked police cars around Aroma Park when he made the 11:28 p.m. call, and he knew they were on to him.

Edwards drove close to home and parked near where Tjarks and Bonness were parked. Edwards walked into an open field area between the two apartment complexes and got his dog. He got back in his van and drove home.

He spent part of the night peeking out his windows, looking to see if he was being watched.

The surveillance was quiet until Nancy Rish left the house at 7:25 a.m. on Thursday in her car. Edwards left at the same time in his van.

Russell and Meitzner followed Rish, while Tjarks and Bonness followed Edwards.

Rish drove to her ex-husband's house at 1321 Franklin Street in Bradley. A few minutes later, she came out with her son. The police followed as she drove the boy to LeVasseur Elementary School. Then she drove home. Russell and Meitzner went back to surveillance in a parking lot across from Stratford Drive, in the Bourbonnais K-Mart plaza.

Edwards drove nowhere in particular. His motive was to see if that car would follow him. It did.

Edwards drove to Armour Road and turned into a subdivision. He drove down a dead end street and turned around, driving back toward the FBI agents' car. The agents pulled their car into private drive, backed out, and continued to follow. Edwards pulled onto another dead end street. Tjarks pulled over and waited for Edwards to make the same maneuver. He did. On Armour Road, Edwards crossed the bridge over Interstate 57, drove into another subdivision, went down a street and again came back toward the FBI. Tjarks pulled into another driveway and let him pass.

That is where the FBI lost him. They knew there were two entrances to the subdivision. But there was a third one they didn't know about. They never did see him leave.

Tjarks and Bonness drove back to Stratford Drive at 8:10 a.m. Edwards' white van returned at 9:05 am.

Edwards went inside for a few minutes before coming out and getting his red motorcycle helmet from the van. He spent some time working on the car and the motorcycle on his driveway that morning.

Nancy lay on the couch most of the day because she was tired. Her sister Lori called at 4:30 p.m. Nancy dropped Benjamin at football practice at 5 p.m., stopping at Econo Drugs to get throat lozenges for Lori.

Nancy went to Lori's house with Danny. They stayed 10 minutes.

23

Lori gave Nancy some round steak. Nancy picked up Lori's children and took them to Lori's mother-in-law. Danny went along. Nancy went home and called her mother to get a recipe for round steak.

Danny picked up Benjamin from practice. Nancy sent Danny to the store for mushroom soup and milk for the recipe. Nancy said Danny ate only a bite that night, and he hardly ate or slept that week.

After dinner, Nancy went to Jewel to get ice cream for Benjamin. She also got 7-Up for Danny because he looked ill. She said Danny was sweating and had the shakes.

Benjamin and Nancy had ice cream and watched TV. Nancy got a call from her mother and they talked about Lori's health. Nancy told her mother she would come to clean her windows on Friday and she would take Lori to the doctor, if necessary, for her strep throat.

The police kept Edwards' townhouse under surveillance. Some officers were playing softball in a park across the street and others were helping a neighbor paint and build a patio. They did all sorts of routine activity, trying to not be noticed.

They were noticed.

"When me and Nancy got home, I saw the cops staking out the place," Edwards said in his 2013 prison interview. "I knew it was over."

"The cops thought they were fooling me. They were across the street the next day throwing the ball around."

"When I drove around, (Sgt. Ralph) McClellan followed. He thought he was fooling me. The female agent was sitting next to him. When they noticed I saw them in the mirror, she scooted over to pretend like they were lovey dovey."

State Trooper Gary King and FBI agent Dave Riser were parked in the lot east of Route 102, south of a McDonald's restaurant. This was in the Bourbonnais K-Mart plaza, across the road from the townhouse and within eyesight.

Thursday was garbage day, and the police wanted to see what Edwards and Rish were putting on the curb that day,

A truck from Apollo Waste Systems came down the street at 2 p.m. Lawrence Zelhart drove, while Eugene Torres Jr. tossed the garbage bags in the back. There were three white plastic garbage bags on the curb in front of 756 Stratford. When the truck pulled up to the house, Edwards came from the garage and tossed a pair of blue jeans in the back. Edwards had another bag and was about to toss it into the back of the truck when Torres took it from him, saying he wanted to see if the bag had anything like fluorescent bulbs that could flash back at him. He checked it out. He didn't see any bulbs, but he did see some plastic straps under the bag.

Torres tossed the bag in the back and proceeded down the street.

He turned onto Route 102, went to Latham Drive, and then turned back into the subdivision through another entrance. King and Riser followed the truck and stopped it.

The police already had stopped the garbage truck before it got to Edwards' block. They identified themselves as police officers, and they asked Torres to empty the hopper on the back of the truck. After collecting so much, the garbage is dumped from the open hopper into the enclosed back of the truck, where it is compacted. The open hopper was empty when it picked up the garbage on Danny Edwards' block.

After Torres picked up the garbage on the block, and while the police stopped Torres and were talking to him, Danny Edwards slowly drove past in the blue Buick. He had seen the police observing him and he had seen the police follow and stop the garbage truck.

Edwards stared at the agents as he drove by. The agents looked back at him.

King and Riser had Torres drive his garbage truck to the Getty's Truck Stop at Route 49 and Interstate 57. They searched Edwards' garbage bags in the back of the truck. They found a pair of brown gloves, a number of plastic tie-straps, a caulking gun, and a Radio Shack receipt for a cassette tape.

Chapter 3
Arrest and Interrogation

"You know, in the state of Illinois, that if we find Stephen Small and he's dead, you're getting the death penalty."
ISP Sgt. William Willis, September 4, 1987

It was Friday morning, September 4. Stephen Small had been missing for two full days. Danny Edwards told Nancy Small that her husband was buried in a box and had 48 hours of air. Was that true?

The FBI decided it couldn't wait any longer for Danny Edwards to lead them to Mr. Small. Edwards had not gone to check on his hostage since they started observing him at 1 a.m. Thursday, and it appeared he was not going to do so.

A search warrant was drawn by Sgt. William Willis. He showed it to the state's attorney for his approval. Willis got Judge Edward McIntire out of bed early that morning to sign it.

Danny Edwards walked his dog in the yard at 10:30 a.m. It was his last taste of freedom. He went back inside. The FBI and local police had their warrant and they decided to move in.

Police surrounded the townhouse. There was a knock on the door at 756 Stratford Drive East at 10:35 a.m. Danny Edwards opened the door.

Kankakee Police Lt. John Gerard identified himself as a police officer and told Edwards he had a search warrant. Gerard put his foot in the door so Edwards could not slam it shut.

Gerard handed Edwards the warrant and stepped inside. He grabbed Edwards by the shoulder and turned him around and frisked him.

Edwards started freaking out.

"Are you f...ing nuts?" he cried. "What the f... is this all about?" As Edwards read the warrant, he told Gerard, "You f...ers are crazy!"

Edwards told the officers, "I could see if it was drugs, but not kidnapping."

A number of other law enforcement officers filled the townhouse. More cops covered the building so no one could escape through a back door.

Nancy Rish was asleep upstairs in bed. She heard noises and looked up to see a man in Army fatigues pointing a gun in her face.

Rish was led downstairs by Sgt. Maurice Meitzner.

State Police Sgt. Ralph McClellan sat next to Rish on the couch and gave her a copy of the search warrant. He gave her a copy of her Miranda rights, read it to her, and she signed it.

Rish was in her nightgown and a blue bath robe. FBI Agent Elizabeth Lamanna, who had been doing surveillance with Agent James Furry, took Rish upstairs to get dressed. Rish got a blouse from the closet, put on a pair of blue jeans and her shoes. Lamanna asked Rish if she wanted to clean up or brush her teeth before they went downstairs.

Lamanna and Rish got in a state police car with State Trooper Sgt. Ralph McClellan and Kankakee Police Detective Rick Gilbert. McClellan drove to the Bourbonnais Police Department. It was across a street and a small field, within view of the Stratford Drive townhouse.

Kankakee Police Sgt. Bob Anderson put the handcuffs on Edwards. Detective Gilbert led Edwards from the house. Bourbonnais Police Sgt. Bill Stark and Bourbonnais Sgt. Myron Devine put Edwards in the squad car.

"I am filing a f...ing false arrest," Edwards shouted at police officers.

At the Bourbonnais police station, Edwards asked officers, "Who is it I am supposed to have done this to?" Police did not reply.

Edwards asked, "Is Nancy being arrested, too?" Police did not reply.

Edwards was put in a holding cell. Sgt. Devine removed the handcuffs.

Danny Edwards held out his right hand calmly and defied police. "Do I look f...ing scared?"

At the Bourbonnais police station, Edwards was asked if he wanted a lawyer. Edwards asked for Joseph Yurgine.

Yurgine represented Edwards' wife in their divorce. Edwards had driven Yurgine and his wife to the airport on a few occasions, something underlings like Danny Edwards would do for big shots in Kankakee.

Yurgine was close to the Small family. He was one of Steve's best friends, and he was godfather to one of Small's twin sons. On the tape, Stephen Small ad-libbed a comment that "this was not a joke or a party at Yurgine's." It is believed Mr. Small was trying to tip police to his location, since Yurgine lived in the Aroma Park area.

Yurgine, who also was the Bourbonnais village attorney, walked into the building. He talked to Edwards and tried to convince Edwards to cooperate. Edwards said he didn't know anything. Yurgine declined to represent him.

Illinois State Police Sgt. William Willis started questioning Edwards. His account comes from conversations with CBS-TV producers who produced a show in 1990 about the kidnapping.

Willis said Edwards was very argumentative, denying any knowledge of the kidnapping.

"I very quietly reminded him, gave him a cigarette, very soft-spoken voice, explained the facts of life," Willis was quoted in the transcript. "I don't tell him nothing I know."

"I told him I had an agreement with the state's attorney that we want

Stephen Small back alive. 'You help us get Stephen Small back alive, I'll cut you one helluva sweet deal. But I want him back alive. If it means a walk, you walk.'"

The conversation went back and forth, with Edwards denying involvement and Willis saying he knew better.

"I quietly reminded him, 'You know, in the state of Illinois, that if we find Stephen Small and he's dead, you're getting the death penalty, pal. I want you to think about that.'"

Willis said he told Edwards, "I want Stephen Small back alive. I'll cut you a helluva deal. You don't believe me? Call the state's attorney. Which he did, right there from the police station. Ficaro told him the same thing."

"Then I go in and talk to Nancy. She says, I don't know nothing. Playing that shit. I tell her, 'Next seat you might be sitting in is a hot seat.' She says, 'Huh?' I said, 'Electric chair, girl. If this guy dies, you're going down. We're going to ask for a death penalty.'"

All this was in Willis' transcript with TV producers in 1990.

Willis said he tried everything to "sweat" Edwards and Rish to get them to talk. He told TV producers that prosecutor Michael Ficaro had told lawyers for Edwards and Rish that the state's attorney would let them go if Stephen Small was rescued alive. The lawyers later denied this was said.

When Nancy Rish was brought into the Bourbonnais police station, Detective Sgt. Bill Stark spoke to her briefly. He gave her something to drink and he put her in his office.

"I spoke to Nancy a little that day," Stark told me in 2013. "I recall how small and scared she looked. She and I didn't discuss the case or any details concerning the case, as Willis had given everyone strict directives not to speak with them. I put her in my office and I asked if I could get her anything. I do recall she was softly sobbing, and I got her some tissue and asked if she would like anything to drink. I told her I knew her sister."

Nancy's older sister was a high school friend of Stark's younger sister. Stark mentioned that to Willis as perhaps a means to ease Rish into talking. Willis abruptly turned him down, telling Stark that this was a case for the state police, not the Bourbonnais police.

"Nancy sat quietly and never really said much at all," Stark said. "Edwards was a different matter. Cussing, screaming, demanding, just being an overall jerk."

Nancy Rish was questioned separately from Danny Edwards. Her interrogation was much more lengthy and detailed than the interrogation of Edwards. That is because she willingly talked to the police, giving eight separate interviews over more than 13 hours from September 4 to 7.

Kankakee Detective Rick Gilbert and Sgt. Ralph McClellan told Rish they were investigating the kidnapping of Stephen Small and that they knew

28

she was present during a ransom call Wednesday night in Aroma Park.

Rish told them she didn't know anything about a kidnapping, and this was the first she heard about it. She said she was willing to talk.

Rish answered a few questions from McClellan and Gilbert before she told them she wanted a lawyer present. The first lawyer who came to mind was Leonard Sacks of Kankakee. He was called, but he declined because of possible conflicts with the Small family. Sacks recommended attorney Larry Dirksen from Olympia Fields. Police could not reach Dirksen. Rish told them to call J. Scott Swaim, a local lawyer she once used to get child support from her ex-husband.

FBI Special Agent Elizabeth Lamanna later testified, "I took her to another room. Nancy sat on a chair in a small room. She said she didn't know why she was there and didn't know why there was a search of her home. I asked her if she knew which attorney she wanted to call. She said she had never been in trouble before and didn't know any attorneys. The only time she had an attorney was when she went through a divorce, and again recently when she was seeking child support. After we sat there awhile, she gave me the name of Leonard Sacks. She said she didn't feel comfortable talking to him on the phone and asked if I would call, that I would do a better job explaining the situation. I called, left a message, and he returned the call. He indicated there was a conflict of interest, that he could not represent her. He spoke to Nancy Rish on the phone. She gave the phone back to me. Sacks gave me the name of another lawyer from Olympia Fields, Dirksen. I asked Rish is she wanted me to contact this man. She said yes. I called but couldn't reach him. It was an hour and a half and I still couldn't reach anyone. Nancy Rish finally suggested Swaim. I called him and explained. He agreed to come."

While waiting for Swaim to show up, Rish started talking to Lamanna. Lamanna said she would not talk to Rish about the case without Rish's attorney. "It's not my job to take a statement from her. I had no role in interviewing. I was there to baby-sit her, as the only female," she later testified.

But Rish talked about other things. Rish told Lamanna she didn't get along with Edwards. She said she had been living with him for some time with her son and they fought all the time. She said she wanted to leave but could not because of her financial situation. His name was on the lease and she had nowhere to go. Rish said Edwards never told her about his comings and goings, and she thought he was having an affair. She was so suspicious that she went out at nights looking for him. She said their fights were so noticeable that their neighbors knew about it. She talked about selling Mary Kay cosmetics, getting pregnant and having a baby at 16, and never completing high school. Rish said her father had been murdered, but she didn't want to talk about it. She said her mother is alive and two of her sisters lived in the area. Rish was offered food and drink, but she declined. Rish talked about her son, and she told Lamanna she was concerned because it was getting close to the time school was getting out. Lamanna said, "She didn't know who would tend to her son and was concerned he would come home and there wouldn't be anyone there. So I had officers make arrangements to be there when her son came home." Rish told Lamanna she had a good relationship with her former in-laws. She talked about wanting to go back to school, that she hadn't completed high school.

Rish was still waiting for Swaim to arrive when -- she later said -- a police officer came in and said to her, "Next seat you might be sitting in is the hot seat. Electric chair, girl. If this guy dies, you're going down. We're going to ask for the death penalty."

Swaim was in his office at about 2:05 p.m., on the phone, when the operator broke into his call. Lamanna told him he needed to come to the Bourbonnais Police Department to confer with a client.

When he got to the police station, Swaim greeted Sgt. Robert Anderson. He knew Anderson because he had done the legal work for Anderson's divorce in 1976. Swaim went into the room where Nancy Rish was being held.

Swaim spoke with Rish for about five minutes. Rish told him she wanted to help. Swaim came out and told Anderson, "The defendant is ready to cooperate and make a statement."

Swaim said Lamanna told him, "Miss Rish wishes to cooperate. If she gives us a statement, she can go home." Swaim said he told Rish she did not have to give a statement, but Rish said she wanted to tell what she knew so she could go home.

Rish signed several papers, including a consent form to search her house. Later in the day, she asked to see a doctor for her ailments. No doctor came.

Swaim was present during the interviews. FBI agents Elizabeth Lamanna and John Osgood were there for some of the interviews.

Swaim telephoned State's Attorney William Herzog. Swaim later said he thought he had an understanding with Herzog and with the police that Nancy Rish could go home after making a statement. Swaim said he believed Rish knew nothing about the kidnapping plot.

The interrogation of Nancy Rish was done by State Police Sgt. Ralph McClellan and Kankakee Police Detective Rick Gilbert. She told them that on Sunday, August 30, she spent most of the day at her son's midget football game, including working at the concession stand. That evening, she and Danny went to the state park for some hot dogs. They met Tracy Storm there. Tracy stopped by their home, then Tracy and Danny left together.

Danny did not come home until 1 a.m.

About ten minutes after Danny left, Nancy said she got a strange phone call from a man asking for Danny. The caller asked if Danny was there. No, he isn't, Nancy replied. Who is this?

"Does it really matter?" the caller asked.

The caller asked again if Danny was home. Nancy said no. The man hung up.

A similar call came on Tuesday evening, she said. When Nancy asked the man his name, he said, "What is it to you?" She said she mentioned it to Danny when he got home, but he did not react.

Nancy told the officers what happened on Monday: she got her son off to school and later went to Julie Enright's house for most of the afternoon. She told police it was on Monday that she noticed the plywood box in the garage was gone.

Nancy told police she stayed home and cleaned her house on Tuesday. After a conversation with Danny, she rescheduled a hair appointment for later that afternoon. She said Edwards drove to some railroad tracks he wanted her to remember. That afternoon, Nancy said she accompanied Danny to Englewood Electric and stayed in the van while he went in to get something. At 5 p.m., Nancy dropped her son off at football practice and then went to get her hair done. Then she went home, had supper and helped her son with his homework.

What she told the police about those routine activities was true.

But she decided to lie to the police about Tuesday night.

Rish said Edwards left the house in his van at 10:30 p.m. She thought he was cheating on her, so she left in her car at 11:30 p.m., driving past Edwards' ex-wife's house, the Dam Tap and Leo's bar to look for him. She came back home after midnight, and then left again at 1:30 a.m. to look for him. She returned home at 3 a.m., she said.

That was a lie. The true scenario was mentioned in the previous chapter -- she followed Edwards' van in her car to South Greenwood Avenue and then drove him to the gas station where he made a phone call. Then she dropped him off at Cobb Park. She picked him up in rural Pembroke at 3 a.m.

At home, Rish said she noticed Edwards was nervous, jumpy and panicky. At 3:30 a.m., Edwards left in the van and was gone 20 minutes.

Rish went to bed upstairs. When Edwards returned, he spent the night downstairs.

In the morning of that same day, Wednesday, Rish told police she woke up and got her son off to school. She dropped the dog off at the groomer and then Edwards drove to a ranch. He told her to pick him up in an hour. Rish drove to her sister's house and stayed there 45 minutes. Rish said she and Edwards picked up the dog at 4:30 p.m., and on the way home, Edwards stopped the car at a pay phone at a Phillips 66 station at Aroma Park. Even though it was a drive-up phone, Edwards parked away from the phone and walked up to it. She said Edwards' back was turned toward her.

He was not on the phone long. When the call ended, they went home. He was in and out of the house all evening, she said, and he was pre-occupied, tense and very nervous.

Rish told police she dropped her son at his grandmother's house, and later in the evening Edwards put her bicycle in the trunk of her car, telling her they were taking it to the shop of a friend named Jack to get the bike repaired.

Rish told police she did the driving. Edwards told her to stop at a pay phone near a gas station, across from Ruffini's Super Value in Aroma Park, at about 11:30. Edwards got out and said he wanted to call Jack to see if he was home. Rish sat in the car. Edwards had his back to her at the out-door phone. She did not hear what he was saying.

At that point, Detective Gilbert stopped her. He read her Miranda rights. She signed it and continued.

After the phone call, Rish said Edwards told her to drive to Sandbar Road. Along the way, he had her stop the car and he took a duffle bag from the back seat and put it in some evergreens. They took Sand Bar Road to Route 17, went east to Route 1 and then south to Jack's house. A sign in his yard said "Precision Repair." Rish said when they got there, no lights were on, so they drove away. She said Edwards told her Jack wasn't home because he worked second shift. They drove back through Aroma Park, then to Kankakee.

Then stopped at another pay phone at a Marathon gas station in Kankakee. Rish parked the car 10 to 15 feet from the phone booth. She kept the car running. She did not overhear his phone conversation. She told police that after this call, Edwards was panicky and angry. He said, "Something is wrong. Something is not right." Rish said she was "bewildered, confused and scared." Edwards then drove back to Aroma Park and past the phone booth across from Ruffini's. Edwards said he saw a car there, did not like it, and drove away.

That scenario was true. FBI agents on surveillance in Aroma Park saw Edwards make the call at the gas station pay phone while Rish stayed in the car. The trunk was open, with a bicycle in it. The agents did see the car drive toward the area where Jack lived, and then back to Aroma Park and on to Kankakee.

After the phone call at the Marathon station, she said they went back through Aroma Park, past Jack's place again. Edwards had her stop and he drove from that point.

Rish said they arrived home at 1 or 2 a.m. She said Edwards took the bicycle from the car and put it in the garage. He then left in the van by himself and told her that he was going out for cigarettes. He was gone 20 to 30 minutes. When he returned, he seemed somewhat relieved. After some conversation, Rish said she went upstairs to bed and Edwards stayed downstairs.

Rish told police details of her routine activity on Thursday morning. At the same time she left to get her son from his grandmother's house, Edwards left in his van. Edwards got home at 10:30 a.m. He had the duffle bag from the previous evening. He told her what was in the bag and what to do with it. She told the officers that it made no sense to her and she had no idea the significance of the bag and its contents.

Then she told the officers a few other things she did not mention about Wednesday's activities, concerning the dog groomer, her sister, taking her son to football practice, going out for lozenges for her sister, getting ice cream for herself and her son, watching TV, and making a few phone calls before going to bed.

The questioning went back to Thursday's activities. Rish said she and Edwards spent most of the day cleaning the garage and washing the car. At 4:45 p.m., she and Edwards took Benjamin to football practice, then went to Lori's house, picked up Lori's children and took them to their grandmother's house. Then they went home. They picked up Benjamin at 7 p.m. Later, Edwards went to Jewel to get soup and Rish went to get groceries. All were in bed by midnight.

McClellan asked Rish if she knew anything about a tape recorder used by Edwards. She said she didn't know anything. McClellan had an idea.

He said, "Nancy, what if your fingerprints are on that tape recorder?" McClellan said she "began to cry and dropped her head into her hands."

McClellan and Gilbert left the room for 10 minutes. When the officers returned, Rish told them she lied about the tape recorder. She said there was one in the house and it belonged to Danny's son Brandon. She said he left it there two weeks earlier and that her fingerprints might be on it because she moved it.

Rish said Edwards built a large box in the latter part of May or early June. Edwards told her it was for his brother Duke, then he said it was for firewood.

She said Edwards sold the box to a black man who came with his wife, "big boned and wearing a dress." The man came back two weeks after buying the dryer, asking about the washer. Instead, she said he bought the plywood box. That story was a lie.

Nancy Rish took a ride with the police officers twice -- on September 4, to show them the route she and Edwards drove in Aroma Park, and again on September 7, to show the area where Edwards tossed the tape recorder.

The officers said Rish was confused in her directions, and the route did not match the time line. However, she did correctly point out the places she mentioned, including Jack's house.

33

After the second ride on Friday evening, they all returned to the Bourbonnais police station. Rish gave another taped interview. At 8:15 p.m., Rish was taken to the county jail by Gilbert and Lamanna.

Nancy Rish gave more details to police during her lengthy interrogations. She said Danny was leaving the house all the time without telling her what he was doing or where he was going. She started thinking that he was seeing another woman.

About a month before the kidnapping, Danny left and was gone quite a while. Nancy got in her car and went looking for him. She went by his ex-wife's house on Hawthorne Lane and she saw his motorcycle parked there. Even though Danny explained that he went there to spend time with his kids, they still had an argument. She told him, "Well, you know, couldn't ya let me know?"

"He was already going out the door when I really wanted him to stay there, and I wanted to have this out with him, and he was just, 'I went and saw my kids.'" They argued about this until Nancy said, "Well, it's just that you're gone and you don't tell me." Danny yelled, "Well, right now I'm telling you where I'm going. I'm going over to Tracy's and I'm helping him move and I will be back later."

They talked more when Danny returned. "Danny, tell me if you're seeing someone else. Cause you're gone all the time and you don't tell me. I never know what's going on with you."

She said Danny said, "Nancy, you just don't understand. You don't know what's going on."

"He says, 'Forget it.' He says, 'I gotta tell you. There's something that's gonna happen. There's something I have to do.' He says, 'I have to do it.'"

The officers asked if he told her what it was. No, she said.

Nancy said Danny's personality started to change during these weeks. "He became very nervous and started talking about large sums of money. He kept saying, 'There's something I have to do.'" She thought he was getting back into drug dealing. She didn't want that to happen, so she tried to find out what he was planning.

"The argument got worse that night," she told police. "I mean, it got rrreal bad. He just wanted to keep avoiding the fight and I wanted to bring it out. I wanted it out and open and done with."

Nancy's son Benjamin watched his mother and Danny argue, so they went upstairs.

"We went upstairs. He tore my shirt off. It just got bad."

"And then he ended up leaving that night. I told him I was calling my mom over, and this and that. We were going back and forth, then he just left."

Sometime after 1 a.m., Danny came home after having a little too much to drink. "Oh, I didn't want to fight with him, I mean after that I was just

34

scared. I was sitting on the couch waiting for him to come home," Nancy told the officers.

"'Nancy,' he says, 'There's something I have to do. I can't really hide it from ya, with you and Benjamin here, it's just hard. It's hard. I can't explain why I'm leaving. I can't tell you these things, there's something I have to do. But it'll be OK. You have to trust me.'"

"And I kept saying, 'No, Danny, don't get into dealing again, don't do that.'"

"No, it's not that. It's just a one time thing," Danny told Nancy.

"It's not anything to do with drugs," Danny told her.

"We started fighting," Nancy said. "He started yelling and threatening me. He says, 'You just don't realize how important this is. You don't realize. This is my life. You don't realize I have to do this.'"

"And he ran upstairs and got a gun. He says, 'I guess I'm gonna have to show you.' And he held the gun up to my head and he says, 'You know your little boy up there in bed? I'll take you up there right now. I'll blow your brains out, I'll blow his brains out and I'll blow my brains out. And I'll do it. Because if anything goes wrong, we're gonna be dead anyway."

Nancy Rish told police she noticed the box was gone on Sunday, August 31. On that day, Edwards said whatever was going to happen was going to happen that week, and he needed her help on Tuesday. He didn't say what for. She said he again threatened her. "They know you and Benjamin and they know you know too much."

Danny was gone a good part of Monday. "He kept telling me he had some things to do, 'and you just don't worry about it,' he says. 'I have some things to do. I'll take care of it. Cause you don't need to know any more.'"

Nancy had a hair appointment on Tuesday at two o'clock. Danny told her to make the appointment for later in the day.

"I want to bring you out to a place," Danny said. "I want to show you somewhere that I want you to pick me up." Nancy called Anita Hamilton (her hairdresser and cousin) and changed her hair appointment to five o'clock.

Early that afternoon, Danny drove Nancy and showed her a place along the railroad tracks. "Be there," Danny said. "I'll tell you later what time. It'll be tonight. Remember this and be right there."

Danny and Nancy went home. Nancy helped her son with his homework, and took him to football practice on the way to Anita's beauty shop. Nancy came home and they all had a quiet evening. Nancy helped Benjamin with more homework before putting the boy to bed at 10:30 p.m.

Nancy then told the police the events of Tuesday night. This time, her story was true.

"Later that night, he told me that he wanted me to follow him in the van," Nancy said. "He was going to leave his van."

This was about midnight, Wednesday morning.

Nancy said Danny drove his van to Greenwood Avenue and she followed him in her car. He parked his van on South Greenwood Avenue. Nancy pulled her car next to the van. Danny got out of his van with a duffle bag and he put the bag in the trunk of her car.

"He got in my car and then he says, 'Wait a minute. Turn down here. I want to go to the gas station to make a phone call.' He got out and made a phone call, got back in the car and he says, 'Hurry up. Bring me down to Cobb Park.'"

As he was dropped off, Danny said, "Babe, if I'm not there when you get there, go ahead and just go home."

"And I said, 'What do you mean, just go home? Why won't you be there?' He says, 'You just go home. But come back the next day and get me at noon. But I should be there.' I drove away and went home."

"Didn't this seem strange to you?" McClellan asked.

"Everything seemed strange to me. Yes," Nancy said.

"He says, 'Nancy, you don't wanta know no more.' He just kept telling me I don't wanta know no more."

Danny was waiting there alone when Nancy picked him up at 3 a.m. He told her to drive him back to the van on Greenwood Avenue.

"I brought him back to his van and he says, 'I'll meet ya home.' Somehow he got home a couple minutes before I did."

Danny was waiting inside the house when Nancy walked in. "I just looked at him and I said, you know, not really saying anything, just looking at him and he says, 'It's OK. Didn't I tell you it'd be OK? Everything is OK. All you had to do is pick me up. Everything's OK. It's all right. Everything's fine, don't worry about nothing."

McClellan asked, "Did you inquire what this is that's fine?"

Nancy replied, "He just says, 'Never mind, you don't have to know. Just never mind.'"

"And then I went upstairs and he says, 'I'm gonna leave. I'll be right back.' I said, 'Now where you going, where you going?' He says, 'I'll be right back. I'm gonna leave just for a minute.' He was gonna get cigarettes or something. And he was only gone for maybe ten minutes. Ten or fifteen minutes."

Nancy went to bed upstairs. Danny slept downstairs.

As morning broke on Wednesday, Nancy said she got up and took Benjamin to school. Danny woke up about noon. He told Nancy they needed to bring the dog to the groomers for a bath. Nancy called Pat's Groom & Clean in St. Anne.

As they drove to the St. Anne and Aroma Park area in eastern Kankakee County with their dog, Danny drove down an isolated rural road and stopped near a horse ranch. He told Nancy to drop him off and pick him up in an hour. At the horse ranch, Nancy noticed two black men. One man was wearing a cowboy hat.

Danny and Nancy went home. Late in the afternoon, they left to get their dog.

"After we picked up the dog, he went through Aroma Park and he stopped at the Phillips 66 station and he made a telephone call."

Danny asked for two quarters. Nancy gave it to him.

McClellan asked Nancy if she knew who Danny called. She said no.

They went home. Later in the evening, Danny asked her to get a babysitter for Benjamin. Nancy told him she didn't like having a babysitter on a school night.

"What is it I'm saying we are gonna do?" she asked.

"Tell Benjamin we're gonna go to the show or something," Danny replied. "You know, give him a reason, cause he's gonna ask."

Nancy agreed.

"Don't worry," Danny told her. "After tonight, you know, this will be it. You don't have to worry about nothing else. It's gonna be over."

What was "it?" McClellan asked.

"This thing he was doing," she replied.

"You had no knowledge of it?" McClellan asked.

"I had no knowledge of it," she said. "He said he didn't want me to know."

Nancy took Benjamin to his grandmother's house at 8:30 p.m. for him to spend the night.

"I came home. He said again he wanted me to drop him off some-where. Then later on he changed his mind. He says, 'I've been thinking more about this. I think it'd be too dangerous.' I says, 'What do you mean too dangerous?' He says, 'I don't want you there tonight.'"

"Tonight I don't want you there. I think it'd be too dangerous," he repeated. "What I'm gonna do is, I'm gonna use your bike," he said.

Danny told Nancy to drop him off somewhere and he would use the bike from there. She didn't have to pick him up after that.

Nancy became suspicious of this strange behavior and she insisted she go along. Danny then told her he would take her bicycle to his friend Jack's place to be repaired.

The night before, he had Nancy pick him up in the middle of nowhere at 3 a.m. Tonight, he wanted her to drop him and the bicycle off somewhere in the middle of the night and she didn't have to pick him up. Then he said he was taking the bike to a repair shop close to midnight. All of that was more strange behavior that would get no explanation if Nancy asked. However, she learned by now not to ask.

Danny put the bike in the car's trunk. He had to tie down the hood.

Still, the bicycle stuck out.

Danny told Nancy to drive. She said Danny was carrying a tape recorder and a duffle bag.

Nancy told the officers that Danny had her to drive to Aroma Park. He asked Nancy for more quarters. Then he got out of the car and made a call from a pay phone at the gas station.

This was the 11:28 p.m. call.

When he was finished, he got back in the car and put the tape recorder under his seat.

"When he got back in the car, he was real panicky," Nancy told the officers. "He says, 'Something's wrong.' I says, now what? What do you mean something's wrong? He says, 'Something's wrong, something's not right.'"

"Just drive, turn around here, just start driving," he ordered. Nancy asked where. "Go to the stop sign. Turn on Sandbar Road," he said.

"Then we drove down Sandbar Road and he kept saying, 'Drive faster! Drive faster!' And I said, well, you drive! You drive! And he says, 'No, I don't want to change it. Just keep driving. I'll tell you where to go.'"

Nancy turned on Day Road, then drove to Waldron Road and drove until turning on Baker Road.

"Then he says, 'Stop! Stop right here!' Nancy stopped the car and Danny got out with his duffle bag. He ran and hid it under an evergreen tree. He got back in the car and told Nancy to drive to the Marathon gas station on the east end of Kankakee.

Danny got out and made another phone call. When he got back in the car, Nancy asked if they could go home now. No, he said, drive back to Aroma Park.

"We went through Aroma Park again," Nancy said. "He just kept circling that area there, by where he made the phone call."

"He kept saying, 'Something's wrong.' And he wanted to go back by there. So we went by there a couple times."

McClellan asked Nancy if they saw anything. Danny "noticed a car there, yeah, by the phone."

"He said he noticed a car. Finally, he says, 'I don't like that.' And I said, well, who is that? And he says, 'I'm not sure.'"

Danny had Nancy drive around a number of rural roads.

"He was just real panicky. He was just, I mean, he kept telling me, 'Drive here, drive here, drive here.' So anyway, we were coming in, I'm not sure how we got back around, to be going up Birchwood Lane. We turned onto that road, I went aways. He said, 'Stop the car. I'll drive now.' And that's when I saw him take the tape recorder and he just flung it. And he got in the driver's seat."

Danny drove through Aroma Park again before heading home.

"After we got home Wednesday, Danny told me that it was done, everything was over. He said that a few times. I was very much relieved. I thought nothing more, you know, nothing had happened."

However, Danny had a few more words that night. He told Nancy to lie about certain things if anybody asked. He told her to say a black man had purchased the wooden box in the garage. And he told her to say they were bringing the bicycle to Jack's house to be fixed.

The next day was Thursday. Nancy told the officers she picked up Benjamin from his grandmother's house and took him to school.

There were a few unusual occurrences that day, which was usual for the Edwards-Rish household. Danny told Nancy he had to leave to see if his duffle bag was still where he hid it. He said it was very important. He was gone about an hour.

"He was real nervous all day, and God, I was, too," she said.

Danny cleaned out the garage, he washed Nancy's car, he kept busy.

The officers asked about Danny's statement about anticipating a large amount of money from Mitch Levitt. Nancy told the officers about Danny's agreement to help trap Mitch, but Danny tipped him off, and she said Mitch was going to reward him.

After Friday's interrogation, Rish was taken to the county jail. She was in solitary confinement for four days. Her cell was a dark room with a stainless steel sink and toilet and a metal bed. She was offered food, but she could not eat. Two days later, she still had not received a change of clothes.

Chapter 4
Finding the Victim

"Oh no, oh no, he can't be dead."
Danny Edwards, September 4, 1987

The police did not know much more on that first day, Wednesday, other than Stephen Small had been kidnapped and he was being held for ransom. They did not know who kidnapped him. They did not know where he was being held.

But they did know that his distinctive new maroon Mercedes was taken. They started to look for the car, hoping that it was not hidden in a garage or elsewhere out of sight.

One of the calls Nancy Small made just after learning her husband had been kidnapped was to next-door neighbor George Ryan. Ryan made some calls and got the government to bring in the Nightstalker surveillance aircraft. Nightstalker is a special MU-2 aircraft with electronic infrared equipment to track vehicles in the dark. The government officially does not confirm nor deny use of the Nightstalker aircraft, as a matter of security.

The high-tech Nightstalker searched from the air for the car and for the victim.

However, it was an old-fashioned aircraft that led the police to Stephen Small.

Sgt. John Dittmer, state police aircraft commander, was at the Bloomington airport when he was notified at 10 a.m., on Wednesday, September 2, to fly to the Kankakee airport. Sgt. Bill Willis sent Dittmer and Detective Robert Anderson to fly surveillance in the single engine, high wing, four-passenger Cessna 182 plane along the Kankakee River and the state park, looking for Small's car.

After a long search, they returned to the Kankakee airport. Dittmer was told it might be a long detail of several days, including night flights. He also was told the FBI had the Nightstalker on its way.

Various crews of state police pilots flew search missions, in shifts, all day Wednesday, Thursday and Friday. The Nightstalker flew by night.

State police flew over the area doing what they called a grid search, section by section, looking for Stephen Small's Mercedes. They looked at places where a car might be hidden: along wooded areas, tree lines, fence rows, abandoned buildings and quarries.

Sgt. Dittmer took off from the tiny Kankakee Municipal Airport just after 6 p.m., on Friday. On board with him in the Cessna were Mark Teske, the assistant aircraft commander, and State Trooper Thad Lillis.

The Cessna had been in the air about 45 minutes when Teske caught a reflection of the sun glaring off an object on the ground, in an area with trees and high weeds. He pointed Dittmer in the direction and the plane swung around. It turned out to be a refrigerator, laying face up, with its door removed.

The plane swung around again, and Teske saw another reflection. The plane dove to 200 feet and the officers could see the reflection was coming off the right section of the trunk of a car. It appeared to be a maroon color.

Teske radioed the command post and said they found a maroon automobile under some trees. The location was desolate, and the sandy soil made it almost inaccessible by regular vehicles. The air crew was told to stand by until ground units arrived, so they could direct them to the location.

Police arrived and verified at 7:40 p.m. that it was Stephen Small's maroon Mercedes.

It turned out the car was parked a short distance from the burial site.

Police at the jail told Edwards a short time later that the car had been located. Edwards began to panic when he heard the news.

More than eight hours after his arrest, Edwards finally decided he had better talk.

Danny Edwards' first thought, however, was to try to make a deal for himself.

Edwards yelled that he needed to talk to Bill Herzog, the state's attorney, to discuss a bargain.

At about 8:30 p.m., as Nancy Rish was being booked, Danny Edwards could be heard all over the county jail, screaming.

Edwards was screaming that he needed to talk to his lawyer Gus Regas or to Bill Herzog. Edwards' screams were ignored until he yelled at Sgt. Ralph McClellan and Detective Rick Gilbert.

Gilbert responded. Edwards said he wanted his attorney right away.

McClellan and Gilbert listened to Edwards' statements. Edwards said Kent Allain, a friend, planned the kidnapping for two months. Edwards told the police a story about Allain and unnamed black men who were involved in the kidnapping. He said Small was buried in Pembroke Township and two black men were there with shotguns guarding the site.

"We'd better hurry! I know where he's at! He's buried out at Pembroke! We don't have much time!"

Edwards asked McClellan what time it was. McClellan said 8:30.

"We have to hurry!" Edwards cried. "We have to hurry! We only have until 10! I need to talk to Mr. Herzog!"

Edwards kept yelling he needed to talk to Herzog to make a deal, and again emphasized that the police had better hurry.

McClellan told him he didn't know where Herzog was.

"It's 8:30, Friday evening," McClellan said. "He said he wanted to talk to Gus Regas. I saw Swaim. I asked him if he knew where Regas lived. I called, the line was busy. I called the operator and told her to break in."

It was Regas' father's phone. The elder Regas told McClellan to call the other number. McClellan did. It also was busy, so he had the operator break in again. Regas' wife answered. McClellan asked if Gus was there. No, she said, and she didn't have the faintest idea where he is.

McClellan told Edwards he couldn't find Regas. And McClellan said he could not talk to Edwards without his attorney.

"F... my attorney!" Edwards shouted. "We got to go right now! We don't have much time! Let's go, let's go!"

McClellan started to read Edwards his Miranda rights, for him to waive. Edwards said, "We don't have time for that. Forget it." McClellan read it. Edwards waived his rights, but didn't sign it, saying there was no time. Edwards later tried to use the fact that he didn't sign it to suppress evidence.

From his cell, he told police he would take them to Stephen Small, and he again yelled, "We'd better hurry!"

McClellan and Gilbert took Edwards from the county jail to the city police station, getting there at 9:05 p.m. Lt. Gerard briefly talked to Edwards, and Edwards told him he kidnapped Stephen Small and buried him in a box in Pembroke.

Edwards said Kent Allain and two black men forced him to do it. Allain was a local criminal known to police. The plan was hatched at Fat Rats bar in Kankakee, Edwards said. He told Detective James Fisher at 9:30 pm., that if Allain didn't get a call from him by 10 p.m., the two black men who were guarding the site on horseback would shut off air to the box.

Edwards said he would tell police where Small was buried, but he wanted to know how much prison time he would get, and he said he did not want to go to Stateville penitentiary. Gerard said he could not and would not promise anything. But, he added, he would tell the state's attorney of any cooperation.

Edwards asked Gerard to send policemen to his ex-wife Peggy's house on Hawthorne Lane to protect her and the kids from the other people involved in the kidnapping.

Edwards said Small had just 72 hours to live. He told officers they would need a 4-wheel drive to get to the location, and he would have to show them because they wouldn't be able to follow his directions. He said he needed different shoes than his jail sandals.

Gerard told Edwards to accompany police to the site.

As he was being escorted from the jail to be taken to the site, police said Edwards said to Nancy Rish, "I'm sorry, honey, I didn't mean to hurt or kill anybody."

Patrolman Wally Rokus drove one squad car, with Lt. John Gerard in the front seat and Patrolman James Fisher, Sgt. Maurice Meitzner and Danny Edwards in the back seat.

In the other cars were FBI Agent Alan Medina, Detective James Fisher, Detective Robert Anderson, Patrolman Bruce Stevenson and Patrolman Wayne Trudeau.

Edwards, who was handcuffed to Sgt. Meitzner, led them to the spot where he buried Small.

The first thing police saw at the site was a pipe coming out of the ground. Medina and Fisher started digging with their hands. Edwards said, "You're digging in the wrong place." He pointed to a spot 25 feet away and said, "Dig here."

The ground there is almost all sand. Medina and Gerard began digging with their hands. Some others officers joined. Edwards told them, "It will take you too long to dig him out, he's buried too deep. Use the shovels that were left behind."

Edwards showed them two shovels -- a large scoop shovel and a spade shovel -- on the ground by a tree, several feet away. A leaf rake also was there.

Detective Robert Anderson got the shovels and the men started digging as fast as they could. Edwards fell to his knees and helped dig with his hands.

The men dug about two or three feet down. Medina saw a piece of plywood. They cleared more sand from the top.

It was apparent this was the lid of the box. Gerard asked Edwards if the top was nailed shut. Edwards said no. Gerard knocked on the lid and heard nothing. Stevenson used the point of the scoop shovel to pry a corner of the lid open. He lifted the lid enough to get a hand under it. He and Anderson lifted it off.

The officers could see the body and it was not moving. Other officers shined their flashlights into the box. They saw a white male who appeared to be dead.

Police recognized the victim as Stephen Small. He was lying on his left side, still wearing the red shirt and blue jeans he wore when he left his house. His leather loafers were off his feet, but inside the box. He had handcuffs on his wrists, but the link between them was cut. He wore a gold watch on his left wrist. His light jacket was wadded under his head, as a pillow. In the wooden box was a jug of water, candy bars, gum and a light hooked up to a car battery.

Fisher, the smallest officer, got into the box. He picked up Small's left wrist. He looked for a pulse and found none. He told the other officers that the body was cold and that *rigor mortis* already had set in.

Edwards asked Meitzner what *rigor mortis* is.

43

"It means he is stiff and was dead for awhile," Meitzner replied.

"Oh no, oh no, he can't be dead," Edwards said.

But Gerard and Meitzner both noticed that Edwards' emotional outburst lasted no more than a minute before he was back to acting normal.

The lid was put back on the box.

Sgt. Melvin Trojanowski, crime scene technician with the Illinois State Police, collected evidence and soil samples from the scene. He also took photographs.

Edwards was placed in the back seat of an FBI car at 10 p.m. FBI Agent Michael Evans sat in the front of the car with him for 45 minutes while the area was searched and evidence was gathered.

While Edwards was in the car, he talked freely with Evans. The statements were voluntary. He was not being questioned. It was not much help because Edwards was lying. It all was part of a web of lies about being forced to kidnap Mr. Small that Edwards was weaving to build a case to minimize his own involvement. He elaborated to Evans the story he started telling Gerard, about Allain and black men. That story is detailed in the chapter on "Black Cowboys, Rumors, and Odd Coincidences" later in this book.

Edwards seemed to be putting more thought into his alibi of lies than he put into his kidnapping plot.

Kankakee County Coroner Jim Orrison came from his home in Herscher to the Pembroke crime scene and pronounced Stephen Small dead at 11:30 p.m.

Police secured the site, and they left Small's body in the crude grave overnight.

Kankakee Police Detective Kevin McGovern and Patrolman Hank Williams, with State Troopers Neal Sherman and Thad Lillis, stood guard through the night.

Danny Edwards was brought back to the county jail. He was filthy from being at the crime scene. Food was brought in to him and he was given a shower.

In the morning, police came back with a video camera. The videotaping began with scenes of branches, as an unseen cameraman walked through the woods, in a sort of spooky amateur production. The videotape showed a police officer's hand opening the lid of the box. Small's body was partially covered with sand because the top had been opened and closed several times during the previous hours by investigators.

The Mercedes 560-SEL was towed away Saturday morning. The late model car had just 6,910 miles on it.

Mr. Small's body was taken to Riverside Hospital in Kankakee for the autopsy on Saturday afternoon.

The state police air crew flew from Kankakee at 8:25 a.m. to pick up

44

Cook County Medical Examiner Robert Stein at Meigs Field in Chicago. They flew him to Kankakee for the autopsy.

Dr. Stein did the examination, assisted by Jim Orrison and his son Tom (who was a deputy coroner), Kankakee Police Sgt. Ed Jackson, Kankakee Police Detective Robert Anderson, State Police Investigator Melvin Trojanowski, photographer John Kelly of the medical examiner's office, and Douglas Childress, the chief autopsy technician.

The examiner read the police report from the grave site, that Mr. Small was wearing a red shirt, blue jeans and was barefoot, with his head facing north. On his left wrist was a gold watch with "Stephen B. Small" engraved on the back. He was lying on his left side with a gray jacket bundled under his head. He had handcuffs on both wrists, with the link between cut. Stein observed that Small had bruises and cuts on the top of his head, on his right elbow, ankles, left leg and right hand.

After the autopsy, Stein's conclusion was that Mr. Small died of suffocation and the manner of death was homicide.

Tommie Rish drove to the Stratford Drive townhouse on Saturday morning, September 5, with her grandson Benjamin. She wanted to get his clothes from his home. Bourbonnais Police Sgt. Brian Milone called Sgt. Bill Willis, and Willis said to not let them inside. Milone sent them on their way.

Milone said a black Ford pickup truck was parked in front of the townhouse on Stratford Drive. The license on truck was 5462 AF. It was registered to Tracy Storm.

Milone and Bourbonnais Police Officer John Griffith went in the house though the garage. They did not find anyone inside. Bourbonnais Police Chief Joseph Beard and the officers sealed the doors with police tape.

Later that day, Griffith and Milone were on patrol and they saw a man on a bicycle stop at the pickup truck. The man was attempting to unlock the truck when the officers approached him. It was Tracy Storm.

Storm told police he had been in the townhouse earlier in the day and he said he took a motorcycle helmet from the garage that belonged to Danny Edwards and himself. The police took him to the Bourbonnais police station to be questioned.

Storm did not tell them much. He said Pam and Ron Geekie told him at 10 a.m., Saturday, September 5, about Danny's arrest for kidnapping. Storm said he was planning to ride Edwards' Honda motorcycle that weekend, so he went to Edwards' house in his truck to pick up the bike. Storm said he went in the garage. The bike had the key in the ignition. He pushed the bike out, pulled down the garage door, rode it to his home on Sand Bar Road, and put it in his garage. Storm said he then got on his 10-speed and rode back to Bourbonnais to get his truck. It was then that the Bourbonnais police stopped him and took him to the police station.

Storm said he did not know Kent Allain and he had no contact with any black people through Danny Edwards. Storm said he was Edwards' best friend and they were out drinking a few days before the kidnapping.

Based on information from Danny Edwards which implicated Kent Allain, Kankakee police started looking for Allain on Friday night. Stake-outs were set up at his auto body shop, his home, even at Fat Rats bar.

Police found him entirely by accident.

Patrolman Robert Green was sitting in River Oaks restaurant at 1940 E. Court Street at 5:16 a.m. Saturday when he looked up and saw Allain at the cash register. Allain was picking up a food order.

Green knew Allain from previous arrests for auto theft and drug possession. Green got up from his table and walked over to him.

Allain said, "Hello, Bob."

Green told Allain to put his hands on the counter.

Allain asked, "Are you kidding me? For what?"

The officer grabbed Allain's right hand and placed one cuff on him. Allain started to pull away. Green grabbed his other hand and bent him over the counter and cuffed the other wrist. Green told the restaurant manager to call the police station for a backup unit.

Patrolman Larry Osenga was a block away. He got there a minute later, as Green was walking his prisoner outside. Osenga asked Allain if he had a car in the lot. Allain told him they were standing next to it.

Allain refused to get in the back of the squad car, demanding to know why he was being arrested. He had to be forcibly put inside. Green read Allain his rights and told him he was under arrest for investigation of murder.

Osenga had Allain's 1979 Chevrolet Caprice towed while Green drove Allain to the police station.

Allain refused to cooperate in the booking process. He refused to be fingerprinted or sign anything until he made a phone call. He was put in a cell.

Police searched Allain's home, auto shop and vehicles. They found cocaine and seven cartridges for a .357 Ruger and for a .22-caliber rifle in his truck. They found a loaded .357 Ruger revolver under his mattress in his house at 368 S. Foley Avenue. They found nothing at his business, Precision Automotive, at 260 S. Main Street.

Allain at first denied knowing Danny Edwards, and then he admitted it. They had known each for other six or seven years and they smoked pot together. He later admitted he knew Danny from Pyramid Electric, and then later said Danny dug a trench at his mother's house. He said he knew Danny was a drug dealer.

Allain told McClellan and Gilbert that he didn't know Stephen Small. He also changed that story, saying he had personal contact with Small in a traffic accident.

Thomas McClure, Allain's lawyer, arrived. Allain continued to deny any knowledge or involvement in the kidnapping.

Allain was charged with kidnapping and murder, possession of a controlled substance, and unlawful use of a weapon by a felon.

The Small family owns the daily newspaper and radio station in Kankakee. They did not mention the kidnapping in its Wednesday, Thursday or Friday editions or broadcasts. They were concerned that the publicity might scare the kidnappers and jeopardize Stephen's life.

The Chicago media did find out and they did their job, asking questions.

The first Kankakee newspaper story about the kidnapping was on Sunday, September 6. This was after the body was found and the suspects were arrested. It was the day before Labor Day.

The story said three suspects -- Edwards, Rish and Allain -- were arrested, and police were looking for two others.

The police searched Edwards' home on Saturday afternoon. They found his boots hidden behind the washer-dryer, with traces of the sandy soil of Pembroke Township. They also found a telephone book with Stephen Small's name circled. And they searched Edward's white van, which had sand in the back cargo door.

Edwards later told police he invented the story about Allain. Police had no evidence to link Allain to the kidnapping, so those charges were dropped and he was held only for drugs and weapons charges.

Edwards was uncooperative for more than 10 hours on Friday, until police found Mr. Small's car that evening. Edwards knew they would find the body nearby, so he took them to the burial site and later gave a bogus story about being forced to kidnap Mr. Small.

Early Saturday, Gus Regas' secretary called and told him Stephen Small was found dead and Danny Edwards took the police to the burial site.

Sgt. Anderson heard Edwards' statements on Saturday. Edwards said Rish was driving the car and he told her to pull over to a pay phone in Aroma Park. He said he called Nancy Small and played the tape recording over the phone. He said Nancy Rish did not see him do this.

Edwards said he thought Nancy Small was stalling him on the phone, so he hung up. He had Rish drive to another pay phone at the Marathon station in Kankakee and he called Mrs. Small again. Edwards drove back to Aroma Park to see if any police were staking out the pay phones. After they got home, Edwards left and went to the Checker gas station and pretended to use the phone, just to see if he was being followed. He went home and spent part of the night peeking out his window.

At the police station, Edwards continued his tale about other people who forced him to kidnap Mr. Small, this time to Sgt. McClellan and Detective Gilbert. The story grew even more elaborate. Nobody believed it.

The police interview lasted three and a half hours. It was the only interview Edwards gave to police.

Edwards agreed to sign a written statement about what he said. Detective Gilbert typed it up. About an hour later, Gus Regas, telephoned and advised his client not to sign it.

Regas went to the jail and told Edwards they needed to talk about retaining him as his lawyer. Regas said, "He was reluctant to call his family. I told him goodbye. Then McClellan asked if we could talk. Until the family retains me, I'm not in."

Edwards cut his wrist with a torn Pepsi can on September 9. The newspaper called it a suicide attempt, but it really was not serious.

He was taken to St. Mary's Hospital for eight stitches and was returned to his cell a short time later. Kankakee County Sheriff Bernie Thompson said it "didn't seem to be a sincere attempt to commit suicide."

Dorothy Smith, a registered nurse at St. Mary's, treated Edwards for what she listed as a "superficial laceration" on his left wrist. While tending the cut, she asked him how he was being treated at the county jail.

"Oh, fine," he replied. "I deserve to die, though. I murdered a man. I didn't mean for him to die."

Edwards asked the nurse about his cut wrist. "Did I come close?"

"Not even remotely," Nurse Smith told him.

"Where should I have cut to have done the job right?"

The nurse did not reply.

An unusual request came to Sheriff Thompson on September 28. Danny Edwards asked to see the sheriff because he wanted to tell him where he hid the gun used in the kidnapping.

It was unusual because the sheriff had talked to Edwards' brother several times, trying to find out where the gun was hidden. Edwards said he was concerned that children might find the gun.

"Edwards wanted to tell me about the gun, but he said his attorney (Gus Regas) said no," Thompson said. "I told him he should follow the advice of his attorney."

Initially, it was Dr. Eiberger, the doctor at the jail, who mentioned to the sheriff that he was concerned about Edwards' mental health. Dean Edwards also talked to the doctor about this, and he said the sheriff and Danny should talk. Somehow, this changed into Danny wanting to see the sheriff to tell him about the gun.

"Danny asked me how he could relate that information to me," Thompson said. "I said an anonymous call could lead to the location of the gun. He asked me how he could make that phone call. I told him he was smart enough that I figured that he could figure a way through a relative or friend or whatever."

He said, "The hell with it. I will just tell you where it is at."

"I told him to stop there, that if he told me face to face where the location of the weapon was, at some point and time I would have to testify to the fact of where I came about the information that led to the recovery of the weapon."

"He said he was going to tell me, but he wanted to be taken to show me. I said, tell me and if we can't find it, we will get back to him."

Edwards started to tell Thompson about a "hit" on his life. Thompson already had heard the rumor from his brother in California. The sheriff said there was no substantiation of this story and he believed Edwards was trying to manipulate him. The manipulation came when Edwards started asking the sheriff for special treatment.

"He told me he wanted to see Nancy Rish (in her cell) to discuss some unpaid bills. I told him that was ridiculous."

Edwards later tried to deny the conversation took place, and he denied volunteering information, in an effort to suppress the evidence. But an "Inmate's Request Form," dated October 23, 1987, was introduced as evidence. It was signed by Danny Edwards and read, "Important I talk to him today," in his own handwriting.

Police found the gun in the area near the burial site -- next to a telephone pole, in the weeds, in a nylon holster, wrapped in a towel -- where Edwards told them it could be found. The gun was loaded.

A further search turned up the bolt cutter 100 paces from the burial site on October 7. This was the bolt cutter used to cut the link in Small's handcuffs. It was stolen by Danny Edwards from his brother's business.

On the visitors list at the county jail for Nancy Rish were her mother, her sisters Lori, Linda and Paula, and Kathy Goodrich, Alicia DesMarteau, Terry Rish and son Benjamin. On the visitors list for Danny Edwards were his brothers Dean, Duke and Donnie, and Bill Mohler and Tracy Storm.

Chapter 5
Stephen B. Small

Stephen Burrell Small was not just an average citizen of Kankakee, Illinois. He was a member of an extremely wealthy and influential family in Kankakee.

The family fortune was built by Stephen's great-grandfather, Lennington Small. He was governor of Illinois from 1921 to 1929. It grew into a national media empire of newspapers and radio stations, worth tens of millions of dollars.

Stephen Small was born in Kankakee on March 18, 1947, to Burrell and Reva (Gray) Small. He had a brother, Leslie Small, and a sister, Susanne Small Bergeron.

Kankakee adjoins the towns of Bradley and Bourbonnais, essentially forming one community. Bradley and Bourbonnais are slightly upscale villages, where many people have moved to escape the declining Kankakee.

When the Small family media empire of newspapers and radio and cable TV stations was divided in 1965, Stephen's father Burrell got the radio stations and Burrell's brother, Len H. Small, got the newspapers.

Small Newspaper Group owned newspapers in Kankakee, Ottawa, Streator, Moline and Rock Island in Illinois; in LaPorte, Indiana; Rochester, Minnesota; and Pacific Palisades and Roseville, California. *Crain's Chicago Business* reported the company's revenue was $40 million in 1986.

Burrell Small formed Mid America Media. Radio station WKAN started in 1947, and about a dozen more broadcast properties were acquired over the years. The Kankakee Cable company started in 1965.

Stephen Small joined the Kankakee Cable TV corporation, a Mid America Media property, in 1966. He became program director in 1972 and manager in 1973. He was made vice president of Mid America Media and its subsidiaries in 1973. He retained that position until the corporation was sold in 1986.

The family sold most of its broadcast properties for $64 million in 1986. It included radio stations in Indianapolis, Tulsa, Davenport, Peoria, and a TV station in Hilton Head, North Carolina, plus Imagery Inc., another media service company.

Susanne Small Bergeron bought Kankakee stations WKAN-AM and WLRT-FM when the other stations were sold.

Sue Bergeron was the primary person who ran the radio station, along with Reva Small. Renee Dorsett, a copywriter at WKAN, said Reva was "an absolute delightful person. She had a big heart and was down to earth. She gave me a pair of shoes once. We had the same size small feet.

She saw I liked her shoes, so she said follow me out to the car. She gave me the shoes and drove home in her stocking feet."

Steve Small was quiet, gentle and had a good sense of humor, Dorsett said.

Stephen Small married Nancy Pedersen on July 26, 1969, at St. Patrick's Catholic Church in Kankakee. She was the daughter of Mr. and Mrs. Neil Pedersen of Kankakee.

The wedding rehearsal dinner was hosted by the groom's parents at Yesteryear restaurant, the historic building that Stephen later would buy and begin to remodel as the B. Harley Bradley House.

Stephen and Nancy Small had three sons: Ramsey, and twins Barrett and Christopher.

Stephen's nephew -- Bruce Small, the son of Leslie and Susannah Small -- committed suicide by shooting himself on March 15, 1998, at age 31. He was married and a certified nurse's aide in Hendersonville, NC.

Stephen Small bought the B. Harley Bradley House, a historic Prairie-style house built in 1901 by famed architect Frank Lloyd Wright.

B. Harley Bradley was the grandson of David Bradley, founder of the farm implement manufacturing company. When David Bradley ran out of space at his Chicago factory and looked for a place to expand, numerous cities courted him. He chose the village of North Kankakee, for a number of lucrative concessions and the promise to rename the town for him.

The Bradleys originally named their house the Glenn Lloyd House. Lt. Tom W. Jones, a Kankakee police officer from 1950 to 1972, told me a story in 2012 about the building of the Bradley House and the Hickox House next door, which was built for Kankakee banker and judge Warren Hickox, the brother-in-law of Bradley. Jones' mother Mable was the daughter of Kankakee lumberman Charles Wertz. Charles was a friend of architect Frank Lloyd Wright, and Wright stayed at the Wertz house on Grand Avenue in Bradley while building the Bradley and Hickox houses in Kankakee. Mable told her son, "If Wright didn't like something about the house as it was being built, he would take a hatchet and start chopping, smashing windows, ranting and raving. He was very temperamental."

B. Harley Bradley shot himself to death in a Chicago hotel room in 1914, after writing a suicide note to his wife. She got the note while waiting for him at an Iowa train station.

The Bradleys moved from Kankakee to Iowa in 1913, selling the house to a realtor named Albert Cook and his wife Christina. Two years later, Cook sold the house to Joseph Dodson, a member of the Chicago Board of Trade and president of the American Audubon Society. Dodson was a bird fanatic. He manufactured birdhouses on a large scale and he kept as many as 400 birds at his house. Dodson died in 1949, leaving the house to his secretary. The house was bought in 1953 by Marvin Hammack and Ray Schimel, who ran it as a high end restaurant called Yesteryear until 1983. The building fell into disrepair, and some of Wright's unique designs and art glass were sold. Stephen Small bought the building in 1986. The renovation ended with his death a year later. Four lawyers bought it in 1990 for their law offices and dramatically altered the interior. The building and carriage house were in danger of demolition until Sharon and Gaines Hall bought it in 2005 and restored it to Wright's specifications. A not-for-profit corporation called "Wright In Kankakee" bought the property in 2010. It is now open to the public as a museum and for tours.

It was on Labor Day 1986 that Stephen Small announced he was going to buy and restore the historic house. The purchase was complete on September 15, 1986, and he had workmen there the next day.

He was duplicating the leaded windows that had been sold from the house by previous owners, locating a company in Chicago that could do it. There was speculation that Small was considering making the historic building on South Harrison Avenue into a bed and breakfast, or perhaps his personal residence or a museum for his paintings and antiques.

Small also bought the Schobey House, later known as the Granger House, directly across Harrison Avenue from the Bradley House. Theodore Schobey's father founded the tiny village of Union Hill (today's population: 58), just west of Kankakee, in 1861.Theodore became a prominent citizen of Kankakee. Claude Granger, a Kankakee lawyer, bought the Dutch Colonial Revival-style house, which was built in 1923, and it became known in historic terms as the Granger House.

Mr. Small was using the Granger House as his office while he directed the renovation of the Bradley House. Small's house was just a couple of blocks away.

The Daily Journal said Stephen was enthusiastic about restoring the historic building, "even though he said he was not a big fan of the Wright Prairie School style."

Stephen's renovation of his own Queen Anne-style house at 917 Cobb Boulevard won national honors in the 1975 Burlington House "awards for interiors." The house was built in 1899 by Capt. Winfield Scott Campbell, who served with General Ulysses S. Grant in Kentucky, Tennessee and Mississippi, including the battle of Vicksburg. Campbell later became a banker in Kankakee. His son was a judge in Kankakee.

Stephen Small was named to the board of directors of Meadowview Bank in Kankakee in April 1981, to fill the vacancy created by the death of his father.

Stephen served a number of civic duties: he was a past director of the Kankakee Community College Foundation, a member of the Kankakee County Historical Society, on a committee for the Bicentennial Celebration in

1976 and he was on the advisory board for the Kankakee Community Arts Council. He was a member of the Kankakee Country Club and was a past director of the Illinois and Indiana Cable Association.

Stephen was a graduate of Lake Forest Academy, Mark Hopkins College in Brattleboro, Vermont, and he attended Drake University and the Brooks Institute.

Stephen Small owned a motorboat, a Mercedes Benz automobile and a red Ferrari Testarossa sports car. The Ferrari cost about $200,000. His wealth was no secret.

Stephen collected dollhouse miniatures and was organizing a miniature club at the time of his death.

Despite his wealth and prominent family name, Stephen Small was low key. He did not seek publicity or attention.

Stephen Small's neighbors, on what was called "Silk Stocking Row" in the historic Riverview neighborhood, had nothing but kind things to say to after his death. The neighbors told the newspaper that Stephen was a nice person, he never hurt anyone, he had no enemies, he was a good husband and father and he helped his neighbors. August Meyer said, "He was one of the good guys. I don't think anybody ever had anything against him. He used to come around when there was snow and plow everybody's sidewalk." George Ryan said Stephen was a "kind, gentle guy...a good neighbor and we're going to miss him in the Ryan household. He was close to all my kids, and they had a good relationship with Steve, and everybody here is sad-dened by his death." Alderman Rosalind Lind said, "I've never seen the man do anything to hurt anybody. It's pretty rare you can say that about some-body." Suzy Ruder said, "We slowly got to know Steve and found him to be a wonderful parent. He often was the cook at home. He was a private per-son, but he spent a lot of time with his kids and my kids. He had his priorities straight. He didn't just say his family was important, he showed that they were by spending a lot of time with them."

The sensational story of the murder came as the community was putting on its annual Labor Day weekend Kankakee Valley River Regatta. The event, just a few blocks from the Small house, continued as planned.

Stephen Small's funeral service was held on Labor Day, September 7, in a private ceremony at Mound Grove Gardens Chapel. Rev. Randy Van Fossan, pastor of Grace Community United Methodist Church in Bourbonnais, officiated. Small was interred in the mausoleum at Mound Grove Cemetery.

Chapter 6
Danny Edwards

Despite any later opinions, Danny Edwards was not a born loser. A better assessment would be that Danny Edwards was born with a silver spoon in his mouth. It wasn't close to the solid gold spoons with jewel-encrusted handles the Smalls had. But his family was hard working and prosperous and did not want for anything. The Edwards family was part of the country club crowd in Kankakee. Danny's brother Duke was president of the Kankakee Country Club.

Danny had everything he needed and he had every advantage to become as successful as his parents or any of his brothers.

But despite his advantage, there was no way his life was going to turn out well. Danny just wouldn't allow it. The only questions were, how much damage was he going to do and how many people was he going to take down with him?

Danny Edwards was born in Kankakee on January 10, 1957, the youngest of six children of George and Gertrude Edwards. George worked as an electrician and he later owned Edwards Star Grocery in St. Anne. Gertrude taught Sunday school at Central Christian Church.

Danny's friend, Jack Karalevicz, said Danny didn't quite measure up to his father's expectations, and his father often would belittle him. When Danny was a child, he stuttered a lot. Karalevicz said when Danny would start to talk and stutter, his dad would say, "When you learn how to talk, come back and I'll talk to you."

Danny's older brother Duke told police that Danny was an unreliable worker and that he skipped most family functions.

Danny didn't finish high school. He married Margaret "Peggy" McKenna on Friday, February 6, 1976, when he was 18. They were married at St. Patrick's Catholic Church in Kankakee. Bill Mohler was his best man.

Danny didn't seem to be able to hold a steady job, and he didn't seem to want one. He worked for the family's Pyramid Electric in Kankakee, but only as a helper. Because he didn't finish high school, Danny couldn't get into the electrical workers union. He eventually earned a GED (equivalency diploma), but the union wouldn't accept it. The few and petty jobs he had were obtained through connections.

Without a high school diploma, and unable to get an electrician's card like his father and brothers, Danny was handed a second chance by his father.

"I had opportunities," Danny said in 2013. "My father bought a grocery store in St. Anne. That was for me. I could have had it when I was 28.

54

But I didn't want to work in a grocery store. I wanted to work construction."

"I wasn't going to get a job 40 hours a week punching a clock when I could make $3,000 a week just by answering a phone and meeting someone," he said. "It doesn't get any easier than drug dealing."

"I didn't finish high school because I had ADD (Attention Deficit Disorder). I was a million miles away. I fell behind and wasn't going to graduate with my class."

Danny dropped out of school in his last semester. He said he was a poor student and would have had to go another year to make it all up. He said he didn't know if they were aware of ADD in those days, and they thought it was just a manifestation of being stupid or lazy.

"I got a job with a natural gas pipeline company, putting in pipe from Crete to Paris, Illinois. After the job was over, the next place was North Dakota. I didn't want to go there. You're there a few months and then move on to somewhere else. That's no kind of life."

"After that job ended, I worked for Kankakee Enterprise to get a union card. I worked as a welder at the power houses at Braidwood and LaSalle. The job was finished. I worked in the warehouse at Pyramid. I had a sound card, so I could do alarm systems, the bottom of the ladder."

Danny went to classes to get an upgrade, in order to get into apprentice school, the path to become a journeyman electrician.

But drugs got in the way. Danny started selling pot as early as 1973, while at Eastridge High School in Kankakee.

Peggy and Danny separated for six months in 1978 because Danny was using and selling cocaine. They got back together, had a second child, and then separated again in April 1986. Danny and Peggy were divorced on July 3, 1986. Peggy became a registered nurse in pediatrics at Riverside Hospital in Kankakee.

When FBI agents interviewed Peggy Edwards at her home shortly after the kidnapping, she said she hadn't seen Danny in two weeks. It was unusual he hadn't visited his kids in that time. He owed her child support. She knew about his drug dealing, but thought he was out of the business.

Peggy said Danny was "a nice kid who never grew up."

They broke up because Danny was having sex with other women.

Danny met Nancy through his friendship with Terry Rish. They were in school together and they rode dirt bikes together.

"I started seeing Nancy after her divorce. There were many women, and I told my wife I would never leave her for another woman. But Nancy was the final one. It was her liveliness, her personality. I loved being with her. I couldn't keep away. It was something to leave my wife and kids, especially Gina, who I adore."

Danny was a small time cocaine operator until 1986. His parents gave him their house on Eagle Street when they retired to Florida. Danny and

Peg and the kids lived there. After the divorce, Danny had $20,000 as his half from the sale of the house. An old friend from high school who was selling cocaine showed Danny the business opportunities in selling drugs. It was a lot more than the $12 an hour Danny was earning at Pyramid Electric.

"He made a better offer. He was right. I was making money hand over fist," Danny said in 2013.

The friend said he had a connection in Chicago who could turn that $20,000 into $100,000. He introduced Danny to a drug dealer from Chicago named Mitch Levitt. Danny's first purchase of cocaine was his entire $20,000.

Danny said he started making $3,000 a week selling marijuana and cocaine. He fancied himself as a glamorous gangster, a drug kingpin in the twisted Hollywood sense.

Danny discovered that destruction paid better than construction.

On Monday, August 31, the night before Danny Edwards went on his murderous mission, he stopped by a party at the house of Dave DuBois at 1198 S. Fifth Avenue.

This is something else the police never knew. Danny never told the police because he was uncooperative. Nancy Rish couldn't tell the police about it because she didn't know about it, since this was one of those times Danny disappeared without giving her an explanation.

A man who was at the party who did not want to be identified said, "Danny spent most of the night upstairs alone, wired on coke. Nancy was not there. Danny would occasionally come down to do more blow with people, but mostly went back upstairs."

"Nancy was guilty of nothing other than becoming hooked on drugs and letting him ruin her life," he added.

In his 2013 interviews, Danny said he and Dave shared an apartment together for three or four months. He said he does not remember being at this party, probably because drugs have fogged his memory. He also said he does not remember Nancy Rish driving him to the pay phone or to Cobb Park on the night of the kidnapping. He said he thought he drove himself.

Danny Edwards went home after a night of snorting cocaine at that party. The next evening, he had Nancy Rish drive him to begin his evil deed.

People saw two sides of Danny Edwards. He was a loyal friend to some, a violent thug to others. It all depended on which side of the cocaine line one sat.

Bob Crawford was Danny Edwards' next door neighbor on Sand Bar Road in 1986. "To me, he was a very good guy. He did favors, helped me out several times," Crawford said.

An insight into Danny's early life came in a 2013 interview with Randy Irps. Randy was Danny's best friend in high school. Danny was the best man when Randy married Beth Wadley at St. Patrick's Catholic Church in Kankakee on September 23, 1978.

"I had to wake him up an hour before the wedding," Randy said "I went to his house and he was asleep. I said, 'I'm getting married in an hour!' Danny said it's all right, we have time. He took a shower and got dressed and we got there 10 minutes before the wedding. He was that relaxed about everything."

Randy and Danny met at Eastridge High School in Kankakee.

"The Danny who did the kidnapping is not the Danny I knew."

"You couldn't pick a better guy for your friend. He was a lot of fun. He would do anything for you. He was a normal guy in high school. We went to games, and so on."

But, "He wanted to be somebody, to do something big. He was full of himself. He wanted to be the center of attention."

"He'd go the last mile for you. He'd be the first one to defend you."

Randy said it was in 1972 or 1973 when "some black students started beating up a white girl. Danny got off the bus and kicked the black guy's ass. That took a lot, to go into a crowd of black guys."

Danny recalled the incident when I mentioned it to him in December 2013. It happened in his junior year at Eastridge High School.

"A couple of black guys were pushing her around in the hallway. I remember her name. It was Alexia. They didn't hurt her because I jumped right in. I kicked their asses. Her mother called my parents that night and thanked them. When I came home, my dad asked me what happened at school. He said a couple of black guys were beating up a girl and you stepped in. I said, of course I did, that's what you taught me to do. At the time, I was one of the tougher kids. I grew up with four older brothers, so I knew how to take care of myself."

Alexia Chambers Helm was surprised when I told her that Edwards remembered the incident. She said in 2013, "Yes, that's true, he saved me. I was 14 and a freshman. It was right around when they had the racial riots. A couple of black guys in my art class were bothering me and had locked me in the art supply room with them and shut off the light. I started screaming. We had a sub that day, so naturally she did nothing but open the door. No punishment or nothing. When class was over, they followed me to the bus area and started shoving me into glass doors. Here came Danny and beat the tar out of the main one. Kids were circled around cheering Danny on, even the black kids. They never bothered me again."

Randy remembered, "I would pick Danny up for school. One day I went to his house and his mother told him I was there to pick him up. He said, 'I'm not going, I quit.' It was his junior year. I'm not sure if he went back, but he did quit before he graduated."

Randy said, "The Department Of Corrections website says he has no tattoos or marks. I know he has two burn marks on his arm. I put them there. He would do anything for a bet. I said, I'll put a twenty dollar bill on your arm, and if I can burn a pinhole through it with a lit cigar, you can have the bill. I was doing it and it burned his arm. It made a mark, but not a hole. He said, do it again. He wanted that twenty."

Danny also recalled that incident nearly 40 years later when I mentioned it to him. He said he thought it was a hundred dollar bill. He showed me the scars he still has on his right arm. He wanted that money.

Randy and Beth echoed the words of so many others about the drug scene in Kankakee. "In the 1970s and 1980s, everybody was doing pot. You were a bit of an oddity if you didn't."

"If you didn't do cocaine in the 1980s, you were almost an outcast," said another survivor of that Kankakee era, who preferred not to be identified. He said it was his lawyer who got him into cocaine. Some of the lawyer's clients paid him in cocaine. "Judges, assistant state's attorneys, everybody was doing it. On weekends you'd see people in bars going into the bathrooms for 15 minutes to do cocaine."

Beth Irps also noted another Kankakee fact of life: "When I was 17, I was told I had to sign an affidavit swearing I would vote straight Republican if I wanted to get a certain job. I wouldn't sign it, and I didn't get the job."

Randy smiled when he said Danny stole Peg from him. Randy was "sort of dating" Peg, but she chose Danny. "So I stopped dating Peg and started dating her sister, Carol McKenna. Then I went in the Army."

It all turned out all right because Danny introduced Randy to Beth. She was 14 and Randy was 16. Randy wasn't able to be best man at Danny's wedding because Randy was in the Army. After he got out of the Army, he met Beth coincidentally at a wedding they both happened to attend.

Beth Irps said, "Danny was very charismatic with the girls. He was well liked."

"His parents were great people. But they coddled him, since he was the youngest," Randy said. "When he was 16, they bought him a new car, a Buick Grand Sport, blue and white."

Randy remembered the time Danny was chased by the River Patrol. "There was a no-wake zone because of flooding, but Danny didn't think it meant him. He outran the River Patrol boats. He ran his boat onto land and beached it. He was a daredevil. We called him Gator for that."

"There were several reasons why Danny and I stopped hanging around," Randy said. "I got married, he got divorced, and he started with cocaine. He hid that from me because he knew I didn't do that. I settled down and he was still riding dirt bikes."

"At Danny's trial, he told me in the courthouse, 'I will not go to prison.' I thought he was going to commit suicide, maybe jump over the third floor railing on the day he was convicted."

Randy said he was subpoenaed to testify as a character witness at Danny's sentencing. He said Danny was too ashamed to look at him in court, but he noticed the Smalls were shooting daggers at him with their eyes.

"When one of Danny's parents died, he could have gone to the funeral home. He would have to be handcuffed and have two guards, and everybody else would have to cleared out of the funeral home, even the parking lot. It would cost $6,000. The family was willing to pay it to bring Danny from Pontiac, but Danny said no, he did not want to embarrass the family."

Danny confirmed the story. He said he did not want to disrupt his mother's funeral by having the police clear the place so he could show up in handcuffs with two armed guards. He wasn't going to do that.

At Danny's trial, prosecutor Frank Nowicki said, "Since the day he was born, Danny Edwards had everything his way." He said the record "didn't indicate that Edwards turned bad because of bad upbringing, it showed he turned bad in spite of good upbringing. All testified how good his life was. His brother, David, told you when he was growing up that Danny was like the rest of them. But look how the rest have turned out. Danny Edwards wasn't a person that was abused by his family. He wasn't beaten. He didn't do without. The defense hasn't come here and told you this kid never had a chance, that he had such a rough life. What they told you is, since day one, Danny Edwards has had every break."

At his trial, Danny's lawyers tried to paint a sympathetic picture of a disadvantaged youth, a poor student who had a difficult childhood because his father traveled a lot, and who was teased by his brothers. But not all his family supported this argument. George Edwards III, known as "Duke" and 14 years older than Danny, testified that Danny "got off to a bad start. He quit high school when he was a junior. He worked for my dad in his grocery store, but that didn't work out." Duke said Danny worked at Pyramid Electric with his other brothers, but he couldn't get into the union and basically was an "errand boy."

It can be argued that Danny Edwards was lucky in several respects. He was lucky his life of cocaine abuse was stopped before it killed him. He was lucky he was not executed. He was lucky to go to a government facility that would take care of him for the rest of his life, including providing free medical care that included a number of heart operations. And, as he will tell you, his greatest gift was when he found salvation for his soul.

Chapter 7
Nancy Rish

Just how did a good Catholic girl end up in a maximum security prison with a life sentence for kidnapping and murder?

Nancy Rish was not much different from other girls at the time, no better or worse than any of her female friends. Most of them faced the prevalent drug scene in 1970s and 1980s Kankakee. There were other girls in her social circle who made many of the same choices she did, good and bad. They came through life's problems, and many found success and happiness.

But none of them had the misfortune to hook up with Danny Edwards.

Nancy Rish was very insecure despite her beauty. Like most beautiful girls, she knew it and she accentuated it. She was no different in that respect, either. She dressed well and had her hair fixed stylishly. One woman who knew her said, "She looked like a Barbie. She definitely liked to have a good time. Danny was a partier. He always had a nice sports car, dressed nice and was a huge flirt. He had no problem getting women. Amazing what drugs can do to someone."

Nancy Rish was born on the day after Christmas in 1961, the youngest of four daughters of Paul and Genevieve Woodrich of Kankakee.

Genevieve was born in Kankakee in 1929 to Lithuanian immigrants John and Petranella Garski. Her father worked at Radeke Brewery and died when Genevieve was six years old. Petranella and her seven children raised poultry, tended a garden, and the children went to work when they turned 16. Genevieve worked at Lecour's women's store in Kankakee, in the shoe department. Paul Woodrich drove a truck, and he made a delivery there one day. They were introduced by his sister, who also worked at Lecour's.

Genevieve contracted polio in both legs in 1952 at the age of 23, when she was eight months pregnant with her daughter Linda. Her oldest daughter Paula was eight months old at the time. Genevieve was in the hospital and in rehab for a year. She suffered the effects of polio for the rest of her life.

Coping with young children and her illness put a strain on the marriage. Paul became an alcoholic and started his downward slide. The marriage was crumbling by 1961 when Nancy arrived, which was pretty much a surprise.

Paul and Genevieve were Catholic and did not believe in divorce, which made for some very rough years before they separated. Parents always teach their children lessons, whether it be good or bad. Nancy said she "learned at a very young age to not ask questions, and pretend as if everything was fine. I guess I just stuffed it. Uncertainty was the norm, and has continued to be throughout my whole life."

Paul Woodrich finally left the family house at 183 W. Longwood Avenue in 1968 when Nancy was six years old. Genevieve divorced him in 1972. Paul was not a part of his family's life after that, and the family never spoke about it. Genevieve raised her daughters while working at Armour Pharmaceutical for nearly 33 years, starting work when Nancy was one year old. She retired in 1995. The family attended St. Teresa Catholic Church.

Nancy's father sold cars at Romy Hammes Ford for a short time and he worked construction at times, but mostly he was an alcoholic and a bum. For a while, he lived under the Schuyler Avenue bridge.

Paul Woodrich drifted around town and was arrested several times over the years, usually for trivial and bizarre acts. For example, he was arrested in 1973 for not paying cabbie Danny Wagner for a ride. When his case came to court three months later, he was placed on six months conditional discharge, fined $50 -- and was ordered to pay the cab driver $2.85.

Woodrich was working pumping gas at a Shell station at 1171 E. Court Street in August 1974 when he got into a dispute with a customer about how many gallons was requested. Woodrich pulled a gun and threatened to kill the man. He was arrested for aggravated assault and weapons violations. The charges later were dropped.

Paul Woodrich got in a fight with another man in June 1985 and was pushed off the Schuyler Avenue bridge into the Kankakee River. Two men rescued him.

The limited contact Nancy had with her father was not pleasant. He wasn't physically violent, but she said he was emotionally abusive. Her childhood was not easy.

Nancy knew George Ryan's daughters.

"I went to school with George Ryan's triplets at King Upper Grade Center. I never met George. At my 13th birthday party, the triplets were invited and they spent the night."

Nancy attended Mark Twain Elementary School for the first three grades, Lincoln Elementary School for two years, and then King Upper Grade Center for two years before entering Eastridge High School in Kankakee. She left in her sophomore year in November 1977, after she became pregnant.

"When I became pregnant at 15, I was too scared and ashamed to tell anyone, especially my mother. Even the day my mother asked me if I was pregnant, I couldn't bring myself to tell her. I eventually did. I then quit school. I could never face going to school pregnant."

"So it was decided that the best thing was to get married. At sixteen years, who does that?"

Nancy said she was surprised that Terry Rish agreed to marry her, because his parents were opposed to the marriage.

Nancy Woodrich married Terry Rish on January 7, 1978. Their son Benjamin was born June 2, 1978. Nancy and Terry were divorced on June 24, 1981.

"I got pregnant at 15 and was married at 16," Nancy said. "We were divorced three years later. We were just both too young, and we got married for the wrong reasons. We were not each other's high school sweethearts."

Adding to the strain on their marriage was the fact they lived in the other half of a townhouse in Bradley where Terry's parents, Odie and Tommie Rish, lived. The Rishs often did not get along well with her.

"To no one's surprise, our marriage lasted less than three years. I basically left a loveless marriage."

"I really had no ambition," Nancy said. "He was 18. He worked at the A.O. Smith factory and he had no ambition in life. I could not see a future for us. So we got a divorce and I was on my own."

"Then I found out how hard it really was."

Around the time of her divorce, Nancy was diagnosed with Guillian-Barre syndrome, a condition of the central nervous system.

"It was frightening not knowing what was happening to me. One morning I awoke and felt numbness in both my hands and feet. It quickly progressed, hindering my motor skills. It also impaired my vision."

Nancy got custody of Benjamin and was awarded child support. Terry paid it for a year and a half, until he was laid off from A.O. Smith. The water heater manufacturer was one of Kankakee's biggest industries. It closed in the early 1980s, along with the Roper stove and lawn tractor factory and a number of other large industries. The factory town of Kankakee lost most of its industry during that decade. The city still has not recovered.

Nancy moved into an apartment at 894 S. Main Street after her divorce. She got unemployment checks for awhile, until she found a job in the men's clothing section at Alden's department store. She lived in the apartment for a year and then lived with her mother for six months.

She then moved to Dallas, Texas, with a girlfriend, leaving her son with her mother until she found a job and apartment. A month later, her mother brought Benjamin to Dallas. Nancy worked at Dillard's clothing store. She also worked as a waitress at Spats and at Dial America Marketing. That lasted three months before she went back to Kankakee because she was ill with Guillian-Barre syndrome. She was sick until June 1983.

In Kankakee, she worked at The Other Place tavern for six months. Then she got a job at American Body Wrap in Bradley for a few months. She also sold Mary Kay cosmetics. In March 1985, she and her son moved to an apartment at 694 S. Greenwood Avenue -- a few blocks from the Small and Ryan houses. She worked part time in the Jewel supermarket deli on South Washington Avenue and at Starnco as a receptionist. But she was let go very quickly from Starnco because she lacked typing skills.

Nancy quit her job at Jewel in August 1985 to take a job at Municipal Trust & Savings in Bourbonnais. She worked there for 10 months. She was fired because her drawer was short on three different occasions. After the first time, bank president Merlin Karlock had Nancy take a lie detector test and he sent her to a hypnotist. She passed the lie detector test, given by Robert W. Cormack & Associates of Oak Brook, on December 16, 1985. Court records show that, "Mr. Karlock stated after checking the bank records, no shortage could be found." But an error was reported two more times.

In April 1987, Nancy worked at The Addition as a laborer for a week. She quit because her hours conflicted with the availability of the babysitter.

It was in that same time period that her father was murdered. Paul Woodrich, an alcoholic who hit bottom and stayed there, was living with Jimmy Holmes, the owner of a Kankakee men's clothing store. Holmes often took in people who needed help. Also living at Holmes' residence at 2708 Cooper Drive was Noble Smith, a 23-year-old mental patient who recently was released from Manteno State Hospital. Smith had many run-ins with the law over the years. He was considered so dangerous that an assistant state's attorney started carrying a gun after being threatened by Smith in court. Smith and Woodrich got into an argument outside the house on April 13, 1986. Smith beat the 59-year-old Woodrich to death and then dragged the dead body down the street. Smith was found sitting across the street from the body. Woodrich died of a ruptured heart, with his entire chest cavity crushed, Coroner James Orrison said. Smith was found not guilty by reason of insanity and was sentenced to 20 years in a mental facility. The judge was John Michela.

The bizarre death of her father became even more bizarre in this dysfunctional family. "When my dad was killed, I wasn't even sure what I was supposed to feel," Nancy said. "I was sad, always shame was there, and strangely enough a little feeling of relief, I think. My father had no one for so many years, which he brought on himself, but nonetheless it was sad to me. His parents were deceased, he never remarried, he was estranged from all his family, and was beat to death at the age of 59. I can remember being at the inquest with my three sisters. It was the strangest thing. It was as if we were discussing someone of acquaintance. This was our father. I had good memories, but they were so few and long ago. My father never had a funeral service. He was cremated and left at the funeral home. I mostly felt sad. I, being the youngest, just went along. I never felt I had a voice in most matters, that my feelings weren't valid."

At the age of 19, Nancy Rish was a single mom working part-time at Jewel and at Municipal Bank, plus selling cosmetics and cleaning houses to support herself and her son.

Nancy said she had little ambition or direction as a youth. Nancy was pretty, charming and smart, and she should have been able to become anything she wanted. But she was insecure and damaged. There was no positive male figure in her life. And, like many young women in that position, she had no example to show her what a real man should be. As a result, she made bad choices.

Her worst choice came in 1985, when Nancy met Danny Edwards at the Dam Tap, a bar on South Washington Avenue in Kankakee near the hydroelectric company dam on the Kankakee River.

Danny noticed her in the bar. He pursued her, but she said no. He was married at the time, with two children.

"I was aware of who he was. I met him at the Dam Tap, but I had seen him in other bars. He was very persuasive," Nancy said.

She finally relented and started dating him.

Danny separated from his wife and started divorce proceedings. And he kept pursuing Nancy. Danny rented a house on Sand Bar Road in Aroma Park which was owned by Nancy's sister and brother-in-law, Lori and Larry Guimond. Danny eventually convinced Nancy to move in with him.

Danny kept telling Nancy that she worked too hard and that she should quit her jobs and take it easier. Nancy liked the idea of someone taking care of her and her son and helping with the bills.

In the meantime, Danny had some money from his share of the sale of his house after his divorce. He decided to invest that money to become a bigger dealer in the cocaine business.

But Nancy and Danny had a rocky relationship. He dominated her and sometimes abused her.

Danny offered to pay the rent on a townhouse for Nancy and Benjamin in Bourbonnais. She moved into 756 Stratford Drive East in the Briarcliff subdivision in December 1986. Danny remained in his house on Sand Bar Road, where he could continue his drug dealing.

"He wanted me and my son away from what he was doing."

Danny's cocaine sales brought enough cash for him to buy a motorcycle, a used speedboat and more. He took Nancy on a 10-day vacation to the Virgin Islands in December 1986. It was intended to ease the rift in the relationship.

That vacation was a disaster for the relationship, mostly because it highlighted the problems that had been building for a long time. It signaled the end for them, she said.

"We had been fighting before, but from that point on, it was over."

The rest of December wasn't any better. On Christmas Eve, Nancy said she and Danny were supposed to finish Christmas shopping. "He was supposed to pick me up and then go to my mother's house for dinner. I called him a few times. There was no answer, so I drove to his house on Sand Bar

Road. He was in bed, and it was obvious he was up all night partying. He said he had no intention of going shopping, and he was upset that I interrupted his sleep. We argued. I went and finished shopping."

"When I got home, there were things missing from my house. An hour later, Danny came over, very mad. He wanted to know where his presents were that he had already bought for his children. They had been in the trunk of my car, and I was gone while he came over, because I think that is the purpose he first came over, to get the gifts. I told him where they were. I said, you promised we would have a nice holiday Christmas. He said, 'That is beside the point. I come for my gifts. We are through. We are over. Just give me the gifts.' He started taking the gifts under the Christmas tree that were there for my son, and some gifts he bought me. He was just taking everything out of the house. I tried to call the police. He ripped the phone off the wall. Ben was in his bedroom. I ran next door and had Baughman call the police."

It should have been all over for Danny and Nancy at the end of 1986. She was in Bourbonnais and he was in Aroma Park. However, a few weeks later, Danny was busted for cocaine. The police took his cash and his drugs. Danny had no money and no place to go. So he went to Nancy's place with a sob story. He was in a panic. He said he was facing 30 years if he was convicted on the drug charges unless he cooperated with the police in trapping Mitch Levitt. And he told Nancy he couldn't go back to the house in Aroma Park because he was afraid of Mitch, since he said it was Mitch's money and cocaine that the police seized.

Suddenly, the relationship was not over.

Nancy let him move in.

"He was paying the rent on the place and I was not working."

But they were no longer close. He slept downstairs and she slept upstairs.

Nancy said she started to look for a job to gain a little independence and a little distance from Danny Edwards. But she didn't know he was pulling yet another scam on her.

"He did not want me talking to friends. I was pretty isolated. I was looking for work and I wondered why I wasn't getting any calls back. Danny always answered the phone. He took the calls. I didn't know until later that I was getting calls for jobs. He always said I wasn't there. A friend later told me she called but couldn't get through."

By that time, Nancy said she lost all her confidence in herself. She said her self image always was low, which is why she got into drinking and drugs, and it was why this attractive young woman went for someone like Danny Edwards. She had no high school diploma, no skills and she hadn't worked until after her divorce. And now they both were doing drugs.

"Everything was so crazy after he moved in," she said.

Things went very bad. There was a fight on May 1, 1987 when the police were called. "He told me to get out of the house, I was no longer to live there. He took every piece of clothing and every shoe, everything out of the closet, my drawers, and threw it on the front lawn. I went to the police station. By the time the police came, everything was on the garage floor."

Nancy said they fought again in July 1987. "Danny ripped my shirt off, grabbed me and knocked me against the wall. He grabbed ahold of my neck and shirt and tore it off. It left bruises on me." Nancy and her son left the house after that. There was another altercation, and Nancy and Ben stayed with Julie Nanos for a few days.

Nancy Rish said she did not know anything about the kidnapping until the day they both were arrested and charged.

"I never even heard of the Smalls at that time," she said in 2013. "I guess I heard of Governor Small Park, but I was in my own world. I didn't know who they were."

But she started seeing changes in Edwards that made her think something out of the ordinary was going on with him.

Nancy saw him building the box in their garage that summer, but he told her it was for his brother to store pool chemicals and equipment.

There was an incident, an outburst three days before the kidnapping that really showed Edwards' pent-up stress.

"He was like a caged-up animal. He was making comments that his back was up against the wall. He left all the time, and was gone for hours at a time."

Edwards had "mood swings" with a "frantic desperation." The days just before the kidnapping were worse.

"He really was acting very out of character. I would ask him what was the matter and he would say, 'You don't need to know. You don't want to know.' He said, 'There's something I have to do.'" She said she begged him to not get back into cocaine dealing. "No, it's not that," he replied. "It's just a one-time thing."

At one point, he jumped to his feet and started screaming, "You just don't realize how important this is!"

This was when he waved a gun in her face and threatened to kill Nancy, her son and himself. Edwards had been drinking that night and he fell asleep. Nothing was said about the outburst the next day.

And then, it all became evident why Danny Edwards was acting so frenetic during the previous weeks. He kidnapped a man, buried him alive, the man died, and the police did not need to do a lot of footwork to find the perpetrator. Danny's ineptitude led the police right to their front door.

When the police arrested Nancy and took her to the Bourbonnais police station, they asked her if she wanted to call a lawyer.

"The only name I thought of was Leonard Sacks," Nancy said in 2013. "He suggested two lawyers from Olympia Fields. I later realized he had the honesty to want me to get a lawyer from outside of Kankakee."

"The cops called those lawyers, but they said they couldn't get through to them. They pushed for me to get a local attorney. They kept pushing for me to get an attorney so they could get on with the interrogation. I had met Scott Swaim through a neighbor. So he came to mind. I called him and he got there quickly."

"He talked to me for five minutes and then he said, 'Let's talk to them. Tell them what they need to know so you can get home.'"

The police file shows that Swaim was called at 2:05 p.m. He arrived at the police station at 2:15 p.m. He started talking to Nancy Rish at 2:20 p.m. The interrogation by the police, with Swaim present, continued at 2:30 p.m.

Rish said Swaim was a civil attorney, not a criminal attorney.

"He kept telling me, 'Do you want to go home?' He never spoke or objected or said don't answer, during all four days. He never said don't answer."

In the state police file transcript of the 13 hours of police interrogation, Swaim does not speak up in Rish's defense once.

The arraignment in court was on the following Tuesday.

"Five minutes before the arraignment, he told me, 'The court will appoint an attorney for you. Your family can't afford me.' Then it was good luck and good bye."

So how did a young lady who never was in trouble, except for the poor judgment of living with a man who sold cocaine, end up in prison for life?

Certainly there was nothing in her life to indicate this. The arrest for kidnapping and murder was the first trouble Nancy had with the law. She had no juvenile record. The only problem she had as an adult was speeding tickets on December 10, 1986, and on April 24, 1987. She pleaded guilty both times and was fined $23 plus $27 in court costs.

There never was any behavior on her part to indicate she would participate in a crime. Her family and friends testified at her trial in 1988 about the kind of person she was. Her sister Lori Guimond said Nancy often needed money as she struggled as a single mother, but she would never ask for help. Nancy dated men who would be demanding on her because she didn't like to be the one who made all the decisions. Her mother told the jury how Nancy held three jobs at a time to support her son.

Terry Rish said Nancy was a good mother and wife. He said money was not important when they were married. He said Nancy never used drugs while they were married. She started that after meeting Danny Edwards. He said Nancy loves her son, and her son loves her.

"According to Terry Rish, Nancy Rish is incapable of hurting any-body or being involved in any criminal activities," a court document from a December 9, 1988, interview said. "Also, Mr. Rish stated he believes the defendant could not be involved in anything like this because it does not fit her character."

The interview also included, "Mr. Rish stated that he knew Danny Edwards for approximately 15 years, and he was a forceful man and could scare a woman and put fear into her to do what he wanted."

Danny Edwards, from the day of his arrest and throughout all these years, has maintained that Nancy Rish knew nothing about what he was planning. In the brief statement Edwards made to police on September 5, 1987, "Edwards stated that his live-in girlfriend Nancy Rish inquired as to what he was building and he told her that he was building a box to store fire-wood." The police report noted Edwards "made up a story" about taking her bicycle to be fixed. And he played the tape recorder into the telephone and "he did not think Rish saw him doing this." As for selling the box to a black man, the 1987 police report noted that Edwards said, "The black male pur-chased the box for $100, as well as the white Maytag dryer for $75. Edwards stated that Rish was home at the time and witnessed this transaction. It should be noted that Rish stated that this was not true, that that was a lie Edwards had told her to say."

Anita Hamilton told the court about Nancy Rish's hair appointment on Tuesday, September 1. She gave Nancy a cut, color and perm. They chat-ted and "she was calm, friendly, just simple talk." Hamilton was asked if Rish showed any evidence of anxiety or nervousness. "None whatsoever," she replied.

A number of Nancy Rish's friends testified in her behalf. They testi-fied at the time, and they swear in statements today, that Nancy acted nor-mal and was not upset or nervous in those last weeks before the kidnapping. That testimony is in the chapter on the trial and in the chapter on her inno-cence.

Chapter 8
The Barn Boss

*"They had Jack Daniels, they had syringe needles, a bag of weed.
I opened the door. I said, damn, what's going on in here?"*
Kankakee County jail guard Troy Whitlow, December 7, 1987

One would think that a person in jail on charges of kidnapping and murder, and facing a possible death sentence, might be frightened and even humbled.

Danny Edwards, ever the wise guy, was not humbled.

Edwards was the center of national attention in a very high profile murder case for burying a prominent multi-millionaire alive. Yet, he continued to act like the small town thug he was, and he used the corrupt local system as if no one was watching.

Kankakee has always been a corrupt city. It isn't just Governor Len Small of Kankakee, who sold pardons to Al Capone and other gangsters in the 1920s, and who bribed a jury to win an acquittal for embezzling millions of dollars. And it isn't just Governor George Ryan of Kankakee, who sold driver's licenses, took payoffs and kickbacks from connected contractors, and who went to prison on racketeering and fraud convictions. Favors and justice have always been for sale in Kankakee.

Anyone who wanted a job at the large mental hospitals in Kankakee and Manteno had to make a payoff to Len Small, and later make a contribution to the local Republican party, work in the campaigns, buy a car from the McBroom dealership and buy prescriptions at Ryan's pharmacy.

Otto Kerner, one of four recent Illinois governors to go to prison, was caught only after the woman who bribed him deducted the bribe from her income taxes as a business expense. She was astonished to learn that the taxman did not consider bribery as a normal cost of doing business in Illinois.

Governor Rod Blagojevich similarly was surprised to find it is not legal to sell a vacant U.S. Senate seat to the highest bidder, or to shake down a children's hospital for a $50,000 campaign contribution if it wanted to continue receiving state funding.

Corruption in Kankakee is what George Ryan has called "business as usual."

It was business as usual a quarter of a century earlier when Kankakee County Sheriff Carl McNutt ran his jail with an open door policy, letting favored prisoners out to chauffeur him to local bars and on out-of-state vacations. One prisoner used his free time to commit burglaries before checking back in for the night. McNutt was indicted on 13 charges of outrageous acts, including conspiring with the operators of the gambling joints and houses of prostitution in Pembroke Township.

Kankakee always has been famous for its whorehouses. Nell Clark was the most prominent madam, with her West Avenue brothel operating openly from the 1890s to the 1940s. The U.S. War Department put Kankakee off-limits to military personnel during World War II because of this. The isolated Pembroke Township became a "wild west" haven for whorehouses, gambling joints and other unbridled vice.

McNutt's indictment came after the *Chicago Tribune* reported in 1961 that "law enforcement had collapsed in the county during McNutt's three years as sheriff. The county harbors wide open brothels, horse betting joints, slot machines and payoff pinball games. Gamblers and vice patrons, some in their teens, flock to the county from Chicago and other cities in northern Illinois and Indiana. The county prosecutor's investigators were said to be seeking evidence of alleged payoffs which permit the gambling machines and bordellos to operate unchecked in the county."

Nothing was done about this long time situation and McNutt's scandalous administration until two deputies found a sack in the jail's pantry with $8,000 cash that could not be explained. That is when local authorities decided to begin an investigation.

McNutt hired as his chief deputy Paul Leathers, a shady local character and gambler who was murdered in his Kankakee home, allegedly by a Mob hit man. The crime was never solved. McNutt also hired as an assistant deputy Dean Bauer, a telephone company lineman with no law enforcement experience, but with connections to local political bosses such as the McBrooms and Ryans.

The only thing unusual about all these charges, in the universe that is Kankakee County, was that Carl McNutt was forced to resign after pleading guilty to "official misconduct" in 1962. McNutt then was given a state job as a meat inspector.

After being arrested on the most serious charges, Danny Edwards ran the Kankakee County jail as if it was still the McNutt era.

"Danny Edwards got preferential treatment in jail. He was able to leave the cell block to take care of his business. And with his friendships with the correctional officers, he was getting things done that we couldn't get done, in terms of phone calls, mail going out, things of that nature."

That is what Thomas James, a 43-year-old burglar, told the police and the court when all this came to light.

"He told me arrangements had been made for him to be taken care of by certain correctional guards because money was being paid for these particular services." The money came from Danny's brother, "Duke" Edwards, who was a close friend of the Smalls and the Ryans.

James said jail guards Troy Whitlow and Del Williams got $100 a week from Duke Edwards for "taking care" of Danny. James said he understood this to mean letting Edwards visit Nancy Rish in her cell and ordering special meals from Dale's Pizza and Lil Robert's rib joint.

"He said he had charge accounts at two places (Dale's Pizza and Lil Robert's)," James said. Meals were ordered and brought to the jail. Edwards treated the other inmates in the cell block to the bounty.

This was the man who was behind bars for committing one of the most heinous offenses in Kankakee history, a man who still was in the glare of publicity from local reporters, Chicago newspaper photographers and TV cameramen.

James was in the Kankakee County jail after being stopped by local police, who found he was wanted on a warrant from Tennessee for jumping probation on a burglary conviction. He met Danny Edwards in the Kankakee County jail.

"He asked if I wanted to get high, and he produced a marijuana cigarette and we smoked it," James said.

Danny Edwards could get anything he wanted in the Kankakee County jail -- marijuana, cocaine, even sex.

Troy Whitlow, Del Williams and Joe Tharpe were guards at the jail. It was surprising how little it took to bribe these men.

Marijuana and cocaine were smuggled in empty cigarette packs and inside cassette tape holders. Edwards even paid the guards to scrape mayonnaise off his sandwiches, since he didn't like mayonnaise.

This wasn't some special power that Danny Edwards possessed. This was business as usual in the Kankakee County jail, and it had been going on long before Danny Edwards went behind bars. He just knew about it and he used it.

Daniel "Squirt" Dunigan and Rick Kibbons were in jail with Edwards. Dunigan was caught with a kilo of cocaine and got a 12-year sentence. Kibbons got a four-year sentence for burglary, was released, got a five-year sentence for theft, was released again, and was awaiting sentencing on another burglary conviction.

It was just after the prisoners watched a TV newscast about the kidnapping that Edwards approached Kibbons.

"I am the guy. I am the one that they arrested for that Stephen Small murder," Edwards said.

"Danny Edwards talked to the guards a lot," Kibbons later testified, under a promise of immunity. "He said he had connections and could get a couple of guards jobs at Armour (pharmaceutical company) or with his brother's electrical company."

Kibbons said Tharpe gave Edwards drugs, packed in a roll of toilet paper. "Marijuana came right from Troy's front pocket in a plastic baggie. He shared it with me and Daniel Dunigan."

Kibbons said Edwards told him he paid Troy Whitlow $100 to get a key to Rish's cell. It was late October or early November when Kibbons saw Whitlow lead Edwards out of his cell. When Edwards came back, Kibbons said Edwards told the other prisoners that he and Rish had sex in her jail cell.

Edwards told Dunigan and Kibbons they could bring their girlfriends in for sex if they paid the guards $100. Dunigan called his girlfriend, Brenda Berry, and told her to buy marijuana and cocaine from a friend, put it in a cigarette pack, and give it and $100 to jail guard Del Williams. Kibbons called his wife Lauren and told her the same thing.

It was the day before Thanksgiving 1987.

Kibbons said, "On that particular day, Troy Whitlow came up and he pulled a key out of his pocket, and he said, 'This is the key. Set it up. Tonight's the night. Call your ladies and have the money.' We called them."

The Berry and Kibbons women came to the jail. They had the drugs and some Crown Royal whiskey in a Pepsi can. But both women had only $50 each. That was enough for the guards

Williams led the women to a third floor classroom in the jail building. Their men were waiting for them with blankets on the floor. The women gave the marijuana and the cocaine to their men. Then the couples had sex.

Williams came in ten minutes later and said, "Time's up." Dunigan took Brenda's panties as a souvenir. The guard led the women back to the visitor's room.

Brenda Berry and Lauren Kibbons testified to this at Edwards' trial.

Two days later, Brenda visited Dunigan in jail, and he put a letter in her pocket. He had given her another letter three weeks earlier.

Dunigan told her to type and mail the letter, the same as she had done with the previous letter.

The first letter mystified Berry.

"It was…it was stupid," she later testified in court. "It was a friendly note, asking how he (Danny) was doing, and was he OK, was his girlfriend OK. It was…it was strange. It was…I couldn't understand it."

"He asked me not to ask any questions, just mail it. Just -- he asked me to type it and mail it from downtown (Chicago)."

She did.

"It's a way to pay the telephone bill," is how Dunigan explained it. He meant that the Edwards family would help them pay their bills if they helped with the letter.

Edwards also told Dunigan that if he beat the death penalty, he would make a movie about his life and pay Dunigan from the royalties. But Dunigan and Berry never did see any money from the Edwards family.

The first letter was written by Danny Edwards, mailed to him in jail with a Chicago postmark, in an attempt to convince police that it came from the drug dealers who really were behind the kidnapping. Edwards told Dunigan he wanted to make police believe it came from the "real" kidnappers, so he could avoid the death penalty.

Thomas James said Edwards showed him the first letter and admitted he had it sent to himself. The letter said that Edwards "was doing fine in conducting himself, and as long as he kept names out of the investigation, as long as he continued (to do so) he would be taken care of, and had nothing to worry about. And in terms of Nancy Rish, because she knew nothing, therefore there was no way she could be convicted or sent to prison."

And then Edwards showed James a draft of a second letter. Danny Edwards, the high school dropout, wanted James to help him write it.

Even the convicted burglar, Thomas James, could see it was poorly written. "There were grammatical and spelling errors, so I helped him," James said.

"He was going to send it to the Smalls, to give credibility to the other letter," James said. "I told him I thought it was wrong, that he should leave the Small family alone, that they had suffered enough. I wanted no further, anything to do with it."

Edwards gave James marijuana and cocaine for helping him with the grammar and spelling.

After having sex in the jail, Dunigan phoned Berry that night. He told her to type up this second letter and mail it from downtown Chicago. This letter was to be addressed to Nancy Small in Kankakee.

Dunigan asked her several times to do this before she finally did it. Berry was a janitor at Argonne National Laboratory. She used one of the typewriters there. She finally put the letter in the mail on December 15, addressed to Nancy Small, 917 Cobb Boulevard, Kankakee, Illinois.

In the meantime, Thomas James tipped off the police. Sgt. William Willis told Nancy Small the letter was coming. She got it on December 16.

The letter read:

"Dear Mrs. Small, It is felt that the time has come for us to write this short correspondence to you. To begin with, allow us to express our condolences to you on the loss of your husband, for it was not meant that he should pass away. However, we felt that a blood debt was owed by the Small family in this, and rest assured that the matter has not been resolved, and sometime in the future the debt must be satisfied. At such time, the Small family must remember two rules that will not be compromised. One is that no authorities are to be brought into the matter. Two, you should be prepared to pay money requested without hesitation, money that you stole from us some years ago. It would be to your advantage to make some arrangements to gather the money now or in the immediate future so that no attention will be drawn to the act that you are in immediate need of that great sum of ready cash. In closing, it needs to be said that this matter will be resolved to our satisfaction, whether it be in Kankakee or in Arizona or wherever we deem it necessary to reclaim what we feel is justly ours."

(signed) "With Regards."

Arizona is where Leslie Small, Stephen's brother, and family lived.

Edwards denied he wrote the letter to Mrs. Small, in a telephone interview with a *Daily Journal* reporter at the time. Edwards said, "I don't know about the letter. They are trying to make me look as bad as they can."

Edwards was lying to the reporter.

Guards found a hole broken in a third floor window at the jail on December 1, 1987. A home made rope from torn strips of a jail blanket was fastened through the window, down the outside wall.

The next day, inmate Sherman Akins Jr. told police he saw prisoners Brian Keller and Danny Edwards pulling a small brown bag on a string, through the window from the outside, on November 29. In the bag was a hypodermic needle and marijuana. The prisoners smoked the weed and used the needle to shoot up crushed sleeping pills.

There also was a plan to tie a gun to the string for Danny Edwards to pull up.

Sgt. Gary Dams was making a routine security check on December 2, when he smelled marijuana. He and Officer Chris Benn searched the cells and found marijuana in Edwards' cell.

On December 8, there was a shakedown of the cells. Guards found three marijuana cigarettes hidden in a plastic baggie inside a sandwich in Edwards' cell. Guards also found a hypodermic syringe hidden inside a toothbrush holder. And inside a Shower To Shower body powder bottle in Dunigan's cell, the guards found cigarette rolling papers, six Ibuprofen pills, two Xanax pills, one Adapin pill -- and Brenda Berry's souvenir panties.

A prisoner told investigators that they would burn tissue paper coated with deodorant or baby powder to cover the smell of the marijuana smoke.

"The guards would always say that particular cellblock was where the money was," the prisoner said. "I knew it was going to catch up to them."

Sheriff Thompson questioned guard Troy Whitlow before suspending him on December 7. Participating in the interrogation were Chief Investigator Gary Mitchell, Assistant State's Attorney Clark Erickson and Chief of Corrections Ken Lockwood.

Whitlow was asked if he wanted a lawyer. He asked for Alderman Steve Hunter, and then he signed a waiver that he didn't want a lawyer.

Whitlow admitted Danny Edwards promised to get him a better paying job. He said Danny sent him and Del Williams to see Duke Edwards twice. Duke gave Whitlow $50 for cigarettes, with half of that for the guards. Dean Edwards met Whitlow in the library parking lot and gave him another

$50, telling him to bring Danny pop and cigarettes every now and then.

Whitlow did so, even making sure there was no mayonnaise on Danny's sandwiches.

He had a lot more to tell.

"I came to work one Saturday. I looked in the cell. They were drinking Jack Daniels on ice. They had Jack Daniels, they had syringe needles, a bag of weed. I opened the door. I said, damn, what's going on in here?"

Whitlow said Del Williams brought the drugs and liquor into the jail.

Whitlow seemed to think he was exonerating himself by saying he saw other guards bring in drugs and he knew all about it, even though he didn't bring it in himself.

"I'd go in there and they had more than a party house. You name it, they had it up there!"

Whitlow said guard Joe Tharpe tried to get him to bring a cake to Dunigan. It had marijuana cigarettes in it. Tharpe had a wife, but he spent his money on drugs. "He shot some shit in his arm and then, you know, and after he shot up, you know, just you know, he started going into spasms, and then he just fell on the floor and just became to himself, you know, right in his basement."

"When Sgt. Daniels was off, it was just me, Del and Joe. Joe would go crazy. Joe would just go crazy up there. He had envelopes, cigarette packs, Joe done brought cocaine up there, before Edwards was brought in here. When you first hired me, Chief, Joe was bringing weed up here."

Of Joe Tharpe, Whitlow said, "No, that's just a lost cause. I don't know what he do, he's on it too bad. He leave work, man. One day, he couldn't function, he just had to leave, but nobody else downstairs know what was his problem, because he kept trying to count the inmates and he couldn't do it, he couldn't even count the inmates. He said, 'Why don't you do it.' He was sweating and a little blood was running out of his arm, but didn't nobody in the office know. Sgt. Daniels didn't know. He got wrote up for that, too."

Whitlow said marijuana was smuggled in cassette tapes by removing the screws and taking the tape out. Marijuana was brought in deodorant cans. Prisoners would hug family members to pass drugs.

It was this interview that Whitlow told the sheriff the plan to tie a gun to a string for Danny Edwards to pull up through the hole in the window.

Just after the interview of Whitlow, Edwards and his lawyer Sheldon Reagan asked to meet Thompson in the sheriff's office. Edwards said there was a plan by three inmates in his cell block to escape in the early morning hours of December 10. He said one of the inmates got sick and had a jailer rush into his cell, leaving the door open. Edwards said the plan was to repeat this and then bash the jailer's head against the bars, steal his keys and uniform, break the window in the visitation room and escape.

Danny did admit that Del Williams and Troy Whitlow took care of him by bringing pop, pizza and ribs, and he arranged for them to meet his brother Duke to get better paying jobs. Danny said he had them set up a charge account at the ribs joint and pizza place so they could just sign for the food. Duke would pay the bill. Danny said Joe Tharpe brought in the drugs, and he tried to exonerate Williams and Whitlow.

Del Williams was fired in December.

Troy Whitlow and Del Williams were indicted and charged with official misconduct, obtaining personal advantage, bribery and soliciting a bribe, all felonies. Both men pleaded guilty to all counts on June 19, 1990. They were sentenced to 24 months probation by Judge Daniel Gould.

On top of all that, investigators learned that someone working in the state's attorney's office was tipping drug dealers about upcoming search warrants. The employee refused to take a lie detector test. She was fired and then left the state.

Sheriff Thompson admitted he found, in May 1987, a guard stealing bond money and cash from prisoners to support a $200 weekly cocaine habit. Thompson promised on January 7, 1988, that he would have mandatory drug testing for all sheriffs' department employees. He blamed low wages for the low quality of jail guards.

It shouldn't have surprised Thompson. When Larry Hildebrand became sheriff in December 1974, he conducted a shakedown at the jail on his first day. Officers found hundreds of contraband items, including a five-foot television cable, an 18-foot cloth strip made from blankets and towels, batteries in socks as weapons, bottles of caustic peroxide and more. Several jailers were suspected of allowing prisoners to have the contraband items. It also shouldn't have surprised Hildebrand. This is Kankakee.

However, Danny Edwards just kept showing he was oblivious to everything going on around him.

He wrote a letter on Christmas Eve to jail administrator Lt. Ken Lockwood, complaining of conditions at the jail, after his special privileges had ended.

"Myself and all other inmates are getting very tired of eating cold food and having nothing to drink but water. I have talked to my attorney about this problem and he assured me he would talk to state health inspectors and get something done. It is very difficult to live under these conditions. You would be very surprised at what your urine smells like when you have nothing to drink but water. We need juices or Kool-Aid or something besides water. It gets pretty bad when a man would kill for a can of pop. Under our Constitution, a person is innocent until proven guilty, and I haven't been proven guilty of anything. And I'm getting very tird (sic) and pissed off of having to live under these conditions. We have no laundry service so we are forced to wash our clothes in the shower. Therefore we need clothes lines in our cells to hang our clothes to dry. When your toy soldiers have a shake-down they tear down our clothes lines and throw our clothes on the floor. There are many reporters who want to interview me. And I am going to give them their wish. And it is going to be about this jail and the conditions under we are forced to live."

Prisoners were offered coffee or milk with their meals, but got only water between meals. Edwards again was oblivious to reality in his choice of words, that "a man would kill for a can of pop."

Inmates were issued new jail overalls once a week and clean towels twice a week. Relatives were responsible for providing prisoners with clean underwear and, Edwards wrote, "for that reason, most don't wear any. So that takes care of that problem."

Edwards brought in his personal barber for a haircut. Roger Hill, of Gary's Hair Unlimited at 858 W. Broadway in Bradley, had never been inside a jail. But this was a couple of weeks before the trial and Sheldon Reagan wanted his client to look clean cut before going to court.

Whether he was toying with Danny or not, apparently one of the guards told Edwards that Nancy Rish still had feelings for him. Edwards was able to send a note to Nancy Rish in her cell. It read, "Hi, Baby. I just got the best news in the whole world. One of the guards came in and told me you still love me. Nancy, I hope you are hanging in there okay. As you know, I tried to kill myself. It was a foolish thing to do and it won't happen again. Nancy, somehow we are going to get through this and we are going to get married and have kids and be happy. I didn't think you loved me anymore and that's what hurts more than anything. But now that I know you still do, it feels like I want to live again. Please write back. I love you more than anything. Dan. P.S. I hope you are with some good ladies and that they are treating you okay." She did not return his message.

Prosecutor Frank Nowicki made the most of Edwards' brazen behavior in the local jail. In his argument during the sentencing phase of the trial, Nowicki called Danny Edwards "the Kankakee County jail barn boss."

Nowicki told the jury, "He had easy access to drugs. He was able to secure and procure drugs for other people at the jail. While in jail, he had accounts at local restaurants. He was able to order ribs or pizza or chicken. Nancy Rish was on a different floor, but he was able to have sex with her."

"With a little planning and a little manipulation, Danny Edwards didn't think there was anything in the world he couldn't do. And he did it all in the Kankakee County jail."

Chapter 9
The Trials

"The murder and kidnapping of Stephen Small is what brought us here today. The evidence will show that this murder was a result of the cold and calculated plans of that man (Danny Edwards)."
Prosecutor Michael Ficaro to jurors, May 16, 1988

Danny Edwards and Nancy Rish were arraigned in Kankakee County Circuit Court on Tuesday, September 8, 1987. It was the first business day after the Labor Day weekend.

State's Attorney William Herzog appeared for the state. Assistant Public Defender Larry Beaumont was there with Edwards.

Scott Swaim was supposed to appear for Nancy Rish. But he met with her that morning and he said goodbye just before her court appearance. Her family could not afford his fee, Swaim told her. It was his way of bowing out, as every other local attorney would do. She faced the judge alone.

It was Stephen Small's wealth and prominence that made him a target of Danny Edwards. It was those same factors that would make it difficult for the accused to find someone to defend them.

Nancy Rish discovered that finding a lawyer to defend her would be even harder than it had been to find a lawyer to advise her when she was arrested four days earlier.

She started with Swaim on the day of her arrest, but he was not there for her arraignment. Assistant Public Defender Michael Kick appeared in court on behalf of Nancy Rish on Oct. 1, 1987, at her indictment. He was there on October 9 and 23.

Kick withdrew on November 6, because he was going to run for state's attorney. Judge John Michela, in the court transcript that day, called Kick "everybody's candidate for state's attorney. Both parties asked him to run."

(Kick did run for state's attorney in 1988, as the choice of George Ryan and Ed McBroom, the bosses of the local political machine. It was the same political machine started by Stephen Small's great-grandfather, Governor Len Small. The local Republicans were having an internecine battle, with younger members rebelling against the boss rule of Ryan and McBroom. Also backing Kick were Republican leaders Tom Ryan, Larry Power and Bruce Clark, Ryan's nephew. Kick ran against incumbent William Herzog in the Republican primary. Herzog won.)

Michael Ficaro, Frank Nowicki and Timothy Reynolds of the Illinois Attorney General's office had been on board from the beginning. Ficaro, 41, was contacted on September 3, the day before the body was found and before the suspects were arrested. Nowicki, 33, also was an experienced prosecutor. Reynolds, 28, was new in the office.

They took over the prosecution from Herzog, who cited a conflict because of his friendship with the Smalls.

Gus Regas was Edwards' first lawyer. He didn't file an appearance in court, saying Greg Morgan, one of his law partners, was a close friend to the Smalls. Assistant Public Defender Edward Glazer withdrew; he was a partner with Regas, and he left for the same reason. Assistant Public Defender Allan Kuester withdrew because he rented his office space from Jerry Bergeron, Stephen Small's brother-in-law.

Edwards had another problem with lawyers. He had no money, and while his family was wealthy, they would not pay his legal fees.

Sheldon Reagan, a Kankakee lawyer in private practice, agreed to defend Danny Edwards.

Sheldon Reagan Jr. was born in 1935, the son of a doctor who once served as a staff physician at the state asylum in Kankakee. Reagan Sr., who died in 1962, also was mayor of Aroma Park for awhile. Reagan Jr. chose law over medicine, taking night school courses for eight years before earning his law degree in 1966. Reagan was working for an investment banking firm in Chicago when he was persuaded to attend law school at night by Terry Brennan, Notre Dame's head football coach. Reagan was appointed a magistrate in Kankakee, entered private practice with Ackman & Benson in Kankakee, and he became corporation counsel for the city. He did not specialize in criminal law. Reagan came on board on September 29, 1987. He was paid by the taxpayers.

But who in the public defender's office would represent Nancy Rish? There were too many lawyers who had connections to the Small family, as was the case with Edwards.

Assistant Public Defender James Burns' wife worked for Susanne Bergeron. Ken Leshen was the public defender for Noble Smith, who murdered Nancy Rish's father. Rish didn't want Leshen, and Leshen's secretary was engaged to marry Gary Mitchell, chief detective in sheriff's office.

Judge Michela said "there was no one left" in the office except William O. Schmidt. He appointed Schmidt as Rish's attorney on November 10. But Schmidt soon withdrew, saying he once represented Small's cable company.

"Unfortunately, in this case, the canons of ethics have precluded any member of my office from representing any individual charged," Schmidt told the local newspaper.

Bourbonnais attorney Vincent Paulauskis said he was willing to take the case, so Judge Michela appointed him on December 7, 1987. Sherri Carr, a young new lawyer, joined the team on September 22, 1988.

"The court finds that the public defender's office cannot represent the defendant," Judge Michela said as he appointed Paulauskis.

One of the first issues in pre-trial hearings was a motion to separate the trials of Edwards and Rish. Ficaro wanted the pair tried together; Paulauskis wanted his client tried separately.

"The discovery basically indicates that insofar as Miss Rish is concerned, her involvement in this matter was peripheral, unknowing," Paulauskis argued before Judge Michela. "I believe the court would certainly find that the defenses of the two are extremely antagonistic."

Paulauskis said he intended to subpoena Danny Edwards to testify on behalf of Nancy Rish, and he couldn't do that if the cases were joined. Paulauskis said if Edwards was tried first, he wouldn't be in jeopardy at Rish's trial. Ficaro countered with his objection, but severance was granted.

Dean Edwards, Danny's older brother, told police he found threatening letters in his mailbox in October 1987. More letters were sent over the next several months, and signs were put in his yard twice.

One letter, misspellings and bad grammar included, read: "Is the whole f...ing family of Edwards druggies and murderers? A family that likes to run with the upper crust and then kill them. Why didn't the family put this guy in a rehabilitation center, or were they afraid of their own reputation? Now the neighborhood has to wonder if they are going to find their kids or there wifes in a box if you suddenly need money. What makes you any different. It runs in the blood. What does it feel like to have a cold blooded brother for a murderer. The neighborhood doesn't need scum like the Edwards. Pack up and get lost. Druggies & murderers are the Edward family. Bums."

Another letter read, "Edwards, Rumors have it all over town that you's are a major supplier for cocaine and anything else you want. You would think after your brother is a murderer and is costing the taxpayers ½ million dollars you would learn. Your family is dirt, your daughter is putting out all over town and you still feel you are better than other people. They need to fry your family, just like your brother is going to be fried. Your name is trash and your killing people off with your drug pushing."

There were a number of pre-trial hearings, as Edward's lawyers fought to suppress statements and evidence.

In a pre-trial hearing to suppress evidence on January 25, 1988, Danny Edwards' testimony didn't exactly match statements given by the police, concerning the morning raid when he was arrested.

Edwards said Lt. Gerard "barged in, grabbed me by my right shoulder, leaned me over a chair, frisked me and cuffed me."

Did he say anything? No. Did you say anything? No, but then Edwards admitted, "I asked him what was going on, what is this about?"

Edwards said he was calm when he said it. At the Bourbonnais Police Department, "I said I don't know what this is about, this is just bogus."

Nowicki said, "Then you looked at the warrant and said, 'You're f...ing nuts. If this was drugs, I could see it. You're f...ing nuts.'"

"I don't remember saying anything about drugs, no."

"Did you say, 'Do I look f...ing scared'?"

"I don't recall."

"Did you say to Bourbonnais police officers, 'I want a f...ing attorney right f...ing now. I'm filing a f...ing false arrest.'"

"Something to that manner, possibly yes."

Edwards took the stand on March 7, 1988, at a hearing to suppress his confession. He said Sheriff Thompson told him on September 9 that they released Kent Allain because there was not enough evidence. Edwards said he told Thompson that Allain "had nothing to do with it, it was just a wild goose chase I put him on." Thompson was upset because of the time and expense looking for Allain and two other men implicated by Edwards.

Edwards said he asked Sgt. Daniels to talk to his attorney or to Herzog.

Edwards was asked if he saw a Miranda waiver.

"No, I have never seen one of these before."

Ficaro asked, "Do you remember telling Sgt. McClellan that we don't have time for this?"

"No, I don't."

"You weren't in a hurry at 8:30 or 8:47 that night?"

"I wasn't in a hurry, but they sure were," Edwards replied.

"You weren't in a hurry?"

"No."

"Time wasn't important to you?"

"Not as important as it was to them, no."

"Do you recall saying at 8:47 that evening, 'F... my lawyer, I don't have time for this?'"

"No, I don't remember saying that."

"So up to 9 p.m., no one advised you of your constitutional rights?"

"That's right."

"You weren't hurt (when Edwards cut his wrist) too bad, were you?"

"I was," Edwards said. "I was up all night. I was very tired. I was on pain pills. I was pulled out of bed to talk to him (the sheriff) and I was sleeping."

Edwards said the sheriff offered him a less harsh prison location if he cooperated.

"You told them you could take them to the body?"

"Yeah."

"And you took them to the body?"

81

"Yes."

"You told the police there were black men on horseback out there guarding Small's body, isn't that right?"

"Yes, I did."

"And you told the police Kent Allain and these black men made you kidnap Mr. Small, is that right?"

"At that time, yeah."

"That you were under the threat of death and that's why you did this?"

"Yeah."

"Under the threat of death from Allain and these black men, is that right?"

"Right."

"And on September 5, you gave the same statement to Sgt. McClellan and Officer Gilbert?"

"Yes, I did."

"That you were forced to do this, that they were going to kill you and your family?"

"Yeah."

Edwards added that Mitch Levitt told him there was a hit on his life for "rolling" on him in March 1987, and that Mitch put out the hit.

It was decided to bring jurors from outside Kankakee County, due to pre-trial publicity and the possibility of local jurors with connections to the Smalls.

A jury was selected from Winnebago County. Judge Michela and the lawyers went to Rockford from May 10 to 13 to choose the jurors.

Sheldon Reagan wanted the court to find Mitch Levitt. He filed a motion on March 30, 1988, claiming Levitt was an important material witness. Reagan said Levitt was under arrest, but he didn't know where he was incarcerated or on what charges. What statements did he make? Who's his attorney? Have any deals made with him? Reagan wanted to know.

Ficaro told the judge that Levitt was "a defendant with various narcotics violations in Cook. We are not going to call him."

Jed Stone joined the defense team in April 1988. He withdrew in May and was replaced by Thomas Allen.

The trial hadn't even started, but Judge Michela was getting annoyed by the crowd of reporters.

In a pre-trial hearing on April 15, 1988, regarding more money for the lawyers for hours, train fare, in court and out of court time, Judge Michela showed his irritation.

"Does the law allow me to put a gag order on the lawyers? I can't gag the press. I cannot personally destroy the press. Maybe I can gag the lawyers from talking to the damn newspapers."

Stone: "You (judge) called Reagan earlier this week, and he told me not to talk to the *Tribune.*"

Judge: "The papers. I said the papers."

Stone: "I was unaware of a gag order, but I would comply."

Judge: "Not to the *Tribune,* the *Sun-Times*, the Lake Forest paper, the Kankakee *Daily Journal,* the *New York Times...*"

Michela added, "It's going to be enough of a circus when it starts. I don't need you guys participating in the damn circus."

The prosecutors agreed.

Michela said, "Well, Ficaro was, or went in the article last night, I didn't read it. My wife told me there was an article in the *Journal* last night concerning the article that was in the *Tribune*. I mean, they just build on each other. It's unbelievable."

The *Daily Journal* ran an unusual editorial on May 15, 1988, the day before the trial started. The editorial, signed by publisher Jean Alice Small, explained that the newspaper would cover the trial with "honesty and fairness." There was "an extra burden for the paper to avoid conflict of interest because of my unique personal involvement" as editor-publisher, as the aunt of the victim and as a witness for the prosecution.

"Complications have made things even more difficult. Despite this situation, *The Journal* has made and will continue to make every effort throughout the trial to maintain the highest levels of professional standards."

"*Journal* readers will be completely informed on all aspects of the trial, but there will be no editorial comment or opinion pieces published until the trial is concluded. *The Journal* pledges total commitment to the people's 'right to know.'"

It was an unintended irony, but in the *Daily Journal's* May 16 edition -- on page 3, right next to one of the stories about the first day of the trial -- there was a picture and caption of the Grace B. Small Young Artists' Piano Competition. Included in the photograph was Reva Small, the mother of Stephen B. Small.

Danny Edwards' trial began on Monday, May 16, 1988.

The jury of seven men and five women from Winnebago County included a drafting department manager, an electronics company employee, a machinist, a cable installer, a maintenance man, a quality control inspector, a case worker for the public aid department, a machine attendant, a mother of six, and a man whose cousin's daughter was brutally murdered by a man with a machete.

The judge and lawyers went to Rockford for the jury selection. So did Danny Edwards. Kankakee deputies Barry Thomas and Harry Powell guarded Edwards, who spent his time in the Winnebago County jail playing racquetball and basketball, a different life from the marijuana and pizza he enjoyed in the Kankakee County jail.

Jurors were bused to Kankakee and sequestered in the Days Inn motel in Kankakee. They were transported each day, under heavy security, to the third floor court room of Judge John Michela in the downtown Kankakee courthouse.

The two sets of lawyers really were mismatched. Not only were Ficaro and Nowicki more experienced and skilled than the small town defense lawyers, they also possessed a fiery command of the theatrical and a passionate courtroom presentation. Their dramatic arguments could sway a jury.

And, of course, they had an overwhelming mountain of evidence that proved Danny Edwards' guilt.

Ficaro's opening salvo set the tone.

"The murder and kidnapping of Stephen Small is what brought us here today. The evidence will show that this murder was a result of the cold and calculated plans of that man (Danny Edwards)."

Ficaro said that while Stephen Small was restoring a historic home, Danny Edwards was building Small's coffin.

"It was Danny Edwards' try for the big score…the big score is what brought Danny Edwards here. Stephen Small was murdered because this man wanted a million dollars."

Ficaro said the evidence would show "he buried Stephen Small alive in a box to get rich quick so he could live in the fast lane. The evidence will show you from the very beginning that Danny Edwards never intended Stephen Small to live."

Sheldon Reagan's opening statement for the defense was a lot more subdued.

"The case begins in June of 1986, when Danny Edwards, just divorced, sold his house and he had some money," Reagan said. "As luck would have it, with this money, he ran into a local drug dealer."

Reagan went through the tale of Edwards' arrest for cocaine, his agreement to help police trap bigger drug merchants in Chicago, and the alleged "hit" on Edwards' life.

Reagan said it was a "tragic but accidental death" for Stephen Small. He said Edwards provided a water jug, candy bars, and a rudimentary system of a light and an air tube, which showed Edwards did not intend for Small to die.

Thomas Allen's opening statement also was subdued.

"The evidence will show that this is a case about kidnapping and a tragic but accidental death. It also is a case about drugs, about drug dealing, and money."

Allen repeated the story of the tragic set of circumstances which started in June 1986, when Edwards was divorced and had money from the sale of his house. He ran into local drug dealers in a tavern. He saw them making money so he took the money from the sale of his house and decided to get into the illegal drug business. He met Mitch Levitt and got started.

In January 1987, Allen said, a friend of Edwards was arrested downstate for selling drugs and he turned informant. He set up Edwards for a drug bust. Edwards then cooperated with police. He wore a wire and went to Chicago to trap Mitch Levitt. It didn't work because Mitch found out, Allen said. Word on the street was that there was a "hit" on Danny Edwards' life, he told the jury.

Allen said the fact that the wooden box had a gallon of water, five candy bars, a pack of gum, a light with a switch attached to two car batteries, a flashlight and an air tube, all proved that he intended to keep Small alive. Small died because the design was faulty, Allen said, not because Edwards intended for him to die.

Reagan's and Allen's statements sounded more like a surrender than a defense. This no doubt was because they knew the evidence was so overwhelming that they weren't going to attempt to deny Edwards' participation or guilt. They would have been fools to do so. They were saying Edwards did the kidnapping, but the death was accidental, and that there were other circumstances to consider. The plea they entered was "not guilty," but the lawyers never claimed that in court. It seems that Reagan and Allen were going more for capitulation with mitigation rather than going for an acquittal.

But what else did they have?

The witnesses brought by the prosecution set up the sequence of events of how Danny Edwards planned the kidnapping and how he acquired the items entered as exhibits.

The first witness for the prosecution was Ramsey Small. He testified that he answered the telephone when it rang sometime after midnight. The man said he was with the Kankakee Police Department and there was a break-in at the Bradley House. Ramsey went into his parents' bedroom and woke up his father.

His father picked up receiver. Ramsey saw his father walk down the hall and down the steps. He heard him open the greenhouse door, which divides the house from the garage, and he heard the garage door open and close.

"I went to sleep about 12:30. I woke up at 2:30 and wondered where my father was. He wasn't home."

A second call that came at 3:30 a.m., "sounded like another male. I picked it up the same time my mom did."

"It sounded like a male voice, and the voice said that he had my father for ransom for a million dollars, and he said not to contact the FBI or the police. And around that time, I hung up the phone and went into my mother's room."

After the boy's testimony, the wooden box -- Stephen's Small coffin in the sand hills -- was wheeled into the courtroom.

Allen vigorously objected. The box was on a carriage commonly used for caskets at funerals. Allen said it was "inflammatory and prejudicial."

"It hit me over the head the first time I looked out there," he told the judge. "There is nothing subtle about it."

Ficaro said it was just a device to bring in the box. The judge overruled the objection.

Terry Dutour of Aroma Park testified that he saw Edwards at the phone booth at the Phillips 66 gas station at 5 p.m. on Wednesday, September 2, at the same time police said a ransom call was being made from that phone to the Small house. Dutour said he recognized Edwards because he knew him from the electrical business. He said he saw a blonde woman sitting in the car, six to eight feet from the phone, while Edwards was making a call.

Jeff Westerhoff, the man who helped Danny Edwards get the wood for the box, had known Edwards for 20 years, since their days in elementary school together. Westerhoff worked as a self-employed carpenter for 12 years. He said Danny asked him for job in January 1987.

"He was just a helper, he handed me tools, would bring material to me. It was part time, couple of days a week, from January to June 1987," he told the court.

"Danny said he needed help building a box. I asked what for. He said it was for his brother's pool in Florida."

"He said he wanted it to be six-by-three feet, close but not exact. He asked for help. He brought it up once a week or so. Whenever we would run into each other, he'd say 'Let's get going on it and get it started.' I was going to help him, but I didn't."

"On June 1, after a half day of work, we went to Security Lumber and bought two sheets of ¾-inch plywood, 4x8s, and six 2x4s, two drill bits and a hinge. I charged it to my father's account, and deducted the cost from Danny's wages."

The bill came to $75.

Westerhoff testified that they took the wood to his parents' house, where he was living, and stored it in the basement. It was there about eight weeks until Danny stopped waiting for Jeff's help and decided to build it himself.

"Well, Danny was getting kind of anxious to get it going and he wouldn't wait any longer," he said. "He came over to pick the wood up himself. I helped him load it in his white van." Danny also borrowed a Skil saw and a hole cutter saw.

About ten days before the kidnapping, Westerhoff said he saw Edwards at his townhouse in Bourbonnais. Nancy Rish and her son were there.

"It was a social call, and to pick up my hole saw. We went into his garage. I saw his box. I said, 'Oh, you got it finished.'"

"He said, 'Yeah, that is it.'"

"I said, 'It is kind of big.'"

"He looked like he might have been kind of proud of that, that he got it together by himself," Westerhoff said.

Allen objected. It was sustained. The judge told the jury to disregard that last remark.

Benjamin Rish was next on the stand.

Outside of the presence of the jury, Judge Michela told the lawyers that Benjamin's grandmother sent a letter, asking not to compel the boy to testify.

"She asked me not to disclose it to anybody because Benji is afraid of your client," the judge said. "Her letter didn't influence me."

Reagan showed no surprise to the comment that Benjamin Rish was afraid of Danny Edwards.

Since his mother's arrest, Benjamin was living with his father in Rolling Meadows.

Judge Michela began by asking the boy if he believes in telling the truth, and if he believes in Santa Claus and the Easter Bunny. Benjamin said yes.

The boy answered questions from the lawyers. He said he had lived in Bourbonnais with mother and Danny Edwards. The box was in the garage. It was built by Danny Edwards. It is the same box as shown in court.

"Do you see Danny Edwards in court?" Ficaro asked.

No.

"Have him stand up," Ficaro said.

The boy still would not acknowledge anything.

Ficaro asked, "You don't want to look at him?"

No, the boy replied.

Jeffrey Senesac lived next door to Edwards and Rish in the other half of the townhouse, at 758 Stratford Drive East. He testified about seeing Edwards in the driveway in July, building the box.

"I said, 'What the hell are you building, a lemonade stand?' He said, 'I must be doing a pretty good job if you can tell what it is already.'"

Senesac also said Nancy Rish came next door on at least one occasion to spend the night because of fights she had with Danny.

Ronald Baughman, Senesac's room mate, also saw Edwards building the box.

Baughman testified he was in bed just after midnight on Wednesday

September 2. His bedroom window was open. The door at 756 Stratford slammed and he heard Edwards say, "Let's go. Let's hit it." Edwards got in his van and drove away.

The foreman of J&B Vegetables in Pembroke Township told the court that he saw a white van in the vicinity of where Small later would be found. It was on Tuesday, September 1, at 11:30 a.m. Small would be abducted late that night.

James Witvoet Jr. was in charge of production for J&B Vegetables, managing the leased farms. He said people sometimes came to ride four-wheelers, dune buggies and motorcycles in those sand hills.

On that morning, Witvoet was driving his produce truck when the white van came toward him, heading into the remote area. There were two people in the van. The driver was a white male and the passenger was white with light colored hair.

But Witvoet testified he couldn't tell if the passenger with the light colored hair was male or female.

It was unusual for anyone to be in that particular area.

"Unless you are one of our employees, you have no business being on that road," he said.

Witvoet said he saw the white van again between 2 and 2:30 p.m., a mile south at Cable Line and Cemetery Road. The van was coming away from the site. The grave site was about half way between the two spots, in the woods.

The word "road" is a bit of a stretch, he said. The roads there are not maintained and are nothing more than beach sand. Cable Line is a deserted road, used only by Illinois Bell Telephone Company. The road got its name because a big telephone cable is strung there.

Karen Thacker lived in Small's neighborhood, next to George Ryan, with her husband and three children. She worked as a teacher's aide for mentally retarded children. She told the court about seeing a van in the neighborhood in the summer of 1987.

"I saw a light colored van parked, then coming down the alley, headed south," she said. "I saw a blonde lady in the van, with a white male driving."

Thacker said she made eye contact with the woman, and the woman immediately looked at the driver.

"She was very startled and then she looked back at me."

Thacker said she saw the van in the alley eight to ten times over the summer, from approximately June 21 to August 28.

Nowicki asked if she knew who the woman was. Yes, Thacker said, it was Nancy Rish.

The defense lawyers did not object.

Thacker said she told State's Attorney William Herzog about it two days after the kidnapping. Herzog lived behind Thacker's house. Thacker said Herzog told her he would have the police interview her, but no police called her until November 11. By then, she had seen Nancy Rish's face in the newspapers and on TV.

Caroline Mortell lived a block south of the Smalls. Nancy Small telephoned her just a few minutes after getting the first ransom call at 3:30 a.m.

Mortell testified that she saw a white van coming slowly down her street at 11 a.m. Wednesday, after the kidnapping. The driver was a white female with blonde shoulder length hair curled around the face. Her complexion was dark, or she had makeup, and she was in her late 20s or early 30s. The woman was driving slowly and observing, looking around, Mortell said. The van turned off her street, onto Cobb Boulevard, toward the Small house. She said she saw the same van that afternoon, between 1:30 and 3 p.m.

At Nancy Rish's trial six months later, Mortell said she could not tell if the van she saw in the afternoon was the same van she saw in the morning.

Virginia Gordon, another neighborhood resident, testified that she woke up after midnight on Wednesday and looked out the window. She saw a white van parked outside her house that she did not recognize. She woke up again at 4 a.m., and looked out again. The van was gone.

Janice Krizak, a sheriff's deputy, lived on the same block of 800 S. Greenwood. She said she was up with her children that night until 3 a.m. She said she heard a car coming down Greenwood. It stopped. She heard a car door slam, then heard another vehicle door slam. She got up to take a look. She said she saw a white van parked there, and a car stopped in the middle of the street. The van backed up and pulled out. Its lights didn't go on until it pulled away,

David Denton told the jury about Danny Edwards coming into Jet Boat Specialists in Momence. The business buys, sells and trades new and used boats, and repairs them.

"He had a 1973 Marlin and I sold him parts to fix it," Denton said. "It was kind of beat up, and every once in a while he would need parts to fix it."

Edwards came on October 19, 1986, and they came to terms on a 1986 Sleek Craft SST that Danny had wanted for a while. The total was $19,200. Edwards made a $1,000 deposit in cash. He made a total of four $1,000 payments, all in cash.

The following April, Edwards told Denton he couldn't afford it, and he wanted to know if he could get his deposit back.

"He said he was just arrested for drugs and he needed the money for lawyers."

Denton said Edwards often stopped in to look at boats, mostly by himself, and a couple of times with Nancy Rish.

"Danny was looking at a 23-foot SS Taylor, a more expensive boat,"

Denton said. "Danny climbed in the boat to look around. He wanted Nancy to climb up there and she wouldn't. She was wearing a short skirt. I was standing behind her. I walked over to the other side of the boat so she could climb up there."

While Edwards came in often over several years, Denton said he didn't see Nancy Rish until August 1987. She was there with him only twice.

Denton said that on August 5, 1987, Stephen Small was in the boat shop at the same time as Edwards and Rish. Small was on his way home from his cabin up north, picking up something to clean his boat. As Small drove away in his red Ferrari Testarossa, Denton heard Edwards remark, "Boy, it sure would be nice to afford stuff like that."

Jean Alice Small gave her testimony about the phone call she got from Danny Edwards later in the day of the kidnapping, where Edwards told her to tell Nancy Small to "quit f...ing up." Edwards said he made his living going to towns and kidnapping rich people. He threatened to kill Jean Alice Small's husband, Len H. Small, not aware that he died seven years earlier in an auto accident.

On May 18, the jury got the biggest shock of the trial when they watched a five-minute videotape made by the police, showing the recovery of Stephen Small's body from the crude grave.

The tape was made the morning after police dug up the body. Small's body was lying on its left side, with his jacket under his head. The video opens with a wide shot of the wooded area, then moves through the brush, to a close-up of the wooden coffin in the ground.

The Daily Journal quoted a lawyer, in the spectator's gallery, describing it as "the opening scene of a horror movie."

Both Reagan and Allen objected to showing the video, calling it inflammatory and prejudicial. If nothing else, they wanted to edit out pictures of Mr. Small's body and the sand that fell on him when the lid was lifted. Judge Michela allowed the tape to be shown in its entirety.

The jury also heard the tape recording Stephen Small made at gunpoint at his grave site.

(Sgt. William Willis, in notes with TV producers in 1990, said the jury did not hear everything that was on the audio tape Mr. Small made. "The judge wouldn't let us play the last part of the tape for the jury. I said it's too much, it would be too prejudicial. Cops are all off in the ante room of the court. What the f... is this guy doing? It's the guy's last words in life. Why not...the whole truth, nothing but the truth, so help me God, as soon as we clean it up. We're pissed. We're ranting and raving, ready to kill the judge.")

Other witnesses took the stand to nail Edwards to the evidence. Jeff Drury said he owed Edwards $1,500 for cocaine, so Edwards came to his house and stole his .357 Magnum revolver. That was shown to be the gun Edwards used in the kidnapping. Michael Kerouac testified that he also owed a drug debt to Edwards, and Edwards took a number of his possessions, including a pair of Smith & Wesson handcuffs. Those handcuffs were proven to be the ones used on Mr. Small.

Charles Juarez testified that Edwards bought a Delco Freedom II car battery from his New Era Auto Parts on Monday, August 31. Juarez ran the salvage auto parts yard with his dad and two brothers.

"I asked if he was going to use it for his van. He said no. He said it was for his brother," Juarez said. He identified the battery in court.

William Mohler testified that Edwards borrowed his battery charger later the same day. Edwards picked it up 15 minutes after calling, and he returned it the following evening. Mohler, the service manager for Messier's Yamaha, was a friend who rode dirt bikes with Edwards in the same Pembroke area where Small was taken. Edwards and Mohler were the best man at each other's weddings.

Loren Flouhouse, a salesman at Radio Shack in the Bourbonnais Town Center on Route 102 -- next to K-Mart and across from the Bourbonnais Police Department and the Edwards townhouse -- testified that he sold Edwards a Realistic brand cassette tape. Edwards' name and address were on the receipt. It cost $2.79.

Lonnie Martens, the warehouse manager at Englewood Electrical Supply at 1224 Grinnell Road, testified that Danny Edwards bought plastic straps. Martens knew the Edwards family for 20 years because of their electrical business. He also was a close family friend. Martens was a groomsman at the wedding of David and Vicki Edwards in 1972, along with Duke, Donald, Dean and Danny Edwards. David Edwards was a groomsman for Lonnie and Judy Martens later in 1972.

Martens said Danny Edwards came in the store on Tuesday, September 1. He wanted to buy just a few plastic straps, but Martens said he only sold them in a bag of 50. Edwards said that was fine and he bought a bag. It cost $10.62.

The 11-inch straps are made by Thomas & Betts, made to bundle cable wires together. Martens said they are unique, and Englewood was the only business within 100 miles that sold them. He identified the straps in court.

Martens said a woman was sitting outside in the van when Edwards came in the store. Martens asked who she was. Edwards said it was Nancy Rish.

Prosecutors were not as solid when they called witnesses to prove Edwards and Rish bought the water and candy bars that were found in the box. Linda Forestier testified that a man and a woman came into Village Hardware in Aroma Park on Monday or Tuesday of that week. The woman asked if they had distilled water. Forestier said no, but she told the woman it was available at Ruffini's Super Value market. The man asked if they had any pipe. Forestier asked her boss, Mike Lergner. He said no.

Lergner testified to the same thing.

Both Lergner and Forestier said that neither of them could identify the couple as being Danny Edwards or Nancy Rish.

Arlene Bires testified that Danny Edwards came into Ruffini's on Tuesday, September 1, to buy bottled water and candy bars. She said Nancy Rish was not with him.

Donna Jordan told the court that on one of the last days of August or the first days of September, Danny Edwards came in the Convenient Food Mart in Briarcliff subdivision near his townhouse and asked for bottled water.

After the testimony tying Edwards to the materials used in the kidnapping, the expert witnesses were called.

Lauren Wisevic, a forensic scientist with the Illinois State Police who specialized in latent prints, told the court that the fingerprints on the PVC pipe, the duct tape and the light in the box belonged to Danny Edwards. None of the fingerprints collected belonged to Nancy Rish.

Blair Schultz specialized in trace chemistry for the Illinois State Police at the Joliet crime lab. He said caulk found in Edwards' garbage bag on a caulking gun, a spatula and brown gloves all matched caulk used in the wooden box.

Ralph Meyer, who specialized in microscopy at the Joliet crime lab, said hair from the stocking cap matched Stephen Small. None of the hair in evidence matched samples taken from Danny Edwards or Nancy Rish.

Robert Hunton, a forensic scientist at the Joliet crime lab, was an expert in firearms identification and tool mark identification. He said Edward's gun was loaded and in operating condition. The Smith & Wesson handcuffs had a link missing and the bolt cutters in evidence could have cut the link. Lawyers on both sides stipulated that the bolt cutters came from Pyramid Electric, Duke Edwards' company.

FBI agent Ronald Rawalt said the FBI lab in Washington matched the soil and other substances on Edwards' boots to the crime scene.

"My opinion would be that the soil on these boots originated from the burial pit described to me as the burial pit for Stephen Small, and the chances of it originating any place else is virtually nonexistent."

Nancy Rish's shoes did not have traces of the sandy soil.

Danny Edwards, the high school dropout whose knowledge about the world did not extend much further than the business of cocaine, thought the narrow PVC pipe from the box underground would give Stephen Small 48 hours of air.

He was wrong.

Small likely died within three or four hours after being buried, if he even lived that long.

That more educated assessment came from Robert J. Stein, chief medical examiner of Cook County.

Stein, a doctor since 1950, specialized in forensic pathology. He had performed more than 1,000 autopsies by 1987, and he gained national fame from his work in the suburban Chicago case of mass murderer John Wayne Gacy.

Stein was flown into Kankakee and was driven to the burial site. He said he observed a shallow grave with wooden box. A body, partially covered with sand, wearing a red shirt and blue jeans, was in the box. The man's head was turned to left, his left leg was flexed and his left arm bent across the chest. The left side of the face was discolored from blood settling after death, Stein said.

Stein conducted the autopsy of Stephen Small at Riverside Hospital in Kankakee on September 5. He testified about the particulars at the trial.

The examination at the hospital showed Small was 5'9" and 150 pounds. His teeth were in good shape and he had braces. The internal organs looked normal. "There were no marks on the scalp, the skull was intact, no evidence of any fractures or any other abnormalities," Stein said. "And upon removal of the skull, the dura, that is the covering membrane of the brain, was intact. Meninges membrane covering the brain, nothing there, the brain itself was perfectly normal."

There was hemorrhage in both eyes, the epiglottis, the throat, lungs and heart -- a bursting of blood vessels from a lack of oxygen.

The body had abrasions and contusions on the knuckles and elbows, possibly from struggling to get out. There was a metal handcuff on each wrist and a yellow watch on the left wrist.

Ficaro asked, "What does this tell you about the victim, Stephen Small, in relation to his death?"

"Just this one thing," Stein replied. "The man suffocated to death. The cause of death was asphyxia, due to suffocation. The manner of death was homicide."

Ficaro asked Stein to look at pictures of the abrasions on Small's ankles. Stein replied that these could have been made by rope or straps.

Allen asked the judge for a sidebar. Judge Michela had already ruled out the straps as evidence since they were found loose in the garbage truck and not inside a garbage bag from Edwards' house.

Allen asked for a mistrial.

Ficaro said he wanted to use Stein's testimony to bring in the straps. Lonnie Martens had testified he sold them to Danny Edwards and said he was the only one who sells them, which make it relevant now, Ficaro said.

Allen called it "a flagrant direct intentional violation of a court order in front of the jury."

"If the defense pulled that stunt, I would be calling my wife in Chicago for bond money right now," Allen said.

Ficaro said the court refused to admit it as evidence because it was not relevant or material, but he argued that it was now relevant because of Stein's testimony.

Judge Michela denied the motion for a mistrial.

Stein continued his testimony, saying the marks on the ankle could be consistent with a strap.

And Stein said that, based on the size of the box and the tubing, Small died in three or four hours.

But there was another problem beside the small size of the pipe's diameter. The pipe went out the side of the box and sideways underground before coming to the surface 25 feet away.

Stein said the box provided for no exchange of air. Even if air was pumped in with a motor, he said, it was a one-way street. There was nowhere for the carbon dioxide to go when Small exhaled.

Ficaro asked, "In fact, Doctor, there is no breathing system there, is there?"

Stein answered, "That is correct. No breathing system."

Ficaro said this was not like a snorkel with a short pipe, and Small couldn't get his mouth to the pipe, right? Right, Stein replied.

The final witness for the prosecution was the victim's widow, Nancy Small.

She took the stand on Friday, May 20, the fifth day of the trial. Mrs. Small told of taking the 3:30 a.m. ransom call and of hearing her husband's voice on the tape in a later ransom call. That tape was then played for the jury. The sad, heartbreaking conversation, with Edwards interrupting to demand the ransom, affected the jury and the spectators in the court room.

The state made its case with 45 witnesses before it rested. When it came time for the defense to make its case, it called just one witness.

Ernest Richardson, a drug enforcement agent, testified on May 21, 1988, about working with Edwards after the arrest for possession of cocaine on January 23, 1987. Richardson promised a lighter sentence if Edwards would help try to trap a higher level drug dealer in Chicago. Edwards still got probation for his cocaine arrest, even though no arrest of a higher drug lord was made.

But Richardson was limited to what he could say in court because Michela ruled that Richardson could not mention Mitch Levitt by name.

Mitch Levitt figured prominently at the beginning of this case, as the drug dealer Edwards was supposed to set up, and who Edwards said put him up to the kidnapping.

But he played no part in this investigation or in this trial. Ficaro objected to calling Levitt as a witness. A subpoena was not issued.

There was a lot of damning evidence introduced at the trial. Police

found a telephone book in Edwards' house with Stephen Small's name circled. There was the soil on Edward's boots and van, caulk on the gloves,
Edwards' fingerprints on the box, the handcuffs, the bolt cutters and more.

Danny Edwards' trial came to a close when the defense rested on
Saturday, May 21, 1988.

Sheldon Reagan tried his best in his closing arguments, given the
overwhelming evidence against his client.

He said the "evidence indicates" Danny Edwards built the box that
Stephen Small was found in, and Danny Edwards was at the burial scene
because of the sand on his boots.

"The rest of the evidence is circumstantial."

Reagan asked jurors if they were sure it was Danny Edwards' voice
on the tape.

He said there were no fingerprints on the gun and then asked, "Was
a gun used in the kidnapping? The state wants you to believe it was. What
evidence can you draw upon to form a reasonable inference that a gun was
used? Was a gun necessary?"

"Remember the tape of Mr. Small. You heard it twice and you read
a transcript of it. Remember Mr. Small saying on the tape, 'God, I thought this
was a joke or something, but it is no joke. This is not some party at Yurgine's.'
Now, if a gun was used, ladies and gentlemen, would Mr. Small say, 'God, I
thought this was a joke?' Is it a reasonable inference to draw that Mr. Small
would think it was a joke if someone had a gun pointed at him?"

"This raises another question I would like you to think about. Why
would Mr. Small say he thought it was a joke? Did he know his kidnappers?
What could possibly lead him to believe that this was a joke? And if he did-
n't believe it was a joke, why would he say it? Is it a reasonable inference,
ladies and gentlemen, that Mr. Small did know his kidnappers? Yes, I think
so. And I think the evidence shows this for two reasons. There is no physical
evidence, or evidence of physical abuse to Mr. Small by the kidnappers, and
by the tapes of Mr. Small's voice saying that he thought it was a joke."

"What proof is there that the person on the tape is the same person
who lured Mr. Small to the scene? None."

Reagan continued. "From the tape, you can tell the exact moment
when Mr. Small realized that it was not a joke. It was the moment when he
realized that he was going into the box and the box was underground. Now,
ladies and gentlemen, if a stranger had a gun on you and led you to believe
that you were going to be kidnapped, you wouldn't think it was a joke. And it
is a reasonable inference that Mr. Small knew his kidnappers and was not
afraid, and thought it was a joke, up until the time he saw the box. Mr. Small's
own words, ladies and gentlemen."

"Is there anywhere in any of the evidence, is there anything that

95

would lead you to believe that Mr. Small knew, had ever met, or even talked to Danny Edwards? And the answer to that is an emphatic no. There is none."

Reagan asked jurors if they thought it reasonable that the kidnappers would know the air pipe wouldn't work.

"This is very tragic. It was very stupid. But it is an accident. It is not intentional murder."

Reagan said if Edwards just wanted to kill Stephen Small, he would have just taken him out there, killed him, put him in the hole and covered him with sand.

Frank Nowicki was having nothing to do with theories of accidents, intentions or mitigation. He had all the evidence on his side, and his closing argument was forceful.

He quoted Danny Edwards own voice from the taped phone call.

"I ain't gone this far for nothing. If she don't pay the money, you are dead. I want to get that through your head right now. And I ain't coming back to dig you up. You have got two days of air, and that's it. And it is going to get real stuffy in there."

Nowicki said, "These are the words of a murderer, a man who intended and planned to kill another man. These are the words of a man who made greed his god. These are the words of Danny Edwards."

"If Stephen Small walked out, the first words out of his mouth would be he was buried in a box. He couldn't do that. If Stephen Small walked out of that box, Danny Edwards could never get away with this."

Nowicki noted that a lot of people saw Edwards building the box. He bragged about it. He joked about it. He was proud of it. "Why? Because no one would ever know anything about it because no one would ever find it. Nobody would ever see it and nobody would ever see Stephen Small again. Stephen Small never had a chance."

Edwards knew he was "made" by the police the same day, he knew he was being watched, Nowicki said. The ranting phone call proved it.

Edwards knew couldn't go there and dig up Small because he knew he was being followed. He could have made an anonymous call to have them dig up Small, Nowicki said, but he didn't.

"He didn't have to turn himself in. There is a million ways. Only your imagination would limit the ways. But what did he do? Nothing. From Wednesday night, he did nothing. Remember that talk, about there is two days worth of air, there is 48 hours worth of air, wherever that figure came from? Danny Edwards did nothing. He sat on his hands while Stephen Small died."

"The first words out of Danny Edwards' mouth were, 'I am going to sue you for f...ing false arrest.' In the cell, he said 'Do I look f...ing scared?' Seems to be a favorite word of this guy. Every other word on some of these telephone calls when he is talking is 'f...ing.'"

Ficaro gave a powerful performance when his turn came to make his closing argument.

"This murder was the product of a cold, callous and calculating plan motivated by greed. The last big score. Life in the fast lane. Easy street. For Danny, the million dollar jackpot. And all Danny boy had to do to cash in on that jackpot was take Stephen Small, a living, breathing human being, and put him in a box, and then the fast lane was his."

"Don't ever lose sight of why Danny Edwards did this. It wasn't a moment of passion. It wasn't in an instant of excitement. It wasn't the result of jealousy. It was cold. It was callous. And it was inhumane."

"Danny Edwards prepared this box like he prepared his plan. He got the materials. He got the handcuffs. He got the pipe. He got the gun. He got it all ready, and he took the American dream of Stephen Small and turned it into an Edgar Allen Poe nightmare. He put a man alive in this box."

"Danny's greed, his lust for the big score, formed that plan, drove those nails into the box, dug that grave and buried Stephen Small alive. Don't ever for one second lose sight of that."

"This wasn't an accident. You don't make a box by accident. Stephen Small didn't wander by and fall in."

Ficaro said Edwards' threats on tape showed he knew there was a strong possibility this would end in death. Edwards' intent was proven when he used the word "grave."

"I never saw anybody come out of a grave alive," Ficaro said. "You bury people who are dead in graves. 'Get this through your head, if she doesn't pay the money, you're dead.'"

Ficaro continued, "He said to Jean Alice Small, 'I am going to kill your husband, too.' Also."

Holding a gun on Stephen Small wasn't enough, Ficaro told the jury.

"What he had to do is play upon the fears that we would all have. So what did he do? He baited the box. He lured the victim. Want some candy, little girl?"

Allen objected to that statement. The judge sustained the objection and told the jury to disregard it.

Ficaro said many people knew Edwards built the box.

"He had the body disposed of in the remotest part of the county. The only thing that could stop him from enjoying that jackpot was to let Stephen Small out alive."

The proceedings adjourned for the weekend after the lawyers made their final arguments. When the jury returned on Monday, May 23, it took them just one hour and three minutes to return a verdict.

Guilty.

Guilty of aggravated kidnapping and murder. Guilty on all counts.

That same day, the penalty phase of the trial began. Lawyers on both sides gave their arguments to the jury, for the death penalty or for a life sentence. A number of witnesses testified.

David Pinski, son of a prominent Kankakee doctor, met Danny Edwards in June 1986 on the river. They both had boats. Pinski said he bought cocaine from Edwards at the house on Sand Bar Road every two weeks or so, from August to December, $50 for half a gram. Pinski was given immunity for his testimony.

Lisa Harms was a school friend of Nancy Rish. She met Edwards through Nancy Rish, at the Dam Tap. Lisa testified that she and her boyfriend, Allen "Chin" Graves, went to Nancy's apartment on Greenwood Avenue one night. She saw a big tray of cocaine on the kitchen counter.

"Danny asked me if I wanted some. I did."

The Chin and Nancy took some, but Danny did not. The Chin bought cocaine from Edwards, Lisa said.

"I saw Danny Edwards in the summer of 1987 near Aroma Park. He was on a motorcycle, ranting that David Young owed him money, and he threatened to beat him."

Lisa Harms was the daughter of Virginia Gordon, who testified about seeing the white van outside her house on Greenwood Avenue on the night of the kidnapping.

David Young was working security at the boat races in 1986. Edwards asked if Young wanted to buy some cocaine. Young said yes and he paid for a half gram. After that, Young said, he bought cocaine from Edwards 20 to 30 times. Young worked in Michigan and made $470 a week. He came back to Kankakee on weekends and spent $300 a week on cocaine, buying it from Edwards on Sand Bar Road. He said he owed Edwards $800 at the time of Edwards' arrest for cocaine possession.

Matthew Mullady worked at Sears and was a fishing guide on the Kankakee River. Married with two children, he had known Edwards since high school. Mullady testified that he was in Beckman Park at the annual Labor Day boat races in 1986. He bought a half gram of coke from Edwards for $50. He bought two more grams for $200 at Edwards' house on Sand Bar Road in October or November. Mullady said he didn't know Nancy Rish.

Thomas Mascher, a carpenter and a friend of Edwards since childhood, also testified about buying cocaine from him.

Jeff Drury met Edwards through Pinski. He owed Edwards $1,500 for cocaine. Edwards came to his house and took clothes and other items, including a Ruger .357 magnum, the gun Edwards used in the kidnapping.

Michael Kerouac bought cocaine from Edwards at Sand Bar Road maybe ten times. He owed Edwards a $175 cocaine debt. Edwards came to his house and took his clothes, suits, jewelry and more, including a set of handcuffs. Kerouac got his clothes back when he paid his debt but he didn't get his handcuffs back. Those were the handcuffs used on Stephen Small.

Debra Geekie told of going to Edwards' house on Sand Bar Road a dozen times to buy cocaine.

"Do you know Nancy Rish?"

"Yes, I've met her."

"Are you a friend of Nancy Rish?"

"No, she doesn't care for me."

Thomas James testified about Edwards buying marijuana and cocaine when they were in the Kankakee County jail, about Edwards ordering food from the outside, about Edwards being able to bribe the guards to get anything he wanted, including sex. Daniel Dunigan and Rick Kibbons told the same story about the bribery at the jail. Brenda Berry, one of the girlfriends of the prisoners, testified about bringing drugs and money to the guards and having sex in the jail. She also testified about sending the second threatening letter to Nancy Small, on Edwards' request.

Sherry Oetter testified about the time Danny Edwards came over to collect a drug debt. Edwards was afraid of getting caught violating his probation, so he gave her husband, Jeffrey Oetter, $500 to make a buy for him. Jeffrey Oetter was a user and a seller of cocaine, and he used Edwards' money for his own drug use.

Danny kept calling, saying he would beat Jeffrey with a baseball bat and take his TV and other items. Sherry had a two-year-old daughter, was pregnant with another child, and was just becoming aware of her husband's deep involvement in the drug world. "I was nine months pregnant and just found my husband was a coke addict. I needed help," she testified. Sherry divorced Jeffrey in July 1987.

"Nancy offered to take me to my lawyers and the bank because I was going to get a divorce," Sherry said. "At the bank, I found we had no money. Our checking account was overdrawn $2,000, our savings was gone, our money market was gone. It was about $10,000 total. I confronted Jeff. He broke down crying and told me he was a cocaine addict. Up till then, I didn't suspect heavy drug use."

Jeffrey Oetter did not testify because he was in prison at that time.

Not all the character witnesses were bad news. Rev Jonathan Dygert of Calvary Baptist Church in Kankakee said Edwards participated in his jail ministry. Doug Thornton, associate executive director of the Kankakee YMCA, said Danny Edwards was an assistant coach for floor hockey when his son was in it. But Thornton admitted he really didn't know Edwards. Edwards was "prompt…and an acceptable floor hockey coach."

Randy Irps told of Danny being best man at his wedding in 1978, and that Danny ran with a different crowd after his divorce from Peggy. And Peggy testified that Danny was good with their kids and he supported her decision to go back to school to study nursing.

Duke Edwards tried, but didn't help much. He said Danny got off to a "bad start" and said basically nothing worked out for his little brother. Ficaro asked Duke if he gave jail guard Troy Whitlow the bribe money. "After a fashion, yes," said Duke.

Another brother, David Edwards, said, "There is a side to Danny that is different from the Danny seen in the testimony last week." David, a lawyer -- and a former prosecutor -- lived in Washington state. He was near tears when he testified.

Kankakee Lt. John Gerard testified that it was Danny Edwards who led police to the burial site.

Gerard and Sgt. Maurice Meitzner both testified that Edwards cried, "Oh, no, oh, no," when Mr. Small was found dead. However, both police officers said Edwards was "back to normal" a minute later.

Ficaro asked Gerard if he thought Edwards was faking his anguish. Gerard said he didn't know, but "no longer than a minute after, Edwards was acting so normal that I figured he was one of us."

Peggy Edwards would not allow her children to testify in the death penalty phase in front of the jury about their father. Thomas Allen told the court, "All they know is Daddy is in trouble and he is in jail and somebody died. And we all, sitting here, know that we would do the same if we had kids."

Ficaro shot back: "Is that why Benjamin Rish had to testify?"

Reagan: "No, he had to testify because you brought him in."

Ficaro: "Because you wouldn't stipulate to him and you know it."

Reagan: "You didn't need him and you know that, so don't go throwing that off on me."

Ficaro: "You refused to stipulate."

Reagan: "You got that right. You got that right."

Ficaro: "Don't be talking about bringing kids in, Mr. Reagan. That was the most despicable and lowest thing I have ever seen, having to drag a nine-year-old in here."

Reagan: "That is what I thought when I saw his name on your list. Are you going to bring him in and use him against Nancy, too?"

Ficaro: "No."

The defense did try to have Edwards' children give statements on videotape about their feelings for their father. The prosecution objected, saying the children were not competent to testify and their comments were not made under oath and were not subject to cross examination. Judge Michela upheld the objection. The defense declined an offer by the prosecution to stipulate to the substance of the children's statements.

Prosecutor Frank Nowicki gave a powerful argument in the sentencing hearing, arguing for the death penalty. He called Danny Edwards "the barn boss" of the Kankakee County jail, reciting the evidence about Edward's ability to bribe guards to bring in food, drugs and sex. And he mentioned Edward's ability to send letters to try to fool police into thinking he wasn't the mastermind of the kidnapping plot. Nowicki mentioned how Danny Edwards continued to terrorize the Small family from the county jail.

"While Danny Edwards was in the Kankakee County jail, he wasn't done with the Stephen Small family. He hadn't done enough. He wasn't done torturing them yet. Remember Danny Edwards the planner, the manipulator, the conniver? Well, as he sat in the Kankakee County jail, he had a lot of time on his hands. And he decided, 'It's time to work on my defense. How am I going to beat this case? I better come up with something.' And what he came up with, you heard a little of it at the trial. You know those mysterious kidnappers that are still on the outside, they're still out there? That was going to be his defense. 'Yeah, I was involved maybe, but there are other people that are really responsible. They're the ones that did it. I'm in jail and they're still out there.' He manufactured evidence, wrote the letter to himself. He sent the letter to Nancy Small, 'You still owe us the money. You can expect another member of your family to be taken.'"

Nowicki dismissed the notion that Edwards turned bad because of his upbringing.

"Danny Edwards had everything in the world going for him. Since the day he was born, Danny Edwards had everything his way."

Nowicki said all the testimony in Edwards' behalf wasn't mitigation, it was aggravation. It didn't indicate that Edwards turned bad because of bad upbringing, it showed he turned bad in spite of good upbringing.

"All testified how good his life was. His brother, David, told you when he was growing up that Danny was like the rest of them. But look how the rest have turned out. Danny Edwards wasn't a person that was abused by his family. He wasn't beaten. He didn't do without. The defense hasn't come here and told you this kid never had a chance, that he had such a rough life. What they told you is, since day one, Danny Edwards has had every break."

Nowicki pointed out testimony that Edwards started selling cocaine in September 1978, "so this isn't a man crushed by divorce, and started leading a different life. He got a break in January 1987, and then went back to dealing."

Nowicki again mentioned the letter to Nancy Small.

"What Danny Edwards did was the result of a diabolical mind. This wasn't a spur of the moment activity. Danny Edwards planned this out."

"And he knew exactly what he was going to do. And anybody, anybody that could do what he did, anybody that could even imagine putting a living human being in a container this size -- take a look inside and imagine living on the inside. Anybody that could do that and bury someone alive is capable of anything."

Nowicki asked the jury to imagine a worse way to die.

101

"Imagine Stephen Small when that lid closed. Imagine as every shovelful of sand hit the top of this box. Imagine not being able to do anything to save your life."

"Before he was put in this box, Danny Edwards tortured him, made him kneel there, made him read these instructions."

"Compared to doing something like that, pulling a trigger is easy. And if that isn't enough, then he sends that letter. As if he hasn't inflicted enough grief to the Stephen Small family."

"What Danny Edwards did was not the actions of a human being, a civilized human being. They are the actions of something less. And by his actions, Danny Edwards has forfeited his right to continue to live in civilized society. Danny Edwards, by his actions, has sentenced himself to death by doing things that no one else would ever do. And I ask you to impose the appropriate sentence, in this case, to sentence him to death."

Michael Ficaro told the jury, "The Edwards family is not on trial. The man who put Stephen Small in this box alive is on trial. And here's the reason why. Money. So that he could get money that he didn't earn fast enough selling drugs. Money he didn't earn like the rest of us working for a living. He doesn't want to go through what the rest of his family went through. He wanted it now. And selling drugs wasn't fast enough. The jackpot."

Ficaro pounded his fist on the wooden box in the court room in front of the jury. "This was a cheap investment for Danny. A couple of shovels, $85 worth of wood, a few quarters for a couple of phone calls, and he was ready to collect a million dollars. All he had to do was kill Stephen Small."

Edward's lawyers, on the other hand, had no stronger argument against the death penalty than they had against acquittal. They just had no weapons in their arsenal. Sheldon Reagan told the jury that the Kankakee County jail was a "cesspool of corruption." The guards were on dope, and the guards were bringing in drugs, liquor and women, "you name it." Reagan said it had been going on before Edwards got there.

Reagan said after Edwards' divorce in June 1986, he met the dope dealer and his life fell apart.

"Fourteen months later, he commits the most stupid and bungleable crime imaginable. As a result, Mr. Small died, and here we all are."

Thomas Allen tried to convince jurors not to impose death because "there was no intent to kill Mr. Small." The air tube, water and candy proved Edwards did not intend for Small to die, he said.

"The state can't have it both ways," Allen said. "On the one hand, they can't say that he is a rocket scientist, and on the other hand, the facts and the physical evidence show something different. They show he's not so smart."

102

The jury retired to deliberate the penalty. They did not take long in recommending their sentence.

They were out for just 11 minutes.

"The jury unanimously finds no mitigating factors sufficient to preclude the imposition of the death sentence. The court shall sentence the defendant, Danny Edwards, to death."

The form was signed by jury foreman John Stover, and jurors Janice Winter, Edgar Hervey, Francis Mandell, Lee Rodewald, Blanche Hutchison, Eleanor Vernetti, Betty Romonouski, Robert Kuczek, Robert Featherston, Brian Petersen and Susan Casarotto.

Duke Edwards told the press he was surprised by the sentence, but he was not upset with the jury. "My own personal observation was that the box was hard to overcome."

"When they rolled that box in on Day One, I would say his fate was decided at that time," Thomas Allen said to the newspapers.

Duke Edwards went further. "The court has done its job. I would think that most people would be satisfied with that."

Duke went to school with Leslie Small (Stephen's brother) and Len R. Small (Stephen's cousin). "We've known the Smalls for a long time. Hopefully, we can still be friends. They are not spiteful and neither are we."

The Daily Journal news story said some members of the Small family "seemed nervous before the jury's decision was made known, others of them had an air of vindication after the decision was announced."

Judge Michela thanked Sheldon Reagan, "a local lawyer who was the only lawyer who was willing to take on his constitutional duty as a lawyer to represent this defendant."

Nancy Rish's trial was next.

There was every reason for her lawyers to believe she would be acquitted. Edwards had confessed, saying Rish had nothing to do with the crime. Rish's lawyers told her she had nothing to worry about. They assured her she would be going home.

It didn't work out that way. The jury took just 63 minutes to find Edwards guilty in May 1988. Rish's jury took 90 minutes before coming to a guilty verdict in November 1988.

These should have been two very different trials. However, Nancy Rish's trial was essentially a repeat of Danny Edwards' trial. But there were three big differences: it was before a different jury, there was no real evidence against her, and the prosecutor suddenly accused her of acts he previously ascribed solely to Danny Edwards.

Edwards clearly was guilty. The forensic evidence nailed it down: his fingerprints on the box and other evidence, his voice on the tape, the sandy soil on his shoes.

That wasn't the situation with Nancy Rish. There was no forensic evidence to tie her to the crime. Her fingerprints were on none of the pieces of evidence -- not on the box, not on Small's car, not on the pipe. None of her hair was found on any piece of evidence or at the scene. Soil from her shoes was not from the burial site in the sand hills of Wichert.

All the state had was the fact that Nancy Rish was living with Danny Edwards, that the box was built in their garage, she was in the car when he made the ransom calls, and she lied to the police about a few things when she was questioned. But the state had better skills than its opponents, and it brought the courtroom theatrics that sways juries.

Prosecutors put a number of people on the witness stand, but none of them positively connected Nancy Rish to the crime.

The prosecutors said they did not have to prove that she participated in the kidnapping or the burial. They said they only had to prove that she aided Danny Edwards or that she had knowledge of his plans.

Rish's jurors also were chosen from Winnebago County. Judge Michela and the lawyers met in Rockford on October 19, 1988. There were 67 potential jurors waiting.

The judge told the lawyers, "Find out who they are, find out if they can go to Kankakee, find out what they know. She has another batch coming in tomorrow. My thinking is, you got 14 jurors, 14 challenges, that is 28. Ten throwaways and two nuts, is 42. We build a pool of 40. We ought to be able to pick the jury."

When the jury was brought in, Judge Michela told them, "I have a couple of things to tell you while you are here. I am fidgeter, if you didn't notice. I will read. I will twist. Well, I just did that, too. I will twist paper clips. You know. Don't pay any attention. It is not a comment on the witness or on the evidence. It is merely me. I can talk to the clerk and listen to the witness and read, all at the same time. So, you just worry about what is happening in the witness chair and not to what is happening here."

Rish's lawyer, Vincent Paulauskis told the press, "We can't wait to start to let the public know the whole story. Up to this point, the public has only been told what other people have said, what Danny Edwards has said, and what Danny Edwards has done. That's going to change October 24."

Before the trial began, Ficaro said he would not seek the death penalty because "murder by accountability" wasn't a death penalty case.

The trial started on October 24. Outside the presence of the jury, Judge Michela granted a motion made by Ficaro that prevented Rish from testifying about her father being beaten to death in 1986.

Michael Ficaro made his opening statement. His theatrics had not lost a step since he ended the Danny Edwards trial five months earlier.

"Murder! Murder is what brought us here today! The murder of Stephen Small. A member of this city, this county, this community. A citizen of the state of Illinois. Murder brought you here from your homes some 150 miles away. A murder the evidence will show was the result of a cold, callous, calculating plan of Nancy Rish and Danny Edwards for the big score. The million dollar jackpot. First degree murder and aggravated kidnapping was the price they were willing to pay. The burying of Stephen Small alive was what they were willing to do for that million dollars. That ticket to life on east street. Life in the fast lane. Murder is what brought us to this courtroom. And it is justice that must take us from this courtroom."

"We will prove to you that Nancy Rish, before or during the kidnapping of Stephen Small, aided or abetted or attempted to aid, or agreed to aid, Danny Edwards in the kidnapping of Stephen Small. In its simplest terms, ladies and gentlemen, we will prove that Danny Edwards is guilty of aggravated kidnapping and murder and that Nancy Rish helped him."

Ficaro went through the particulars of what the jury would hear from witnesses, and what happened.

Sherri Carr made her opening argument for the defense.

"Believe it or not, this is a murder mystery. They would like you to believe the mystery is solved. They don't even believe all of what they just said. The mystery, ladies and gentlemen, focuses around who helped Danny Edwards."

Edwards had an accomplice, Carr said, but it was not Nancy Rish.

"There is a blonde person walking the streets," she said. "The mystery is why this young woman is sitting before you. Who is it? We'll let you know."

She alluded to Tracy Storm, a blond-haired man who was Danny Edwards' best friend.

Carr said Edwards was drinking in a tavern on Sunday, August 30, breaking $100 bills, in the company of a man with shoulder length blond hair. This was Tracy Storm, Carr said. She said Storm did not show up for work the next day.

"Edwards is tense, nervous, anxious. He is not sleeping, he is not eating. Nancy Rish is carrying on a normal life. She is helping a friend clean an apartment, she is having her hair done, she is talking on the telephone with friends, she is visiting her sister, she is having her dog groomed."

"It is not only the actions of Danny Edwards and Nancy Rish that are in contrast. It is their disposition. When Nancy inquires of Danny as to his unusual disposition, she receives the response, 'You don't want to know.' However, ladies and gentlemen, we do want you to know, and we are going to tell you. We are going to give you the clues. This response of Danny Edwards is indicative of his unusual behavior, magnified during the week, however unusual, for many months."

Carr said conflicts and arguments between the two sometimes ended in physical abuse. Nancy didn't leave, Carr said, for a number of reasons. She had a nine-year-old son from a pregnancy at 15. She did not have a high school education. Her options were slim.

But, Carr said, Nancy was trying to get away. She moved out in December 1986, into the townhouse on Stratford. She took Edwards back in March 1987, "when gone were the fast cars, the boats and the fast life style." She left again in July 1987, but returned.

Carr said none of the evidence had Nancy Rish's fingerprints or hair samples, and soil samples from her shoes did not match the crime scene.

"I believe you will realize during this trial that the mystery is why this young woman is sitting here before you today, and that there is a blond person walking the streets. Who is this person? They don't want to tell you. We will tell you. "

The witnesses at Nancy Rish's trial were the same one who testified at Danny Edwards' trial.

David Denton was the first to take the stand. He was the boat store owner who said that Edwards saw Stephen Small in his Ferrari and remarked, "It sure would be nice to afford stuff like that." Karen Thacker testified about seeing Nancy Rish in a van in her neighborhood. Ramsey Small told of picking up the phone at 12:30 a.m., and a "deep voice" told him there was a break-in at the Bradley House. The caller at 3:30 a.m. was a different voice, he said, but it also was a man. Eight other witnesses took the stand the first day of the trial, repeating their testimony from the previous trial.

Kankakee Police Detective Rick Gilbert was on the stand the next day. He testified to Rish's lies and inconsistencies when she was interviewed after being arrested. Gilbert said Rish told him she was not with Edwards the night he abducted Small. He told the court the story Rish told him the day she was arrested, that she drove around looking for Edwards at Kankakee taverns, went home, and left again to look for him in Aroma Park. This was not true. She later changed her story to say she followed Edwards' van to Greenwood Avenue.

Illinois State Police Sgt. Ralph McClellan also told of Rish's inconsistent statements.

The officers told the details of what Rish said happened that night, from her interview statements. But she didn't mention the call at 12:30 a.m. until a later interview. McClellan said she told him she forgot to mention it.

Gilbert and McClellan asked her about the tape recorder used by Edwards to force Stephen Small to record a message for his wife. Rish said she didn't know anything about it. McClellan asked her, "What if your fingerprints were found on it?" With that, she remembered touching the recorder, McClellan said.

The officers said Rish told them the wooden box was sold to a black man long before the kidnapping, then admitted seeing it in the garage a few

106

days before the kidnapping. McClellan said Rish admitted to being with Edwards when he made the 5:03 p.m. ransom call and said she did not mention the 11:46 p.m. phone call in the initial interview.

In another police interview, which was taped and played for the jury, Rish said she was with Edwards when he made two phone calls on Wednesday, but she said she thought it was to someone who would repair her bicycle.

FBI Agent Elizabeth Lamanna testified that she saw Rish when the phone booth in Aroma Park was under surveillance. She said Rish spotted her and had a look of "fright or panic." Other officers testified that Rish was driving the car, but Lamanna testified Rish was on the passenger's side. Lamanna said, "The passenger turned and looked at me and she had a look on her face of, it was either like fright or panic, because I just looked back at her and it startled me. And then right after she did that, she turned around to look out the back window of the car, and I thought that was so unusual, I thought why, what is she looking at?"

Paulauskis objected to Lamanna's testimony about Nancy Rish's state of mind. Judge Michela sustained the objection and told the jury to disregard that part.

Donna Jordan said she was mopping the floor at the Convenient Food Mart when Rish and a man came in sometime during the week before the kidnapping. She said the man asked for bottled water. On cross examination, she said it was possible the woman was not Nancy Rish. Linda Forestier told of a man and woman coming into Village Hardware in Aroma Park for distilled water, but she also could not identify the woman as Nancy Rish. Loren Flouhouse testified that Danny Edwards bought a cassette tape from him at Radio Shack, but Rish was not with him.

Forensic scientist Ralph Meyer testified that hair samples from the crime scene did not match Nancy Rish. Lauren Wicevic, a forensic fingerprint expert, said none of the fingerprints at the crime scene matched Rish.

One witness testified that she was hypnotized before testifying.

Janice Krizik, a Kankakee County sheriff's deputy and a neighbor of the Smalls, admitted to being hypnotized in order to better remember the car and a van outside her house on the night of the kidnapping.

Paulauskis was surprised to hear that. That fact wasn't mentioned at Edwards' trial. The prosecution did not inform the defense about it, as they are required to do under the rules of evidence. Paulauskis objected to the testimony because he said he didn't know if Krizik's statements were different before or after the hypnotism.

Judge Michela conferred with Krizik and the lawyers, with jurors removed from the courtroom, and then decided her testimony was not affected by the hypnotism.

Krizik said she heard a tornado siren and called the sheriff's department to see if it was *bona fide* warning. It wasn't. She then heard a vehicle drive down Greenwood Avenue, heard a door slam and then heard another door slam. She looked out and saw a parked van. A car was sitting in the middle of the street. The car left, then the van.

It was Krizik's idea to seek a hypnotist. Father Joseph Tremonti, a priest, a doctor of psychology and a hypnotist, tested her a week and a half after the kidnapping.

He later swore in an affidavit dated November 9, 1992, taken during the appeals process, that Krizik "related further facts she had not related initially."

Lonnie Martens testified about selling straps to Danny Edwards and seeing Nancy Rish sitting in the van outside. James Witvoet testified about seeing a van in the area of the burial site a few days before the kidnapping.

Jean Alice Small testified about her phone call from Edwards.

Ronald Baughman, who lived in the other half of the townhouse on Stratford Drive, said he saw Edwards building a box. Edwards told him it was for his brother in Florida. Baughman identified the same box in court.

Baughman said he heard arguments between Edwards and Rish, and a lot of yelling. The police were called two or three times. He said Rish stayed with him once. He said Rish confided to him a couple of times about wanting to leave Edwards.

He said Rish came to his door around Christmas 1986, at a time when the police were called. She was crying, even hysterical, he said. Baughman said he talked about buying a house and having Rish move in. He said he advised her to leave Edwards.

Baughman, a jewelry representative for a New York company, said he was lying in bed just after midnight on Wednesday, September 2. His bedroom window was open. He heard a door slam and he heard Edwards say, "Let's go, let's hit it!" Edwards got in the van and took off.

Kathy Highfill gave her testimony about Danny Edwards' behavior at the Dam Tap on Sunday, August 30. She said Edwards came about 7 p.m. and sat next to a pay phone. He used the phone several times that night. He was with another man, and they broke $100 bills -- a very unusual situation for that bar.

They were drinking beer and shots. They did five shots in a row, reordering one right after another, and they had three or four beers. They did leave the bar a few times that evening. One time, they went across the street to the Shell gas station and got in a car -- a Camaro or Firebird or TransAm, she said.

They left about 10 p.m., came back 10:30 p.m., and left at midnight. They left an $18.75 tip, and that was large for that bar, she said.

Edwards was not with a woman that night, she said.

Who was the man he was with?

Highfill said he was a "tall man, with long blond hair, shoulder length blond hair. Feathered."

Was his hair like a man or woman? Could go either way, she replied. Tight to his head?

"Not tight, it was feathered, a shaggy type. Wind blown look."

Ficaro asked if the man's hair was like Sherri Carr's hair.

"Not quite as fluffy." He was maybe 190 pounds, Highfill said, and definitely a man.

Carr asked Highfill how close she was to this man. About two feet away, Highfill said. He was muscular, dark and tan, Highfill said.

Was he attractive?

"Very."

Paulauskis and Carr maintained that the charge against Nancy Rish was a case of mistaken identity. The blond man seen with Edwards just before the kidnapping was the real accomplice, they said.

Carr tried to make the case that the blond seen with Edwards in the van was Tracy Storm.

Kathy Highfill identified Tracy Storm as being in the bar that night drinking with Danny Edwards. Bourbonnais Patrolman Jack Griffith said Storm was at Edwards' townhouse the day after the arrests, and Storm took a motorcycle helmet from the garage.

Storm worked at Paschen Construction. His boss, John Hammond, testified that Storm did not show up for work on Monday, August 31, but he did work eight hours on September 1 and 2. He said Storm was "tall, thin, 6'1, with blond hair tied with a rubber band in a pony tail…and dark, from a tan."

"Is he a good looking young man?" asked Paulauskis.

"Very. I thought he was a very handsome guy, yeah."

The court files contain a statement that Tracy Storm gave on May 6, 1988, to investigator George Clodfelter. Storm said that on Sunday, August 30, he was on his way to Irwin, between Kankakee and Herscher, to pick up his truck. He said he and Edwards stopped at the Convenient Food Mart on Route 102 in Bourbonnais so Edwards could show him a blonde female employee named Gina Greene. Storm said Edwards was infatuated with Greene and often went there to buy something just to look at her. They left and went to Irwin to get Storm's truck, and then went to the Dam Tap.

When Storm was called to testify in court, friends were surprised to see him show up with close-cropped dark hair. He did not look like the young man with "shoulder length, feathered blond hair" as his friends knew him.

And on the witness stand, Storm invoked his Fifth Amendment right against self-incrimination, and he did not testify.

Luann Barisa, Tracy Storm's mother, testified that her son didn't have shoulder-length blond hair at the time of the kidnapping.

James Witvoet Jr. repeated his testimony from the Edwards trial, saying he saw a white van on the road to the burial site at 11 a.m. on the day before the kidnapping, and there was a passenger with blond hair -- but he could not tell if the passenger was a man or a woman. Witvoet said he saw the same van leaving the site at 2:30 that afternoon.

Thad Wells, who worked for Witvoet, testified that he saw three men, including a blond man, in the van near the farm. His truck and the van both had to slow down when passing. He said he was within four feet and noticed a heavy-set passenger with shoulder-length blond hair. The driver was a dark-haired white man. The other passenger was a black man.

"As I was getting by the van, I looked at them and they looked at me," Wells said. "And they gave me a suspicious type look, very much. They kind of like frightened me, to be honest with you." Wells said he saw the van again later in the evening.

Forensic scientist Laura Wicevic testified that Storm's fingerprints did not match any from the crime scene. Ralph Meyer testified that Storm's hair sample also did not match.

Carr painted Danny Edwards as a violent man who intimidated Nancy Rish. Bourbonnais Patrolman John Griffith testified about a domestic disturbance where Edwards threw all of Rish's clothing on the garage floor. Lori Brault, a close friend of Rish, testified that Rish often spoke about problems she was having with Edwards.

"She was very confused and unhappy, mostly because she was not happy in her relationship," she said.

Linda Sue Mailloux, Nancy's sister, testified that Nancy was crying and upset in July 1987 when she came with her son to spend the night. Nancy's friend Julie Nanos testified that Nancy was crying and bruised when she spent a night with her in July.

Mailloux, Nanos and Nancy's mother testified that Nancy acted normal during the week before the kidnapping.

A tape of Rish's police interview was played. Rish said she questioned Edwards about his strange behavior the week before the kidnapping. He told her he couldn't tell her what he was doing. She thought he was back dealing drugs, he said no, they continued to argue, and he pulled a gun and threatened to kill Nancy, her son and himself.

In a major case such as this, both sides hire investigators to find evidence that will help convict or acquit their client. The state had the unlimited resources of the attorney general's office, the FBI, the county sheriff and the city police. All Nancy Rish had was a local private investigator and ex-cop from Manteno named George Clodfelter, who was paid by county taxpayers.

Clodfelter, like Nancy's lawyers, found himself at a disadvantage from the start. He was supposed to have the authority of the judicial system

110

in the discovery phase of the case. However, many of the people he wanted to interview would not make themselves available. Clodfelter told Paulauskis he believed it was because of a letter sent to witnesses by Frank Nowicki.

The letter read: "You were recently subpoenaed to appear before the Kankakee County Grand Jury investigating the homicide of Stephen Small. As you may now be aware, the Grand Jury returned Bills of Indictment against Danny Edwards and Nancy Rish for murder and aggravated kidnapping. As a result, you may be called to testify again at the trial of these individuals. Should you receive a subpoena requiring your attendance in court, obviously you must appear. You may be contacted by persons outside of court, for example, members of the news media, who wish to question you about your grand jury testimony or your potential trial testimony. You should be advised that you are under no obligation whatsoever to discuss your testimony with any of these persons. Along with your right to refuse to discuss the case, you also have the right to discuss your testimony if you choose to do so. If you have any questions about your rights, feel free to contact either Michael A. Ficaro, Timothy C. Reynolds, or myself, Frank P. Nowicki, Assistant Attorney General."

Was this proper legal instruction or was it intended to intimidate? Did it chill anyone who was approached by George Clodfelter? Paulauskis complained about the letter in court, but Ficaro said his office was just giving advice on the law.

Clodfelter believed otherwise. A number of people who spoke freely to the prosecution would not talk to him. He called Ronald Baughman on four different occasions, and Baughman put him off each time. Clodfelter went to the house and knocked on the door. No one answered, but Clodfelter noticed someone peeking through the blinds.

Clodfelter called on Karen Thacker, who said she saw the white van in the alley. She also resisted several times before finally telling Clodfelter, "I'm not going to speak to you or anyone else about the case until I reach the witness stand."

Clodfelter tried to interview Gina Glogowski, the woman who was in Danny Edwards' house on Sand Bar Road when drug agents arrested him in January 1987. She said she would answer no questions about drugs. Her lawyer, L. Patrick Power, told her not to talk. She didn't.

Jeff Collette, a 16-year-old boy who worked at the Phillips 66 gas station in Aroma Park in the summer of 1987, told police he saw two black men making calls from the pay phone there at about 5 p.m., on September 2. He would not talk to Clodfelter, on the insistence of his mother.

Clodfelter interviewed William Herzog on March 2, 1988. As state's attorney, Herzog knew better than to be intimidated by a formal letter warning witnesses about talking. Herzog told Clodfelter, "Karen Thacker called me week of September 7, and said she saw a light colored van several times in the area. This was after the (newspaper) story was published. The van was going down the alley." Herzog said he called officers Willis and Gerard. Herzog said he next saw Thacker at a Halloween party at Alderman Rosalind Lind's house. Thacker told him she hadn't been contacted by police yet, and Herzog told her he would tell them again. Herzog met with Nowicki the first week of November and told him what Thacker said.

It only was after Clodfelter asked John Skimmerhorn, the investigator for the public defender, to come along that he got statements from witnesses such as the store clerks. Skimmerhorn lived in Bradley.

Nancy Rish took the witness stand in her own defense on November 1. That was something Danny Edwards did not do at his trial.

The story she told in court was almost exactly the same story she told to police in her initial interviews after her arrest more than a year earlier -- except for the initial lies she told about her whereabouts on the evening of the kidnapping. Parts of those interviews were taped, and the tapes were played for the jury during the prior week.

Here is a summation of her testimony about what happened the week of the kidnapping. It is condensed here, from the questions and answers on direct examination by her lawyers. Unlike the questions and answers during the police interrogation, the sequence of events in her testimony was in chronological order.

Sunday, August 30: Nancy said she took her son to his midget football game in the morning. The night before, her son's coach called and asked her to work in the concession stand. She did.

Danny later showed up on his motorcycle and they rode to Kankakee State Park. Nancy said she and Danny went to Tracy's house on Sand Bar Road. Later, Tracy came over, and Danny and Tracy left in Tracy's car. Ten minutes after they left, Nancy said she got a strange phone call from someone asking for Danny. Nancy said he wasn't home. She asked the man for his name. "Does it really matter?" he said.

Monday, August 31: Nancy got Benjamin off to school, and spent the afternoon at Julie Enright's house at 557 S. Alma Avenue. In the evening, Nancy and Benjamin went to the video store. Danny was in and out all evening.

Tuesday, September 1: Nancy called Anita Hamilton to schedule a hair appointment. A previous appointment had to be rescheduled because Nancy's color wasn't in. Nancy made the appointment for 2 or 3 p.m. Danny came home at noon. Nancy said she wanted to go to Julie Enright's house, but Danny told her to reschedule the hair appointment once again. Nancy called Anita back at 12:30 p.m., and rescheduled it for 5:30 p.m.

Nancy said she and Danny left the house in the afternoon and went to Englewood Electric to get supplies for Pyramid Electric. Danny then drove her to a remote area and showed her some railroad tracks on Rehoboth Road. Then they went home.

Nancy took her son to football practice and then went to Anita Hamilton's place and got her hair done. It took an hour and a half. That evening, Nancy helped her son with his homework. Nancy talked to her mother and to Julie Nanos that evening.

Danny left at 8 p.m. and came back not long after. Nancy said he was nervous and tense, and was in and out of the house all evening.

Nancy said that at 11:45 p.m., Danny drove his van and she drove her car to Greenwood Avenue. Danny parked the van while Nancy stayed in her car in the middle of the street. Danny got out of the van. He had a bag, which he put in the trunk of her car. Danny got in the car. Nancy drove to a nearby gas station. Danny made a call at a pay phone. He got back in the car and told Nancy to drive to Cobb Park and to hurry up. Nancy said she did.

Danny got out and took the bag from the trunk and told Nancy to drive home. She stayed home until 2:30 a.m., watching a video, *Crocodile Dundee*. Nancy left in her car at 2:30 a.m. and drove to the railroad tracks. Danny got in the car and he told Nancy to drive him back to his van. She did. Danny got out of the car, went to his van and said he would see Nancy at home. "I was surprised, he got there before I did," she said.

Nancy said Danny was "nervous, antsy, jumpy, panicky."

Danny left in the van at about 3:30 a.m. He was gone about 20 minutes before coming back home. "He slept downstairs, I slept upstairs."

Wednesday, September 2: Nancy helped her son get ready for school. Danny slept late. Before noon, Nancy called Pat's Groom & Clean and made an appointment for her dog. Danny left in the van after 11 a.m. He was gone a half an hour.

Nancy and Danny dropped the dog at the groomer at noon. Danny stopped the car in front of a horse ranch. He got out of the car and told Nancy to pick him up in an hour. Nancy went to her sister Lori's house for 45 minutes and then picked up Danny at the horse ranch. Then they went home.

Nancy and Danny left home at 4:30 p.m. to pick up the dog. They went in Nancy's car. Danny did the driving. They went through Aroma Park and Danny stopped at a pay phone at a gas station to make call at about 5 p.m. She said his back was turned toward her. She said she didn't see any tape recorder when Danny was making the call. They went home after that.

Benjamin was playing outside. They had dinner. Benjamin talked with Grandma Rish on the phone and he made arrangements to stay with her that night because Danny and Nancy were planning to go to the movies.

Danny was "tense, nervous, preoccupied."

Nancy took Benjamin to his grandmother's house at 8:30 p.m. Danny did not come along. Nancy went home. Danny went to sleep.

Nancy said Danny put her bicycle in the trunk of the car about 10:30

p.m., and they left at 11 p.m. Nancy said she didn't know where they were going. She drove toward Aroma Park, to the Precision Repair place Danny previously had pointed out.

At 11:28 p.m., they stopped so Danny could make another call. It was in Aroma Park, across from Ruffini's. Nancy said his back was toward her. She did not see a tape recorder.

Danny got back in the car. Nancy made a u-turn and drove on Front Street, then to Sand Bar. Road and then to Baker Lane. Danny told her to pull over. Danny had a duffle bag in the back seat. He took it and hid it among some evergreen trees. They drove to Kankakee and stopped at a Marathon gas station, and Danny made a call from a pay phone there.

Nancy said that after the call in Aroma Park, Danny was nervous and panicky, but he also was mad. He said, "Something is wrong. Something is not right."

And after the Marathon call, she said Danny still was mad.

"I was feeling bewildered, confused, scared," she said.

It was after the 11:28 p.m. call that Nancy said she saw a tape recorder in the car. Danny put it under the seat. When he got out of car to switch drivers, he took the tape recorder out from under the front seat and he flung it out the car window. She said she recognized the tape recorder as belonging to Brandon, Danny's son.

After the Marathon call in Kankakee, Danny drove back to Aroma Park. Nancy said Danny drove past the phone booth. He just kept looking at the phone booth. He had noticed a car there and he said he didn't like that.

After midnight, they drove home. Danny took the bike out of the trunk and put it in the garage. Danny then got in the van and left, saying he was going out for cigarettes. He was gone 20 minutes.

Thursday, September 3: Nancy picked up Benjamin from his grand-mother's house and took him to school. Later in the day, Nancy went to Lori's house with Danny. Lori gave Nancy some round steak. Nancy went home and called her mother to get a recipe, and Nancy sent Danny to the store for soup and milk. Nancy said Danny ate only a bite that night, and he hardly ate or slept that week. Nancy went to Jewel to get ice cream for Benjamin and 7-Up for Danny. She said Danny was sweating and had the shakes.

Benjamin and Nancy had ice cream and watched TV. Nancy got a call from her mother and they talked about Lori's health. Nancy said she would come to clean her mother's windows on Friday and she would take Lori to the doctor, if necessary, for her strep throat.

Friday September 4: Nancy sent Benjamin off to school and then went back to sleep. At 10:30 a.m., "I was awoken by some noises and voices downstairs. I proceeded to get out of my bed, and as I was getting out of bed, there was a man in Army fatigues who met me in my doorway of my bedroom and he had a gun pointed at my face."

Rish said Lamanna got her dressed and they went to the Bourbonnais Police Department. She was questioned by Sgt. McClellan and Detective Gilbert.

Paulauskis asked, "Did anyone else talk to you?"

"I believe he is a detective. Detective Erickson. I will never forget him. He is about 6'4, maybe 250 pounds."

"What did he say to you?"

"He came into the room and said, 'Young lady, do you realize your next seat could be the electric chair?'"

"How did you feel at the time you were being questioned?"

"I was very confused and very scared."

"Have you ever been arrested before?"

"Never."

Rish said she asked for a doctor. "I had Guillain-Barre Syndrome and I felt it coming back on real strong and that scared me because it gets in stages where it can be very bad, paralyzing, and with female problems, also."

She said no doctor ever came. She spent four days in solitary confinement. She was too upset to eat.

Rish said she felt better after seeing her mother and two of her sisters. Rish said that during the interrogation, she didn't get to ask questions. Everything she said was answers to questions.

Paulauskis asked, Did the police say something that upset you?

"Yes. They kept telling me that I was lying. They didn't believe anything I said."

How did this affect you?

"I was just very frustrated. Nothing I said they seemed to believe. I was just told I was lying, I was lying, I was lying."

Did you even understand some of the questions you were being asked?

"No, I didn't."

Why did you tell the police the box was sold to a black man?

"Because that is what Danny told me himself, and if anyone was to inquire about that."

Rish said she moved to Stratford Drive to get away from Danny and the drug dealing.

Did it bother you he was paying your rent?

Yes, she said, but she didn't have anywhere else to go. She said she didn't want to move in with her mother because she didn't want her mother to know the problems she was having with Edwards. Rish said she enrolled Benjamin in Bourbonnais schools and she didn't want to switch to Kankakee schools.

Rish said she knew Edwards was getting his money from drugs, but she also knew he was working with the police. She said Officer Ernie Richardson and other cops were over to her place many times.

What about the cops saying your prints were on the tape recorder, and crying?

"At this time, I was just very frustrated, and everything that I was saying to them, they would just tell me that I was lying, and no matter what I said it just didn't seem to help. He just continued to call me a liar."

How did you feel about Danny during the questioning?

"He used me. I was very upset. I was very angry with him."

You admitted lying to the police about the tape recorder.

"Yes, I did."

Why did you lie?

"Because I realized how Danny had used me and he was putting me in the middle of this without me knowing, and I was scared. I was scared to tell the truth."

Rish said she did not attempt to mislead police in the Aroma Park routes. She said she didn't memorize the routes, and it was dark, rural and there were no street lights or signs.

Rish said she was confused about a question about the battery charger and didn't know the significance of it. She said the question came from out of the blue about seeing Edwards' charger, but she did remember Mohler's name and said Edwards was going to borrow it.

Why did you wait to tell of the 12:30 a.m. call?

"It was just a phone call. I didn't know it fit in with this story."

Why didn't you tell the police about being present at the 3:30 a.m. phone call?

"I was not present."

Why did you wait until the second interview to tell about the dog groomer?

"They didn't ask me. I didn't see the importance of mentioning about my dog being groomed. "

Paulauskis asked about police showing her a photo lineup of black men.

"Danny said something to police about black men. They wanted me to see a lineup. On way back from Lori's, I picked up Danny and I saw a white LTD car with a black man. He had a light beige-colored cowboy hat and another black man was standing by his car."

Rish said she didn't mention the 5:03 p.m. call until later in the interrogation because it didn't dawn on her what Edwards was up to. She said she didn't mention bottled water, bolt cutters or other things because she didn't know what the police were talking about.

Paulauskis asked, "Nancy, you heard some tape recordings in this courtroom last week. On those tape recordings is a voice of a man that you

116

indicated to me that you recognize. Whose voice was on that tape record-ing?"

"Danny Edwards."

Could you have ever believed it?

"Believed that it was his voice on the tape recorder?"

That he could have done this?

"No."

When Nancy Rish was done testifying in her own behalf, prosecu-tor Michael Ficaro cross-examined her for more than 90 minutes.

"When you were given the search warrant for aggravated kidnap-ping, did you know it was about Stephen Small?"

"That is what they said."

"You knew who Stephen Small was?"

No, she said.

"You didn't know who the Small family was?"

No, she said.

"Do you remember being in the boat shop when Danny made the remark about it would be nice to afford something like that?"

No, again.

"Do you know the Small family is wealthy?"

No, again.

"You knew Edwards sold drugs from Sand Bar Road, and you were there?"

Yes, she said.

Ficaro asked about Detective Erickson's remark that her next seat might be the electric chair. She said yes, he said it in the Bourbonnais police station. She knew it was Erickson because he was the biggest policeman on the force.

Ficaro didn't pursue it any more. He was saving the "electric chair" incident for later.

Ficaro focused on the lies Rish told police after being arrested.

Ficaro: "When you gave your first statement, you tried to trick them."

Rish: "I wouldn't say trick them."

Ficaro asked if she lied to the cops. She said yes.

Ficaro: "You told the cops you watched TV Tuesday, September 1, and then went to bed. Was that was a lie? "

Rish: "Yes. I was scared to tell the truth."

Ficaro: "You wanted McClellan and Gilbert to believe what you said in that first statement, so they would let you go home, true?"

Rish: "Yes, because I didn't feel I should be there."

Ficaro: "You were pretending to tell them the truth, weren't you?"

Rish: "I didn't know what to tell them."

Ficaro: "Were you pretending to tell them the truth?"

Rish: "I guess I would have to answer that yes."

"And when you told them, what you told them in the first statement, you included some facts that were true, isn't that correct?"

"Yes."

"You gave them an explanation based upon what they told you they knew at the time, isn't that correct?"

"I don't remember what it is that they told me."

"Well, do you remember them telling you that your car was seen at the 11:30 p.m. phone call, with you in it?"

"They asked me where I was on Tuesday evening. That is how I recall it."

"Do you remember telling Sgt. McClellan, Detective Gilbert and Agent Lamanna that you watched TV on Tuesday night, September 1, and then went to bed?"

"Yes I did."

"That was a lie, wasn't it?"

"Yes, it was."

"You were attempting to deceive them, weren't you?"

"I was scared to tell the truth after... "

"Answer the question, Miss Rish."

"Yes."

Paulauskis stood up. "Your honor, I object to rephrasing the question, which seeks to solicit the same answer."

The objection was overruled.

The questions and answers became a sparring match between Ficaro and Rish. Ficaro kept asking his questions in different ways, until he got the answer he wanted. Rish tried to dodge, until she gave up. The young woman clearly was outmatched by the older, experienced and more aggressive man.

"You told the police you didn't know if Danny left that evening, didn't you?"

"Yes"

"And that was a lie, wasn't it?"

"Yes, it was. Part, yes."

"You said Danny left the house at 10:30 in the van."

"Yes."

"And when he left, you thought he was cheating on you. That was a lie, wasn't it?"

"That particular night. Yes."

"And you told Sgt. McClellan that you went out looking for Danny at 11:30 p.m. That was a lie, wasn't it?"

"Yes."

"And when you told McClellan that, you were trying to deceive him, weren't you?"

"Yes."

"You told Sgt. McClellan that you returned home at midnight, is that correct? Is that a lie?"

"Yes."

"Then you told Sgt. McClellan that you had gone to Danny's ex-wife's house to look for him. That was a lie, wasn't it?"

"Yes."

"That was an attempt to deceive him, wasn't it?"

"I told you in the beginning that I was scared. Yes, it was."

"You told him you went to a couple of bars, the Dam Tap and Leo's, looking for Danny, and that was a lie, wasn't it?"

"Yes."

"You told him that you went out at 1:30 or 2 a.m., looking for Danny, that was a lie, wasn't it?"

"Yes."

"So, you were just telling lies to get the statement over with so you could go home, is that right?"

"Because I didn't know what was going on. Danny was the one who knew what was going on."

"You said upon your arrival home at 3 a.m., Danny said to you, 'Well, where have you been?' Is that a lie?"

"Yes."

"Did you tell the police the box remained in the garage for a month, and that was a lie?"

"Yes."

"You told the police a black man bought the box for $100."

"That is what Danny told me."

"You weren't there when the black man bought the box?"

"No."

"Sgt. McClellan asked you whether a tape recorder was present at any of the phone calls, didn't he? That you hadn't seen a recorder recently and never saw Danny with one? That was a lie."

"Yes."

"You lied to Sgt. McClellan about when the box was gone, didn't you?"

"Yes."

"And you told him you lied after being confronted with what Benjamin said, isn't that the truth?"

"Yes."

When Ficaro was finished with Rish, he put Kankakee Police Detective Thomas Erickson on the stand.

Erickson testified that he went on surveillance in Aroma Park on September 3, and he went to Pembroke Township the next day to look for Stephen Small. But he said he never went to the Bourbonnais police station that day. He said he did not make the "electric chair" comment to her. He said he had never spoken to Nancy Rish.

The Daily Journal probably did not intentionally portray the court-room scene as an out-of-control prosecutor pummeling a weak woman until she was beaten. But that is how the coverage seemed in print.

Even the courtroom sketches by Daily Journal staff artist Ken Stark showed a weary Nancy Rish on the witness stand. The caption read, "Nancy Rish appears worn while being questioned by prosecutor Michael Ficaro, who subjected Rish to more than 1-1/2 hours of cross examination. Ficaro focused on statements made by Rish after her arrest." Another sketch showed Ficaro pulling on the wooden box during his argument to the jury.

In the cross examination, and later in his closing arguments, Ficaro argued with Rish as much as he questioned her. He yelled, he pounded on the wooden box, and he dragged the box across the courtroom for effect.

Judge Michela sat silent, giving much latitude throughout the trial to the prosecution.

The trial continued on Saturday October 29. Judge Michela seemed to have more on his mind than a murder trial

"I checked the football schedule and it is just unbelievable," was the first thing Michela said to the jury. "ABC had a choice between Illinois and Indiana, and Minnesota and whomever, and they are putting Minnesota on, so we might as well be there. Ready to go?"

Both sides stipulated to Karen Williams' testimony about Illinois Bell Telephone records.

Paulauskis moved for a directed verdict of not guilty because he said the evidence was insufficient.

"There is no physical evidence linking Nancy Rish to the kidnapping and death of Stephen Small. Not only does scientific evidence exclude Nancy Rish as a participant in the mad, insane scheme of Edwards, it points an unmistakable finger of guilt to at least four other individuals. So-called eye-witness testimony is convoluted, contradictory and self-impeaching, as to give that type of testimony little more than speculative value."

"Nancy's statements, the last portion of the evidence from yester-day, at least Sgt. McClellan's version of those statements, is not enough to overcome the severe deficiencies in the state's case."

Ficaro countered, "Apparently, Mr. Paulauskis and Miss Carr have been attending a different trial than I think everyone else has been. The evidence has been overwhelming as to the defendant's guilt."

Paulauskis' motion was denied.

Nancy Rish's lawyers brought a number of witnesses to tell jurors what kind of a woman she was, and what her behavior was like the week of August 30. Unlike Edward's witnesses, Rish's people had good things to say.

Lori Brault knew Nancy Rish since childhood and was one of her best friends. She said she first saw Nancy with Danny in April 1987 at Two Doves restaurant in Wheeling.

Brault was an employment counselor in Hinsdale. She wanted Nancy to work with her in sales in Hinsdale, to get her out of Kankakee. Nancy came to Brault's business in Oak Brook in July 1987.

"She was rather despaired at the time, and needed a friend," Brault said. "She was very confused, unhappy. Mostly, she was not happy in her relationship at all. She did cry. When she left my house, she was very frightened, and it was more in the sense of confusion."

Julie Enright, a mental health technician at Shapiro Developmental Center in Kankakee, said she saw Nancy on Monday, August 31, 1987. "She came to my apartment. I just moved into new apartment and she came to help me clean windows. She came about 1 or 2 p.m. and stayed until 5 p.m. She was gone about 20 minutes when she left to get some celebratory wine."

Enright said she didn't notice anything different about Nancy's mood. She said Nancy did not have any "anxiety, preoccupation or tension."

Julie Nanos of Bourbonnais told of an incident in the first week of July 1987. "She came to my house, and she was very upset. She had her suitcase and she asked me if she could stay with me for awhile."

Benjamin was with her. There were bruises on her arms.

"She was very upset, very frightened."

She came on a Thursday and stayed until Sunday. When she left, she was "confused and frightened."

Nanos said she talked with Nancy on Tuesday, September 1 -- three times that day, in the evening and late evening. Her demeanor was no different from any other time, she said.

Another friend, Kathy Goodrich, said she saw Nancy in last week of August 1987. Nancy came over to the house that Kathy and her husband and two children had just moved into at 595 W. Mertens Street. Later that night, Nancy came back for a surprise housewarming party.

Nancy was alone when she came and she stayed until 2 a.m.

"She was the same Nancy, calm, and seemed to be fine to me," Goodrich said.

Kathy talked to Nancy again on Wednesday, September 2. "I called her up at 5:30 or 5:45 p.m., to invite her to a party. She was fine. I asked her if she could come to the party. She said yeah. She had just stepped in the door from taking Porsche from getting groomed. She said she'd bring a covered dish. Her voice was just fine. She was relaxed, seemed fine to me over the phone, no nervousness or anything in her voice."

Beth Tomsic said Nancy and her son came to her apartment in the last week of August 1987. At first, Nancy seemed OK, but after Benjamin went outside to play with Beth's children, Nancy started crying and hugged her. Ficaro objected to Tomsic testifying about the details of the conversation. Tomsic said she told Nancy she could stay with her. Ficaro again cut her off.

Penny Lee Parks of Bradley, married with three children, knew Nancy Rish for 12 years, and said she was her best friend. She was living in Texas in the spring of 1987 and she wanted Nancy to fly to Texas and drive with her and the children to Illinois. She said Danny Edwards prevented her from speaking to Nancy in August 1987.

Parks said Danny Edwards would not let Nancy talk to her. Lori Brault said Nancy was unable to leave Danny and he wouldn't let her leave. They both said Danny didn't want Nancy to have friends or to talk to them. They said they saw bruises on Nancy that were made by Danny.

Anita Hamilton told the court that Nancy Rish's hair appointment on Tuesday, September 1, was set for 2 p.m., but it was changed to 5 p.m. She gave Nancy a cut, color and perm. They chatted and "she was calm, friendly, just simple talk." Hamilton was asked if Rish showed any evidence of anxiety or nervousness. "None whatsoever," she replied.

Nancy Rish's family all testified there was nothing unusual about her demeanor before the kidnapping.

Her mother, Genevieve Woodrich, spoke to her daughter several times between August 30 and September 4. She said Nancy was fine, normal and there was nothing unusual about her voice over the phone. They went to Orland Park to shop at the mall.

"Same Nancy, no nervousness or tension."

Nancy's sister, Lori Guimond, and her husband Larry owned the house on Sand Bar Road that Danny Edwards leased. Lori told the court they rented the house to Edwards after Danny and Nancy started dating. She said Edwards moved out in March 1987, and then Tracy Storm bought the house. Lori said she saw her sister during the last week of August 1987, at a birthday party for another sister. Nancy was normal, talkative, outgoing and there was nothing different about her.

Lori saw Nancy on Wednesday, September 2, from noon to 1:30 p.m. Nancy came to Lori's house and stayed 45 minutes to an hour. She saw Nancy the next day, Thursday, at about 4 p.m. Nancy was not nervous. She was calm, in a good mood. Lori was ill, and she asked Nancy to bring the kids to her mother-in-law's house, and she did.

Nancy's sister, Linda Sue Mailloux, program director at the YMCA, saw Nancy before July 4, 1987, during her troubles with Danny. Nancy was crying, upset, shaky, with eyes swollen.

Linda saw Nancy at a family birthday party on Sunday, August 22. She came with Danny Edwards. She was fine and they joked around.

Frank Nowicki gave his closing arguments on November 2.

"The defense has painted a picture of this woman as an ostrich. They painted her as an ostrich who hid her head in the sand the week of August 31, 1987. They have painted for you a picture of this woman as the fourth monkey to go along with see no evil, hear no evil, speak no evil. They have attempted to paint for you a picture of Nancy Rish as a very simple, very unfortunate young lady. Ladies and gentlemen, I submit to you nothing, nothing in this world could be further from the truth."

"You have before you probably the finest example you will ever see of a gold digger. You have as fine an example as you will ever see of a girl that will do anything for money. You have before you a woman with a 10-year-old son who will live with a drug dealer. A man that didn't earn an honest day's living in over a year."

"Danny Edwards may not have been Nancy Rish's dream, but he certainly was good enough until somebody better came along, until somebody with more money came along."

"Defense witnesses told you that in the last week of August, all of a sudden she is now calm, now she is her old self, she is laughing on the phone with Julie Nanos, everything is fine. What happened the last week of August? She was this far from that million dollars. Things were going to change. She was going to have what she wanted. The big score was about to happen."

About Rish's statement that Danny Edwards used her, Nowicki asked the jury, "Does any one of you believe for a second that anybody could use that woman, that anybody could tell her what to do?"

"This woman is a pathological liar. From the minute she opened her mouth when she was arrested, till she stopped talking on Tuesday, all she could do was lie. She lied often, she lied repeatedly. How do you know she is a pathological liar? Well, the evidence tells you that. But once again, there is a better test than what other people come in and tell you what happened. You got to see her. Each and every one of you got to listen to her. And you are in a position to decide in your own mind, is this woman a liar or is she telling the truth."

"What kind of things help you? Well, how about when she admits to you, oh, I lied, I lied in that statement, or sure, I lied about that -- she freely admits it. She smiles as she says it, with her little giggles as she testifies. No big deal, it is only a lie."

"And when she tells you, I was so flustered when they were taking these statements from me, the police were being so mean. Her lawyer was sitting right there. She never admitted anything unless the police already knew it or she was confronted with facts she couldn't deny. Once a liar always a liar."

"She read the warrant, and knew it was for kidnapping Stephen

Small. She tells the police I was home all night, never went out. A lie. She went out looking for Danny Edwards. A lie."

Nowicki said she lied about the route and lied about seeing a tape recorder. She leaves things out and only mentions them when asked, Nowicki said. She forgot the 12:30 a.m. phone call that lured Small out, until a statement on the following Tuesday, a "convenient lapse of memory," Nowicki told the jury.

"At every turn during this scenario that was acted out that week, during every second of this spectacle, who was at Danny Edwards' side? Who was there Tuesday night, who was there Wednesday, who was there Wednesday night, who was there Thursday, who was arrested there Friday? Try as she might, she can't hide from that. The evidence is uncontradicted. It is her. She was there from the beginning. She was there till the end."

Nowicki said Nancy Rish picked Stephen Small because she once lived in that neighborhood. Nowicki said that Danny Edwards went to Jeff Westerhoff for wood because he is Nancy Rish's cousin. She was in boat store when they saw Stephen Small. And that means "she is involved in every phase of this case, from the early planning till the final conclusion."

Nowicki said Danny Edwards and Nancy Rish were there at the 12:30 a.m. call, they were there at the van on Greenwood, they were there at Cobb Park where she left him off, she went to pick up Danny Edwards after he buried Stephen Small, and she took him back to the van. Danny Edwards knew the police were at Small's house the next morning because Nancy Rish drove the van there, looking, Nowicki argued. She was at the other calls from Aroma Park.

"From the very beginning, from back in the planning stage, this crime was never meant to be just a kidnapping. From the very beginning, Danny Edwards and Nancy Rish meant this to be a murder. Stephen Small was never coming out of that box alive. How do we know that? What did Danny Edwards call the box, what did he call the area, what did he call the site? Before he even put Stephen Small in? Remember Steve Small saying I am in a box, and you hear a voice in the background say, no, grave. You don't put people in a grave and then let them out."

"How could Danny Edwards and Nancy Rish ever let him out? You heard from all the people that had seen the box. Two neighbors saw the box, Danny joked about it being a lemonade stand. Benjamin had seen the box. Jeff Westerhoff had seen the box. How do you bury a man alive and then let him out so he can tell everybody about this box, and this pipe and this water? How could they ever get away with it if they left any witnesses? There could be no witnesses. There could be no Steve Small coming out."

Nowicki said the only reason for the pipe, the candy, the water, was to get Small's cooperation. They needed him to make the tapes and to get in the box. "It was bait, it was the lure."

Nowicki went through all the evidence that made Danny Edwards guilty and then said, "Under the law of accountability, we, the people, are only required to prove that Nancy Rish committed one act to aid or abet Danny Edwards in the kidnapping and murder of Stephen Small. In the eyes of the law, if we can show that one act, Nancy Rish is then legally responsible for anything that Danny Edwards does that follows."

"We only need prove one act. We have shown you at least 25 separate things she did -- drop him off, pick him up, go to the phone calls with him, the water, shopping for the pipe, and every one of those items alone is sufficient to prove her guilty on the theory of accountability. You see, the theory of accountability is based on the fact that the law does not allow an individual to escape responsibility by not performing the ultimate or most serious act. In other words, if two people undertake to commit a crime, they are responsible for everything that follows. You can't say, well, I am not the one who pulled the trigger, or I am not the one that put him in a box, to escape your responsibility. You are equally responsible. That is the law of accountability."

Paulauskis gave his closing arguments for the defense.

"Murder brought you to this court room, justice will lead you from this courtroom. Where have you heard those words? You heard them from a gentleman at the counsel table at the start of this case. In the next few moments, I am going to demonstrate to you why that isn't true. I am going to demonstrate to you why it was not Nancy Rish using anyone, and it is not Nancy Rish who today is trying to use you. It is the police and the prosecution trying to use Nancy Rish. Why? They need you to convict her. It is the Danny and Nancy show and nothing else. It is all Danny and it is all Nancy. They have got no other answers. They can't solve it. They can't make sense of it unless they put the two of them together. So I am going to show you it is not murder that brought you to this courtroom, but that Danny Edwards did it."

"At the start of the case, the prosecution said they would place Nancy Rish several feet from the grave, that she participated in the phone call that lured Stephen Small, that the kidnapping was a plan they conceived, that Nancy Rish helped Danny Edwards try to collect the ransom -- none of which was proved."

"We asked you to pay attention as each witness was called and each exhibit was introduced: what does this have to do with Nancy Rish?"

Paulauskis said Rish would legally be responsible if she knowingly aided Edwards.

"The key word Mr. Nowicki left out was 'knowingly.' I am going to show you why Nancy Rish did not know, why she couldn't have known."

"The eye witness testimony showed nothing more than that Danny

125

Edwards planned this, he conceived this in his own mind, and he executed this on his own and that it was he that used others to help him unknowingly."

Paulauskis said Edwards planned to build the box as early as January 1987 after he was arrested in his Sand Bar Road home. Edwards bought wood, finally, on June 1, but Paulauskis said it was Westerhoff who was there to buy the wood with him, not Nancy Rish.

Edwards finally took the wood to build it himself, on his driveway, "right under the nose of the Bourbonnais police who were across the field about a block away," and in full view of the neighbors, and Nancy Rish and Benjamin Rish.

"Now, why Nancy Rish is somehow charged with the knowledge of what Danny Edwards is going to use that box for, when the police, the neighbors, when Jeff Westerhoff are not charged with that knowledge, the state doesn't explain," Paulauskis said.

"The seed is in Danny Edwards' mind in January when he loses his money and his drugs and is watched by the police," Paulauskis said.

He cooperates with the police, wears a wire, they are in his house and Nancy Rish cooks for them, Paulauskis said. "How ironic, during the time that Danny Edwards' plot is taking shape, the police are sitting in his house. They are using him. But he is using them."

"Jeff Senesac made a remark about the box looking like a lemonade stand. "'I must be doing a good job if you know what it is.' That is the voice of Danny Edwards, not Nancy Rish."

Paulauskis noted that Nancy Rish was not there when Edwards bought the car battery, borrowed the battery charger or when he bought the cassette tape. The bolt cutters came from Duke Edwards' business, and had nothing to do with Nancy Rish.

The first participation of Nancy Rish, Paulauskis said, was when she sat in the van when Edwards went to buy the plastic straps. The woman at the Aroma Park hardware store couldn't identify Nancy Rish as being there, and the woman at Ruffini's said a blonde and a man bought four gallons of Hinckley & Schmitt water, not the bottled water found at the grave site. And, Paulauskis said, what does Denton's remark about Edwards saying, "I wish I could afford that boat," have to do with Nancy Rish?

Paulauskis questioned Karen Thacker's sighting of the van that summer, and the woman who was in it.

He questioned Witvoet's timeline of seeing the van in the sand hills of Pembroke Township. Witvoet said he saw the van coming into the area on September 1, between 11 and 11:30 a.m., and coming out between 1:30 and 2 p.m. That was about the same time a man was looking for bottled water.

Phone records showed that on September 1, an 8:12 a.m. phone call was made from Nancy Rish's home phone to Anita Hamilton, her hairdresser. Nancy also called Anita at 12:49 p.m.

126

"The state wants you to believe Nancy Rish is at the grave site from 11 a.m. to 1:30 p.m."

Paulauskis pointed out several odd facts:

Police saw a bicycle in the car trunk at 1:20 a.m. at the Edwards-Rish house.

When Edwards made the calls, he got out of the car, when he could have easily made the call from the car at the drive-up pay phone. That was because he didn't want Nancy Rish to hear what he was saying.

The forensic experts all linked evidence to Danny Edwards, but not to Nancy Rish. As for the 12:30 a.m. phone call, Nancy Rish had no idea this call was to the Small house, he said.

Paulauskis said Nancy took Danny in, after he was arrested for drugs, when the money, the boat and everything else is gone.

He said Nancy talked about her hair appointment, she was talking with friends, and all her activity was normal on Tuesday.

"Could Danny Edwards have possibly trusted her with any portion of the knowledge of his unholy plan? He could not, he could not."

"What could he say to her, what could he promise her, why could he be so sure that her conscience -- she is the mother of a nine-year-old son, has never been in trouble with the law before -- hey, we are going to kidnap a millionaire and bury him alive. But, so make your appointment with the hairdresser a little later. It doesn't make sense. She'd be a nervous wreck through that entire week. She would be a nervous wreck. She couldn't take it. She'd have the blinds pulled, she wouldn't want to talk to anybody on the phone, her sisters, her friends, her child, taking her child to the midget football game, bringing the child home, cooking, helping with homework, getting her hair done, going to the dog groomers."

"He couldn't trust her, and that is why he wouldn't dare clue her in. His instructions to her were simple. Drop me off here. Pick me up here. Something I gotta do. You don't want to know."

Paulauskis pointed to the fingerprints and hair samples the experts could not identify.

"They still have 15 fingerprints and four hairs in search of a suspect."

Michael Ficaro used his final plea to the jury in a dramatic manner.

"Why would Nancy be with Danny in all these places? Answer, because she is guilty. Why would Danny trust Nancy and take her along? Because she is part of it. Why would Nancy help Danny? Well, there is a mil-llllion reasons why."

"Why wouldn't she be a nervous wreck? Because she was part of a well-thought plan to kidnap and never, ever let Stephen Small get out of that box."

"Why would Nancy Rish lie? Because she is guilty."

Paulauskis previously told the jury the heavy plywood box was too heavy to be carried by two people, so there must have been other accomplices. Ficaro took that statement to grab the box and pulled it across the court room. "I'd venture to say you'd drag that all the way to Minnesota by yourself for a million dollars."

"This isn't a case of who else helped Danny Edwards. That is not why we are here. The indictment says, as Mr. Nowicki told you, Nancy Rish aided and abetted Danny Edwards, helped him in the kidnapping of Stephen Small. That is why we are here. Let's never lose sight of that single issue."

"Danny Edwards on September 2 took Stephen Small from the sanctity of his home and buried him in this box. Take a long, hard look at the box. While Stephen Small laid in that box, his lungs bursting in hemorrhage for oxygen, the defendants -- not defendant -- Danny Edwards and Nancy Rish circled Kankakee County, traveled from one end to the other, like vultures waiting for their blood money."

"You know, some people kill out of passion. Some out of revenge. Some out of frustration. There is no greater evil than to kill for money. That is what we are talking about. Easy street, life in the fast lane, the cars, the boats, the Virgin Islands. Who was Danny Edwards going to share the million dollars with? Who was he going to be with when he picked it up in a satchel? Who was going to be there when he counted it? His partner, his companion, his live-in."

Ficaro said the remark in the boat store, "It sure would be nice to afford stuff like that," was not for the salesman in the store, it was an "inside joke" to Nancy Rish.

Ficaro told jurors, "We have her in the afternoon buying electrical straps here."

Paulauskis objected.

Ficaro said "Why didn't Nancy Rish tell you she was back by the grave of Stephen Small? Because she is guilty."

Paulauskis failed to object.

"You have to get Stephen Small from the sanctity of his home. You can't make your million unless you get him out the door. You have got the box and now you need the man. Who do you pick to lure him from his home? Danny Edwards on the phone? No. You need someone who could sweet talk him out, fast on their feet, an accomplished liar, an actress, someone who could convince the man to leave his house at 12:30 at night and respond to a burglary. You heard her lie on tape, you heard her lie in person."

Ficaro flat out told the jury that Nancy Rish made the phone call that lured Stephen Small from his house.

There was no testimony that Rish made the call. In fact, the person who answered that call -- Ramsey Small -- said it was a man's voice. And yet, Paulauskis again failed to object to a statement like that.

128

It was a mistake that even Paulauskis realized was significant. He acknowledged it as a big error in an appeal brief filed by Rish's new lawyers six years later.

"Oh, what a tangled web we weave when first we practice to deceive," Ficaro spun to the jury. "Aid, abet. Right there on the phone, sweet-talking Nancy, the spider to the fly, come on, come on out, my million's waiting for me."

"What does the evidence mean, that she was OK? It means exactly what you saw. She is a cold, callous, calculating, capable of lying, deceiving, putting on a show, pretending, fabricating, concocting, she is capable of murder and kidnapping."

Ficaro said Rish lied to protect herself.

"Innocent people don't lie. They don't. Innocent people don't forget important facts like boxes and recorders and phone calls unless they are guilty. Innocent people don't continue to lie over and over and over again. Innocent people don't need to make up lies or excuses to explain."

And then Ficaro brought up Detective Erickson as the "best example" of her lies.

"She says she is scared because someone threatened her with the electric chair. This is not a death penalty case for her. If you are going to be afraid of somebody, make them big."

"That one lie alone -- forget about this long string of lies, forget about it. That one is good enough for you not to believe her."

"Detective Erickson wasn't even around her. And at the time, wasn't even involved. Her next seat would be the electric chair. Stephen Small wasn't even known to be dead yet. His body wasn't even recovered at that time. There was no murder."

The jury came back with a verdict on November 2, 1988, after deliberating less than 90 minutes. It was the ninth day of Nancy Rish's trial.

The verdict was guilty.

Rish broke down in tears when the guilty verdict was read. She was embraced by her mother.

Judge Michela polled the jurors: foreman Barbara Baumgartner, Howard Hendershot, Linda Sukala, Maryelyn Burkman, David Anderson, Steve Brunson, Pauline Booker, Norman Schesvold, Kenneth Dean, Robert Farrey, Anthony Delmont and Gudrun Erickson.

Ficaro told reporters, "The jury's verdict was swift and just. Hopefully, this ends a terrible nightmare for the Small family." Paulauskis told the press he was surprised the verdict came back so quickly because there were so many exhibits and so much testimony to consider.

Paulauskis filed motions in December 1988 asking to set aside the verdict and for a new trial. His grounds included 25 points. Several of them were technicalities. However, there were a number of substantial arguments -- he cited the "inflammatory and prejudicial" showing of the video of the grave site made on the morning of September 5; the fact that the court would not allow Nancy Rish to testify to what Danny Edwards said; and the state "knowingly misrepresented evidence to the jury" by saying Nancy Rish made the 12:30 a.m. phone call "in direct contravention to the evidence, especially Ramsey Small's testimony that it was a male caller with a deep voice." His motions were denied.

Hearings began to determine a sentence. Nancy Rish was facing a minimum sentence of 20 years or a maximum sentence of life in prison.

It started with Victim Impact Statements, written by members of the Small family, read to the jury.

Susanne Bergeron: "Steve was a quiet, shy, kind and loving brother who never caused hurt to anyone."

"We now live with an elaborate security system at home and at the office. We drive locked cars day and night. We live in fear when the phone rings, particularly when there is no one there. Neither my husband nor I have slept through one night since being awoken at 3:30 a.m., with the news of Steve's kidnapping -- not once." Their children, she said, "have fears one of us will be harmed or killed."

Leslie Small: "For days, we lived behind locked doors, rarely letting our children out of sight. We jumped at the sound of a telephone. Each stranger represented a potential threat. Every noise in the neighborhood was another kidnapper."

He said his 10-year-old daughter has nightmares about his safety and his teenage son sleeps with the doors locked.

Nancy Small's four-page letter was the most heart-wrenching.

"Every day, each and every one of us relives the agony of the final hours of his life. The memory of the horrible way in which he died never leaves us for a minute. At night, when our heads hit our pillows, we find ourselves inside that box as we wrestle with our nightmares throughout the night."

"Steve's murder has brought another dimension to our lives that was not present before -- fear. When the phone rings, I find myself reliving the ransom calls. When the mail arrives, I shudder to open it, ever since we received the letter from Danny Edwards. We are constantly reminded of the chaos in our lives by crank mail and phone calls still being received today."

She said her sons were traumatized they will be kidnapped.

"None of us will ever be the same because of what these two people did. Life will never again have the beauty or warmth it once had. It will always be somewhat cold and scary. We will never be at peace again."

Reva Small wrote, "I have bitterness, anger and resentment toward Nancy Rish and Danny Edwards, and also toward the brother of Danny Edwards and toward the system that allowed him to purchase a new $70,000 car while the legal bills were paid by the taxpayers."

"I am depressed and lonely. I have a constant fear of overexposure of the family or exaggerated financial worth."

Lawyers for both sides brought witnesses to make statements, in support of a severe or a lighter sentence.

The state put on Lisa Harms, Suzanne Lagesse and Michael Kerouac, all of whom spoke of doing cocaine with Nancy Rish and Danny Edwards, in order to make Rish look bad. Kerouac was under a contempt citation for not obeying a subpoena to show up at the Rish trial.

Nancy Rish's mother and sisters gave their statements for the defense. Paula DeBetta, a hospice nurse, was asked what goals Nancy had.

"She wanted a family and a home."

Would you describe her as a gold digger, someone out for money?

No, she said. Nancy had a good personality and was "outgoing and naïve."

Linda Sue Mailloux said Nancy was "friendly, sensitive, out going, trusting." She said Nancy had "no positive male figure, so she didn't know really what was normal."

Lori Guimond said it was a "disruptive family" and that "things started getting really bad about time Nancy was born."

She said Nancy was happy when she got pregnant at the age of 15 because she thought she finally would have a happy family.

Would you say Nancy was someone who wanted a lot of money?

"No, she just wanted a husband, and she would love to have more children. And just a good home for her kids, a stable home."

Lori said Danny Edwards was self-centered and was always was bragging about himself, "and he seemed to be able to tell her what to do all the time. She was dependent on him."

Genevieve Woodrich said Nancy was a good mother who had three jobs at a time, at a bank, at the Jewel deli and selling Mary Kay cosmetics.

Nancy Rish gave her brief statement.

"I just want to say I am not guilty of these charges and never was. I am very sorry for what's happened to someone who I was associated with. I am upset with the people who took the stand under oath, because, as I did myself under oath, and I told the truth. At the times I did lie, I admitted what I lied and for what reasons. But then, I watched one by one by one go up there under oath, officers, detectives, and they did not tell the truth. I feel that had a lot to do with my conviction, and having to get a conviction the way they did was very, very unfair."

Ficaro asked for a life sentence, repeating much of what he said in his closing argument.

Paulauskis pleaded for a perspective.

"Whatever case Mr. Ficaro is on, you can bet it will be the worst defendant he's ever seen and the worst crime he's ever seen. But that is his job, and he has a right to perform his job. Mr. Ficaro had tried to characterize Nancy Rish as a vicious, cold blooded, lying gold digger. He must have a real good thesaurus or dictionary, licking his chops, and the jury came through for him."

He asked, "How can you penalize someone for lack of remorse if they are innocent?"

"She never was in trouble, and now the state is adding on as her criminal history, armed violence, possession of stolen automobile, burglary, residential burglary, even the second letter to Nancy Small."

Judge Michela thanked Vincent Paulauskis and Sherri Carr for their willingness to defend Nancy Rish when so many lawyers in the community refused to defend her.

The judge then handed down his sentence.

"This defendant was involved in every major phase of this event. The box was built in her garage. The box was transported from that garage to its final resting place. The box was transported in the van of Danny Edwards, the person with whom she resided, a van in which she was in often. Evidence would indicate that the defendant had been up and down the alley of the Stephen Small residence earlier in the year, casing the locality, as Mr. Ficaro would say."

"That the defendant was identified by a neighbor person on the day of the kidnapping, the daylight hours after the event. Again, reviewing. The defendant by her own admission took Mr. Edwards to the scene. An inference was drawn from the testimony of Ramsey Small, from the testimony of the defendant, from the physical evidence that was available, that this person made the phone call that lured Stephen Small from his home. That was an inference that the state was allowed to make, it was for the jury to debate whether or not that occurred. Even if that did not occur, this defendant was a part and parcel of this offense."

"She was at 3 o'clock in the morning in the middle of an area where no person should be to retrieve Mr. Edwards. She was there at the phone booths, whether 30 feet away or five feet away. She was there when the calls were made to the Small residence. She was there as the evidence was being thrown out the window of the car. When the police arrived, when the arrest occurred, she was transported to the Bourbonnais Police Department. That the defendant had an excuse for herself and tendered Danny Edwards to the police by saying I don't know what he was doing."

"Having considered that aggravated factors exist, and having considered this offense, this court is going to impose on you, Nancy Rish, a sentence of natural life. That, for the crime of aggravated kidnapping, the court will impose on you a term of 30 years in the Department of Corrections. Those sentences are to run concurrent."

Michela's life sentence added no possibility for parole. He gave Rish credit for the 473 days she already spent in jail, on the 30-year sentence. And he added two-year's supervision after her release.

Nancy Rish entered the women's state prison at Dwight on December 27, 1988, the day after her 27th birthday.

When the state closed the Dwight prison in March 2013, she and the other women prisoners were transferred to Logan Correctional Center in downstate Lincoln.

She has remained in state prison ever since.

Chapter 10

The Electric Chair

"Next seat you might be sitting in is a hot seat. Electric chair, girl.
If this guy dies, you're going down. We're going to ask for a death penalty."
Sgt. William Willis, September 4, 1987

Nancy Rish was not eligible for the death penalty.

The state charged her with aiding and abetting Danny Edwards in the kidnapping and murder. That made her liable for his actions, if convicted, but not eligible for the same penalty he was given.

And even if a sentence of death was imposed, there is no electric chair in Illinois. Lethal injection was the method of execution at that time.

Even so, the electric chair became an important factor in her trial and in her appeals.

Rish said that in the first hours after her arrest on September 4, 1987, a police officer told her that if Stephen Small was found dead, she could go to the electric chair.

"Next seat you might be sitting in is a hot seat. Electric chair, girl. If this guy dies, you're going down. We're going to ask for a death penalty."

It was a threat intended to frighten her into telling the police where Stephen Small was being held. It may have been a good tactic or it may have been an inappropriate threat for a police officer to make. That isn't the issue.

The issue is, did a police officer really say it, and if so, which police officer said it?

If it can be proven that Nancy Rish made up the story, then it is another lie she told. Not an important lie, but a lie. However, if it could be proven that the remark, indeed, was said by a police officer, then Nancy Rish was telling the truth about this.

And that is important because the "electric chair" remark was a key part of the prosecutors' contention that she was a liar who could not be believed about anything.

"That one lie alone -- forget about this long string of lies, forget about it. That one is good enough for you not to believe her," Michael Ficaro told the jury, citing this as the "best example" of her lies.

It was in Ficaro's closing argument, among the last words the jury heard before they went to deliberate a verdict. Ficaro told the jury Rish's whole defense was a lie.

There are a few things to consider about this matter.

First, the subject didn't come up until November 1, 1988, during Nancy Rish's trial. That was more than a year after the alleged comment was made. It was Rish who volunteered the information, on the witness stand, under direct examination by her own attorney.

Ficaro and the other prosecutors did not know about this until Nancy Rish said it on the witness stand.

Nancy Rish testified it was Officer Thomas Erickson who said it. She thought it was Erickson because he was the biggest police officer in Kankakee County.

Ficaro and Nowicki decided to check it out. They found Erickson wasn't in the Bourbonnais police station when the comment allegedly was made. They proved he was on duty elsewhere at the time.

They believed they caught Rish in another lie, and they made the most of it in court.

Rish later said she misidentified the officer who made the remark.

Impossible, Ficaro and Nowicki said. Erickson is 6'8" and 285 pounds. He was "the biggest creature in Kankakee County," Ficaro said. It would be impossible to misidentify him.

The jury believed the prosecutors. It was not the only argument they made to win a conviction, but they did emphasize its importance to the jury.

They later changed their story. In depositions several years later, during the appeals process, Ficaro and Nowicki said it was not an important part of the case they made.

It would have remained a matter of one person's word against another person's word, with the benefit going to the state, until the Stephen Small case became an episode of the *Top Cops* TV series in 1990.

State Police Sgt. William Willis was instructed by his superior officers to cooperate with the TV producers. The basis of the show was police files he sent and a number of telephone interviews he had with producers.

It was a "docu-drama," Willis said, a fictionalization based on a true story. Much of the show was exactly true and some of it was dramatized.

Willis did a short voice-over in the episode. Actors portrayed the principal characters. An actor portraying Willis told an actress portraying Rish, "Electric chair, girl. If this guy dies, you're going down. We're going to ask for a death penalty."

This came directly from the transcript of the telephone interviews Willis had with the TV producers. A 15-page "Bill Willis Transcript" of his statements to the TV producers was entered into Rish's appeal file. The single-spaced transcript went into lengthy detail. It was "replete with information that is highly personal to Mr. Willis that could not have come from any other source," Rish's attorney, Michael Costello, told the court in 2005.

Willis' words were the same words Rish told on the witness stand a year and a half earlier.

In the transcript, dated May 1990, Willis first said that he threatened

135

Danny Edwards with the death penalty if Small was found dead. He said he then made the threat to Nancy Rish.

"Then I go in and talk to Nancy. She says I don't know nothing, playing that shit. I tell her, next seat you might be sitting in is a hot seat. She says, huh? I said, electric chair, girl. If this guy dies, you're going down. We're going to ask for a death penalty."

Willis continued, "Later, in the trial, she accuses some guy 6'7" of doing this. I'm 5'10"."

Willis gave a deposition in Rish's appeal on December 21, 2004, and he testified at an appeals hearing in Kankakee County Circuit Court on January 20, 2005. In both instances, Willis denied he ever threatened Nancy Rish with the electric chair. He said he didn't recall talking to Nancy Rish. He said the transcript was truthful, except for three points: his interaction with other police, the electric chair remark, and a scene at the grave site. He admitted he provided the majority of the information in the lengthy transcript.

However, Willis repeated in his 2005 court testimony what he said in 1990, that he had used the threat of the electric chair in other cases in his career, specifically when he questioned Danny Edwards.

"I told Danny Edwards that if he was involved in this case, he should cooperate with us, words to that effect," Willis testified on January 20, 2005. "Because if we found Stephen Small and something had happened to him, he was killed, he would be facing the death penalty in the state of Illinois."

Willis said he told the producers that Sgt. Ralph McClellan interviewed Nancy Rish. He didn't tell them McClellan made any such threat.

Willis testified he didn't see a copy of the transcript until December 2004, more than 14 years after it was compiled. He said he was unaware his conversations in 1990 were being recorded or transcribed. Willis said he didn't know who compiled the transcript of their telephone conversations.

Willis knew it was going to be in the show. In his deposition in 2004, he was asked about the scene where the electric chair remark was made to Nancy Rish, and he said, "I was there, observed him (the actor portraying Willis) say those words, but I did not say those words."

In more than one answer in that deposition, Willis said he never talked to Nancy Rish. And in more than one answer in that deposition, Willis said he did not recall whether he talked to Nancy Rish.

In a voice-over spoken by Willis on the videotape of the show, he does say that he talked to Nancy Rish.

Rish's attorneys, Joshua Sachs and Michael Costello, said the TV producers' notes of their conversations with Willis was proof that it was Willis who made the threat, and Nancy's only mistake was naming Erickson as the officer who said the words.

If this was the truth, then Nancy Rish did not lie in court about the incident happening -- she just misidentified the officer who said it.

136

Costello told the court that the 1990 transcript did not have any denial from Willis about the electric chair comment, but in fact, he said Willis admitted it.

Michael Ficaro made a strong argument to the jury about Nancy Rish being a liar because of her statement about Erickson. Ficaro also said Rish didn't just lie in identifying the wrong officer, he said she lied about the conversation taking place.

Sachs and Costello contend this was a "presentation of false evidence" by Ficaro.

Sachs and Costello argued it was this false allegation by Ficaro that swayed the jury into coming back with a guilty verdict. Their verdict was based on Ficaro's false claim, not on any lie by Rish, the lawyers said.

Judge Gordon Lustfeldt ruled the transcript from the TV producers was inadmissible because it was not a sworn statement, it could not be determined who wrote it or that Willis knew it was being made.

Swaim said he became aware of the electric chair comment a few months after it was said. In a deposition on October 14, 2004, Swaim said, "Someone, can't remember who, said Bill Willis had threatened her at some point in time." Costello asked Swaim, "What was your feeling about that?" Swaim replied, "I thought it was horrible."

In later appeals by Rish's lawyers accusing Ficaro of misconduct for telling the jury that Rish could not be believed about anything because she lied about Erickson, the Circuit Court said, "For the purpose of this motion to dismiss, the court has accepted as true that Mr. Willis actually made the statements in question." It did not grant her appeal, but it allowed that the threat was made and that Willis made it.

Did Ficaro's "electric chair" argument to the jury, which he called Nancy Rish's "biggest lie," this final impression they took into the jury room, weigh heavily on their decision? Did jurors agree that if Nancy Rish lied about this, that everything else she said was a lie? Did they believe it was a small lie, but the one that tipped the scales?

Was this a misidentification of the officer who made the threat, or did Nancy Rish make up the whole thing?

Consider the possibilities.

First of all, an officer making a threat is not much of an issue. Police often get rough with suspects in an interrogation. In this case, the police were working against the clock to try to save a life. Willis admitted he made the threat to Danny Edwards.

Second, Nancy Rish had nothing to gain by saying this happened. No one paid much attention to it as a procedural issue or as misbehavior on the part of the police.

It didn't become an issue until Erickson was named as the man who made the threat and it was proven he did not. It only became important when the prosecution could use it to undermine her entire credibility, not just for this statement, but for everything she said. In other words, a lie here meant she lied about everything else.

Third, is it believable that Nancy Rish was scared, confused and could have misidentified one of her interrogators? Every officer who threatens a woman in this harsh manner is a "big creature."

Nancy Rish was awakened by a man pointing a gun in her face, and then she was hustled over to a police station where she was accused of kidnapping and possibly murder. She went, within a few minutes, from sleeping in her own bed to being threatened with the electric chair.

Rish's identification of Thomas Erickson can be argued as a misidentification, not a lie. But even if she made up the story about a police officer making this threat, how is that proof that she was part of a kidnapping plot? Ficaro meant to show it proved Nancy Rish a liar. But not this nor anything she said in her interrogation sessions proved she knew what Danny Edwards was doing.

Rish's mention of the electric chair remark, during her testimony, had nothing to do with the charges against her. It was irrelevant to questions of guilt or innocence, it was irrelevant to any issue in the case, it was irrelevant to everything. And yet, it proved a pivotal moment for the prosecution to use to condemn her.

The prosecutors said the electric chair remark was "biggest of all lies" at the trial, but in their depositions in 2004, it suddenly it was not so important. If it is unimportant now, why does the state continue to misrepresent it?

Finally, just where could Nancy Rish have gotten the "electric chair" story if it wasn't true? Willis made the same threat to Danny Edwards. Nancy Rish could not have known he made that comment to Edwards. The remark was made to Edwards on the day of the arrest, outside her presence. It was only at her trial 15 months later when she said the remark was made to her on the day of her arrest.

How would she know about this remark, a year and a half before Willis admitted it in a TV show?

Where did the TV producers get this remark, and where did Nancy Rish get this remark, unless it was true and was said to her by Willis?

In any event, the "electric chair" remark became an important part in convincing the jury that none of Nancy Rish's testimony could be believed.

The jury believed the prosecutor, and it accepted that Nancy Rish was guilty until proven innocent. It was too bad that it was proven too late.

Stephen B. Small

Illinois State Police
crime scene photo
of the box buried in the
Wichert sand hills in
Pembroke Township.
A shovel is in
the sand
on the left.

Stephen Small's new Mercedes, hidden in the brush, just a few feet from the burial site. *Illinois State Police crime scene photo 1987*

This is the box Danny Edwards built, as it was pulled from the Wichert sand hills by the police, days after the kidnapping. *Illinois State Police crime scene photo 1987*

These are the telephones where Danny Edwards made his calls. The left picture shows the pay phone at the Phillips 66 gas station on River Street in Kankakee. Below is the pay phone outside the Phillips 66 at Lowe and Third streets in Aroma Park. Both phones were designed to be used from a car. However, Danny Edwards got out each time because Nancy Rish was sitting in the car, and he didn't want her to hear him.

Illinois State Police crime scene photos from 1987

141

Stephen Small's house on Cobb Boulevard in Kankakee
on Sepember 5, 1987, the day after the body was found.

The Edwards-Rish townhouse (on the left side)
on Stratford Drive East in Bourbonnais.

This is the rented house on Sand Bar Road which prosecutors referred to as "the good life, life in the fast lane, Easy Street." It was an older, rural 1,100-square-foot house behind the garage, with two small bedrooms. *Illinois State Police photo, 1987*

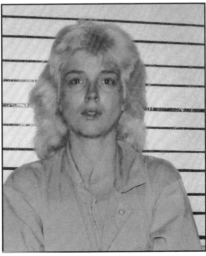

The booking photos for Danny Edwards and Nancy Rish, taken on September 7, three days after their arrest. *Kankakee City Police file photos*

143

A stunned and tearful Nancy Rish is escorted by Sheriffs Detectives Nancy Sullivan and Jo Lynn Fahrow into the Kankakee County courthouse for her bond hearing on September 8, 1987. Below, Nancy Rish is led into the Kankakee County courthouse on October 25, 1988, for the beginning of her trial

The November 2, 1988, *Daily Journal* showed a weary Nancy Rish on the witness stand. The caption reads, "Nancy Rish appears worn while being questioned by prosecutor Michael Ficaro, who subjected Rish to more than 1-1/2 hours of cross examination. Ficaro focused on statements made by Rish after her arrest." The bottom drawing is from the next day's newspaper edition, showing Ficaro at his theatrical best, dragging the wooden box across the courtroom floor as he makes his argument to the jury. *Drawings by Daily Journal artist Ken Stark*

Paul and Genevieve Woodrich family, 1964.
Nancy Rish is in front on the right.

Nancy Rish and her parents, Paul and Genevieve
Woodrich, at her First Communion, 1970.

Nancy Rish in 1964,
1971 and 1984.
*Photos courtesy of
Lori Guimond*

146

Paul Woodrich and his daughters
in 1962. Nancy is on her
father's shoulders.

Nancy Rish was maid of honor at
her sister Lori's wedding to Larry
Guimond on August 27, 1977.

Nancy Rish and her son Benjamin, 1986. *Photos courtesy of Lori Guimond*

Danny Edwards (left) was best man at the wedding of Randy and Beth Irps
at St. Patrick's Catholic Church in Kankakee on September 23, 1978.
Photo courtesy of Randy and Beth Irps.

Nancy Rish and one of the dogs she helped train in the prison "Helping Paws" program, in 2012.

Nancy Rish, upon earning a college degree in Dwight prison in 1999.

Nancy getting a visit from her grandsons Benjamin and Vance in 2012.

Photos courtesy of Lori Guimond and Nancy Rish

Prison ministry
at Pontiac's
Death Row,
early 1990s.
Standing from left:
Jimmy Pitsenbarger,
Pastor Bob Grison of
Christ Church,
Danny Edwards,
Jack Karalevicz
and Chuck Rivard.
In front is
Douglas Oaks.

Photo courtesy of
Jack Karalevicz

Danny Edwards signed an affidavit in Pontiac prison on September 25, 2013, swearing Nancy Rish is innocent and that she knew nothing of the kidnap plot. Edwards maintained it from the beginning, but this was the first time he swore to it in a legal document. *Photo by Jim Ridings*

Chapter 11
The Powers That Be

"The King can do no wrong."
The legal 'precedent' argued in 1922 as to why Governor
Len Small was above the law and could not be arrested.

Kankakee once was a prosperous factory town, a land of plenty, with the promise of a job and a nice house for anyone who wanted to work for it. But the good life started to end as the 1970s came to an end.

Manufacturing was the backbone of Kankakee's prosperity, but factory after factory closed or left town in the 1980s. The reasons are many, and Kankakee was not alone in its decline during that era. It didn't help that Illinois is not a pro-business state and continues today to do all it can to chase away business and individuals with its punishing regulations and taxes. Other areas of the nation, with a better climate, cheaper labor, lower taxes, and public officials who welcome businesses departing Illinois, have benefitted from our loss.

Kankakee, a city of about 27,500 people, lost 4,000 factory jobs between 1977 and 1983 (according to *Crain's Chicago Business*) during the rule of Tom and George Ryan, who did nothing to stop the tide. They simply did not know how to adapt to changing trends and times. Most of Kankakee's factories relocated in the South. Kankakee's 22 per cent unemployment rate in the 1980s equaled Great Depression figures. More than 30 years after the collapse, Kankakee still has one of the highest unemployment rates in Illinois, a state with one of the worst unemployment rates in the nation.

Today, Kankakee is known for its high unemployment, boarded-up houses and storefronts, decaying neighborhoods, its drug scene and its violent street gangs. There is a lot of good in Kankakee County. It still has a lot of thriving businesses. It has two fine hospitals, two fine colleges and an excellent public library. It has a beautiful river and state park. It is blessed with rich, productive farm land. But the city is plagued with a corrupt political system, drugs, a defeated attitude, no vision, and a municipal bread and circus to mask the dreary reality.

Kankakee has always been ruled by political bosses who took care of themselves before they took care of the public need. In prosperous times, no one noticed or cared.

In Kankakee, money talks. Money is power. Power can intimidate. And no one in Kankakee speaks louder than the Smalls and Ryans. The Smalls own the daily newspaper and they control the political apparatus and more. "The Powers That Be" gives orders, and a whole lot of people jump.

The jobs are gone, but the power is still there. The machine is still in place. The poverty has gotten worse, but the fat cats are still fat.

Kankakee was born from corruption. Kankakee County was formed in 1853 as the Illinois Central Railroad was building a line through that prairie. The county was established after railroad workers in the Limestone area voted fraudulently and frequently. Another vote to set a county seat was rigged by the Illinois Central to choose a place on their rail line -- a rut in the road that commonly was known as Kankakee Depot, rather than the established Bourbonnais or Momence. The first county board of supervisors meeting was held in Momence because there were no buildings in the primitive railroad settlement called Kankakee Depot.

The village of North Kankakee got the huge David Bradley Implement factory to relocate from Chicago in 1895, only after a deal that included changing the name of the town to Bradley. A couple of miles to the west in Kankakee County, the village of Verkler got a railroad station located there in 1882, only after being shaken down by Thomas Bonfield, a slick Kankakee lawyer (and attorney for the railroad and Kankakee's first mayor) who demanded cash payoffs. Bonfield then renamed the village for himself.

One of Kankakee's proudest boasts is that it is the home of Dairy Queen. It is not. The first Dairy Queen opened in nearby Joliet in 1940. It was another seven years before Kankakee got a Dairy Queen. The city makes its boast based on a Kankakee ice cream store owner's one-day experiment of serving the unnamed treat as it was being developed. DQ corporate headquarters in Minnesota says Joliet is the home of Dairy Queen.

For more than a hundred years, people have abbreviated their town with the initials KKK, oblivious to what outsiders might think of that.

Stephen Small's great-grandfather, Len Small, was governor of Illinois for eight years in the 1920s. He was a progenitor of The Kankakee Way. In a state infamous for crooked governors and crooked politicians of all kinds, Len Small may have been the biggest crook of them all.

Len Small started making the family fortune in the 1890s, using political connections to be named head of the board of trustees of the state insane asylum in Kankakee. Incidentally, it was a shady deal that got the institution located in Kankakee in 1877. It was called the Eastern Illinois Asylum for the Insane until the name was changed to Kankakee State Hospital in 1915. It was renamed Shapiro Developmental Center in 1977 for Samuel Shapiro, another Illinois governor from Kankakee.

It was in his position at the asylum that Len Small rigged coal contracts and shook down employees and vendors if they wanted to get a job or to do business with the large institution. Employee paychecks had a five percent deduction for Len Small's political slush fund. Small built a powerful political machine in Kankakee that ruled for the next hundred years.

Len Small became state treasurer in 1917 and embezzled two million dollars from the state. He did this by depositing millions of state dollars in the "Grant Park Bank," a bank that did not exist; it loaned the money to Chicago meat packers at six to eight percent interest and it paid the state two to three percent. Shortly after taking office as governor in 1921, Small was indicted. He ran from the sheriff rather than be arrested, threatening to call out the National Guard "with bayonets" against sheriff's deputies. Small's lawyers argued in court that, as governor, Small was above the law and was not subject to arrest. The lawyers based their defense on "an old English doctrine" that "the King can do no wrong." The judge rejected this argument and Governor Small went on trial in 1922. He was acquitted after Al Capone's hoodlums bribed and intimidated jurors. Eight jurors got state jobs.

Although a jury acquitted Small of criminal charges, a civil suit filed by the state forced Small to repay $650,000 of the money he stole. Small got the money by shaking down state employees and road contractors. In its decision, the Illinois Supreme Court ruled the Grant Park Bank was a sham.

Governor Small sold as many as 8,000 pardons and paroles, to killers in the Capone organization and anyone else who could pay the price.

Harry Guzik, the brother of Al Capone's bookkeeper and top aide Jake Guzik, ran houses of prostitution for Johnny Torrio and Al Capone. Harry and his wife Alma were convicted of forcing a teenage girl into prostitution, and were sentenced to the penitentiary. But the Guziks never spent one day in jail. They were immediately pardoned by Governor Small.

Robert Emmett Crowe, Cook County state's attorney in the 1920s, said, "Perhaps the worst handicap this office confronts is Len Small's pardon and parole system. He lets them out as fast as we put them in."

Al Capone said in 1927, "There's one thing worse than a crook, and that's a crooked man in a big political job." He added, "There are worse fellows in the world than me."

There may have been no St. Valentine's Day massacre in 1929 if Governor Small had not taken a bribe to let gangster George "Bugs" Moran out of the penitentiary in 1923. There would have been no need for Eliot Ness and the Untouchables if not for Chicago Mayor "Big Bill" Thompson and Governor Len Small; the Chicago police and the state police were so crooked that federal agents had to come to Chicago.

Governor Small aided the Ku Klux Klan, giving them the use of state facilities in Chicago and Springfield for their rallies, and the Klan endorsed all his campaigns. Members of Small's inner circle were Klan members. Among those in the Kankakee chapter of the KKK in the 1920s was Earl Gray, a nephew who lived in Small's house on Station Street (he was assigned robe number 255), and Walter Lowe, who was Lura Lynn Ryan's grandfather (robe number 361). Lowe, a wealthy farmer and seed corn developer, died on January 14, 1933, in a bizarre farm accident. He was on a small electric elevator going to the second floor of his seed house, when he fell. His head and neck extended from the side of the elevator and he was all but decapitated when the elevator reached the second level of the seed house.

Len Small and "Big Bill" Thompson campaigned together in 1931 and 1932. Thompson constantly made vile anti-Semitic speeches against Henry Horner, Small's opponent, who was Jewish. TIME magazine quoted a Thompson's appearance: "On behalf of his snaggle-toothed partisan Small, Big Bill proceeded to give Judge Horner a forensic log-ride. Downstate rural clodhoppers gawped, snickered and nodded approvingly when he shouted, 'My friends, I don't have to tell you that Levys don't eat hogs. If Horner is elected, hog prices are bound to drop. Furthermore, Jews run pawnshops, and the first thing Horner will do if he gets to Springfield is open a pawnshop." TIME added, "In the primary, one-time Mayor Thompson had employed 'stooges' in rabbinical dress to ridicule Judge Horner's racial origin."

Another political mentor and ally was Fred Lundin, who handed out patronage jobs, collected kickbacks and ran much of the show in Chicago from behind the scenes. Lundin went on trial for stealing a million dollars from Chicago public schools but was acquitted, Chicago style. Lundin's most famous quote was, "To hell with the public and our promises, we're at the feedbox now!"

Governor Small wrecked civil service and brought back the spoils system. He had his legislature pass a law exempting him from removal. The *Chicago Tribune* despised him, using names like "unscrupulous, insufferable, flannel-mouth, unprincipled, stupid, a gangster" and more. TIME magazine couldn't write about Governor Small without using words like "malodorous" or "crook pardoner."

A TIME magazine story in 1926 called Governor Len Small "a cold blooded crook." This was for Governor Small's pardon of cop killer Ignatz Potz, who shot-gunned a motorcycle policeman who was pursuing a car of Capone bootleggers in 1921. Potz was sentenced to death, but Small commuted the sentence and later gave Potz a full pardon.

Len Small used his rapidly expanding wealth to buy a bank, farms, railroad stocks and more. He didn't like what the *Chicago Tribune* and the local *Kankakee Daily Gazette* wrote about him, so be bought a struggling rival Kankakee newspaper and turned it into the dominant local newspaper. It started as the *Kankakee Daily Republican* and today is *The Daily Journal*.

Governor Small created the Department of Purchases and Construction and appointed his son Leslie as director, in charge of hundreds of millions of dollars in projects and contracts. Small's son-in-law Arthur Inglesh was named administrative auditor of the Department of Finance, joining numerous cronies and family members on the state payroll.

The machine in Kankakee did not always run smooth. From the beginning of Small's reign, there was an opposition political party. It wasn't the Democrats. It was another Republican party, local political leaders who did not like the corruption of the Small faction. But because the Small faction held the political power (and the power of the press), this group of honest men was called the Anti-Republicans.

One such Republican opponent was State Representative J. Bert Miller of Kankakee. He made a dramatic speech to the Illinois legislature in 1927, when Small was using strong-arm tactics to force his Republican majority to pass a law exempting him from removal.

Miller called the law "an attempt to throw protection around the thief, the perjurer, the jury briber, the traitor that sits in the governor's chair. No one knows him better than I. I have lived in the same town with him for 40 years, and if there is a bigger thief and political crook anywhere, I'd like to see the color of his hair."

He continued, "In January 1917, with uplifted right hand, with perjury on his lips and treason in his heart, Small swore to uphold the Constitution. Within a month, he had his hands up to the shoulders in the state treasury and had removed 10 of the 30 million dollars and loaned it to the packers at 8 per cent."

Miller continued speaking about Small's money laundering scheme, his evading the sheriff to avoid arrest after his indictment, the bribing of jurors and how the governor pardoned the gangsters involved in the jury tampering.

Miller then delivered the lines that were quoted in TIME magazine.

"Caesar had his Brutus, Jesus Christ had his Judas Iscariot, the United States had its Benedict Arnold and Jefferson Davis, and Illinois has Len Small. And if the Judas of Illinois had the courage of the Judas of Jesus, he would return the 30 pieces of silver, get a rope and hang himself and remove the withering blight which will remain upon this state as long as he is governor of Illinois."

Governor Small succeeded in convincing the legislature to pass the legislation exempting him from removal, a law his successor had the legislature reverse. In the governor's case, "Small justice" was to his benefit.

As a parting shot when he left the governor's mansion, Len Small stole expensive silver sets and other valuables.

The Kankakee County Museum today, generously endowed by the Small family, is in Governor Small Memorial Park. Its reverent displays on the governor do not mention anything about his corruption, which was as vast as his fortune.

In Kankakee, people either love or hate George Ryan. The same goes for the McBrooms. Ryan brought a lot of taxpayer money home to Kankakee County and he did a lot of favors for a lot of friends, and they still appreciate him. The majority of people are the ordinary citizens who were bullied and hurt by the strong-arm tactics of the local political machine of George Ryan and Ed McBroom. I hear their opinions in remarks after public lectures I give, in interviews I conducted for this book, in comments on social media and on-line newspaper comment posts.

The local political machine that started in the 1890s with Len Small gained great power in the early 1900s with men like Ed Jeffers, a Kankakee businessman and political boss who was Republican county chairman for 30 years. Jeffers was given control of patronage at the Kankakee State Hospital, and he grew rich from his own state contracts. Victor McBroom married Jeffers' daughter and moved into the top political circle.

McBroom and his brothers owned a restaurant in Kankakee where business and political deals were made. McBroom was appointed head dietician at Kankakee State Hospital by Governor Small, after Small wrecked the state civil service system to make this merit job a political plum. McBroom was paid by the state, but spent most of his time at the Jeffers & McBroom car dealership. Jeffers and McBroom also were on the boards of Len Small's newspaper, bank and Inter-State Fair.

Patronage jobs were given to those who bought a new car from Jeffers & McBroom. Workers kept their jobs by buying a new car when it was time. For decades, Victor McBroom (and his son Edward) would go to a business or a home and throw a set of keys on the counter and tell the man, "You just bought a new car." Other people found new car payments deducted from their paychecks.

Victor McBroom took over as Republican county chairman in 1930 and held it until he died in 1959. Victor was appointed state representative in 1940 and was elected state senator in 1946. His son Edward followed him as county chairman in 1959, and was a state representative or a state senator from 1962 to 1982. Edward died in 1990 at the age of 65.

This was the local political machine George Ryan inherited and took to a new level.

However, just as Len Small's Republican party had an opposition Republican party, George Ryan also had Republicans who opposed the boss politics of the McBroom-Ryan machine. They formed a Lincoln Club. Ryan spoke to the group once in 1985, only to excoriate it as a "rump group."

George Ryan became Ed McBroom's campaign manager in 1962. It was McBroom who picked George's brother, Tom Ryan, to become mayor of Kankakee in 1965. He appointed George Ryan to the Kankakee County Board in 1966, starting him up the political ladder.

Ed McBroom also taught the Ryans the fine art of politics, in giving contracts and favors to those who paid. But George Ryan was smarter and more aggressive than Ed McBroom, and George quickly became the real boss. Those who did not jump when he barked lost their jobs. Others were roughed up by his squad of rogue cops.

Dean Bauer was typical of the men in authority who worked for Ryan. Bauer, a telephone lineman, was appointed Kankakee chief of police by Mayor Tom Ryan in 1970, an appointment that was strongly opposed by several members of the city council. The opposition to Bauer only grew stronger over the years. Bauer's main qualification was that he was a friend of the Ryans. Bauer created his own scandals. Morale on the police department sank so low that it was an issue in Mayor Tom Ryan's campaign in 1977; Harold Rapier said he would fire Bauer if elected. Bauer ran the police department strictly on a political basis. Bauer used his policemen as chauffeurs for local officials and businessmen, taking them to and from O'Hare airport and other Chicago destinations. Important people in Kankakee or those who supported the party had traffic tickets torn up or charges dropped.

This was so common that no one blinked an eye when the *Kankakee Daily Journal* wrote about it in 1974. The story said hundreds of motorists pleaded guilty to traffic tickets and still kept charges off their driving records. They admitted guilt, but no conviction was entered, and tickets were dismissed after a period of "court supervision" to keep them from having their licenses suspended. Defense lawyers and Kankakee judges liked it, but State's Attorney Edward Drolet told the newspaper it was "a shabby, horrible reflection on the whole judicial system" and "a lot is done for political reasons" since it was "embarrassing because of who it is." Of course, political favors and money changed hands.

Bauer told the newspaper he reviewed all traffic tickets before any were sent to the courthouse. Sometimes, a police report was retyped to show different information. The newspaper showed an example where the insurance company was given one police report showing a ticket was issued (so the insurance company would pay off) while the police file showed no ticket or arrest (so the motorist did not have it on his record). And it was never filed with the circuit clerk, as required by law.

The newspaper articles were presented as informative, not scandalous. Kankakee does not recognize the routine as scandalous.

How oblivious are Kankakee politicians? When George Ryan was a freshman state representative in 1974, he voted for a law that allowed legislators and other state officials to continue to receive state pensions after being convicted of a felony (anywhere else, this wouldn't ever be an issue; in Illinois, this is important to politicians). Ed McBroom also voted for the law. Ryan said, "If a fellow is in public office for years and years, I think his wife has a vested interest, she's entitled to that (pension) protection."

Governor Dan Walker vetoed the bill, which he called the "Future Felons Protection Act."

(Walker went to prison in 1987, a decade after leaving office, for irregularities involving a savings and loan association, not for any malfeasance in office. He was one of four Illinois governors who has gone to a federal prison since 1974; the others -- who got caught -- were Otto Kerner, George Ryan and Rod Blagojevich).

Was George Ryan being brazen or prescient in 1974? More than

30 years later, a judge stripped Ryan of his large pension after his convictions on several federal felonies.

Dean Bauer was a campaign issue again in 1985. Russell Johnson said one of his first acts would be to fire Bauer. Johnson beat Tom Ryan 60 to 40 per cent, ending Tom Ryan's 20-year rule as mayor.

Bauer later joined George Ryan in the secretary of state's office as inspector general. Instead of rooting out corruption, Bauer worked hard to cover it up and destroy evidence. He was convicted and sent to prison.

State Representative George Ryan led the fight that defeated a bill in 1976 to require pharmacists to inform the public about less expensive generic drugs. This was while Ryan was forcing Kankakeeans to buy their prescriptions at Ryan's pharmacy if they wanted to keep their jobs. Ryan's pharmacy also sold medical equipment to state facilities, in violation of state law.

Westview Terrace nursing home in Kankakee gave Ryan's pharmacy more than $60,000 in Medicaid scrips each year. It switched its business to another pharmacy in 1982, after it was purchased by Morris Esformes. The Illinois Department of Public Health was investigating neglect and abuse of elderly residents at Esformes' other nursing homes, after an 85-year-old patient died of infected bedsores. But George Ryan intervened and charges were dropped. Ryan's pharmacy then got back its annual $60,000 in business with Westview Terrace.

The nursing home also overcharged the federal government for Medicaid prescriptions and then kicked back part of the payment to Ryan's pharmacy. And in 1981, Ryan got the state to drop regulations that fined nursing homes for being understaffed; Ryan's campaign then started getting big donations from nursing home operators.

George Ryan's 35 years of public corruption only caught the attention of federal prosecutors after a terrible traffic accident in 1994. As Illinois secretary of state, Ryan was putting millions of dollars in his campaign fund by having his driver's license offices sell licenses to unqualified drivers, a "licenses for bribes" scheme. Ricardo Guzman, an unqualified truck driver who paid a bribe to get his license, caused an accident near Milwaukee on November 8, 1994, that killed six children of Rev. Scott and Janet Willis.

That was just too much. A lengthy investigation was launched by federal prosecutors, resulting in indictments and trials for Ryan and 79 of his cronies (76 were convicted).

George Ryan was convicted in April 2006, on 22 counts of racketeering, fraud, tax evasion and other crimes. He was found guilty of giving multi-million dollar contracts based on payoffs, taking illegal gifts from contractors who did business with the state, shaking down state workers for campaign contributions, using state workers to run his campaigns and illegally trying to kill official investigations into his corruption. He was sentenced to

6-1/2 years in prison. He entered a federal prison on November 7, 2007, and he was released on January 30, 2013.

George Ryan has remained defiant, and he has never admitted guilt or shown remorse for anything.

Kankakee is proud of its native sons. Len Small and George Ryan have worshipful displays in the local museum in Governor Small Memorial Park. Streets are named for numerous Small family members. Driving onto the campus of Kankakee Community College, the first thing one sees is the big sign on the George H. Ryan Activities Center gymnasium. Down the road is the George and Lura Lynn Ryan Aquatics Center, commonly known as Splash Valley water park. A brass bench and plaque honoring George and Lura Lynn Ryan is on the front lawn of the Kankakee County courthouse.

Kankakee in the 1970s and 1980s was awash in a sea of marijuana and cocaine. There almost was a correlation between the decline of jobs and the increase in illegal drug use in Kankakee in those years. By the 1990s, Kankakee also was the *per capita* murder capital of the state.

Police described Kankakee in that era as a "shooting gallery." There were 23 murders in 1993, 25 murders in 1994 and scores of shootings. People were shot on playgrounds, in neighborhoods, in the downtown area, in seedy bars and from speeding cars. Almost every victim was black.

To this day, scandals are a normal way of life in Kankakee.

In 2011, a scheme between Kankakee and numerous businesses was revealed. Kankakee had been allowing companies in Chicago and its suburbs to set up sham offices to evade higher taxes in their own communities. Dozens of Chicago-area companies ran their paperwork through offices in Kankakee, which has lower sales taxes; the scheme was sweetened by Kankakee kicking back part of that tax money to the businesses. Kankakee took in tens of millions of dollars in sales taxes, on sales it did not make, from companies that were not there. The scheme had been going on since 1999 but *The Daily Journal* didn't report it until 2011, only after the local African-American *City News* and the Chicago media broke the story. The city of Chicago and the Regional Transportation Authority sued the city of Kankakee. The RTA's lawsuit claimed it was cheated out of $100 million in taxes it was due because of this scheme in Kankakee and a few other towns.

The city of Kankakee vigorously defended its tax scheme. However, the state department of revenue changed its tax code in 2014 specifically because of the Kankakee situation, and Kankakee's windfall went away.

Kankakee was designated in *Places Rated Almanac* in 1999 as the worst place to live among 354 metropolitan areas in the United States and Canada, a designation that certainly was unfair. A CBS-TV survey in 2013 showed Kankakee was the least likely city in America for real estate prices to recover from the Great Recession. The survey said Kankakee needed growth of 39.2 percent to get back to its peak, and its present growth was minus 3.5 percent. Stagnant population and high unemployment were factors.

The official reaction from the city to a long string of bad news over the past several decades has been denial and excuses.

The only major effort to attract industry by Kankakee County leaders in the last several decades has been a continuous push to locate more landfills in the county for Chicago's garbage, an effort that has been opposed by environmental and citizens groups year after year.

The Smalls, Ryans and McBrooms have been only a part of the problem. There is a whole infrastructure of various elected officials, rogue cops, political appointees, government workers and others who know the local political machine is what is important, and who know it is best to go along and keep their mouths shut.

It is essential to know the background of the corrupt environment faced by the people of Kankakee County. This is an overview of "The Powers That Be." These are the powers that ordinary and defenseless people like Nancy Rish have to face.

Chapter 12
Those Lies

"What must be realized about the American justice system is that justice is not necessarily the goal. Winning is the goal."
Jim Ridings, August 2013.

Nancy Rish's trial emphasized the lies she told to the police.

She admitted telling several lies in the first hours of being interviewed by the police. She said she was scared, confused, and in a few instances said she was telling police a story Danny Edwards told her to tell. She said she didn't realize what was happening, but said she told the truth after the enormity of the situation sank in.

Her lawyer, Sherri Carr, pointed out that none of the lies Nancy Rish told proved her guilt. They were immaterial to the case. Not one lie or misstatement incriminated her.

We will look at "all those lies" she told which were emphasized.

We also will look at all the lies others told which were overlooked.

Let's start with the biggest lie Nancy Rish told, which came in her second interview on Friday, September 4. She was asked about her whereabouts on the night of the kidnapping, Tuesday, September 1.

Rish said Edwards left the house at 10:30 that night in his van. She was suspicious of him, thinking he was seeing other women, because she knew he was a womanizer and a cheat. After putting her son to bed, she said she went out looking for Danny. She said she left at 11:30 p.m. and was gone half an hour. She said she drove by Danny's ex-wife's house on Hawthorne Lane and went to the Dam Tap and Leo's bar. She said she didn't find him, so she went home. She said she went out again at 1:30 or 2 a.m., and was gone an hour. She said when she came back, Danny was home.

All of that was a lie.

She soon admitted to police the real story about following his van in her car to Greenwood Avenue and taking him to a gas station where he made a phone call, and then dropping him off at Cobb Park.

Rish told police the box Edwards built was sold to a black man for $100 in May or June. He came with his wife, "big boned and wearing a dress," is what Rish told police. She said it was the same man who bought their clothes dryer. The man came back two weeks after buying the dryer, asking about the washer. Instead, he bought the box. That was not true.

Archie Napper was the man who bought the used Kenmore dryer from Edwards in May 1987. Napper, a fraud investigator for the Illinois De-

161

partment of Public Aid, read in the *Bourbonnais Herald* in September that the black man who bought the dryer also bought the box. He called the police to let them know that he responded to a newspaper ad the first week of May 1987. Napper and his son came on May 8 and bought the dryer from Danny Edwards, and they took it to their house at 833 S. Lincoln Avenue in Kankakee. The dryer cost $100, and Edwards told Napper to make out the check to Nancy Rish. Napper said he did not buy a plywood box.

Rish told police the box was sold a month prior to the kidnapping. The officers told her that her son said the box was still in the garage a week ago. She had no reply.

In statements Danny Edwards gave to the police on September 5, he said two black men came and got the box. Sgt. Ralph McClellan wrote in his report, "It should be noted that Rish stated this was not true, that it was a lie Edwards told her to say."

The officers asked Rish if she ever saw a tape recorder during any of the phone calls. She denied any knowledge of the recorder. The officers told her they didn't believe her. McClellan asked Rish what she would say if her fingerprints were found on the recorder. She then held her head in her hands and started to cry. She asked to consult with her attorney.

The officers came back "a few moments later" and again asked about the tape recorder. She told them that two weeks earlier, Danny's son Brandon visited and he left his tape recorder. It was there for several days, and she picked it up to move it. She said she hadn't seen it recently and had never seen Danny use it.

"I lied to you guys before about the recorder because I was afraid if I told you about it, then it would hurt Danny," she told the officers.

Officers McClellan and Gilbert asked Rish about the route she and Edwards drove on the night of the ransom call. It was a complicated route from Bourbonnais to Aroma Park and it went aimlessly through the country until a frantic Edwards had her drive to the Marathon station on the eastern edge of Kankakee. The account Rish gave did not satisfy the police.

It wasn't only Nancy Rish who said she was confused. The police were, too.

"Due to Rish's confusion on times and route of travel, Rish agreed to show the reporting agent (McClellan), Detective Gilbert, FBI Agent Lamanna, and her attorney Scott Swaim, her and Edwards' travel route on Wednesday evening that she had previously described," McClellan wrote in his summation of the second interview.

They all got into a squad car at 5:50 p.m. and left the police station. Rish gave the directions along the way.

"While the reporting agent was traveling on Court Street, Route 17, eastward, Rish stated, 'This is not right.'" McClellan wrote. She then gave further directions until they got to Aroma Park. She showed the direction they took from there to the Marathon station. It took 10 minutes. She also showed the route past Jack's place, back to Aroma Park and then home.

McClellan wrote that Rish was confused. Despite that, it was counted as another lie because her initial directions were confusing.

The sixth interview was on September 7. The police report begins by saying that the officers "re-interviewed Nancy Rish at the request of her and her attorney, Scott Swaim. The purpose of the interview, according to Swaim, was that Rish had something more to say to the interviewers."

Clearly, Nancy Rish was being cooperative and was trying to tell the authorities what she knew. She added a lot of details in this interview and clarified some previous issues.

One of the issues was about her and Danny dropping off the dog. The police report noted that she previously said she was alone when she dropped off the dog. However, the police account isn't entirely accurate. In her fourth interview on September 6, the official police report written by Sgt. McClellan says, "Rish stated that after she dropped her dog off at Pat's Groom & Clean, she went to her sister's house, Lori Guimond, and visited for awhile." The report does not make it clear if she was alone or if Danny Edwards was with her when the dog was dropped off. In any event, she plainly did not say she was alone.

The police informed Nancy that her son said he was told she and Danny were going to the movies on Wednesday night. Nancy said this was correct, Danny told her to tell Benji this even though they did not go. This was counted as a lie even though it was a lie she told to her son, not to the police.

And her identification of Detective Thomas Erickson as the officer who made the "electric chair" remark was counted as a lie. This was the lie that Ficaro said was the biggest of them all, "forget about all the other lies."

There were other statements which the state counted as lies. These were omissions in Rish's answers to which she added upon further questioning. The questions asked by the police in these interviews were not always in chronological order of occurrence. Some of her answers were cut off with another question before she could finish her answer. This may have added to Nancy Rish's confusion.

In the first interview on September 4, which lasted just 30 minutes, Rish did not mention the 12:30 a.m. phone call or dropping off Edwards at Cobb Park. She was answering questions at that time, and that was not one of the questions. This was an omission, but it was counted as a lie, even though she did include it in the fourth interview.

In the second interview on September 4, Rish volunteered information to fill in gaps she did not mention in the first interview. This information was about taking the dog to the groomer and visiting her sister. But she did not mention the 5:03 p.m. phone call that followed. The question was not asked. But this was another omission counted as a lie.

In her fourth interview on September 6, Rish told about picking up the dog, when she mentioned that Edwards told her to stop at the pay phone in Aroma Park to make the 5:03 p.m. call. The police noted in their report that she had not previously mentioned being with Edwards at this phone call. She later explained that at the time of the questioning, she did not regard the 5:03 p.m. call as significant because she did not know it was a ransom call.

The police report did say that Rish included the 11:28 p.m. phone call in her fourth interview, and it noted that she did mention it previously.

McClellan wrote in the middle of his report about the fourth interview, "At that point in the interview, the reporting agent and Gilbert began to ask Rish specific questions that had not been previously discussed."

It was an admission by the police that the line of questioning never was a straight line. And it explains why Nancy Rish may have omitted some details along that ragged path.

The transcript shows the interviewers skipped around and interrupted. Considering the strain and pressure Nancy Rish was under, her answers can be seen as incomplete either because she did not have an opportunity to finish the answer or because she did not think every detail was important or relevant. She was answering direct questions, willingly, and answers to direct questions do not always include every detail. She was not allowed to ask her own questions or interject details that were not part of the questions she was asked. The record shows that when Rish went over the subject again, she did fill in details. She even remarked several times that she did not include a certain detail previously because she thought it was not important. All this was said in the first few days after her arrest. She did not know the whole story at that time. She only knew what she experienced. She did not have the time to make up a false story. The few lies she told the police were obvious, and she told the truth when she was confronted.

There are factors that were not considered at the time because there was a presumption of guilt and a collective decision to condemn this woman at all costs. If one presumed Nancy Rish was innocent until proven guilty -- something that was not done at the time -- the statements in her eight interrogation sessions, taken as a whole, can be understood in her favor as easily as it can be taken against her.

Nancy Rish said she was confused during her interrogation. This discussion about dropping off Danny Edwards on the night of the kidnapping is just one example that shows that even the interrogators were confused.

This exchange with Nancy Rish is taken directly from the tape recorded transcription in the Illinois State Police file, with Sgt. Ralph McClellan (and Scott Swaim, in one of the few times Swaim opened his

164

mouth in 13 hours of police questioning).

Nancy: "Cobb Boulevard? Was it Cobb Boulevard?"

McClellan: "Somewhere…"

Nancy: "I…"

McClellan: "…by Cobb Park?"

Swaim: "Emery, Emery runs, Cobb runs into the park. That's Emery that runs across the front of it to the (inaudible). (Inaudible) are off of it."

Nancy: "OK, then it's Emery."

McClellan "Somewhere around…"

Nancy: "(Inaudible) is Emery then, but I mean, it's right there at Cobb Park."

McClellan: "Right at Cobb Park you, you're not sure, but you think it might be Emery Street?"

Nancy: "Yeah, I'm just not sure of the name of the street."

McClellan: "OK."

A few minutes later, the exchange about picking Danny up at the railroad tracks went this way.

McClellan: "You picked Danny up."

Nancy: "Uh huh."

McClellan: "Were you in your vehicle or Danny's white van?"

Nancy: "I was, I was in my car."

McClellan: "OK. Then what happened?"

Nancy: "Uhh, after that we went home. He told me to drive home. No, is he (inaudible)."

McClellan: "That's fine, that's fine."

Nancy: "(inaudible)."

McClellan: "…think, think and don't…"

Nancy: "OK. We didn't…"

McClellan: "…worry about the recorder."

Nancy: "OK, we didn't go home. Uh, he told me to bring him back to his van."

And it went on like that through much of the interrogation.

There also were all "those lies" told by Danny Edwards.

It wasn't just all those lies Edwards told to the police about black cowboys and drug dealers up north. There also were all those lies Edwards told to Nancy Rish. And those lies were the basis of what Nancy Rish knew, or thought she knew.

Danny lied to Nancy about the box, telling it was for his brother's pool supplies. He lied when he told her to stop at a gas station so he could make a simple phone call; he lied to her about this three times. He lied when he told her to say a black man bought the box. He lied when he told her Mitch was threatening him, his family and her family. He lied when he had her drop

165

him off at Cobb Park. He lied when he had her pick him up in the middle of the night. He lied when he said he was taking her bicycle to be fixed. He lied when he said he was going out to get cigarettes when he really went out to make another ransom call. He lied when he said he was going out to get his duffle bag from the evergreens. He lied when he said he was going to be getting a large sum of money from Mitch. He lied when he said everything would be all right. He lied to her about everything, and then he instructed her to lie if anyone asked any questions. No wonder she was confused. No wonder why she didn't know what was going on when she was arrested.

Some of what she told police either was a deliberate lie, or it was something that she didn't know was untrue because Danny lied to her.

After their drive to Aroma Park on Wednesday evening, Danny told her it was over and everything was all right. He did add one thing, however. This is from Nancy Rish's police interview of September 8, 1987.

"He did proceed to tell me, though, in case anything should be asked about that night, you know, what we were doing, he said that I was to say, we were gonna say that we were bringing my bike in to St. Anne to be repaired at Jack's house."

McClellan: "So Danny instructed you to lie to anyone that inquired about this?"

Nancy: "Yes, if something was asked about it, yes."

McClellan: "Is that the only lie he told you to say?"

Nancy: "Uh, no. Also about the box being gone."

McClellan: "The box that was in your garage?"

Nancy: "Yes. He told me to say that he had sold it to a black guy who had once bought our dryer from us and he sold it to him for a hundred dollars."

McClellan: "But did this black guy have anything to do with what you were doing, as far as you knew?"

Nancy: "I don't know... I don't know."

McClellan: "That was just the story that Danny told you to tell anyone that inquired about the box? And about..."

Nancy: "Being gone. Yes."

McClellan: "...your travels the night before?"

Nancy: "Yes."

Nancy Rish's emotional state was a factor at the interrogation, but it was not given much consideration in her trial.

At the trial, Vincent Paulauskis asked Swaim about Nancy Rish's disposition when he arrived at the police station on September 4.

"She was very upset, she was crying, she was petrified," Swaim said. "She continued that whole afternoon, evening and late into the evening being upset, crying, confused. There were times when she was not crying, obviously, but that disposition continued throughout that evening and most of the weekend."

Paulauskis asked Swaim about the car ride they took to retrace the route she and Danny Edwards drove on the night of the ransom calls.

"Did she exhibit confusion as to times, dates and routes of travel?"

"Yes she did," Swaim answered.

When she gave the taped interview, she had the same disposition, Swaim said. With the exception of the last interview on September 8, her disposition was the same, he said. Swaim said Rish asked for a doctor on that first evening because she said she wasn't feeling well. They did not send for a doctor. Swaim said Rish was more relaxed by September 8. McClellan was the lead interrogator. "He was forceful, questioning. I mean that in the sense that he wasn't, he didn't appear to me to be buying anything that she was saying. He told her she was lying."

What affect did that have on Nancy Rish?

"She became upset," Swaim said.

Her emotional state not only was delicate during questioning, it was in tatters a year later when she was put on trial. She was taking prescription Xanax for her anxiety, and her family said she did not act her normal self because of the medication.

When Nancy Rish testified at her trial, Paulauskis asked her about her state of mind. She said she was frustrated and upset because the police kept telling her she was lying, and she also said she didn't understand some of their questions. She said she told the police the box was sold to a black man because that is what Danny told her.

Paulauskis asked her, Why did you lie?

"Because I realized how Danny had used me and he was putting me in the middle of this without me knowing, and I was scared. I was scared to tell the truth."

The confusion during the interrogation could be explained, Paulauskis told the jury. He asked the jury to consider why the police recorded only two of Rish's eight interrogation sessions. He said the other sessions were documented only as "Sgt. McClellan's impressions of what she said. When he felt like changing the conclusion around or the summary of what she said, he did it."

"He used words like fronted, ransom, words that he admitted were never used. That was his interpretation of what was said," Paulauskis said.

"If you listen to those tapes, try listening to the background, the screaming and the yelling that is going on," Paulauskis said to jurors. "Gives you a good idea of the environment in which Nancy Rish found herself in. But the first moment of that day, her waking day being looking down the barrel of probably a .357, and then she is asked where are your flashlights at -- how the heck is she supposed to know where the flashlights are at?"

Paulauskis went on. "See the police, as they are uncovering information, they go back to her and ask her questions. Mr. Nowicki criticized Nancy Rish this morning because they asked her about batteries. She said, oh yeah, he (Danny) went out and got one from New Era. Oh, and he got a battery charger from Bill Mohler. Mr. Nowicki said there, she told the police about the battery charger, that proves something right there. Why would she have any reason to think that a battery charger would have something to do with the case unless she was hiding something? Now, what happens if she doesn't talk about the battery charger? Well then, that becomes a checkmark later on that magic chart -- when is the first time she mentioned the battery charger -- she didn't mention it until statement number seven. See how that can be twisted? When she gives information, it is oh, look at that, she didn't tell us that. In statement number two, she talks about taking the dog to the dog groomer. There is a little line with a checkmark. Oh, that is the first time she talked about taking the dog to the groomer. Geeze, got to be lying. Forgetting, of course, that the first statement is 20 minutes long, as she testified yesterday."

"Why on earth would they have to think that taking her dog to the groomer would be relevant to anything? Where is your flashlight at, how big are they, what room in the house? Doesn't mention the bolt cutters, does she? Well, yeah, she doesn't know what they are. But that is one of the taped statements. You recall the question about the bolt cutters. She is asked, do you know what bolt cutters are. She says, now I do. But that evidence is presented to you as a drastic change in her question and answer sessions."

"Did she ever mention anything to you about the 12:30 call? About the 3:30 call? This is the first night. Let's take that 3:30 call, the second one Ramsey heard. When they got back home, Danny went out and bought a pack of cigarettes. Nancy stayed home. How would she even know Danny made a phone call? But the question does come out to the police officer -- did she ever tell you about the 3:30 phone call?"

"How could she possibly tell about the 3:30 phone call if she had no idea it had been made?" Paulauskis asked.

"And what about the 12:30 call? Well, Mr. Nowicki says that is the one she doesn't want to give up at that time. Statement six or seven. But see, even the police don't know what's going on at this point and are trying to figure it out. Nancy, who has no knowledge of these things, how is she supposed to know that Danny Edwards is in the phone booth making a call across from the root beer stand, calling the residence of Stephen Small to announce that he is a policeman, and Mr. Small won't you please come down and check out this burglary? When she volunteers it, you waited. Why? Hiding, hiding information. It is hard for somebody to mention on questions that you are asked that has nothing to do with the topic. Did she mention driving up Cobb Boulevard that day after? She wasn't asked that. Remember, the questioner controls the information that comes out from the person being questioned."

Scott Swaim told *Tribune* reporter William Gaines in 1993, "She told me she wanted to tell them what she knew. I told her she didn't have to. She said she wanted to talk to them and that she had nothing to hide."

Swaim said Rish would give a statement to police and they would come back with other questions. "They asked, 'what about the gun,' and she would remember about the gun. She would change and add to her statement. We would talk and she would cry and want to talk to them again, and I would tell her that she didn't have to. Then they'd say, 'what about the tape recorder' and she'd remember about that. During that time, the police became more and more agitated." Swaim also told Gaines that Lamanna definitely told Rish she could go home if she made a statement to police, even though Lamanna later denied making that promise.

Nancy Rish willingly talked to the police because she knew she committed no crime and she wanted to be helpful. Nancy Rish was a naive young woman who was grilled for four days. Sherri Carr said Rish spoke to police for hours on end and they asked the same questions and didn't always get the same answers. Nancy Rish was caught in lies and inconsistencies because she talked too much without the advice of counsel. Swaim told Rish she did not have to talk, but when she did, he did not speak up.

Swaim said Rish was upset, crying and confused as to dates and routes of travel, and she became more upset when McClellan became forceful and told her she was lying.

Nancy Rish told some lies that first day. After that, she told the truth. No matter what the prosecutor said about lie after lie, the record is different.

Scott Swaim was a friend to the Small family and he was more anxious to find Stephen Small than he was to protect a client. That may be laudable, considering the urgency at that time, but he should have acted as her lawyer. There were other people whose job it was to find Stephen Small. Nancy Rish told Swaim she knew nothing about it. He should have protected her. That was his job.

Michael Ficaro, as might be expected, didn't have much sympathy for Nancy Rish or her emotional state at the time. In a deposition he gave on October 15, 2004, during Rish's appeal process, he admitted Rish wanted to talk to police the day she was arrested, but said he thought "she only wanted to exculpate herself by her statements."

Nancy Rish couldn't win. If she had refused to cooperate, it would have shown her guilt; since she did cooperate, it showed she was trying to talk her way out of it. If she told the police something significant, it was because she knew all about the plot; if she left something out, it was because she was hiding her guilt. Since she was talking and laughing with friends on the phone, it showed she was cold hearted to act this way while planning a kidnapping; if she had been moody and secretive, it would have been because she was nervous about planning an evil act. She couldn't win.

Nancy Rish's friends said her behavior in the weeks before the kidnapping was calm and normal. Nowicki said this behavior showed she was cold and calculating, and Ficaro said she "wasn't a nervous wreck because she was part of a well-thought plan" to kidnap and kill Stephen Small. She just couldn't win.

She was accused of lying because she didn't mention every detail at first. For example, she didn't mention the 12:30 a.m. or 5:03 p.m. phone calls because she didn't know it had any significance at the time of the initial questioning. She didn't mention the dog groomer because she didn't think it had anything to do with anything. She didn't mention the battery charger for the same reason. The police did not know these details at the early point of the questioning, so they couldn't ask her about it. Details such as these were filled in as the questioning expanded. For this, she was accused of lying; if she had known, and told, every single detail in order in the first interview, she would have been accused of having a pat story prepared. But she wasn't allowed to tell every single detail in order. She was only allowed to give answers with no details to the questions that were asked. She couldn't win.

Interestingly, Nancy Small did a similar thing when she didn't mention the Yurgine comment to police initially. Yes, she was a victim and not the accused, but no one called Mrs. Small a liar because she failed to mention a detail she didn't think was relevant at the time.

Ficaro said he did not hear about the "electric chair" comment until Nancy brought it up on the stand in direct examination by her attorney.

"It was during what I refer to as a second box of Kleenex testimony," he said in his 2004 deposition. "She was crying on the witness stand."

Ficaro continued, "Her defense was the dumb blonde defense, looking for sympathy when she was crying on the witness stand on direct examination, because she didn't cry on cross examination. She turned to an angry, volatile, nasty witness. The pretend that went on during direct examination disappeared on cross examination, which was another apparent hypocrisy for a jury to attend in coming to the conclusion of her guilt beyond a reasonable doubt."

The trial transcripts of the cross examination shows that Ficaro perhaps was an angry, volatile, nasty interrogator.

Acting angry, volatile and nasty is a bully's schoolyard trick to elicit an equal reaction.

Nancy Rish told three big lies -- about her whereabouts on the night of the kidnapping, about selling the wooden box to a black man, and about touching the tape recorder. Ficaro said Nancy Rish told at least 30 lies. The

170

omissions in her answers were counted as lies, in Ficaro's summation.

You can call these statements lies or you can accept Rish's explanation that she was frightened, confused and was telling a story Danny told her to tell, and who did not fully understand the situation in those first hours.

Despite his flourish and his dubious flattery of calling Nancy Rish a sweet talker and an actress, Ficaro certainly was wrong about Nancy Rish being an accomplished liar. She was very bad at lying.

So what about the "falsehoods" the prosecution told?

The biggest one in the entire case was told by the prosecutor.

Michael Ficaro told the Rish jurors that Nancy Rish made the 12:30 a.m. phone call to get Stephen Small out of his house.

"You have to get Stephen Small from the sanctity of his home," he said. "You can't make your million unless you get him out the door. You have got the box and now you need the man. Who do you pick to lure him from his home? Danny Edwards on the phone? No. You need someone who could sweet talk him out, fast on their feet, an accomplished liar, an actress, someone who could convince the man to leave his house at 12:30 at night and respond to a burglary. You heard her lie on tape, you heard her lie in person."

Ficaro's claim was not supported by any evidence or testimony.

Ramsey Small took that first phone call, and he said it was a policeman reporting a burglary. He said it was a man's voice.

At Edwards' trial, Ficaro established, from testimony by his own witness, that it was a man who made the call. There was no assertion that the call was made by a woman, or even possibly by a woman.

But when Ficaro was prosecuting Nancy Rish six months later, he said it wasn't a man, Danny Edwards, who made that call. He said it was Nancy Rish who positively made that call.

It was never asserted by anyone, before or during Nancy Rish's trial, that Nancy Rish made that call, until Ficaro's closing argument.

So who made that phone call, Mr. Ficaro?

Was it Danny Edwards or was it Nancy Rish?

Was the caller a policeman, informing Mr. Small about a burglary, or was it a woman sweet-talking a man who was in bed with his wife to come outside? And if Nancy Rish was trying to be seductive on the phone to lure Stephen Small, would she say she was a policeman and use a deep voice?

Ramsey Small testified the caller was a policeman reporting a burglary at the Bradley House. How does anyone construe that as seductive?

You can't have it both ways. But Ficaro did spin it both ways, telling

---

Note: *From a legal standpoint, defendants and witnesses may lie, but lawyers never lie. They may tell falsehoods, they may make false assertions, they may say things that are untrue, they may claim things that never happened, they may tell some fibs and a few whoppers, but they don't lie.*

his second jury that the caller was Nancy Rish, and the jury bought it.

Ficaro also used a stocking cap as "evidence" that Rish made the call, even though no stocking cap as entered as an exhibit. A stocking cap was found on the floor of Small's garage. Tests showed it had Small's hair, but not Edwards' or Rish's hair. What did this have to do with anything? Nothing! Why would Small go out in a stocking cap? It was still summer, it was in the 80s all that week. Ficaro said it was used in the kidnapping. He went to great lengths about this. No proof. His lengthy, rambling, convoluted speech made no sense, beyond enthralling a jury with his performance.

So just how did Ramsey Small's testimony change from Edwards' trial to Rish's trial -- the caller was a man, then the caller had a "low voice?"

The change was subtle and it came mostly from leading questions by the state. The defense tried to square Ramsey's statements from both trials. But it remained confusing -- which was something the prosecution counted on during most of the Rish trial.

At the Edwards' trial, Ramsey said it was a male voice who made the 12:30 a.m. call. But at Rish's trial, he testified, "It was a deep voice. Low."

Could you tell the sex of the caller, asked Ficaro? No, Ramsey said. It left the impression that the caller could have been a woman.

The search warrant on the Edwards-Rish house specified that the caller was a male, and it based that on Ramsey Small's information to police.

Sherri Carr: "You have testified that you couldn't tell us if the caller on the first phone call was male or female?"

Ramsey: "Yes."

Sherri: "Now the second call you said is a different voice?"

Ramsey: "Yes."

Sherri: "Could you describe that voice?"

Ramsey: "It was another deep voice, but it was different from the first phone call."

Sherri: "Do you remember stating under oath in May of this year, the 16th (at Edwards' trial), that the phone call sounded like another male?"

Ramsey: "Yes."

Sherri: "Do you remember also testifying under oath in May that the 3:30 call again sounded like a male's voice?"

Ramsey: "Yes."

Sherri: "Did both voices sound like a male?"

Ramsey: "Yes."

In his opening statement at Nancy Rish's trial, Ficaro said, "We will prove to you that Nancy Rish, before or during the kidnapping of Stephen Small, aided or abetted or attempted to aid, or agreed to aid, Danny Edwards in the kidnapping of Stephen Small. In its simplest terms, ladies and gentle-

172

men, we will prove that Danny Edwards is guilty of aggravated kidnapping and murder and that Nancy Rish helped him."

The prosecution's contention started out with Nancy Rish aiding Danny Edwards. Danny did it, but Nancy is guilty by "accountability" because she aided him. But by the end of her trial, their contention was that Nancy Rish was an active participant, she planned it and she did as much as Danny Edwards did.

Frank Nowicki went further. He ended up telling the jury that Nancy planned all this, and did so as a deliberate and intentional murder!

"From the very beginning, from back in the planning stage, this crime was never meant to be just a kidnapping. From the very beginning, Danny Edwards and Nancy Rish meant this to be a murder. Stephen Small was never coming out of that box alive," Nowicki said in his closing arguments. "How could they ever get away with it if they left any witnesses? There could be no witnesses. There could be no Steve Small coming out."

How did Ficaro and Nowicki go from Nancy Rish simply helping Danny Edwards obtain a few materials, to planning an intentional murder?

Nowicki went even further than that. He told the jury it was Nancy Rish who picked Stephen Small to be the victim, it was Nancy Rish who set up Danny Edwards with her cousin Jeff Westerhoff to buy the plywood, and because Nancy was in the boat store when Stephen Small happened to come in, it meant "she is involved in every phase of this case from the early planning till the final conclusion."

Proof? We ain't got to show you no stinkin' proof!

Just who planned this whole kidnapping fiasco?

Frank Nowicki told Edwards' jurors that Edwards was "the planner, the manipulator, the conniver. What Danny Edwards did was the result of a diabolical mind. This wasn't a spur of the moment activity. Danny Edwards planned this out."

In his opening statement to the jury at Edwards' trial, Ficaro said, "The evidence will show that this murder was a result of the cold and calculated plans of that man. It was Danny Edwards' try for the big score. The big score is what brought Danny Edwards here. Stephen Small was murdered because this man wanted a million dollars."

Danny Edwards. That man. He planned it all. He did it all.

All this changed in his opening statement to Nancy Rish's jury five months later.

"Murder. Murder is what brought us here today. A murder the evidence will show was the result of a cold, callous, calculating plan of Nancy Rish and Danny Edwards for the big score."

It was Danny's cold, calculated plan. Then it became Nancy's and Danny's cold, callous, calculating plan. Same lawyer, same judge, different allegation to a different audience.

173

Ficaro told the jury, "You will hear testimony that she was identified acquiring items found inside the box after Stephen Small was discovered."

That was not true.

"You will hear of a blonde or Nancy Rish looking for bottled water which was found inside the box, for PVC pipe which is the kind of pipe which was attached outside the box."

That was not true.

"And that she is identified in the van a short time after that van was seen in the remotest part of this county way back into the woods where no one would have any business except murderers and kidnappers."

That was not true.

James Witvoet, the farmer who said he saw a van, said he couldn't tell if the blond was a male or female. He said the blond had "dishwater blond hair." Nancy's blonde hair was bright. Elizabeth Lamanna saw Nancy Rish when Danny Edwards was making the phone call in Aroma Park. She said Rish's hair was "white-blonde color."

Phone records proved Nancy Rish was 15 miles away at the time given by Witvoet.

The prosecutors told the jury that Nancy Rish bought materials for the kidnapping. That was wrong. She did not acquire one single item.

In his closing argument, Ficaro told the jury that hardware store clerk Linda Forestier testified that a man and a woman came into the store on Tuesday morning. But that wasn't accurate. Forestier said it was "likely after 10 a.m. Monday or Tuesday" when a couple came in and asked for distilled water and the man looked at PVC pipe.

Forestier said the hardware store didn't have distilled water, so she sent the couple to a nearby grocery store. Arlene Bires, the grocery store clerk, said she thought Danny Edwards bought water and candy. Nancy Rish was not with him.

No one testified that Nancy Rish bought a bottle of distilled water. And yet, Ficaro told the jury she did, and he claimed that proved Nancy Rish bought an item for the box.

What the jury wasn't told was that the water bottle found in the box was not distilled water in a brand name bottle purchased at a store. It was tap water in an old milk jug.

A state crime lab technician's report said he could not test the water because the evidence was possibly contaminated by lab equipment. It was not determined if the water in the bottle in the box was distilled or tap water (Edwards said it was tap water). But that report wasn't introduced in court, and the state did not reveal this to the defense. The prosecutors said the water in the plywood box was distilled water purchased by Nancy Rish.

If distilled water specifically was bought for the box, why didn't the bottle have a label of a brand name of distilled water? Who goes to the detail of buying distilled water and then puts it in an old milk bottle?

The prosecution put pictures of distilled water bottles on a large map of the area. It gave jurors the impression that Rish was buying distilled water all over the place.

But a very important piece of evidence -- the actual bottle of water from the box at the grave site -- was never introduced in court. It was not entered as an exhibit. The prosecution's contention about the water bottle was an important part of the circumstantial evidence that convicted Nancy Rish. The prosecution went to great lengths in court to condemn Nancy Rish for buying distilled water for the box -- and yet the water and the bottle were never introduced.

The Appellate Court at Ottawa, in a decision delivered on November 10, 2003, found that the state "committed a discovery violation when it failed to hand over the laboratory report to the defendant."

Presiding Justice Mary McDade wrote, "The majority finds that the failure of the State to disclose the laboratory report confirming the lab's inability to analyze the water found with the victim was a discovery violation." It didn't affect the appeal because the majority of the justices decided it would not have changed the verdict. McDade wrote a dissenting opinion.

"I cannot agree," she wrote. "The State's case against this defendant was purely circumstantial. Success in prosecuting her was dependent on the State being able to put together enough evidentiary pieces, none of which was dispositive standing alone, that cumulatively made a case for the defendant's guilt. To this end, and knowing that there was no way of tying any water to this defendant, the State produced three witnesses in an apparent attempt to associate the defendant with Danny Edwards and the two of them with the purchase of bottled water of some kind. As is shown in the majority opinion, not one of the three provided any evidence that the defendant, either alone or in concert with Edwards, had purchased any water of any kind."

"The majority acknowledges that the testimony had 'extremely low probative value.' In point of fact, it had no probative value at all, a fact which leaves me wondering why the witnesses were produced at all, if not to bolster the State's case by innuendo, and why the State has battled in the circuit court and before this court to keep the evidence in. I have to wonder if the jury, too, strove, possibly successfully, to find some significance in this testimony which, although admittedly without legal probity, had acquired some worth or utility simply by virtue of having been presented."

Justice McDade got it exactly right. The whole case against Nancy Rish was circumstantial, and it was built on faulty circumstance and flawed arguments, such as the water bottle. Innuendo, guilt by association, empty testimony from witnesses who witnessed nothing, and a lack of evidence. That is what the state used in prosecuting Nancy Rish. It applied to the water bottle. It applied to everything else in her trial.

Ficaro, in his summation to the jury, said that Forestier testified it was Tuesday when the couple came in, and then he made the connection to Bires, who testified a man and a woman came in her store sometime between 11 a.m. and 1 p.m. on Tuesday looking for distilled water.

That fit Ficaro's time line, but it didn't fit the testimony.

If one follows the testimony truthfully, it means the couple at the hardware store and the couple at the grocery store could have been two different couples at two different times -- and neither one was positively identified by the clerks as Edwards or Rish.

Again, their argument was wrong and was intended to confuse the jury, because pipe was not purchased at that hardware store and distilled water was not used in the crime.

Ficaro told the jury that Forestier testified that the man asked if they had bigger pipe, when she really testified the man asked "if that is that all the pipe we had."

Mike Lergner, owner of the hardware store, told police it was Tuesday at 3 p.m. when this couple came in. He couldn't identify them and they didn't buy anything. But the jury was left with the impression that it was Danny Edwards in the store and he bought the pipe for the box.

Lergner went to the police station and looked at a lineup of photographs, but he couldn't identify anyone. Forestier also looked at the photographs. She said a man and a woman's pictures looked familiar, but she couldn't make a positive identification. The pictures were not Danny Edwards or Nancy Rish. Bires said a man bought three gallons of Hinckley & Schmitt nursery drinking water and several candy bars. This was between 11:30 a.m. and 12:30 p.m. on Tuesday. Bires also looked at pictures and said the man might have been Danny Edwards. Bires knew Nancy Rish, and she said Rish was not with the man.

The empty plywood box with the attached pipe already was buried before Tuesday afternoon. The manager's account definitely would have had the couple in the store after the box was buried. His time frame differed from his clerk's time frame. The differing accounts were a problem, and his afternoon time was a bigger problem. The prosecution solved it by calling only the clerk as a witness, not the manager. Lergner testified at Edwards' trial, but he was not called to testify at Rish's trial.

Ficaro told jurors, "Why didn't Nancy Rish tell you she was back by the grave of Stephen Small? Because she is guilty."

That was untrue.

The evidence from her shoes showed she was not at the grave site.

Think about it. Ficaro and Nowicki started out by telling jurors that Nancy Rish was liable because she knew about the kidnapping, and then they ended up telling jurors that Nancy Rish planned it as an intentional murder, made the phone call, bought the materials and was at the grave site!

176

There was more in their summation that was pure speculation, unsupported by any testimony or evidence, and often was contradictory to the testimony and evidence.

Ficaro said, "We have her in the afternoon buying electrical straps here."

Nancy Rish did not buy electrical straps. She was in the van when Danny Edwards went inside. Nevertheless, the prosecutors said this was "proof" that Nancy Rish bought something used in the kidnapping.

And there are two different receipts for the straps. The copy entered as an exhibit at the trial shows the names "Edwards-Rish" as the customers. Sherri Carr went to the store and got a copy of the original receipt. It shows no names on the customer line.

So who wrote "Edwards-Rish" on the receipt and brought it to court?

This is beside the larger point -- the straps were not proven to have been used on Stephen Small, and the judge ruled them out as evidence. And yet, Ficaro convinced the jury that Nancy Rish bought this item and it was critical to the crime. Danny Edwards told me he bought the tie straps to secure a TV cable at home. Yes, some purchases during that week were for simple household items.

Ficaro said Edwards' remark in the boat store, "It sure would be nice to afford stuff like that," was not said to the boat salesman, it was an "inside joke" to Nancy Rish. The boat store salesman didn't testify to that.

Nowicki told the jury, "From the minute she opened her mouth when she was arrested, till she stopped talking on Tuesday, all she could do was lie. She lied often, she lied repeatedly. She never admitted anything unless the police already knew it, or she was confronted with facts she couldn't deny."

The record shows a very different account. After telling lies about her whereabouts in that first interrogation, Nancy Rish told the truth in seven more interrogations over the next three days. When the police asked her questions that were not previously raised by them, she told the truth.

"We only need prove one act. We have shown you at least 25 separate things she did -- drop him off, pick him up, go to the phone calls with him, the water, shopping for the pipe, and every one of those items alone is sufficient to prove her guilty on the theory of accountability."

That was not true. The only instance of Rish aiding Edwards was her driving him to the pay phones where he made his ransom calls, and Rish said she did not know his intention at the time. The law said she had to have the knowledge of his act, so if she did not know who he was calling or why, then the prosecutor doesn't even have one instance of her aiding Edwards.

Nowicki was counting as examples all the steps Edwards took in his process, including buying the wood, buying the water and candy, buying the cassette tape, buying the car battery, borrowing the battery charger, and stealing the gun and handcuffs. Nancy Rish was not with Danny Edwards when he obtained any of those items or any material used in the kidnapping. And every person involved in those transactions testified that Nancy Rish was not with Danny Edwards when he obtained those items.

Nowicki told the jury that Danny Edwards and Nancy Rish had sex in the county jail. It was another statement made without proof. This idea may have been drawn from an inmate's statement at the county jail to police that did not come from first-hand knowledge. It was jailhouse bragging by Edwards to another inmate, and it was not true. And there was no testimony at the trial to support this. Both Danny Edwards and Nancy Rish told me it never happened. A woman who was undergoing the horror of being taken at gunpoint from her home, and jailed on charges of kidnapping and murder, would not want to get romantic with the man who put her there.

Winning a conviction of Danny Edwards was a slam dunk. He had confessed. His fingerprints were on the box and other items. His voice was on the tape of the ransom calls. He led police to the spot where the body was buried. A first-year law student could have won a conviction, even after a weekend of heavy drinking at the frat house.

The elaborate case they presented against Danny Edwards certainly proved Edwards' guilt. But it did not prove Nancy Rish's guilt. They needed an elaborately detailed case against Edwards in order to carry it over to the case against Rish. In fact, the trial of Nancy Rish was a repeat of the trial of Danny Edwards. Everything that proved Danny Edwards guilty was inferred to apply to Nancy Rish at her trial.

At Edwards' trial, Rish's name was not mentioned as an accomplice. She was invisible at Edwards' trial. That, too, is all right, because Rish was not on trial then. But one would think that if Danny Edwards had an accomplice who was helping him, it would have been mentioned in his trial.

Prosecutors didn't have to make any false assertions at Danny Edwards' trial because they didn't need to. But they did have to make false claims at Nancy Rish's trial or they never would have gotten a conviction.

The Edwards trial, to put it in show-biz terms, was a rehearsal for the Rish trial. The Rish trial did not prove her guilty by the evidence. It proved Danny Edwards was guilty, and thus, by sleight of hand, Nancy Rish was guilty by association.

Even Judge Michela admitted he thought Nancy Rish was guilty even before her trial started, based on hearing the evidence at the Edwards trial -- even though there was no evidence and almost no mention of Nancy Rish at the Edwards trial.

There was no evidence to convict Nancy Rish unless you tie together a string of circumstances that may or may not mean anything.

And yet, prosecutor Michael Ficaro said Nancy Rish "was involved in every aspect" of this crime.

Involved in every aspect? Seeing her boyfriend build a wooden box means she knew what it really was for? Driving and stopping so he could make three phone calls meant she knew who he was calling or what he was saying?

Maybe. But not necessarily. Not beyond a reasonable doubt.

Danny Edwards told Nancy Rish and several others that the wooden box was for his brother. That was what she and the others believed. No one else was arrested for knowing that Danny Edwards was building a box.

Nancy Rish sat in the car while Danny Edwards made his phone calls, at a distance from the phone booth, with his back turned to her. These were drive-up pay phones, where he could have made the calls while sitting in the car. He chose to make these calls outside of Nancy Rish's earshot.

Two of the ransom phone calls were witnessed. Terry Dutour saw the 5:03 p.m. call being made, and the police observed the 11:28 p.m. call. In both cases, Edwards was seen making a call at an outdoor pay phone while Nancy Rish was in the car eight feet or more away.

All that sounds like he was leaving her out of his plans, not including her.

Ficaro, in his closing argument, said that Rish was "part of a well-thought plan to kidnap and never, ever let Stephen Small get out of that box."

A well-thought plan?

Burying someone alive is a well-thought plan? Having a narrow 26-foot long air tube was well-thought? A box with no fan to bring in fresh air or to exhaust bad air was well-thought? A convicted drug dealer building a wooden box in an open garage, across the street from the Bourbonnais police station, and then telling the victim's family Stephen is buried alive in a box? Leaving a house full of evidence and fingerprints on everything? Making ransom calls from a phone that is instantly traced, and then going back there to make more ransom calls? Using a cheap tape recorder that breaks down and has to be rewound several times while trying to play a ransom message? Knowing the police are watching you and doing nothing? Leaving the victim's shiny new maroon Mercedes just a few feet from the grave? A plan that ends with the man who did the planning on Death Row?

This was a well-thought plan?

The thinking was done by Danny Edwards, and the prosecutors admitted it. Frank Nowicki called Edwards "the planner, the manipulator, the conniver." Edwards' letter to Mrs. Small "was the result of a diabolical mind," Nowicki said. "This wasn't a spur of the moment activity. Danny Edwards planned this out."

No one accused Nancy Rish of dreaming this up. Not the police or anyone else. They all said Danny Edwards did the thinking. Only his cocaine-addled mind could have thought this was a good plan.

Edwards admits it was all his plan. His lawyer, Sheldon Reagan, told the jury Edwards "committed the most stupid and bungle-able crime imaginable."

It wasn't until Nancy Rish's trial that she was accused of being part of this well-thought plan. And then she was painted as the evil mastermind.

"Right there on the phone, sweet-talking Nancy, the spider to the fly, come on, come on out, my million's waiting for me," Ficaro told jurors.

Her normal behavior prior to the kidnapping was held against her.

"What does the evidence mean that she was OK? It means exactly what you saw, she is a cold, callous, calculating, capable of lying, deceiving, putting on a show, pretending, fabricating, concocting, she is capable of murder and kidnapping."

Ficaro said it was "a murder the evidence will show was the result of a cold, callous, calculating plan of Nancy Rish and Danny Edwards for the big score."

The prosecutors said Nancy Rish is an intelligent person. The one thing they did not explain was how an intelligent person could come up with, or agree to, such a stupid and bungle-able plan.

The prosecution built one false assertion on top of another in his argument for a life sentence for Nancy Rish.

It wasn't just the claim that Rish made the 12:30 a.m. phone call, even though Ramsey Small testified the call was made by a man.

Ficaro said burying Small alive showed "wanton cruelty" on Rish's part. "Even after she was arrested, Nancy Rish continued to lie, and she abandoned Stephen Small in his grave. To this day, Nancy Rish has not told the truth. To this day, Nancy Rish has exhibited no remorse."

The prosecutors condemned Nancy Rish on no evidence and on false assertions, and then condemned her again for showing no remorse for something she did not do.

Ficaro peppered Rish with question after question on the same topic of her lying about her whereabouts on the night of the kidnapping. She told a lie and he made it sound like a dozen lies.

He summed it up by asking her, "So, you were just telling lies to get the statement over with so you could go home, is that right?"

In a way, Ficaro's badgering of Nancy Rish along this line should have helped her case. It explained why she lied at first. She just wanted to make a statement and go home, as she was promised. It was no grand scheme of lies. It was just as simple as wanting to go home.

In his plea for a life sentence, Ficaro condemned Rish for other crimes she did not commit: auto theft, possession of a stolen car, armed robbery, armed violence, residential burglary, home invasion (all of which were committed by Danny Edwards during the kidnapping), plus possession of drugs, narcotics racketeering, failing to report her income to the IRS, and even perjury for her testimony during her trial.

This was submitted by Ficaro as Rish's "history of criminal activity" in considering a sentence.

Nancy Rish never was convicted of these crimes. She never was charged with these crimes and never was accused of these crimes until this argument. Her real "criminal history" consisted of two speeding tickets.

But the court was asked to presume her guilty of these accusations.

There is one more interesting aspect to this idea. When Ficaro argued for the death penalty for Danny Edwards, he named all the related crimes of which Edwards was guilty while committing the kidnapping. It included impersonating a police officer, for making that first phone call to Mr. Small. He did not include that as one of Nancy Rish's crimes in her sentencing hearing, even though he claimed she made the call, impersonating a police officer.

After her trial, Nancy Rish went to the penitentiary. Michael Ficaro got a prestigious position with Hopkins & Sutter, the Small family's top law firm in downtown Chicago.

Judge Michela sentenced Rish to the maximum: life in prison, no possibility of parole. His reasoning, in pronouncing sentence, was that Rish "was involved in every major phase of this event." These were the exact same words Michael Ficaro used in court.

Michela said the box was built in her garage and "was transported in the van of Danny Edwards, the person with whom she resided, a van in which she was in often."

Was she involved or was she just there, unwittingly? And what if she was in his van often? Of course she was.

"Evidence would indicate that the defendant had been up and down the alley of the Stephen Small residence earlier in the year, casing the locality. The defendant was identified by a neighbor person on the day of the kidnapping, the daylight hours after the event."

That was not true. That is something that came from Ficaro, not from the witnesses.

Caroline Mortell told the FBI on September 8 that she saw a white female with long blonde hair driving a light colored van past her home on Emory Street onto Cobb Boulevard, sometime between 10 and 11 a.m. on Wednesday, September 2, and again in the afternoon.

Mortell could not identify the woman as being Nancy Rish. Phone records proved Rish was 15 miles away.

But, what she told the FBI, which was not in her court testimony, was that on the same day, she saw two or three white men with a boy in a wagon at about 5:30 p.m., on Cobb Boulevard. One man was white, blond and muscular. The other was darker and large. Given the defense team's interest in white blond men who may have been an accomplice, this could have been important. But it didn't fit the scenario the prosecution built, so it was left out. Light colored van or white van? It didn't matter.

Michela said, "The defendant by her own admission took Mr. Edwards to the scene."

Just what scene was that? She did not drop him off at Stephen Small's house and she did not take him to Pembroke Township. She took him to the Riverview neighborhood, but did she know he was about to kidnap and murder a man?

"An inference was drawn from the testimony of Ramsey Small, from the testimony of the defendant, from the physical evidence that was available, that this person made the phone call that lured Stephen Small from his home. That was an inference that the state was allowed to make. It was for the jury to debate whether or not that occurred. Even if that did not occur, this defendant was a part and parcel of this offense."

That is not true. Ramsey Small did not testify that Nancy Rish, or any woman, made the call. And it did not come from any physical evidence, and it certainly was not an "inference from the testimony of the defendant!"

"She was at 3 o'clock in the morning in the middle of an area where no person should be to retrieve Mr. Edwards," the judge said. "She was there at the phone booths, whether 30 feet away or five feet away. She was there when the calls were made to the Small residence. She was there as the evidence was being thrown out the window of the car."

As Robert Agostinelli, her first appellate defender, said, all that was easily explainable. And, one should consider the possibility that it just could be true that she did not know what he was doing. There is more evidence, circumstantial and other, to support that contention than there is to refute it.

Ficaro stuck to his story 16 years later in a deposition he made on October 15, 2004. He said Nancy Rish "told at least 30 lies in eight statements" and "she was involved in every aspect, the collection of materials used in the kidnapping, and plus her prior involvement with Danny Edwards in drug dealing, were clearly the indicators of her involvement. She was identified by witnesses as participating in this kidnapping."

All that was untrue.

Testimony and evidence at the trial did not support this statement in 2004 any more than it did in 1988.

Those lies. All those lies. When you look at all those lies Danny Edwards told, both to the police and to Nancy Rish, and when you look at all those lies the prosecutors told in court, it may be that the lies Nancy Rish told to the police on that first day were the smallest and least important lies of all.

There are lies Nancy Rish told. There are lies the prosecutors told. And there are lies built into the criminal justice system.

One thing that must be realized about our system is that the prosecutors were simply doing their job, which is working to get a conviction.

What also must be realized about the American justice system is that justice is not necessarily the goal. Winning is the goal. Prosecuting attorneys seek to get a conviction, even if the defendant is innocent. Defense lawyers seek to get an acquittal, even if the defendant is guilty. It is an adversarial system. The winner frequently isn't which side is right; the winner often is the side that has the better lawyer. The goal is an acquittal or a conviction. The goal is not necessarily justice.

This continues on appeals, even when there is evidence of a wrongful conviction. The state almost always fights any challenge to a conviction, even if new evidence shows that someone who has spent years in prison is innocent. The lawyers' reputations are important.

Judge Michela's rulings during the trials seemed to lean toward the prosecution, perhaps because the prosecution was more skilled.

Remember Judge Michela's words as he sentenced Nancy Rish to life in prison. Michela said "an inference was drawn that this person (Nancy Rish) made the phone call that lured Stephen Small from his home. That was an inference that the state was allowed to make. It was for the jury to debate whether or not that occurred. Even if that did not occur, this defendant was a part and parcel of this offense."

That is an amazing statement. The judge said Rish made the call, but even if she didn't make the call, she is guilty. Even in a case of circumstantial evidence, that is a stretch, certainly beyond reasonable doubt.

This aspect of the judicial system was shown again when Rish's lawyers raised the issue of prosecutorial misconduct in her appeal. Rish identified Erickson as the officer who threatened her with the electric chair. It turned out it likely was Willis, not Erickson, who made the threat, although Willis denied it years later. Rish's lawyers argued the prosecutor wrongfully accused Rish of lying about everything because she named Erickson when it was just a misidentification.

In an appeal in the circuit court, Judge Gordon Lustfeldt said, "For the purpose of this motion to dismiss, the court has accepted as true that Mr. Willis actually made the statements in question."

However, while the court admitted it was a misidentification and not a lie, that fact did not matter.

It should have mattered. If it was a misidentification, then it was not a lie.

The court's opinion read, "The defendant created this problem by misidentifying the maker of the threat. If she had correctly identified Sergeant Willis, the state would have confronted him, and the truth would have come out. If she had not identified any one at all, and merely said it was a police-man, the state could then have inquired of everyone involved in the investi-gation. But when she says it was Detective Erickson and Erickson denies it, there is no obligation on the state to then conduct a further investigation of anybody involved in her questioning. This court has seen Sergeant Willis tes-tify in court. He is nowhere near the size of Detective Erickson. There is no explanation in the record how the defendant came to identify the maker of the alleged threat of Detective Erickson. Ms. Rish identified Erickson. Erickson denied it, and the state put Erickson on the witness stand to let the jury decide who to believe. At that point, the state was entitled to argue its ver-sion of the facts to the jury. There is no evidence that the prosecution knew Mr. Willis had made such a statement. There is no justification for imputing it to them on the facts presented by the post-conviction petition. This court does not believe the state had any obligation to question every witness who might have been involved in defendant's questioning, when the defendant positively identified Detective Erickson as the maker of the statement. The court also notes that the jury is instructed at the end of the case that what attorneys say is not evidence and that any argument not based on the evi-dence or a reasonable inference there from must be disregarded. The court must presume that the jurors follow its instructions."

The judge is saying that because the defendant made a mistake in the identity of the officer in question, the state -- the people of Illinois -- has no obligation to find the truth. It can "argue its version of the facts" instead of finding the truth.

And remember, the electric chair remark is irrelevant to the kidnap-ping. It was Rish's misidentification that undermined her credibility; it had nothing to do with guilt or innocence.

An argument can beat the truth.

And a technicality can allow a lie to pass for the truth.

How? Appeals are decided on what is presented in the trial court. A lie told at the trial becomes a fact in the appeals court. Call it a technicality.

Justice Kent Slater wrote the majority opinion when the Third District Appellate Court in Ottawa ruled against Rish's appeal on November 10, 2003. Slater did make note of the ambiguity of the factors that led to the conviction, but he didn't consider that enough to give Rish a new trial.

"No direct evidence was presented linking her to the kidnapping or death of Small. However, the state was able to enter defendant's eight incon-sistent statements into evidence. Witnesses were also presented who testi-fied that they had seen her at various times with Edwards when he was pur-chasing some of the items that were ultimately found with Small's body."

"Other witnesses reported that they had observed her at various related locations during the course of the kidnapping and ransom calls. Lastly, the state submitted evidence that Edwards had used their garage to build the box in which Small's body was found."

The falsehoods in the trial became facts once the verdict is reached. All further appeals courts accept these as the facts.

The Appellate Court also said that once Rish identified Erickson, the state had no obligation to look further to see if another officer made the remark about the electric chair. The only concession was in a dissenting opinion on just one issue from Justice McDade, who said Swaim's failure to disclose his friendship with the Smalls violated Rish's Fifth Amendment rights.

Nancy Rish's petition for writ of *habeas corpus* was denied in U.S. District Court, Central District of Illinois, on July 24, 2013. The opinion starts out stating the facts of the case, that Rish "was involved in a kidnapping that resulted in the death of the victim." A footnote at the bottom of the page adds, "The Court is allowed to presume that the facts are accurate. On *habeas* review, we presume that the factual findings of the state appellate court are correct in the absence of clear and convincing evidence to the contrary."

But who wrote the "facts" stated in the opinion? And what if those "facts" are not factual?

Nancy Rish said she was not involved. The court's opinion starts out with the presumption that she was involved. How does one have any hope with a start like that?

The presumption that she was involved is not the only wrong "fact" in the district court's initial summation. It contains numerous wrong statements which are based on the state's arguments, granted as "facts" because she was convicted.

But what if Nancy Rish was wrongly convicted? It does not matter in the eyes of the appeals courts. Wrongfully or not, she was convicted, and in a post-conviction a defendant is guilty until proven innocent. The courts are more concerned about procedure than truth.

Justice Slater mentioned "the defendant's eight inconsistent statements." He meant inconsistent statements in eight interrogation sessions. Accuracy apparently doesn't matter in an appellate ruling.

Judge Lustfeldt said, "For the purpose of this motion to dismiss, the court has accepted as true that Mr. Willis actually made the statements in question." U.S. District Judge Richard Mills said on July 24, 2013, that Willis did not make the threats. So which "fact" is true?

It might be dismissed as an academic argument, except a woman's life is at stake.

Michael Ficaro told the jury, "The evidence is brought to you by the people of the state of Illinois. Now, that is who I represent. I represent the people of the state of Illinois. I don't represent Nancy Rish." He added, "Nowhere, nowhere do I have to have a responsibility to prove to you that she aided in every single aspect of the kidnapping, either before, or during, or while Stephen Small was alive in that box, I don't have to prove that. I have to prove one act of aiding or abetting in the kidnapping of Stephen Small."

Frank Nowicki's closing argument was similar: "Under the law of accountability, we, the people, are only required to prove that Nancy Rish committed one act to aid or abet Danny Edwards in the kidnapping and murder of Stephen Small. In the eyes of the law, if we can show that one act, Nancy Rish is then legally responsible for anything that Danny Edwards does that follows."

It is interesting to note that Ficaro said at one point that Rish "was involved in every aspect" of this crime, and he said here that he doesn't have to prove that she aided in every single aspect of the kidnapping.

(A *Chicago Tribune* story on January 11, 1999, *Trial & Error: The Flip Side of a Fair Trial; Some Cook County Prosecutors Break the Rules to Win,* by writers Maurice Possley and Ken Armstrong, looks at what prosecutors have done to get convictions. The story showed that 326 convictions, which include 207 from Cook County, were reversed because of prosecutorial misconduct in the previous two decades. Eight people who were sentenced to death got new sentencing hearings because of prosecutorial misconduct. Ficaro was one of several lawyers interviewed for the story. "That adrenaline rush can push you over the line," Ficaro told the writers. Ficaro prosecuted two of the reversed cases, according to the *Tribune*).

The only obligation the state has in finding who else may be involved is confined only to whom they have a chance of winning a conviction. Prosecutors go after people they believe they can convict. They weren't interested in Tracy Storm or Mitch Levitt or anyone else. They didn't look into their involvement because a conviction would be doubtful. They went after Nancy Rish because it was easy. She lived with him, she drove him on his errands. She was there.

Ficaro and Nowicki were right about accountability -- but only if Nancy Rish helped Danny Edwards while knowing what he was doing.

That was never proven in court.

There also is the matter of what is considered for an appeal.

The most damning things that convicted Nancy Rish was not evidence and it was not testimony -- it was the false assertions by the prosecutors that went unchallenged.

Vincent Paulauskis and Sherri Carr did not object to several false statements by the prosecutors, most notably the claim that Nancy Rish made the phone call that got Stephen Small out of his house. It was such an egregious error that they both signed affidavits in October 1996, backing Rish's plea in Kankakee County Circuit Court, claiming that their inadequacy led to a conviction that should not have happened.

"I was aware that no evidence had been adduced at trial to support this argument, yet I failed to object," Paulauskis and Carr swore in their affi-

186

davits.

Because Paulauskis did not object during the trial, the law assumes he had no dispute with the statement and it is not a legitimate basis for appeal. If Paulauskis had objected and the judge had overruled him, that would be a basis for appeal. The issue -- the objection -- is not in the trial record, so the appeals court can't rule on something that isn't there. This applies not only to the claim that Rish made the phone call, it applies to all the other false assertions in the trial to which the defense did not object.

It comes down to this -- a successful appeal must be based on error in the trial, not on a bad decision of a jury that may not have understood what was happening, or who may have been misled by a prosecutor whose claims went unchallenged. A wrongful conviction stands unless there is new evidence or error at the trial. A poor jury verdict stands. That is our system.

Inadequate legal representation was cited in the appeals briefs of Joshua Sachs and Michael Costello. They claim that Scott Swaim was almost completely ignorant of the case or of possible charges facing Rish when he was advising her. They said Swaim did not review the arrest report, the search warrant or affidavits supporting the warrants; he did not talk to any officers about his client's involvement; he did not talk to Herzog or any assistant states attorney to determine his client's trouble; and he made no attempt to familiarize himself with information the authorities had, or with their intentions. They said Swaim did not tell Rish that any statements could be used against her and he did not give her any advice about answering questions; he permitted her to submit to eight interrogations exceeding 13 hours over four days without advice or instruction.

Sachs and Costello also cited ineffective legal defense in Nancy Rish's trial. Even Paulauskis and Carr agreed, in their affidavits. That is something that almost never happens. A defendant might sue for malpractice or for ineffective legal representation. But never do those accused lawyers agree. This time, they did.

Another point raised by Sachs was that during Rish's trial, she was taking the drug Xanax for severe anxiety and nervousness. Sachs cited legal precedent, in which convictions were overturned when prescription drugs altered a person's mood and affected their testimony. At a hearing in Kankakee County circuit court, nurse Mary Blanchette testified that Rish took Xanax after suffering headaches, heart palpitations, anxiety and insomnia. Rish took 1 milligram a day of the sedative before and during her trial for "increased anxiety and inability to sleep." Sachs said Rish should have been given a medical test to determine fitness to stand trial, but it was not made.

Family and friends of Nancy Rish said she seemed uncharacteristically distant during the trial because of the effect of the drug.

Judge Gordon Lustfeldt ruled against the motion for a new trial in

August 1998, on the matter of medication impairment. The ruling came five years after the petition was made.

The prosecutors told the jury its entire case was circumstantial. They had no evidence that she was guilty, only the argument that she "had to know." However, one does not need to prove an argument. One only need convince a jury of the argument, with or without evidence.

The evidence said she was innocent. The argument was she was guilty. In this case, the argument beat the evidence.

There are plenty of flaws and loopholes built into the system. There are rules about what a jury can and cannot hear, and what evidence can and cannot be admitted. There are good reasons for rules. But they also can be used in illogical ways.

Nancy Rish's entire knowledge of what happened prior to her arrest consisted of Danny's strange behavior and what Danny told her. And yet, the judge ruled that she could not testify as to what Danny said to her. It was considered hearsay. Any time she got close to saying anything close, she was cut off.

Paulauskis: "When Danny pointed out the railroad tracks to you, did he say something to you?"

Rish: "He said that…"

Paulauskis: "You cannot get into that, please."

Rish: "Yes, he said something to me."

But she couldn't say what he told her. And again, later:

Paulauskis: "Did Mr. Edwards say something to you just before you stopped?"

Rish: "Before I stopped? He told me to stop."

Paulauskis: "All right. I don't want you to relate what he said."

Rish: "Okay."

And later:

Paulauskis: "What was Danny's attitude at this point?"

Rish: "He told me not to ask him about…"

Ficaro: "Objection."

Paulauskis: "You can't get into what he said. Describe his demeanor, his attitude."

Rish: "Nervous."

During questioning on the witness stand, Rish said she was "very scared and confused" during the police interrogation.

Paulauskis: "Did you have any idea what was going on?"

Rish: "No, I did not."

Paulauskis: "Were you ever allowed to ask any questions?"

Rish: "No. Every time I wanted to ask something, I was cut off."

Paulauskis: "Were you ever shown any kind of written statement you had given to police?"

Rish: "I know I had signed something, but I don't know I signed a statement. I signed a lot of things."

When Rish testified about the days before the kidnapping, she was reminded several times about what she could and could not say. She said Danny and Tracy talked about what they were going to do that night. But Paulauskis stopped her from telling what they said. It was hearsay.

Shouldn't justice be the goal of the justice system? Not when loopholes can get around it. How could Nancy Rish be expected to explain her actions during August and early September without saying what she had been told by the perpetrator? It didn't leave her much of a defense.

It is especially unfair that she was not allowed to defend herself by bringing in what Danny Edwards' said, and yet the state was allowed to prosecute her by bringing in everything Danny Edwards did.

Much has been said by many people of the theatrical performance of the prosecutor and the show-biz atmosphere on this big stage. Michael Ficaro had the gruesome plywood box brought into court to make an impression on the jury, when Judge Michela said pictures of it would do. The video with horror movie production values was shown to shock the jurors, with the cameraman going through the misty woods until coming upon the corpse of Stephen Small, who had been left in the box underground all night. The lid on the box had been opened and closed so many times that a good amount of sand was draped over the corpse, making the appearance even more gruesome.

Who wouldn't vote to convict a person who the state accused of this monstrous crime after seeing this video?

And yet, despite all the false statements in court, and all the innuendos and accusations about Nancy Rish, none of it proved she participated or knew about the act Danny Edwards committed. And none of the lies Nancy Rish told proved her guilt. They were immaterial to the case. Not one lie or misstatement incriminated her in the kidnapping.

Herzog, Glazer, Kuester, Regas, Burns, Kick, Leschen, Schmidt. Everyone in the public defender's office withdrew from taking Edwards' or Rish's case. They had conflicts of interest or they feared the Smalls -- or maybe they were afraid of what might happen to them if they won their case. Swaim served briefly but poorly. Paulauskis and Carr served ineffectively. They were in way over their heads in a very big case, and they were outmatched. There were powerful forces at work against Nancy Rish from the very beginning. These powerful forces continue today.

Chapter 13
The Road to Damascus Goes Through Pontiac

"I will never get the blood of Stephen Small off my hands."
Danny Edwards, June 28, 2013

The decision to kidnap Stephen Small and hold him for ransom ruined more lives than are known.

Everyone in the Small family, the Edwards family, the Rish family and many others were changed forever.

That one murderous act changed the path for a lot of people and set them in an entirely different direction.

It certainly changed the direction of Danny Edwards' life. But, he said, his path ultimately became a better one than the path he had been on.

Danny Edwards said he was on the highway to hell until a religious conversion in prison saved his soul and put him on the highway to heaven.

His soul desperately needed saving. He was an evildoer who didn't have any morals, didn't have any conscience and didn't care.

Danny Edwards was a user. He was a user of marijuana, of cocaine, and a user of friends. He used Jeff Westerhoff to get the wood for the box, Jeff Drury to get the gun, Bill Mohler for the battery charger, his brother Duke for the bolt cutters, and even his own son Brandon for the tape recorder. He used Nancy Rish to drive him to his ransom calls and he used Jack Karalevicz as an excuse to fool Nancy. He used Kent Allain, Mitch Levitt and "black cowboys" as scapegoats. He tried to use the man he killed, Stephen Small, to make a deal to get a better prison location. Danny Edwards used everybody, and he didn't care who he used or who he hurt.

However, the man who once had a colorful yet limited vocabulary, today does not utter a curse word. The womanizer who sought sex everywhere now shows disgust at fellow inmates who have nudie magazines.

"I was corrupt. I was drinking, doing drugs, womanizing. I had sex with as many women as I could," he said of his past life.

"I was a womanizer my whole marriage. I had affair after affair."

What drove you to such affairs? Is there some deep psychological reason that drove you to such behavior?

"No. It was just sex. I liked having sex, with a lot of different women."

"I have a cookie theory. The reason why so many marriages fail is because we have variety. Today, sex is so free. People have 30 partners before they get married. If Oreo was the only cookie, you'd be satisfied. When you see so many varieties, you're not satisfied with one woman."

"I married the most perfect woman in the world. Peg wanted a husband and a family. Peg forgave me many times. But she could only take so much."

Was a bad childhood to blame for your life turning so wrong?

"No. I had a great childhood. I played pee-wee football, little league baseball. I had a two-parent home. The family trade was electricians, and I was supposed to go into that. The local was in Kankakee. When it was time for me to join, it had moved to Joliet. It was impossible for me to get in. I didn't want to work in the grocery store."

He really had no explanation for his actions, except perhaps drugs.

"I was a pot head since I was 15. I was not much of a drinker, except for social drinking at bars."

"Peg's family was big drinkers. Her father was the Kankakee postmaster (Clark McKenna). He'd drink from morning to night. I always said the McKenna family measured things in beer, not time. If it took two hours to paint a fence, it took 38 beers to paint a fence."

Danny started selling pot while he was in high school. A few years later, he moved up to pushing cocaine.

And he didn't care if he was selling poison to kids.

"If they didn't buy it from me, they would buy it somewhere else."

"Drugs were normal. It was what everybody else was doing. Go to a party, people are snorting cocaine, smoking pot."

"Sin is fun. Satan makes it so appealing."

Danny also didn't care about burglarizing and stealing from people who owed him drug money, and he didn't mind threatening those who did not pay. He had no moral feelings about selling drugs, sexual contacts or anything else he did.

Danny even snorted cocaine at home in front of his kids. When his son Brandon was a toddler, his grandmother gave him a birthday card with a twenty dollar bill. The child rolled up the bill and pretended to snort coke from the table. It was quite a shock for Danny, but the only change he made was to be sure he never snorted cocaine in front of the kids again.

Danny Edwards said he had to be convicted by the state before he could be convicted by the Holy Spirit.

It was in prison that he found God, in a circumstance he sees similar to St. Paul.

"I don't look at Pontiac as my place of incarceration. I look at it as my road to Damascus. This is where I was struck. This is where my eyes were opened."

Saul was a persecutor of Christians. He was on the road to Damascus to find more Christians to torment when God knocked him to the ground and blinded him for three days. Saul was converted and God opened his eyes. He became Paul, one of the greatest saints in all Christianity. St. Paul, in turn, was persecuted for the faith.

St. Paul died in prison.

"I found salvation in prison. You don't find God on the mountaintops, you find him in the valleys, in the depths. Look at all the lives Saul destroyed."

There are a few things people need to know about Christianity.

Christianity teaches that God can reach a sinner and turn him around. The enormity of the sin doesn't matter if the sinner confesses and repents and asks for forgiveness.

Christians believe that Jesus died for our sins and anyone who accepts Jesus as our savior has his sins washed away. That means Danny Edwards' sins of cocaine selling, kidnapping and murder have been forgiven. Are there any Christians who believe there are some people who are exempt? Does the Bible say God forgives this, but doesn't forgive that?

It changes a person. The old Danny Edwards is no more. There is a new Danny Edwards who is as opposite of the old Danny Edwards as Paul is of Saul.

This is something that is hard for a lot of people to accept. Even a lot of Christians.

Christianity teaches that God forgives and that people also should forgive. Hate the sin, love the sinner.

Danny Edwards acknowledges that this is tough for some people to accept, especially if it involves a sinner who killed someone in your family.

Danny's own family has not forgiven him. He said they have disowned him. He hasn't talked to his son Brandon since the boy was 16 years old, more than 20 years ago.

"The world can't forgive me, but God has," he said.

When Governor Ryan was thinking about commuting all death sentences, the Death Row inmates at Pontiac would gather in the prison yard and hold hands in a prayer circle, praying that God would move George Ryan's heart toward clemency.

"I was the only one who wouldn't join them," Edwards said. "I told them they had it exactly backwards. They should be praying for the victims' families to find peace instead of praying for themselves."

"When Ryan commuted the death sentences, I was the only one who wrote to him and said don't do it. Set me free or let me be. I'm ready to die and I'm not afraid to die."

Danny Edwards lost his free lawyer when his death sentence was commuted in 2003. He has no money to continue filing any more appeals. He gave up the idea of any further appeals in 2005. He said he could have filed more, on his own, but he decided to "take responsibility" finally.

"I preach to the guys all the time: if you did it, accept responsibility. Live with it. Stop wasting people's time. You got caught. I wanted to be a good example. Practice what you preach. There are people in the law library working on appeals, and you ask them if they're guilty and they say yes. That's the problem with the world today. They don't want to own up."

Danny's religious conversion began about a month after his arrest. A local preacher with the Gideon Society conducted regular religious studies in the Kankakee County jail. Danny Edwards, in his cell, couldn't help hearing what was being said down the hall.

"Jim Smith was a Gideon. He would come into the county jail. I would lay on my bunk and listen to him. It went on for about a month. One day, I decided to get up and see what this was about. I came up to the bars after his church service and he asked me my name. I told him. He broke down in tears. He said, 'I've been praying God would bring you to me.'"

Smith was a very big figure in Danny Edwards' conversion. "Later, he told me he had terminal cancer. He said he was a soldier for God."

When Jim Smith died, Danny wrote a poem for him. The family was so moved, that the poem was part of the funeral service.

"Half his prayer card was his information, the other half was my poem. That was his gold watch."

Here is Danny's poem, *Soldier For My Soul:*

"I would like to tell you a story about a man I'm glad I met,
He came to me at a time in my life when I was conquered by regret,
My friends they have all scattered, they left me sitting cold,
Now I've met this man named Jim, a soldier for my soul.
The law got so disgusted that they threw me in their jail,
And anchored by the weight of sin my soul was bound for hell.
But locked up behind these bars of steel my Christian life begun,
For this is where I learned of God and Christ His only Son.
Now the man I have to thank for this has become so very ill,
Jim, an advocate of God, whose sickness I pray will heal.
One thing I'll say I learned from Jim is that life will never end,
As long as we keep our faith in God and practice not to sin.
So, Jim, you needn't worry for you have reached your Christian goal,
Because I believe God brought you to me to be a soldier for my soul.

Another great influence on Danny Edwards' religious thinking was a man named William Bracy.

"William Bracy taught Bible studies here in Pontiac. He came up to me in the yard and said we have Bible study Friday mornings. He had a deeper understanding of the Bible than anyone I have known. He had an IQ of 138. He was convicted by the spirit."

"To get in his Bible study, you had to give up the yard (the outdoor prison yard). That separates the sheep from the goats. He was a huge influence on me."

Bracy was another Death Row inmate who found God.

"He was a hit man for the Black Stone Rangers. He was in their royal family. He was cool. When he spoke, you listened. He was an excellent painter. When he finished a painting, doctors would bid on them."

Bracy was convicted of multiple murders and was sentenced to death in *two states*. Bracy and two other men invaded a house in Phoenix, Arizona, on December 31, 1980, and ransacked and robbed the place before brutally murdering a man and his mother-in-law. The victim's wife survived the attack and identified the murderers. Earlier that year, Bracy and two others tied up three men and led them from their Chicago apartment to a viaduct, where they shot them, execution-style. Bracy had the distinction of receiving capital sentences in Arizona in 1983 and in Illinois in 1985. Illinois had the distinction of providing hospitality for Bracy until his death.

As horrible as Bracy was, Edwards said Bracy was an example of how a man can turn his life around when the Lord touches him.

"Bracy died of cancer about six years ago. He refused treatment."

Bracy was convicted by crooked Cook County Circuit Court Judge Thomas Maloney in 1981. Bracy later tried to have his verdict overturned, claiming he was convicted because he did not bribe Maloney. The appeals courts rejected his argument, but the United States Supreme Court in 1997 found that Bracy made a legitimate case for a new trial.

Maloney had a connection to Dino Titone, another Death Row prisoner Edwards knew in Pontiac.

Titone was 24 when he was convicted in 1984 of murder, kidnapping and armed robbery for killing two men in 1982 during a cocaine rip-off scheme. He was sentenced to death in a manner unique to Cook County, but not unusual. Maloney's specialty was taking bribes from street gangs to acquit their members or to find members of rival gangs guilty. Judge Maloney did this for 13 years before being caught.

Titone's lawyer, Bruce Roth, solicited Dino's father, Salvatore Titone, to come up with $10,000 in bribe money for Maloney.

Dino Titone's case came up just as the feds were going after crooked judges in Cook County in the infamous Operation Graylord investigation. This investigation ended with the conviction of nearly 100 people, including 13 judges and 51 lawyers (including Roth and Maloney). Maloney took the bribe money from Titone and then learned of the investigation.

Guilty or not, Maloney decided Titone had to be convicted to prove to the feds he was not crooked.

Ironically, it was Titone's allegation that Maloney took bribe money and did not acquit him that set the feds on Maloney's trail.

Maloney also was known as a "ruthless and heartless" judge who sentenced more people to death than any other Cook County judge.

Titone got a new trial because of this. He was convicted again in 1998, and was sentenced to life. He died in Pontiac prison in 2007.

Maloney, one of 18 Cook County judges convicted of corruption in the previous decade, was found guilty in 1993 of fixing several murder trials.

While still a lawyer in 1977, Maloney directed a $10,000 bribe to Cook County Circuit Court Judge Frank Wilson to acquit notorious Mob hit man Harry "The Hook" Aleman. Because of the bribery, Aleman did not beat the double jeopardy exclusion. He was put on trial again in 1997. He was convicted and sentenced to 100-to-300 years. Aleman died in prison in Galesburg in 2010.

Judge Wilson blew his brains out as the investigation got closer.

Judge Maloney was sentenced to 15 years in prison. He was released in 2007 and he died in 2008.

"When I was sentenced to death, I didn't care."

"I've had four heart attacks. I have twelve stents in my heart now. I had four stents put in August 2000, three more in April 2003 and five on September 10, 2013. One artery was 100 percent blocked, but they were able to open it and put a stent in. I had quadruple bypass surgery in May 2000. I was taken to the infirmary Thanksgiving 2005. I refused treatment. The psychiatrist asked me questions and then said I was in my right mind."

"They said I was going to die. I said I didn't care. I'm leaving here in a pine box, whether it's today or 10 years from today."

Edwards said he stopped taking heart medication in 2004, although he was talked into resuming medication in 2012. He takes four different heart pills and he said hardly day goes by when he doesn't need a nitro pill.

"I don't care. I trust in the Lord. The Lord is testing me. He is asking, 'Is he going to give in at the first sign of a heart attack?' I didn't."

"I'm always in a good mood because of who lives in me and through me. I don't know how I got along so many years without God's favor in my life. And now I have it in abundance."

The only people who are still in contact with Danny Edwards are Jack Karalevicz (from the "bicycle" story) and Dickie LaPorte, a former Kankakeean now living in California. Both men are born again Christians.

"I could not have done my time without Jack," Danny said. "I ask something, it is there. If a guy in here has no TV, and if he attends Bible study and church, about five of us guys pool together and get him a TV. There's nothing worse than being in here with no TV. Twenty hours a day looking at the walls. A guy wants a King James Bible, Jack gets it for him."

Jack still owns Precision Repair near St. Anne. He talks to Danny on the phone about once a month. He used to visit, but Danny finally told him several years ago not to bother because of the hassles visitors go through.

Jack said he met Danny in 1975 through the Yamaha shop where Jack worked. They rode dirt bikes for a while, but Jack said they weren't really friends at that time. Jack said he settled down when he got married, "but Danny kept living in the fast lane."

At the trial, Jack had to testify concerning the false story Danny told about taking the bicycle there to be repaired.

It was several months later when an elder at his Faith Reformed Church on Waldron Road told him that Danny Edwards' soul was saved. "I said I need to get ahold of this guy who is a brother in Christ," Jack said.

Before that happened, Danny wrote a letter to Jack, telling him that no one in his family would visit him, and that he had no one in prison who is a Christian. He asked Jack to write to him.

Danny sent Jack a poem he wrote in February 1989, titled *Our Lord.*

Oh the comfort, the inexpressible comfort of feeling safe with our Lord.

Having Him weigh our thoughts and measure our words.

Knowing some day we will all have to stand accountable before Him.

But in times of haste and anger we quickly

Weigh our thoughts and measure our words,

Pouring them all right out, just as they are.

Chaff and grain together, praying the Lord's faithful hand will take and sift them.

Hoping He will keep what is worth keeping

And with a breath of kindness, blow the rest away.

Praise the Lord.

Jack knew what the Bible said about the importance of visiting those in prison. Still, Jack did not visit or write. He said he prayed that he would be able to send a letter to Danny Edwards.

"The next day while I was driving to church, I was listening to the ONU (Olivet Nazarene University in Bourbonnais) station on the radio. The preacher read Danny's poem on the air. I said, 'Lord, I hear you.' When I got home, I set my Bible down, and it opened to the page where I had Danny's poem. The Lord was making it clear to me, this man is your brother, go see him. I was blessed more than Danny was when I got there."

Jack said, "Danny tells the old story about the man who would hit his mule across the head with a 2x4, just to get his attention. That is what the Lord had to do to Danny."

A pastor who went to Pontiac with Jack to visit Danny later told Jack he would let Danny preach in his pulpit on Sunday if Danny was free.

If only Danny had found religion early in life instead of finding cocaine -- but that was not his destiny.

"The Lord wanted him to witness in that prison," Jack said.

And that is what he ended up doing.

Jack said Danny's letter to Governor Ryan meant that "he'd rather be executed because that's the way he gets to go home (to heaven)."

Randy Irps and Tracy Storm were Danny's best friends in Kankakee, but he hasn't been in contact with them or any other old friends since he was arrested. "God gave me new friends, Christian friends who encourage me to do the right things, to stay in my studies," he said. "You don't put new wine in old wine skins."

Edwards has become a writer of Bible studies and Christian poems. Here is a poem he wrote, titled, *I Could Never Find the Time.*

I knelt to pray, but not for long, I have too much to do,
I must hurry off and get to work, for bills would soon be due.
And when my work is done, and the weekend comes,
This is my time for me to play,
No time, no time, too much to do, this is my constant say,
No time to pray or go to church, oh Lord, what will you do?
At last, it was my time to die, so before the Lord I came,
He looked at me with downcast eyes, this day I am ashamed.
In His hands He held the book of life, and as He flipped another page,
He closed the book and said to me, your name I cannot find.
I remember once I was gonna write it down but I could never find the time."

Danny Edwards has come up with a lot of theories from his studies of the Bible.

"I was on Death Row 15 years," Edwards said. "You don't just read the Bible, you study it. I'll put my knowledge of the Bible against anyone else here, and I'll smoke 'em. And I'm proud of that."

One of his greater interests involves the "End Times," the Biblical signs that predict the end of the age and the return of Christ. In his Bible study, *The Two Olive Trees,* he said God has favored America, but He has lifted His favor because of grievous sins like abortion and homosexuality. Not much upsets Danny Edwards more than the idea of legalizing gay marriage. He also is appalled by the public acceptance of homosexuality and same-sex marriage; however, he said, "The Bible says in the End Times, good will be evil and evil will be good."

He has written numerous Bible study essays of his own, called *Something To Ponder.* He specializes in taking several scriptural passages and linking them together into a larger picture, showing how various Bible passages are interwoven, and nothing is isolated or unconnected.

A reader might find that some are very perceptive and some are off the mark. That is an individual judgment. The Bible is very complicated and each person may have his own interpretation of the same verses.

One Bible study pertinent to this book concerns Danny Edwards' biblical theory on the death of Stephen Small. He asked that his studies on the tabernacle and the olive trees precede the study on Stephen Small because he believes they are connected. These are instructive to knowing more about Danny Edwards, so here they are.

The Wilderness Tabernacle and America is a Something To Ponder essay dated April 17, 2006. In it, Danny Edwards gives his interpretation of how America is the new covenant land.

"Exodus 40:34-38. Matthew 21:33-43. The theory of God's vineyard. Before we can fully understand this parable, we have to know who or what the vineyard represents. The answer is found in Isaiah 5:1-7. In verse 7, we see that Israel is the vineyard. In Matthew 21:41-43, we see where God's vineyard will be taken away from its original tenants and will be given to another people who will produce its fruit. In 1Peter 2:9-10, we see that the Gentiles, who were once not a people, now are the people of God. Romans 11:11-24 tells us that we've been grafted in. Now under the new covenant as God's people, we co-exist with Israel. When God moved His vineyard to a people who would produce its fruit, He was speaking of the largest Christian nation on earth, the United States of America. This new vineyard is His church, the Gentile nation who would eventually carry the gospel of Jesus Christ to the four corners of the earth."

"We are the transplanted vineyard. The question now is, being God moved His vineyard to what is now the United States of America, has His wilderness tabernacle that His spirit dwells in also been moved here, or did He design it into our landscape when He created the earth? When we take the positioning of the tabernacle furniture and overlay it onto a map of America, a very strange picture unfolds. The only entrance to the tabernacle was on the east. When the colonists came across the Atlantic, they landed on the east coast and began building. So, in a similar way, America's historic entrance is on the east. If we place each piece of furniture from the wilderness tabernacle and with its position place it on the map of America, we find an amazing pattern that occurs only in America. It will not happen with any other nation on earth!"

"Moving east to west, the altar of sacrifice, Leviticus 6:8-13, is positioned in the area of Tennessee and the edge of Kentucky and Virginia. Fire was the central feature on the altar of sacrifice. This area of America experienced dynamic revivals before and after the Civil War that impacted the nation. Great revivals burned in Kentucky throughout the 1800s. In 1896 near Murphy, North Carolina, a group of Baptists were baptized in the Holy Spirit. From this experience, the Christian union was formed. The fires of the Holy Spirit that thrived in this area correlates with the fire on the altar of sacrifice."

"Continuing on in a straight line, the next piece of tabernacle furniture is the lavor filled with water. Exodus 30:17-21. On the map of America,

198

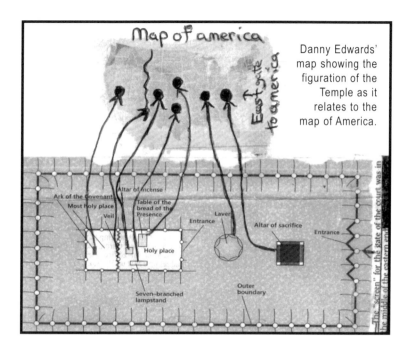

Danny Edwards' map showing the figuration of the Temple as it relates to the map of America.

the lavor would be positioned in the area where the Mississippi River flows. The mighty Mississippi is recognized as the waterway of America. It supports large barges which transport shipping materials and provides irrigation to thousands of farms. The main substance in the lavor is water, and its water correlates with the Mississippi River."

"Going on into the holy place, the next piece of furniture is the table of the bread of the presence. Exodus 25:23-30. Bread was placed on this table daily, made from Israeli-grown wheat. On the map of America, this table of bread would be positioned in the states of Nebraska and Kansas. These farming states are called America's bread basket. The next piece of furniture is the seven-branched lamp stand. Its main substance was oil. Exodus 27:20-21. The positioning of the tabernacle lamp stand would be in the states of Texas and Oklahoma, which are America's two major oil producing states. The next piece of furniture is the altar of incense. Exodus 30:7-8. On the map of America, this altar would be positioned in the state of Colorado. The main substances of the altar were hot coals and incense. Some of the incense from the ancient temple was discovered in Qumran, Israel, along with the Dead Sea scrolls. The incense had a deep red color. Colorado is famous for the Colorado Red River, and it is a coal producing state."

"If all of this seems happenstance so far, then consider the following. Leaving the holy place, we must pass through the veil. This veil separated the holy place from the most holy place. On the map of America, this veil we must pass through would be positioned on the Continental Divide. This divide is an imaginary line that marks the highest regions in the country. It is clearly seen on any map of America and on any satellite picture. The most holy place is our next stop and it contains the Ark of the Covenant, which is overlaid in pure gold. Exodus 25:10-22. On the map of America, the ark would be positioned in the states of Nevada and California, which are famous for their gold rush days."

"The evidence in this study is thought provoking, that America is God's new covenant nation and that we co-exist with Israel."

The Two Olive Trees in Prophecy is a *Something To Ponder* from November 4, 2006. In it, he contends 9/11 was prophesied in the Bible.

"Romans 11:11-24. What's the hidden prophecy of the two olive trees? If the Gentiles have been adopted by God because of Israel's transgression, we will receive God's blessing for doing what's right, and we will receive God's judgments for doing wrong. In Romans 11:17, we read, Because of Israel's unbelief, some of their branches have been broken off, and you (Gentiles) through a 'wild olive shoot' have been grafted in among the others and share in the nourishing sap from the olive tree (blessings). In verses 19-21, we read, You (Gentiles) say then branches were broken off so I could be grafted in, but they were broken off because of unbelief, and you (Gentiles) stand by faith, 'do not be arrogant but be afraid,' for if God did not spare the natural branches, He will not spare you either (judgment). In verse 24, we read, You (Gentiles) were cut out of an olive tree that is wild by nature (outside the Abrahamic covenant) and contrary to nature were grafted into a cultivated olive tree (Israel). In short, we Gentiles now co-exist with Israel because we have been grafted in. In Daniel 9:11 we read, 'All Israel (both olive trees) has transgressed your law and turned away, refusing to obey you, therefore the curses and 'sworn judgments' written in the law of Moses, the servant of God, have been 'poured out on us' because we have sinned against you. In history past, when God wanted to punish Israel (cultivated olive tree), he raised up Nebuchadnezzar of Babylon (Jeremiah 25:1-9). At this time, the Babylon empire occupied the same area of what is now Iraq, Saudi Arabia, etc."

"In Ecclesiastes 1:9 and 3:15, we see where 'history will repeat itself.' On September 11, 2001, the wild olive tree of the Gentiles (America) was attacked by a group of Islamic extremists (Al Qaeda) who occupy the same area of the world that attacked the cultivated olive tree Israel. 'History has repeated itself,' Babylon has attacked 'both olive trees.' The king of Babylon attacked the cultivated olive tree (Israel) and Islamic extremists from Babylon attacked the wild olive tree (America). We find the attack (judgment) on the cultivated olive tree in the book of Jeremiah. Did the Lord also record the attack on the wild olive tree? Could the curses and sworn judgments that are poured out on us in Daniel 9:11 be 9/11? It would be correct to point out that 'all of Israel' in Daniel 9:11 is referring to the southern and northern tribes. But consider this: in Daniel 7:2-7, he uses three beasts to describe kingdoms or powers of 'his day,' leopard, bear and lion. The book of Revelations 13:1-2 uses the same three beasts, leopard, bear and lion to describe an 'end time' kingdom or power. 'All of Israel' has a double meaning as well. It refers to Daniel's time of the two tribes and it refers to the end times, the natural olive tree (Israel) and the wild olive tree (America)."

"I understand that many who read this study might be thinking, 'Why would God want to punish America, His new covenant people?' Because like Israel, the rules are the same -- we do good, we get God's blessings; we do wrong, we get God's punishment. Let's look at some of the wrongs America has done in the eyes of God. We are the number one producer of pornography that goes around the world. We are the number one illegal drug consuming nation in the world. We are number two behind China in abortion. We have taken prayer out of schools and we pass more laws every day to allow same sex marriage. This should answer any question of why God would want to punish America."

"One more point. Many Christians believe that Christ's death on the cross ended all these Old Testament punishments. This paper proves otherwise."

That brings us to Danny Edwards' essay where he sees the death of Stephen B. Small as a "Biblical" punishment from God, and he believes he was an instrument to carry out the Lord's will.

He explained his theory in a five-page letter before we met for our interviews in prison. He later refined it as a Bible study titled, *The Ahab and Stephen Small Factor.*

"I've learned over the years that God gives us truths about the Bible in nuggets," he wrote. "When we research a subject about a Biblical truth, we find bits of information throughout the Bible."

"My mom said the Small family was cursed. Dad said Governor Small was so corrupt and that he built the family fortune on what he stole. God's word says He will punish the sins of the father to the third and fourth generations. Governor Small put his hand on the Bible and swore on it. That is a covenant he made."

Edwards said his Biblical theory became clearer to him after Dino Titone gave him a book about Al Capone that mentioned Governor Small's complicity with the gangsters.

Danny Edwards cites many examples from the Bible where God led people, both righteous and unjust, to destroy other people because of their sins. Many times these people did not know God was directing them. Edwards said he did not realize at the time that God was directing his actions.

But he says he realizes it now.

"When I was 30 years old, did my corrupt evil heart decide on its own to kidnap Stephen Small, or was this decision made for me to carry out a sentence written against the Small family? When you look at the history of the Small family, you have to stop and wonder."

"You are the only person I've shared this information with, and why you, I don't know, but I believe time will tell," Edwards wrote.

He cites Psalm 149, which includes. "May the praise of God be in their mouths and a double-edged sword in their hands, to inflict vengeance on the nations and punishment on the peoples, to bind their kings with fetters, their nobles with shackles of iron, to carry out the sentence written against them, this is the glory of all His saints."

"Here we learn that it is the glory of the saints, Old Testament and Christian believers, who have gone before us, to carry out the sentence written against them who are still on earth."

"You might be saying to yourself, okay, but why me, Danny Edwards?"

Danny said he got a "gut feeling" that came from his uncle, Leonard Edwards. Leonard was the first child of George and Minnie Edwards. He was hit by a car and killed in 1923 when he was three years old. This was when the Edwards family lived in Moose Jaw, Saskatchewan, Canada, before coming to Kankakee.

Just as there was a board meeting in heaven on how to kill Ahab, there was a meeting in heaven on how to punish the Smalls, Danny said.

"When it was decided the sentence was to be carried out against the Small family, First Corinthians says when we leave this world and enter the kingdom of God we will have great authority, we will judge the things of this life. It says the saints will judge the world. Judgment against the Small family was due."

When George Edwards arrived in Kankakee, he worked at the state hospital. This made him beholden to Len Small and Victor McBroom. "Dad told me that every four years McBroom gave grandpa a set of keys and said here's your new car for the next four years. You bought the car or you lost your job."

The McBroom family also has suffered its share of tragedies. Edward McBroom should have had a lock on his seat in the legislature, but he was defeated in more than one election. He went through two wives and became an alcoholic before his death at age 65. His son, Harvey Victor McBroom, also should have enjoyed a privileged life, but he was a drug user whose life spiraled into failure and tragedy before an early death.

Danny explained how he was brought to commit the act. "God cannot move a righteous heart to do an evil act. But I had an evil heart."

When Stephen Small picked up the phone that night, he asked his wife why the answering service didn't pick up the call. I asked Danny if he had a special number and who gave it to him.

"I got his phone number out of the book. Again, things happened then that shouldn't have happened. God wanted me to get through to him. Maybe that's why the Lord has given me Biblical knowledge."

This revelation came to Danny only after many years of studying the Bible in prison, he said. He did not know this when he was committing the kidnapping.

So how do the death of Stephen Small and the imprisonment of Danny Edwards fit into the grand scheme?

No one will know until we get to heaven, he said, but things happen for a reason. "I'm counting on a big family reunion someday (in heaven). One day I'll see uncle Leonard, and he'll sit down with me and he'll tell me why I did this."

The Ahab and Stephen Small Factor is his *Something To Ponder* Bible study, presented here to the public for the first time.

"This Bible study, *The Ahab and Stephen Small Factor,* is a biblical aspect of the kidnapping and murder of Stephen Small. I am by no means saying that this is what happened. The degree of probability will be left up to the reader. The greater the biblical knowledge of the reader, the greater the degree of probability of the biblical aspect. Those with a lesser degree of biblical knowledge will have a lesser degree of the probability of the biblical aspect. I cannot elaborate or emphasize enough the importance of using your Bible to discern the degree of probability in this Bible study (NIV translation)."

"Exodus 34:7 and Numbers 14:18. Yet He does not leave the guilty unpunished, He will punish the children and their children for the sins of the father to the third and fourth generation. When we parallel this verse with the history of the Small family, a *Something To Ponder* Bible study is born. Governor Len Small was not a righteous man, and when this unrighteous man became governor, he had a swearing in, and in this swearing in, he placed his hand on the Bible and made a covenant with God. And to honor this unrighteous man, his son Leslie Small in 1948 oversaw the building of Governor Small Memorial Park and museum. This park and museum, in the eyes of the Small family, then and now, is a memorial to honor an honorable man. They have refused to recognize Governor Small for what he was. They continue to donate money for its upkeep, when biblically speaking, they should be paying somebody money to tear it down."

"Leslie Small was the only child of Governor Small to live a full life of 70 years. His brother Budd Small died at the age of 56 and his sister Ida May died at the age of 55. Leslie Small was the only child of Governor Small to have children. He had two third-generation sons, Len H. Small and Burrell

203

Small. Both of these third-generation sons died an early death."

"'He punishes the children and their children for the sins of the father to the third and fourth generation.' Sometimes His punishment 'on the surface of things' is so subtle (hidden), like His tabernacle furniture, you don't even realize it's biblical. Proverbs 25:2 says, 'It is the glory of God to conceal a matter, to search out a matter is the glory of kings.' To search out this matter, we need to find a biblical parallel to their deaths. We learned from my *Two Olive Trees* paper that when God wanted to punish Israel, He summoned (moved the heart of) the king of Babylon. The Israeli people who died in this attack never knew a sentence was carried out against them, and the king of Babylon never knew his heart was moved to carry out the sentence. No one of that day ever suspected any biblical aspect to this earthly event."

"Another biblical parallel is found in the story of Naboth and Ahab, 1Kings, chapters 21 and 22. In 22:19-23, we see there was a meeting in the throne room between God and His spirit beings (angels). In this meeting, it was decided that Ahab would be enticed onto the battlefield so a sentence could be carried out against him. On the surface of things, Ahab was killed on the battlefield. No one ever suspected any biblical aspect to his death. Another biblical parallel is found in the attack on America that we call 9/11. In my *Two Olive Trees* paper, I more than satisfied the burden of proof that this attack was biblical. The only logical conclusion you can come to is God (like the king of Babylon) summoned (moved the heart of) Osama bin Laden to carry out the sentence against America. And who knew before reading my *Two Olive Trees* paper the biblical aspect of 9/11?"

"Len H. Small, the third generation from his grandfather, was on his way to O'Hare airport, and was at the intersection of Route 113 and Warner Bridge Road, when the driver of another car did not see the stop sign at the intersection and slammed into Mr. Small's car, killing him. It is listed that his brother Burrell Small died in 1981 of natural causes at the age of 63. Is there a biblical aspect to their deaths? On the surface of things, most people would say no. But if we take this perspective, 'on the surface of things,' 9/11 was just an attack on America by a bunch of crazy Islamic terrorists."

"One biblical aspect is very clear: when God wants to carry out a sentence against an individual or nation, hearts are moved. When the king of Babylon carried out a sentence against Israel, was this his decision or was this decision made for him? When the sentence was carried out against Ahab by enticing him onto the battlefield, was this his decision or was this decision made for him? When Osama bin Laden carried out a sentence against America, was this his decision or was this a decision made for him? In each of the biblical parallels I gave, the king of Babylon, Ahab and Osama bin Laden, the decision which prompted their actions was not theirs, the decision came from the throne room, their hearts were moved."

"One final biblical aspect needs to be answered. Was it my decision to kidnap Stephen Small or was this decision made for me? Was a fourth generation sentence carried out?"

"Before we can accurately assess this, we need to look at three more verses. 1Corinthians 6:2-3, says that when a believer (saint) enters the kingdom of God, they are given great authority. It says we will judge the things of this life. Psalms 149:6-9, says it is the glory of the saints to carry out the sentence written against men. In Genesis 28:10-12, we learn about the stairway to heaven where angels are descending and ascending. We know how these spirit beings descended to earth to entice Ahab. Do they also move the hearts of men to carry out sentences? We also learn in 1Corinthians 6:3, that the saints in Psalm 149: 6-9, who carry out the sentences against men, will also have the authority to judge angels. Is there a connection with the saints of God who judge the things of this life and carry out the sentences against men, who also have the authority to judge angels? Are these descending angels being judged by the saints of God for missions they are given concerning the things of this life?"

"When Len H. Small's car crashed on that road in 1980, maybe a descending angel on a mission was at the scene to play a role in judging the things of this life. Mr. Small was the only one killed in this car accident. We know when a sentence to judge the things of this life fell on Ahab, a descending angel on a mission was at the scene to play a role of a lying spirit. The word of God says His punishment will visit the third and fourth generations. And by this study we now know that God and His saints use angels (many angels) and men (king of Babylon, Osama bin Laden, etcetera) to carry out their sentences."

"The Ahab and Stephen Small factor is this. They both have one common factor that links them together. They both were told a lie which lured them to their place of death. Ahab was lied to by telling him he would be victorious in attacking Ramoth Gilead. This lie lured him to the battlefield where he was killed. Stephen Small was lied to by telling him his business was broken into and he was needed at the scene. This lie lured him to the Wichert sand hills where he was killed. The information in this study in no way diminishes my guilt or shame of what I've done. God cannot move the heart of a righteous man to commit an unrighteous act. In 1987, my heart was far from righteous. I was a drug dealer, drug user, womanizer, liar and a big lover of money. I was just the kind of man that God and His saints were looking for."

"I will never get the blood of Stephen Small off my hands, but mingled together, I will never get the blood of Jesus Christ off my heart. With the death of Stephen Small, the fourth generation from his great-grandfather, Governor Len Small, I pray that God's judgment is satisfied, and the rest of the fourth generation of the Small family will be spared the judgment of their sentence."

"I understand that many people reading this will say it's all foolish-

205

ness and deny the biblical aspect within. But to deny the biblical aspect of these Bible studies would be to deny the existence of God Himself. How can anyone say there is no God, knowing how when God created the earth He designed His tabernacle furniture into the landscape of our country? How can anyone deny the existence of God after reading my *Two Olive Trees* paper that shows the attack on America that we call 9/11 is in the Bible? How can anyone say there is no God when you look at the history of the Small family and what the Bible says about their fate?"

"When the author of this book asked me if he could use my *Ahab* paper, I said yes, but my *Tabernacle* paper and my *Two Olive Trees* paper must go along with it because they are interconnected. My tabernacle paper shows that America (not Europe) is the Gentile nation spoken of in Romans 11:17. We are the wild olive shoot. In the Old Testament, the tabernacle stayed with God's covenant people, Exodus 40:34-38. In the book of Matthew, we saw where God gave His vineyard to another people. These people became His new covenant people. To find out who these new covenant people are, just look for His tabernacle, because the tabernacle and God's covenant people go together. And we find God's tabernacle in the landscape of America. It's all about hide and seek. Now that we know we co-exist with Israel as God's covenant people, you can better understand my 9/11 paper."

"With God, the rules are the same for his covenant people, old or new. You do right by God, you get blessings; you do wrong, you get punishment. When the old covenant people (Israel) did wrong and needed to be punished, God raised up the king of Babylon. Likewise, when the new covenant people (America) needed to be punished, God raised up Osama bin Laden and Al-Qaeda (from Babylon). This is God's signature on 9/11. History has repeated itself. Then add in the tabernacle furniture being designed into the landscape of our country, and how this proves we co-exist as 'all of Israel,' and what Daniel 9:11 says about 'all of Israel.' This attack on America gives credit to my *Ahab* paper because it shows a sentence was carried out against this nation. And, being God still carries out sentences against nations, then He still carries out sentences against individuals (Psalms 149:6-9)."

"How can anyone say the Bible is just a book written by man to control man? How can anyone make that statement after reading all the information in this study? I once felt this way, 'If I can't see it, I don't believe it.' But like Elisha's servant, my eyes have been opened (2Kings 6:15-17) and I will never return to my foolish ways. My hope now is that your eyes will be opened and you can see these Bible studies for what they are. I want to thank my brother in Christ, Jim Ridings, the author of this book, for having the courage to put in his book the biblical aspect behind the kidnapping and murder of Stephen Small. My two Bible studies, *The Two Olive Trees-9/11* and my *Ahab* paper are subject matters best kept not said. What I mean by this is: 9/11 killed 3,000 Americans, and my *Ahab* paper appears to show our loving Father still carries out sentences. Not your typical Sunday sermon."

"God is the God of love, but what kind of loving father doesn't punish his children? And as children of God, we must give an account, rich or poor, and nothing is hidden from His sight, Hebrews 4:12-13."

"The contents of these two Bible studies have been seen nowhere else but this book. They are original, and I've kept them to myself until now."

"The main subject in my *Tabernacle* paper, 'the furniture and the landscape of our country,' is not mine. It came from an unknown source. I took this teaching and built on it to make my *Tabernacle* paper. The bulk of my biblical knowledge comes from my 17 years on Death Row, when you think the state is gonna take your life. You don't just read the Bible, you study it. And to my fellow Death Row brother William Bracy, who went to be with the Lord, I say thank you, it was you who taught me how to study the Bible, how to search things out, how to connect the dots. And much love to Jack, Arliss, Chuck, Richard and Marre for all the love and support you've given me over the years. God will have a special place at His table for all of you in His kingdom. And finally, to my uncle Leonard I say thumbs up, I hope you get your family reunion."

"One final question that gave birth to this Bible study: Should the name of Danny Edwards be added to the list of names (King of Babylon, Osama bin Laden, etc.) whose hearts were moved to carry out a sentence written against them?"

"With this in mind, Hebrews 13:3, comes to light: Remember those who are in prison as though you are their fellow prisoner. Maybe there should be many names added to this list. Something to ponder."

"*Postscript:* Many people who have just read this Bible study will be saying that Danny Edwards is crazy for thinking that he was used by God and His saints to carry out a sentence against the Small family, especially for something that Stephen Small's great-grandfather did in the 1920s. To my defense, these are God's words, not mine, 'I will punish the children and their children for the sins of the father to the third and fourth generations.' You want to talk about crazy. Here's a whole bunch of crazy. In 1921, when Len Small became governor, he placed his hand on the Bible and swore an oath to God, and this was after he had already stole two million dollars as state treasurer. Then, while as governor, let's not forget his crazy association with Al Capone. Then his crazy son in 1948 oversaw the building of Governor Small Memorial Park and museum, a place to honor his crazy father. Here's more crazy. The taxpayers of Kankakee County in 1948 paid for the construction of this place of honor. What's even more crazy, the taxpayers of Kankakee County today continue to pay taxes for its upkeep. But what's epic crazy about all of this is that Nancy Rish has been in prison for 27 years, and

207

counting, for something that I did that she had no knowledge of. To all of those who have read this book about her innocence and choose to do nothing about it, add your name to the list of crazy associated with the kidnapping and murder of Stephen Small."

There will be some who agree with Danny Edwards' "biblical" citations about the Smalls, while others will think it's a distortion of scripture, and others will think it's just plain crazy. Nevertheless, that does not have any bearing on his redemption or salvation. Many people misinterpret scripture, and many of them are TV preachers who make millions of dollars doing it. Heaven would be a lonely place if it holds only those who accurately interpret scripture one hundred per cent of the time.

I did discuss his points with him and I offered my opinions. Here they are, briefly:

Len Small was a corrupt politician. But he was far from being the worst human being to hold power. If there is punishment for Len Small, or for anyone, it will come in the next life from a far greater judge. I do not think it is reasonable to believe that God directed a great-grandson to be buried alive for the governor's sins, fifty years after the governor's death. Exodus 20:5 says God "punishes the children for the sins of the father to the third and fourth generation." But Ezekiel 18:18-20 says, "The son will not share the guilt of the father." Is Danny Edwards being punished for what he did, or for what his grandfather did?

People get killed, kids get cancer; it isn't a punishment, not for anything they did or for anything their grandfathers did. Everything happens for a reason, even terrible things. We may not understand why, right now, but we eventually will. We don't have to understand now; we walk by faith, not by sight.

God does know what people will do, but He does not interfere every time a person decides to commit a bad act. He gave us free will, and our actions are our own.

God is love, God is good. While He can lead a person to do good works, He does not force people to do so, and He does not direct a person to commit an evil act.

Danny Edwards' theory on the Smalls is an attempt to make sense of what happened and why it happened. He believes it is an explanation, not an excuse. But it still is amounts to a way out for Danny Edwards. He believes the blame, or at least some of it, rests on a higher power. If this was a reasonable belief, then every horrible act committed by humans could be justified as being directed by God.

God often uses people to do His work. But so does the Devil.

Chapter 14

Filling In Some Details: Danny Edwards Talks

"If anyone else had been involved, there would be no need to put Stephen Small in a box. We would have put him in a hotel room and sat with him. I was working alone."
Danny Edwards, September 25, 2013

There is a lot about this case that has not been known until now.

Danny Edwards said his lawyers would not let him talk because of his appeals. It was only in 2005 that he dropped his appeals. Even so, he had no desire to talk, and he never sought out anyone to talk about this.

Danny Edwards knows he will never get out of prison. As a born-again Christian, he said he is at peace with his relationship with God and with the punishment he knows he deserves.

Before we met in prison for the interviews for this book in August, September and December 2013, and April 2014, we corresponded. Danny Edwards promised to answer all my questions. He did, without hesitation or evasiveness. He has a chronic heart condition and he knows he could die at any time. That does not worry him.

Danny Edwards didn't volunteer to talk to me. He was not forced to talk to me. I contacted him and he agreed to see me only after much persuasion. He is not seeking fame or attention. He wouldn't be talking about it at all if I had not approached him. He answered the questions I asked and he added details where needed.

Danny Edwards has nothing to gain and nothing to lose by telling what he knows. He said his Christian belief is what allows him to confess the truth of what happened and his sorrow for causing so much pain.

There are those who will scoff at him for saying that.

Christian doctrine believes in forgiveness and redemption, no matter how great the sin, if the sinner is repentant. That is not always easy to accept.

I didn't talk to a 30-year-old punk on cocaine who had no morals or conscience. I talked to a 56-year-old man in poor health who has gone through a spiritual conversion and who says he is a new man in Christ.

After spending several days in prison talking to Danny Edwards about the kidnapping, about his life, about the Bible and his beliefs, about his own mortality and what lies ahead, and continuing it through a long correspondence, I believe he told me the truth that he could never tell before. I believe he is sincere in his faith, sincere in his remorse and sincere with the peace he says he has found with the Lord.

And there are those who will scoff at me for writing that.

How did you get the idea for the kidnapping?
"I got the idea for the kidnapping shortly after my drug bust. I was dealing drugs and I became addicted to money because I was making so much. I did the kidnapping because I didn't have money after the drug bust."

"I did it purely for the money. Ficaro said it best, 'Stephen Small had it and I wanted it.'"

He explained it further in a later interview.

"Ever since I can remember, I've had this big thing about money. In the third grade, my mom would drop me off at school. We had a Buick Electra and an old Ford Fairlaine. Sometimes my dad would take the Buick Electra and mom would take me in the old car. I hated being dropped off in that old car. The kidnapping was about money. Dealing dope was about money, so I could have nice things, a big car, nice clothes."

"It took the love of money to do what I did. Now what motivates me and moves my heart is when the Lord gives me a nugget and I build on it in writing my *Something To Ponder* Bible studies."

Why Stephen Small?
"He was an easy target. I knew he had Yesteryear. I knew a phone call saying Yesteryear was burglarized would bring him out."

"He stood out like a red apple on a green apple tree."

Did you consider any other target?
"I looked at Jim Hunt (a wealthy local businessman), but he had too much security around him all the time."

In a subsequent interview, I asked him about this again and Danny said, "I knew he (Hunt) had a lot of money and a big mansion. But I didn't consider him, not really. It was Stephen Small the whole time."

You made the phone call that got Stephen Small out of his house?
"Yes. I made the call to Small's house. I said, 'This is the Kankakee Police Department. Your business at the former Yesteryear has been broken into. Two officers are on the scene. There are things they took that are in their van. You need to come over to identify them.' He said. 'OK, I'll be right there.'"

Why did you bury Stephen Small? How did you get that idea?
"It was supposed to be a holding place for the man."

"Nancy had nothing to do with it, so I couldn't bring him back to the

210

house. And I couldn't sit in a hotel room with him for three days. I was restricted by what I could do. I was limited by what I could do."

He could not remember why burial was the choice that came to mind, except that it would hold his victim without need of a guard.

Was anyone else involved in the kidnapping?
"If anyone else had been involved, there would be no need to put Stephen Small in a box. We would have put him in a hotel room and sat with him. I was working alone."

"It was a Danny operation and no one else was involved."

What about the black cowboys, Kent Allain and the others?
"There were no black cowboys. Kent was not involved. I was just putting the blame on somebody else, to try to get out of a tough situation. It's human nature."

"Kent owed me money for drugs. He said, screw you, I ain't gonna pay. Naming him was payback."

Was Mitch Levitt involved? Did he threaten you or your family?
"No."

What about Tracy Storm?
"Tracy Storm had nothing to do with it. We were drinking the day before. We were so drunk we left a $100 tip. The last time I saw him was when were drinking together that Sunday. Tracy's only mistake was crossing a police tape line to get my motorcycle."

Was Nancy Rish involved, or did she know anything about it at all?
"No."

"Her behavior at that time was normal. She made a hair appointment, she made an appointment to get the dog groomed, she helped a friend put up wallpaper. My behavior was erratic."

"It was hard because I was trying to do two things at the same time. I was trying to plan a kidnapping, and I was trying to keep it from her."

"It would have been a lot easier if she was part of it and was helping me."

You and Nancy lived together. Why didn't you tell her what you were planning?
"Because she wouldn't have gone along with it."

Is it possible that you could build a wooden box without Nancy knowing what you really intended it for? She believed you when you said it was for your brother.
"Of course. I lied to her."

Didn't you know the air pipe was insufficient?
"I didn't know. It was a lack of education. I didn't know people breathed out poison (carbon dioxide). Stephen Small also didn't know it, or he'd never have gotten in the box."

The pipe from the box came up and then went 26 feet sideways underground before coming up. Why?
"I don't know why I did that." (He explained here, as he did with a few other questions, that pot smoking impaired his judgment).

That was a big box. How did you get the box to Pembroke?
"I just picked it up, end over end, walked it along, scooted it along. Over the weekend, I dug the hole. I scooted it to the hole. It was on its side on the edge of the hole and I just kicked it in."
Nancy Rish would not have been able to help lift one end?
"She would be more concerned that she might break a fingernail."
Danny added more in another interview.
"I rolled it till I got to the hole and I flipped it in. People say one man can't do that. Don't tell me one man can't do it, I did it."
(*Note:* Michael Ficaro was able to move that big box by himself, as he dragged it across the courtroom floor with one hand, in a dramatic performance for the jury. Ficaro even suggested to the jury that Nancy Rish could have dragged the box all by herself. Not true. But Ficaro did prove that one man could move that box.)

What about the testimony of the neighbor who said she saw you and Nancy driving down the alley behind Stephen Small's house eight to ten times that summer?
"We never cruised the area. There was no need to cruise the alley. My childhood home was at the corner of Nelson and Eagle. Cobb Park is where I grew up. Why would I have to cruise the area? I knew it like the back of my hand." As for Nancy driving the van the morning of the kidnapping, he said, "Nancy never drove the van. She hated driving it." It was big and clumsy, he said, and she had her own car.
"The worst piece of evidence against Nancy was Karen Thacker. In her statement to the police, she recalled a day when she was back in her alley and she saw a white van with a blonde female in the passenger seat. When she looked at the woman, she had a startled look on her face. She also said the van was parked behind the Small home like we were casing the place. She said *every time she saw the van after that,* she was suspicious. But in her trial testimony, she changed her story. She recalled this day, but said *this was the last time she saw the van.* Ficaro wanted to make it appear like Thacker made us and scared us off."

212

Why did you have Nancy in the car when you made the ransom calls?

"We picked up the dog from the groomer on Heiland Road. I made the 5 p.m. call on the way back after that, from the Citgo station. It was the 'do you have the money' call. Nancy sat in the car."

"Nancy was in the car. I'm standing at a pay phone. She can't hear me."

"Why did I have her along? I just didn't think. You don't think ahead like that."

Why didn't you testify at Nancy's trial?

"My lawyers wouldn't let me because of my appeals."

Danny could not testify to Nancy's innocence without admitting his own guilt. It would be the only way he could know she was innocent. He wasn't about to admit that while his case was being appealed.

And, he said, "Nancy's lawyers didn't subpoena me."

What was the purpose of the foul rant against Jean Alice Small?

"The purpose was to tell her that I knew the cops were there, that I knew the phone was tapped, and to get the cops out of there if they wanted to see Stephen Small again."

How did you know Nancy Small's phone was tapped when you called Jean Alice?

"Nancy Small was trying to keep me on the line, so I figured it was because they were trying to get a trace."

What did you tell Nancy Rish about taking the bicycle on the night you made a ransom call?

"The night of the ransom call, I told Nancy that we were gonna take her bike to Jack's to get fixed. On our way to Jack's, as we were going through Aroma Park, we pulled into the old Sunoco gas station. I told Nancy I was gonna call Jack to make sure he was home, but I did not call Jack because the bicycle story I told her was a lie. At this time and place, I called the Small home for the ransom drop. During the call, I saw an undercover police car drive by. I hung up the phone. I got back in the car and told Nancy Jack wasn't home."

"If things would have went according to my plans, when she would have dropped me off at Jack's on Route One, I would have told her to go home. I would have rode the bicycle to the ransom drop or to Pier 6 in Aroma Park and called Nancy at home to pick me up."

Nancy said you were expecting Mitch to give you a lot of money.
"I told Nancy I was getting a lot of money from Mitch to justify all of the ransom money I believed I would soon have."

Much was made about the tie straps you bought at Englewood Electric and the water bottle in the box. Both items went a long way toward convicting Nancy Rish, even though neither one was entered at trial as an exhibit. What about them?
"The tie wraps had nothing to do with the case, and the water in the jug came from Nancy's kitchen."
I asked if he bought the tie straps with the intent of using them, and if he ever bought bottled water.
"The tie wraps were not used, had nothing to do with anything. I used the tie wraps to secure the TV cable to a 2x4. I did not buy distilled water prior to the kidnapping."

If your cash and cocaine were seized in January, what did you live on until August?
"I was living on drug money that was owed to me, which got me through the summer. Come August, that money dried up, so I did what I thought was time to do."
(*Note:* The police files show that in January, Edwards was required, as a part of his plea bargain, to give the police a list of names of drug customers and the amount they owed, which was considerable. Danny Edwards was very efficient at collecting debts).

Police interviewed Benjamin Rish two days after Mr. Small's body was recovered. He told the police he helped you count $11,000 on the living room couch in August. The cash was in twenties and fifties. Benjamin told police, "Danny said the money was from friends he did favors for, and he said don't tell anyone." Benjamin did tell his grandmother Tommie Rish and she repeated it to the police when she was interviewed. What about that?
"Benjamin and I never counted out any money on the couch or anywhere else. The bank took my 1986 Pontiac Fiero GT, a car that I loved, in August because I was behind in my payments. Now, if I had $11,000, why would I let this happen? It's the wild imagination of a nine year old boy."
(*Note:* No such amount of cash was found in Danny Edwards' possession after his arrest in September).

If there is one aspect to this case that most people find the hardest to believe, it is the idea that Danny Edwards acted alone. They say the box was too heavy for him to move alone, but that is not true. The chapter in this book on "Black Cowboys and Rumors" addresses the theories about co-

conspirators, drug kingpins from Chicago, and more. Danny Edwards unequivocally said he acted alone.

Here is more on that, in his own words.

"The night I took the police to where the burial site was, I made up a story about black cowboys. This story about black cowboys grew from that," he wrote in a letter to me dated February 24, 2014.

"Jim, my brother in Christ, you've gotten to know me well over the last six months, and I'm a deeply seeded Christian man, and in the name of my Lord and Savior Jesus Christ, I ACTED ALONE. NO Tracy Storm, NO black cowboys, NO people up north. JUST ME. This I swear to you in the name of Jesus."

"From the very beginning of our meetings, I told you I would be very truthful, and it's hard for me to admit that I kidnapped a man and buried him alive. I wish there were others involved to help me share my shame and guilt, but there is not. I told you from the very beginning, if I wanted to, I could tell you a big lie about other people being involved and get you to believe it. You told me you doubted that because you're not easily persuaded."

"This black cowboy thing is nuts. Think about it. Stephen Small was buried six feet in the ground with a thousand pounds of sand on top of him. He wasn't going anywhere. What would black cowboys have to guard the site from, termites? And they helped me pick out the burial site? I know that area like the back of my hand. We rode dirt bikes out there for years. Trust me, I needed no help to pick out the burial site."

"I have told you the God almighty truth. I acted alone, I did this! And the only reprisal I fear would be from God because I took His name and then lied to you. This would never happen!"

He added, "Anything contrary to 'JUST ME' is rumorville. The reason he was put in a box and not a tent, if black cowboys were guarding the site, is because I acted alone. If anyone else would have been involved, we would have gotten a hotel room or something. His being put in that box proves I acted alone. Guarding a man in a tent would be just as easy as guarding a man in a box in the ground. No black cowboys guarding the site."

I believe Danny Edwards. He acted alone. No black cowboys, no Tracy Storm, no Kent Allain, no Mitch Levitt, and no Nancy Rish.

And here is something else to consider: remember the letter he had Brenda Berry send to him in the Kankakee jail, and the letter he had Berry send to Mrs. Small? Both letters had a Chicago postmark and both letters had one purpose -- to convince the authorities there were others behind the kidnapping. If there really were drug kingpins or others involved, Danny Edwards would not have needed to have those letters sent.

Edwards took me through the night of the kidnapping, step by step.

"I called and said I was with the Kankakee police, and Yesteryear

215

was burglarized. Two people were being held and he needed to come to identify the stuff they put in the van. He said all right and he came out."

Edwards had a gun, the .357 Magnum he stole from Jeff Drury.

"He came out of the house, into the garage. I waited for the garage door, and for his car to back out. I got in the car in the passenger side. I pointed the gun at him. He said, who are you, what is this, what is going on? I told him to drive. He said, where? I said toward Aroma Park. He said, what is this all about? I said there are people out there who want to see you. He asked, who are these people? I said, you'll find out when we get there. I told him where to drive. Not much else was said."

"On the road that links Waldron Road and Lowe Road, I think it is Laketown Road, I had him stop the car near the railroad tracks. I put him in the trunk. He didn't say anything. I drove the rest of the way. When we got to the site, I handcuffed him. His car was parked about 50 feet away."

"He asked, what's going on, what are we doing out here? That's when I told him, you've been kidnapped."

Danny said he wrote the script that Stephen Small read into the tape recorder. Mr. Small had difficulty because he didn't have his reading glasses. "I had to prompt him. You could hear my voice in the background on the tape. He was kneeling when he read it."

What about that reference to Joe Yurgine? Did you notice that?

"I didn't catch his reference to Yurgine."

"The light was on in the box, and candy and a water bottle were in there. He remarked these were some of his favorite candy bars."

"He asked me how long he was going to be in there. I said it depends on how long it takes your family to get the money."

"He asked me, is this safe? I said, you're not going to be in there that long. You're going to be out tomorrow. I told him you'll be out of here within 24 hours. I get my money and you're gone."

Did he believe you when you said it was safe?

"He must have thought it was safe or he wouldn't have gotten in it."

Was he frightened?

"Wouldn't you if someone was pointing a .357 at you?"

Did you use force or did Stephen Small get in the box willingly?

"Well, it's not willingly when someone is pointing a gun at you."

Did he get in without a struggle?

"Yes. Then I put the lid on it and shoveled sand over it and waited for Nancy to pick me up where I told her to. I didn't wait long."

The prosecutors claimed Danny Edwards buried Stephen Small and left him to die and never had any intention of digging him up.

Danny Edwards said this is not true. The candy, the water, the light, the air pipe were put there to keep Stephen Small alive. He said he never intended for Mr. Small to die.

The prosecutors said Edwards never went back to check and see if his victim was alive.

Also not true. Danny Edwards said he did go out to the grave site to check on Stephen Small.

The police do not know this. They did not know it at the time and they will not know it until they read this book. Edwards said I am the only one he told about this.

It was on Thursday, the day he drove into Quail Hollow subdivision off Armour Road and managed to lose his FBI tail. That part is in the official police files. It was the only time during the surveillance that they lost Edwards. He was gone for nearly 90 minutes before he returned home.

Where was he during that time?

"I lost them and I drove straight out there to check on him. I went directly there. I called into the pipe, 'Mr. Small! Mr. Small!' There was no response. I knew he was dead."

Edwards said in 2013, "I was going to let him out. I was going to dig him out. I was going to tell him to wait a minute before getting out of the box so I could leave, then he could get up and get in his car."

"It was all about money. I'm not a murderer. Was I a rotten son of a bitch? Sure. But that's a long way from being a murderer. I never intended for him to die."

Edwards returned home from checking on the grave site that morning and waited to see what would happen next.

He said when Stephen Small's car was spotted, he knew it wouldn't be long before they found the grave a few feet away. That's when he agreed to take police to the grave site, in a phony attempt to convince them he was trying to save Mr. Small's life in time.

And it was an attempt to make a deal for himself.

"I'm sitting in the drunk tank and I hear on the police radio that the car has been located. I started calling, asking for my attorney. I knew it was a matter of time before they found the grave. I thought I could cut myself a deal. Even though I knew he was dead."

The policemen at the grave site heard Danny Edwards cry out, "Oh no, oh no, he can't be dead." They said a minute later, Edwards was acting normal. This caused the police to think Edwards was faking his emotion.

The police were right.

"When they opened the box, Stephen Small was laying there on his side, with his coat rolled up under his head," Edwards said. "He looked like he was sleeping."

There is one other piece of information that has not been revealed until now. Danny Edwards may have gone to the grave site one other time.

It was at 4 a.m., on Thursday morning, September 3. The police had been staking out Edwards' house. But when the lights went out early Thursday morning, the police assumed Danny was asleep in bed for the night. They terminated surveillance for the night and they went home.

Danny took the advantage and left the house, unmolested by police.

Randy Irps, who was Edward's best friend in high school, was driving a bread truck for Colonial Bakeries. He started his day at 4:15 a.m., at Blue's Café in Kankakee. Sometime after 4:30 a.m., he was on his way to in Aroma Park. He made that run on Mondays, Thursdays and Saturdays.

"It was Thursday morning (September 3) and I was in Aroma Park between 4:30 and 5 a.m. It was still dark. I saw Danny's white van on Birchwood Drive heading east, out of Aroma Park. I know his van. It had a picture of a horse with a naked lady on the back wheel cover. I helped him remodel the inside of that van. I know that van."

Randy went home that day and told his wife Beth, because it was strange to see Danny's van in that remote area at that odd time. The news of the kidnapping was not known then. The story about the crime didn't break until Saturday. The news of the kidnapping and Danny's arrest seared the van sighting into Randy's and Beth's minds for good.

The police do not know this. Randy said he never mentioned it to the police because they didn't ask him about it.

After Randy told me this, I went back to Pontiac to talk to Danny. He said he does not doubt Randy, but he has no recollection about driving his van to Aroma Park in those early hours before sunrise on that day.

Why didn't you dig up Mr. Small when you knew it was over?
"I went out there. I was going to let him go. It was over with. This was all about money. There was no money at that point. It was over. Let the man go. I went out and yelled in the pipe. There was no response."

That was Thursday. Why didn't you dig him up before then?
"I couldn't go and dig him up because I was being watched."

What were you thinking?
"Anybody who kidnaps and buries someone alive isn't thinking straight."

So why didn't you dig him up Thursday when you went there without being followed?
"I couldn't dig him up. What would be the point? I knew they would find the car."

So why didn't you move the car from the grave site?
"It didn't occur to me to move the car."

What gave you the idea the pipe would provide 48 hours of air?
"It was just a number I made up, to make them think he was still alive, to give them a time frame to act."

You told the police someone forced you to do this. You also told Nancy Rish that someone was forcing you to do something, although you didn't tell her what it was. Why did you tell her this, privately and before any act was done?
"I told Nancy a story because she was questioning me about why I was acting strange. I guess I said it in case something did go wrong, she could say it to support my story of compulsion."
So she could honestly say it because that is what she thought?
"Yes."

You knew it was over for you when the car was found.
"When I heard the car was found, I knew the grave would be found eventually. They couldn't find (Gus) Regas (his lawyer), so I told them let's go, and I took them out there. As we were leaving, I saw Nancy (in a holding cell) and I said, 'Baby, I'm sorry I got you involved.'"
"Regas stopped being attorney because my family wasn't going to retain him. They weren't going to spend $150,000 or so defending me. My family threw me to the wolves. (Judge) Michela appointed (Sheldon) Reagan. He was the defense lawyer the state wanted me to have."

In the extortion letter you had someone send to Nancy Small while you were in the Kankakee County jail, you mention that the Smalls still owed a "blood debt" that must be paid. Where did "blood debt" come from?
He said his father mentioned years ago that Governor Small was corrupt and the family fortune was built on stolen money. Danny also said he got a strange letter after his arrest.
"I got a letter in the county jail from someone who praised me for what I did because he said the Small family cost him everything he had years ago. It said, 'anything you need, let me know.' It was signed. I forget the name. Sheldon Reagan took it. Sheldon said it sounded like a set up. It was this letter that gave me the idea for the blood debt."
Reagan declined to comment on this to me, citing attorney-client privilege.

What about writing that the debt will be settled in Illinois or Arizona? Did you know then that Stephen's brother Leslie lived in Arizona?
"Yes, I knew Stephen's brother lived in Arizona."
When the police searched Edwards' house on the day of the arrest, they found a 1986 Kankakee telephone directory, and the name "Small" at

the top of the page was circled. Edwards told the cops that they circled the name. A quarter of a century later, Edwards still claims the cops did that to plant evidence, which is funny to him because they didn't need to do this. They already had more than they needed.

More than 25 years after being convicted of a crime she did not commit, Nancy Rish is still in the dark about some of what really happened.

Danny Edwards was frantic that week because he was planning and carrying out a kidnapping, and he was working to hide it from Nancy.

Danny was leaving the house on another strange errand on the evening of Wednesday, September 2. It was to make a ransom call, but Nancy didn't know that.

His strange behavior was even more bizarre that week, and Nancy suspected he was sneaking out to see other women. She didn't know where he was going, but she said she asked to go with him. Danny said she had been asking to have her bicycle repaired, so he used that as an excuse. He put the bike in the trunk of her car. They drove out to see a man named Jack in a rural area near Aroma Park and St. Anne.

Danny stopped to make a ransom call along the way as Nancy sat in the car. She later realized that taking the bicycle was just a ruse, since she asked to go along.

That wasn't the entire story, Danny said in a 2013 prison interview.

Danny said he insisted that Nancy come with him. He initially told her he was going to use her bicycle, then he told her he was going to take her bicycle to be fixed.

"I told her she was going with me. She had been after me to get her bike fixed. I put the bike in the trunk. I needed to make the call to tell them to make the money drop."

"I made the call and gave them directions to put the money on the railroad tracks on Wichert Road. I was going to have Nancy take me to Jack's, have her leave me and the bike there, and send Nancy home. I would ride the bike from Jack's, pick up the money, bury it, and then ride the bike home. I was able to ride the bike. The gears slipped, but I could ride it."

That was his original intention. And that was the story he was going to tell Nancy when they got to Jack's place.

However, that ransom call went wrong. Danny never told her that story because he changed his mind about leaving the bike. He had seen the cops staking out Aroma Park and he knew they had seen him.

Instead of having Nancy leave him and the bicycle at Jack's, he had her drive him to the Marathon station where he made the phone call telling Mrs. Small that he was calling it off.

Nancy Rish never knew those details.

I asked: How were you going to explain to Nancy why she was leaving you and the bike at Jack's at midnight, in the middle of nowhere, and why she was driving home alone?

Danny said he didn't have an explanation prepared, and he didn't need one, because his whole plan was called off when he saw all those cops in Aroma Park.

Clear and logical, his thinking was not.

"If the ransom drop would have taken place, then I would of had Nancy drop me off at Jack's with the bike, but it never got that far. I only told her what she needed to know when she needed to know it. When I told her Jack wasn't home, the bicycle lie was over. That's all she knew."

The day before the kidnapping, Danny went to the site by himself. It was one of those times he left the house with giving Nancy any explanation.

"Over the weekend, I put the box in the ground and covered it. Tuesday, I went out and uncovered the box."

He said he covered the box so it wouldn't be seen if anyone happened to come near it, and he uncovered it just before he needed it.

On Wednesday afternoon, he had Nancy drop him off near the horse ranch and told her to go to her sister Lori's house for an hour and then pick him up. No one knew what he was doing during that time. Some people speculated he was meeting with the black cowboys there.

No, Danny said. He was looking for the bolt cutters.

"I used the bolt cutters to cut the link in the handcuffs, and then I tossed it. I was worried it would be found, so I went to look for it. I didn't want to take my van because it was a very noticeable van. I customized it. I didn't want anyone to see it out there. I couldn't use my motorcycle because the bolt cutters were too long (to transport on the motorcycle)."

The bolt cutters were about three feet long and heavy. That is why he had Nancy drive him in her car and then leave the area.

No one knew that, especially Nancy.

Danny Edwards told Nancy Rish that someone was forcing him to do something, and was threatening his family. After his arrest, he told the police it was Mitch Levitt because, he said, it was Levitt's money and cocaine that was seized when police raided his house on Sand Bar Road. That was untrue, and it makes no sense. What would Edwards be doing with Levitt's money or coke? Every sale was a completed transaction. They exchanged money for cocaine. The cocaine in Edwards' house was purchased from Levitt, the money in the house was the profit Edwards made from its sales.

Today, Edwards says it was a lie. Levitt had nothing to do with it.

Mitch Levitt told me he had nothing to do with Edwards, except for selling him cocaine a few times. He said he never threatened Edwards or his family. He said it was not his money that was seized in the drug raid at Edwards' house in 1987. He said Edwards did not owe him money.

But to this day, Nancy Rish still believes the story Danny Edwards told her about Mitch Levitt threatening the Edwards family. She still believes it means others were involved. She still thinks Tracy Storm was the blond seen with Edwards in the van. She still believes the lies she was told in 1987, because she was never told the true story.

Edwards told me he moved out of the house on Sand Bar Road in Aroma Park because he lost his money in the drug raid and he couldn't afford that house and the townhouse in Bourbonnais. The townhouse had a lease in Edwards' name, and the house in Aroma Park did not. Simple as that. The story he told Nancy, that he couldn't live in the Aroma Park house because he was afraid of Mitch, was a lie to get her to believe why he had to move in with her. But Nancy didn't know any of that.

It is strange, but after getting inside details from Danny Edwards in 2013 and 2014, details he never previously revealed to anyone, I thought I knew more about the kidnapping and murder than did the woman who was convicted of it.

There is more information to add to the record involving the police report about the ransom call and the attempted set up of Mitch Levitt.

After police traced the 5:03 p.m. ransom call to a pay phone in Aroma Park, Danny Edwards, who didn't seem to think out his plot to grab a million dollars, went back to the same place that night to make his next ransom call. The FBI was waiting for him.

Sgt. William Willis had his own view of this incident, in an account he provided in May 1990 for the TV show, *Top Cops.*

Willis believed Edwards did not see all the police on surveillance in Aroma Park that night. Willis believed it was local teenagers who spooked Edwards into his state of panic. Two local teens pulled their car across the street from the pay phone where Edwards was making his ransom call at 11:28 p.m. The teens parked there in the dark to drink a six-pack of beer. Another car pulled beside it, and the youths shared the six-pack.

Willis believed that Edwards thought these kids were cops.

Willis said Edwards never noticed all the cops all around him in this tiny rural village of 690 people, but he saw these kids and he panicked.

"These kids had no idea there were federal, state and local officers all over the place," Willis said. "They're drinking beer. And that goofy f...ing Edwards thinks it's the cops. They spooked Edwards. They about blew the whole deal for us."

The cops also were perplexed. They thought the teens might be part of the gang, acting as lookouts for Edwards while he made his calls.

"We're assuming the other kids could be lookouts," Willis said. "The cops think it's the bad guys. Edwards thinks it's the cops."

However, Edwards said Willis is wrong. In 2013, Edwards said he never noticed any teenagers in parked cars. But he did see all those cops.

"It was ridiculous there could be so many cops in that small town and I wouldn't see them," he said.

"When I was at the pay phone, I saw one car go by with two guys in it. They were looking at me. Come on, in Aroma Park, late at night, nobody should be driving around."

"That's when I knew it was over."

As Danny and Nancy drove from Aroma Park, Danny was starting to panic. "We left, and I kept thinking, what should I do? I told Nancy to drive to K-Mart. That's was the phone call where I called it off."

Nancy Rish told police in her initial questioning that Danny saw something that night that threw him into a panic. It was cops, not kids, Edwards told me.

Danny Edwards was facing up to 30 years in prison after his arrest on drug charges in early 1987. The police promised probation to Danny if he would set up a higher echelon drug seller. But the meeting with Mitch Levitt did not go as planned. Levitt did not sell any cocaine to Edwards that day.

The police believed Edwards tipped off Levitt.

Edwards said he did not tip Levitt. He said the cops blew the deal.

"The police wanted me to set up Mitch. Normally, I would have the money in my car. We'd meet at a restaurant and then he'd leave and take my car. When he came back, the money would be gone and the dope would be there. That's how he did business."

"If he sees someone coming with me, he knows it's a set up. I told them having a cop come with me wouldn't work. They wouldn't listen. They said drug dealers are greedy. It would be too much money to pass up. It was a $50,000 buy. But I was making $50,000 buys every month."

Levitt had a different view of that day. In interviews in 2013 for this book, he said he took one look at Danny Edwards and knew it was a set up.

"I looked at his nose, and I saw a cut on his nose, and something inside me got the heebie jeebies, and I knew he was trying to set me up."

Levitt said he was suspicious before they met because Edwards had been gone for awhile and he was out of phone contact. Edwards gave Levitt a not very believable story about being out of state on family matters.

"I knew it was a set up as soon as I saw him. As soon as I saw him, I saw he had a horizontal scratch across his nose. I thought he had been busted and roughed up by the cops. It was instantly knowing, an instinct."

Ernie Richardson was sitting in a car outside the lounge, waiting for the deal to be made. He did not go inside. "Danny was by himself. I wouldn't have even talked to him if he was with someone else," Levitt said.

Danny Edwards today said he did not pay the guards at the county jail to bring in drugs, but he did pay to have them bring in food.

"The only pot that came in was from a hole in the window, where inmates would throw out a string. I paid the guard to bring in food. If you had jail food, you'd know why."

Edwards said he doesn't remember saying, "It sure would be nice to be able to afford something like that," after seeing Stephen Small drive away from the boat store in his red Ferrari Testarossa.

"I saw Stephen Small only once. It was at the boat store. I said, 'That's a sharp car,' and he said, 'Thank you.'"

Edwards said he once worked for Kankakee Enterprise, where he helped install burglar alarms. But he said he never tampered with the alarm at Yesteryear/Bradley House.

"When they took me to Bourbonnais (police station), they brought in Joe Yurgine," Edwards said. "Joe knew me because I took him to the airport several times. He was best friends with Stephen Small. He said, 'Let's have a heart to heart talk. Danny, did you do this? We want Steve back.' I said I had nothing to do with this. That was the end of our conversation."

Edwards' own lawyer, Gus Regas, came to the county jail the next day. By this time, Edwards already had led the police to Small's body. "I was giving a statement and Regas stopped me."

Despite a mountain of evidence -- fingerprints, sand on his boots, tape recordings of ransom calls, being seen making a ransom call, and taking the police directly to where the body was buried -- Danny Edwards still believes he could have been acquitted.

And while he said the prosecutors lied in court, Edwards wanted his lawyers to lie as well, with a "compulsion defense. Compulsion is not a defense for murder. But the compulsion defense would say I was forced to do the kidnapping, so I would have been found not guilty of kidnapping because of compulsion. And if I was not guilty of kidnapping, then I would be not guilty of murder."

What about producing the people you said forced you to do it?

"It's not my attorney's job to go out and arrest people. Mitch would have hired a high powered attorney. The arrest was bogus. The search warrant would have been thrown out. Everything they got, I gave them. It all resulted from the search warrant. It's called fruits from a poisoned tree. It all would be thrown out."

Edwards said Levitt's attorney would have quashed the search warrant, and that, he said, is why prosecutors refused to bring Levitt into it.

"If they went after Levitt, they might have lost everything (the search warrant). There was no way Reagan was going to present a compulsion defense. Michela ruled against it because he said there was no evidence. There was no way they were going to let me out. At the federal level, they rule only on it if it's constitutional. They agreed it was just good police work.

That's how much reach the Small family had, how much influence they have."

That is Danny Edwards' theory.

Edwards said the prosecutors lied when they told the jury he had sex with Nancy Rish in the county jail. "The police let me down there to talk to her once or twice, but they never let me in the cell."

He said the jurors weren't able to sort out as truth what the opposing lawyers said. "This is why we need professional juries. They should be retired judges and lawyers who know how to listen to the facts. Now they get twelve of the most naive, stupidest people to be on a jury, twelve naive housewives who stay home and watch Oprah. This is why lawyers don't want black people on a jury. They know how the system can be misused. White people trust the system. Black people don't."

"When someone is arrested and accused of murder, they should be given sodium pentothal (truth serum). You can't lie. They should be asked one question, did you murder Joe Smith? If they say no, then drop the charges and give him $20,000."

He agreed when I mentioned that this could only be done with the person's consent, and guilty people would not do it.

Edwards had harsher words for his defense lawyer than he had for the man who put him on Death Row. "Sheldon Reagan gave the defense they wanted him to give. He wanted his judge's job. If Sheldon Reagan had been on my side or if I hired a lawyer who fought for me, I would have got things on discovery that I didn't have until later on appeal."

"Sheldon was there to make sure I got convicted and that I didn't put up any kind of a fight. I could have used Mitch to file a compulsion."

Judges in the appeals courts did not agree with Edwards' legal reasoning or his opinion of Reagan. Reagan was complimented in several rulings for his work.

Sheldon Reagan took the unenviable job of defending the most hated man in Kankakee. And my reading of the record shows he did a very good job in what was an impossible task.

Edwards concedes, "He did try to save me from the death penalty."

It is preposterous to believe Danny Edwards could have beaten the rap on technicalities, given the overwhelming evidence against him. But he believes otherwise, even to this day.

"I could have kept lying and I could have beat this," he said.

But, he added with a laugh, "then I'd be going to hell!"

And as for Michael Ficaro? "He did his job. He was out to win and he was out to put me on Death Row, and deservingly so. I've got nothing against him. You use all the tools you have. Be honest, I kidnapped a man and buried him alive. They're not going to be nice to me, and they shouldn't."

I asked, Didn't you want to base your whole case on lies?

"Of course. But I still believe it could have worked if I had a high-powered attorney."

If you had been acquitted, would you have gone back to your lifestyle, selling cocaine and so on?

"Oh, sure. And I'd be back on the path to hell."

He explained more about his biblical aspect of this crime.

"If the state would have executed me for the kidnapping and murder of Stephen Small, would this have been an evil act or just punishment? Answer: just punishment. In God's eyes, some acts of evil are so grievous, it requires punishment to the third and fourth generation from the person who committed the grievous act. God does not look at Stephen Small's murder as an evil act, he sees it as just punishment. God moved the heart of the king of Babylon; this was not an evil act, it was just punishment to a people who would not heed His word. You quote Ezekial, "Punishment will not visit the son," but as long as the son keeps God's law and follows His decrees. Leslie Small did not do this. He oversaw the building of Governor Small Memorial Park and Museum, a place of worship for an evil man."

"I'm being punished for an evil lifestyle that led to the kidnapping of Stephen Small, but my punishment has been a good thing. It led to my redemption. And because of my redemption, the punishment stops with me. But more important, my son will not build a memorial in my name."

"If Leslie Small had not built a monument to his father, if he had said he was sorry for what Governor Small had done and built a church on the grounds of Governor Small Park instead, all this (the kidnap and murder of Stephen Small) never would have happened."

"The actions of the king of Babylon, Osama bin Laden and Danny Edwards, in God's eyes, were not horrible acts, they were acts of just punishment by a holy God who is bound by His word. And no, not every horrible act is directed by God. If it's biblical, there will be indicators. The kidnapping and murder of Stephen Small is loaded with biblical indicators, as well as 9/11. And we know with a certainty that the punishment Israel received was just punishment from a holy God, as well as the punishment that fell on Ahab."

"Trust me, there will be a lot of non-pacifist people who will commend you for printing my Bible studies."

"There are 31,102 verses in the Bible. It's very hard for me to believe all the information I put forth in my 9/11 paper is just happenstance. Daniel 9:11 parallels 9/11. And this was not an evil act from the devil, this was just punishment by a holy God because the people refused to obey His word. His punishment on America was parallel with his punishment on Israel, and for the same reason. You are right, God cannot direct a person to do an evil act, but He can direct a person to carry out a just punishment. You have to know the difference by searching out the matter. What may appear to be an evil act in our eyes may be just punishment in God's eyes."

The **Illinois Supreme Court** upheld Edwards' conviction and death sentence in 1991. It denied his petition for *writ of certiorari* in 1992. Edwards appealed again in 1992, and the circuit court dismissed the petition. The state Supreme Court ruled against Edwards again in 2001.

Edward's numerous appeals over the years rested on procedural technicalities rather than on a claim of innocence. His main contention was that the original search warrant was flawed and should have been thrown out, and therefore everything that followed should have been thrown out.

Edwards' legal briefs presented a large number of issues on appeal. It is hard to believe that any lawyer would present them in a court of law, but they did.

For instance, his lawyer argued that the search warrant should have said Mrs. Small heard a tape recording of her husband's voice instead of saying she heard his actual voice; and the warrant should have stated the victim said he was handcuffed instead of being handcuffed; and that the 11:46 p.m. phone call was made at a Marathon gas station in Kankakee, not at a Sunoco station in Aroma Park.

And most astounding, Edwards' appeal lawyers claimed the FBI recordings of the ransom calls should not have been admitted as evidence because they violated eavesdropping laws!

Edwards claimed he had ineffective counsel because his lawyer did not get a second lawyer on the case quick enough and because his lawyer would not present a compulsion defense. He also criticized his lawyer for failing to call as witnesses police officers who saw his grief at discovering that Mr. Small was dead when the box was uncovered.

His argument of ineffective counsel included a failure to object when the prosecutor said Edwards was not a civilized human being and that the jury should not consider sympathy in making its decision.

These arguments were dismissed by the courts at every level of appeal. The Supreme Court said the issues raised in his appeals were irrelevant and would not have helped his case or made a difference in the verdict.

In another filing, Edwards' lawyers demanded the Department of Justice provide the Nightstalker surveillance reports in the search for Mr. Small's car. The government denied the request, saying Nightstalker is classified information. Harlington Wood Jr., a judge in the Seventh Circuit U.S. Court of Appeals, upheld the government's decision to deny the release of the reports in 1994.

Judge Wood's seven-page decision concluded with comment that could have applied to every argument Edwards' lawyers made: "Now, what else is it you want me to do? It's a dry hole, gentlemen."

Chapter 15

Scared and Confused

*"The first I knew about it was when the cops burst into the apartment.
I woke up with a gun in my face."*
Nancy Rish, March 6, 2013

Nancy Rish told the police some conflicting information on the day she was arrested and brought in for questioning. Some of the things she told them were honest misstatements. Some of the things she told them were deliberate lies.

The reasons for the lies, she explained, were that she was scared and confused.

She said that to the police on the day she was arrested, and her explanation has not changed.

It was these lies -- none of which incriminated her -- along with the false accusations of the prosecutors, that convinced a jury she had guilty knowledge of what Danny Edwards was going to do.

Nancy Rish was a 25-year-old woman who had never been in trouble with the law. She awoke one morning, took her son to school, and found her life changed forever within a matter of minutes.

Nancy Rish spoke to me in a series of interviews in 2013 in the Dwight Correctional Center and the Logan Correctional Center.

After being divorced at the age of 19, Nancy found herself raising her young son alone. "I knew I had to figure things out on my own. Our lives were now our own. So I did not always make good decisions for myself. There came many dark years ahead that I could never have imagined for myself. Running from an abusive boyfriend, all the way to Dallas, Texas, only for him to follow me months later, then becoming sick and having to come back home less than a year, later to be diagnosed with Guillain Barre Syndrome. I didn't have a choice but to stay at my mom's until I was well again, which was less than a year. I found work and moved Ben and I into a place. I thought life was about to turn for the better. I was clueless what was down the road for me, that would change my life forever."

I wanted to know what attracted her to Danny Edwards. She said it wasn't that she was attracted to him, it was more a case of him pursuing her in the Kankakee bar scene until she gave in.

"I would go to happy hour, ladies night with girlfriends. I'd see him out. He'd want to buy me a drink. I'd brush him off. He pursued me. I knew he was married."

"He was manipulative. He wore me down. He was separated from his wife. It was a sad story. He had nowhere to go. She threw him out. One day he showed up at Greenwood (Nancy's apartment) with a brown paper bag and he said, 'she threw me out.' There was a way about him that made you feel sorry for him."

Was there a little pity involved? Yes, she said.

"I was still young and naive and just lost. I was just making my way. Unfortunately, there was a bit of the bad boy in the attraction. I always saw myself as a nurturer, someone who could change a bad boy. It makes you feel like you are helping them, like they need you, but they are manipulating you."

"When he met me, I was working and self sufficient (at Municipal Bank and at Jewel). He said I worked too hard, take the summer off. He had me quit my jobs."

After awhile, Nancy moved into Danny's house on Sand Bar Road. Danny later signed a lease on a townhouse for Nancy and her son on Stratford Drive East in Bourbonnais, so he could continue his cocaine business at the Sandbar Road location alone.

However, the relationship went downhill fast. Even though Danny was paying Nancy's rent, it was over. Danny made one more attempt later in December 1986, by taking Nancy on a trip to the Virgin Islands.

"At the Virgin Islands, we argued a lot. It was paid in advance, so we went. But it was over. Once I moved out of his house, it was over."

A month later, Danny was arrested at his Sandbar Road house. After the bust, Danny asked Nancy to take him in again.

"When Danny came to move in (at Stratford), I felt like I didn't have a choice. His name was on the lease, he was paying the rent."

What was happening the week before the kidnapping?

"On Sunday, Danny and I were on his motorcycle at the state park. Tracy (Storm) just happened to be there. Later, Danny said Tracy wanted us to come to his house. Danny and Tracy spent some time together, maybe 30 minutes. He said Tracy wanted to get his mother's car, in some small town. About 4 p.m., Danny left with Tracy."

"He came home at 2 or 3 a.m. But through the night, Danny was calling me, saying 'We're at the Dam Tap.' At the time, Tracy was dating Brenda Milk. She and I were on the phone. There was call-waiting, so I got these calls from Danny. I thought it was strange, Danny was calling and checking in. He didn't do that. When he was gone, he was gone. It was odd."

"The bartender testified they were at the Dam Tap, buying drinks, breaking hundred dollar bills and tipping big. Danny wasn't working and didn't have any money at that time."

That also was odd. But despite whatever odd behavior Danny was showing, Nancy was becoming more afraid to confront him about it.

In the weeks before the kidnapping, "Danny made it pretty clear not to ask any questions."

Danny gave her a story that Mitch Levitt was threatening him if he did not do something for him. "Danny was concerned about Mitch," Nancy said. "Danny was worried about his ex-wife and his kids, but not about me and my son."

Danny told Nancy to change her hair appointment to later in the day because he wanted to show her a place where he wanted her to pick him up later. Danny and Nancy went to Aroma Park and stopped at Ruffini's market. Danny came out and put a bag in the back seat. Then he drove and showed her the spot. This was the same afternoon they stopped at Englewood Electric. "At the supply store where Pyramid bought supplies, I was in the van. Someone asked Danny who's in the van. He said that's Nancy. I was never in a hardware store buying pipe."

What happened that Tuesday night?

"It probably was around midnight (early Wednesday, September 2). Danny told me he wanted me to follow his van, in my car. He drove his van and parked it (on Greenwood Avenue). He took a duffle bag out of his van and put it in my car. He got in the car and we drove to the Phillips 66 gas station. It was the gas station near Jaenicke's drive-in. He got out and made a phone call, at the pay phone at the station."

That would have been the phone call where Edwards impersonated a police officer to lure Stephen Small from his house.

"I took him a half block to Cobb Park. He took the bag out of the car. He told me to go home and to pick him up in the country at 3 a.m. at a certain road. It sounded strange, but the strange is usual when you're in the drug world."

Since Danny parked his van near the house of another drug dealer friend, Nancy said she "thought Danny was back doing drugs."

Danny "was being frantic, desperation with mood swings. He insisted I be there at the road. It was not a casual request."

"I went home. At 3 a.m., I picked him up and took him home. First, I picked him up and took him back to get his van."

Nancy said she was suspicious about being asked to drive Danny to pay phones and to pick him up on the isolated road near Wichert at 3 a.m. But when she asked, he would say, "Nancy, you don't want to know."

When they awoke later on Wednesday morning, there were a number of errands they had to run. "Danny and I dropped our dog off at the dog groomers, then he took me to Lori's house. Then Danny left. Danny picked me up and we got the dog. Later, he had me drive him. I knew something was going on, he was not typical."

On the way home from picking up the dog, Danny had Nancy pull over so he could use a pay phone. This was the 5:03 p.m. ransom call.

"Later that night, he had me drive to another phone booth. He got out and made a call. I waited in the car. That wasn't always unusual. I thought it had something to do with his setting up a drug dealer as part of his deal with the police. I thought something was going on this night, it was not typical."

"Friday morning, I was sleeping. I had taken my son to school and went back home to sleep. The cops burst in. There was a gun in my face. They told me to get up and get dressed. They took me to the Bourbonnais Police Department. It was 10:30 a.m., but I wasn't arrested until 8:30 pm., then by 2 a.m., I was fingerprinted and processed. So much of it was a blur at the time."

At the police station, she said, "I was getting upset when they were going to arrest me. He (Swaim) kept telling me I had nothing to worry about. He had me show them places, where the calls were made, the route we took. We took two cars. Swaim got in the car with other cops, not in the same car I was in. We drove around to where he (Danny) drove, looking for the tape recorder. I told them he threw something out the window."

"It didn't take too much to confuse me. They tried to intimidate me. They played good cop, bad cop."

What did you go through in those first days after being arrested?

"I had Guillain-Barre Syndrome, and I felt it coming back on, real strong, and that scared me because it gets in stages where it can be very bad, paralyzing." She asked for a doctor, did not get one, and spent four days in solitary confinement without eating, because she was too upset.

Nancy said that during the interrogation, she didn't get to ask questions. Everything she said was answers to questions.

What about telling the police the box was sold to a black man?

"I didn't know what was going on. The first story I told was what Danny told me to say."

"The cops told me I should have a lawyer present. The only lawyer's name I could think of was Leonard Sacks. He was called and the word came back that he declined, but he offered the names of two lawyers in Olympia Fields. I can see now that he was the only one with enough integrity to decline and to subtly suggest that my lawyer be from outside Kankakee."

The police could not reach the Olympia Field lawyers. They asked Nancy again to give them a name of a lawyer to call. "They were pushing for me to call a local attorney so they could get on with the interrogation."

"I knew who Scott Swaim was. I had met him once, through a neighbor. His name came to mind. He got there so quick, he must have rushed there as fast as he could."

Swaim "talked to me for about five minutes, then he said, 'Let's talk to them. Tell them what they need to know, so you can go home.'"

Swaim was not a criminal attorney. He did not confer with her about

231

anything. He did almost no objecting to any questions or answers. He basically just sat there, she said.

"He was not there to represent me. He was there so that an attorney could be present. When Swaim took the stand, he said he was my attorney, but he was not. He said he was my attorney, there for my constitutional
rights at questioning. I was brought up respecting authority, to listen to them
and do what they say, that authority was in the right."

Here was the extent of Swaim's legal work during the four days he
was on the case: his testimony in court on October 3, 1988, was, "I told
Nancy Rish she did not have to talk with police. She said she wanted to cooperate and give a statement. I had no problem with her cooperating."

She was taken into court on Tuesday, September 8, to be arraigned
on kidnap and murder charges. "Five minutes before the arraignment, he
told me he wouldn't be my attorney that day. He told me, 'The court will
appoint an attorney for you. Your family can't afford me.' Then it was good
luck and good bye."

For the meager effort Swaim put into Nancy Rish's case, he sent
Nancy's mother a bill for $3,000. She wouldn't pay it.

Years later, Rish filed a motion for a new trial, claiming Swaim provided ineffective counsel. Swaim, who by then was a judge in Kankakee
County, took the stand and testified that he never was Rish's attorney. He
said he was there to protect her constitutional right to have a lawyer during
questioning, but said he never represented her.

Judge Gordon Lustfeldt ruled in favor of Judge J. Scott Swaim, and
against Nancy Rish.

"I was so scared, I didn't want to say nothing. I was being questioned without an attorney present, when I was threatened with the electric
chair."

"I never was in that van in Small's neighborhood."

"Danny told me what to tell them."

How did you feel about Danny during the questioning?

"He used me. I was very upset. I was very angry with him. He put
me in the middle of this without me knowing, and I was scared."

One of the main points hammered by the prosecutors was the lies
and inconsistencies in her stories when she was brought in for questioning.
She said the first stories she told were what Danny Edwards told her to say,
in the event she was asked. Once she realized the situation, she told what
really happened.

She still did not know anything about the kidnapping of Stephen
Small when she was brought in. She didn't know why the police were at her
house that morning.

"The first I knew about it was when the cops burst into the apartment," she said in 2013. "I woke up with a gun in my face."

As far as the conflicting statements of Scott Swaim and Elizabeth Lamanna about being told she could go home if she made a statement to police, Nancy Rish said Lamanna did tell her she could go home if she made a statement. And she said Lamanna did pat her knee and say "honey."

It was, Nancy believes, Lamanna's role in playing "good cop" to Sgt. McClellan's "bad cop" at the interrogation. Nancy said she was too naive to realize it at the time.

"She (Lamanna) was playing the role, acting like she was there to protect me. That's what I felt. They were coming at me, and she would say this isn't necessary."

As for Detective Erickson, "There were so many police officers, FBI, detectives, plain clothes, so many in and out of that room. It was Willis who said it (the electric chair). I was confused and not sure of why I said Erickson."

She said the same thing in 2013 as she said in 1987 about the lies she told the police in the early interrogation. "Whatever statements I made were what Danny told me to say. I was scared and didn't know what else to tell them."

Nancy Rish said it was not her idea to testify at her trial. She said she does not express herself well, not even during our interviews in prison, and she was feeling ill at the time.

"I did not want to testify. Vince (Paulauskis) talked me into it. He felt the jurors needed to hear from me. They had conflicting statements and needed to have me explain it. I did not express myself well."

"I was so scared at my arraignment, I couldn't speak. The judge told me to shake my head."

"I was on high doses of Xanax (an anti-anxiety drug) when I testified, and Vince gave me two Valiums. He later claimed they were placeboes. They weren't. I felt like I was intoxicated. It made me answer in a monotone."

It was not a favorable impression to the jurors.

"Vince told me I was going home. But I never felt that in my gut. I was taken from my home at gunpoint and I never returned."

Chapter 16
Broken Image

"It isn't what Nancy saw in Danny, it was what she couldn't see in herself."
Lori Brault, October 10, 2013

The prosecutors, in order to build their argument to get a conviction, had to manufacture an image of Nancy Rish as a greedy, scheming, dominating, manipulative, controlling mastermind.

The truth is just the opposite. Nancy Rish was a naive, frightened, insecure woman who felt she had no control.

Her father abandoned the family by the time Nancy started school. She had almost no relationship with her father except brief negative encounters. He was an alcoholic and a bum, and Nancy lived with the embarrassment and shame that came from the other children who knew it.

"In the 1960s, there was not so much divorce. I carried the shame. When kids would ask, where's your dad, I would say at work."

"Dad never abused me. He never put his hands on me. It was verbal. When he was sober, he was a good man. When he drank, he became sarcastic. When he came home, we didn't know what to expect. He came and went as he pleased, until mom divorced him. It set a lot of fear in me. It was always the unknown."

"Not having a father figure, growing up without a father, was difficult," Nancy said. "A father and a daughter are supposed to be close, for protection, security and love. We never had a relationship."

"He lived with his parents (Carl and Jennie Woodrich). Mom went to work when I was six months old. His parents watched me while she went to work. I spent a lot of time at their house on Hammes Avenue. Directly from work, she picked me up. He had a room there. He didn't ignore me, but he didn't acknowledge me. He'd be in and out. You didn't know when he'd be back. I think that's where my feeling of rejection came from, my feeling of abandonment. I just wanted to fill that void."

"By the age of six or seven, I had prominent characteristics of guilt, shame, fear and abandonment, which in turn gave me very low self esteem and self worth. Admitting this to you, I feel shame."

It was that longing for love that brought Nancy Woodrich and Terry Rish together. She got pregnant at 15 and left high school after her freshman year. Nancy hoped for the happiness and the love she had lacked.

Divorced and on her own at 19, Nancy was insecure about her lack of education and skills and about her inability to get a good job because of it. She worked at Alden's Department Store in Kankakee for awhile.

Nancy moved to Texas briefly with her friend Kathy Bowman.

"When Kathy divorced, she came back to Kankakee for me to drive back to Texas with her. I did. I was just divorced, and Alden's had closed. She said there's work, so I went to try it. But I came back a few months later when I developed Guillain-Barre."

Nancy and her son had to move back in with her mother. Nancy was sick, she had no money, no possessions, and her relationship with her mother was tense. Her relationship with her former in-laws was worse.

Nancy got a job at American Body Wrap salon in Bradley in 1984. It turned out the owner was mostly interested in the pretty girls he hired. The women ended up quitting and the owner ended up committing suicide in Florida.

With no male role model as an example to show her what a real man should be, Nancy made poor choices. She married a boy because he got her pregnant, and she moved in with a cocaine dealer because he showed her attention. These choices were as much a manifestation of her poor opinion of herself as anything else. She felt she had nothing to offer, and she was willing to grab anything that passed for love and happiness.

Janet Woititz, Ph.D., wrote in her book, *Adult Children of Alcoholics*, "Throughout life, to keep others from finding out that they don't know what they're doing, they guess at what is appropriate." They "have no frame of reference for what it is like to be in a normal household. You have no frame of reference for what it is OK to say and feel." It prevents normal intimate feelings from forming.

"As a result of your fear of abandonment, you don't feel confident about yourself," Woititz wrote. "So you look to others to feel OK. Needless to say, you give away a great deal of power. You give the other person the power to lift you up or knock you down."

Nancy never was into drugs until she met Terry Rish and Danny Edwards. She went from being a chubby child with insecurities and a bad body image, to being slim from cocaine use, described by friends at one point as having hair like straw and black circles under her eyes.

An insight into Nancy Rish came from her friend, Lori (Papineau) Brault, in interviews for this book in 2013 and trial notes she wrote in 1988.

Nancy and Lori grew up together and had a lot in common. Nancy was pregnant and married at 16. Lori was pregnant and married at 17.

Lori said their circumstance was common to young girls whose self image was damaged and who made bad choices while looking for acceptance and love.

That was especially true in Nancy's situation, Lori said.

Nancy and Lori worked together briefly in Bradley. Both women were divorced at a young age, with small children, and neither received child support money from their ex-husbands. They leaned on each other, listened to each other's problems and babysat each other's kids.

If there is one feature about Nancy Rish that Lori and other friends have agreed upon, it is her naivete.

"Nancy was extremely beautiful, but very naive. Nancy was one of the most naive people I ever knew. She never had a decent role model or a father figure. She was always looking for love in all the wrong places."

Part of the damage done to Lori Brault came from being molested several times as a child, by a total of five men. One man was the first husband of her oldest sister.

"I was molested in fourth grade. We were all being molested. It set the course why we settled for men who were abusive. We were strapped with the last bad decision we made."

"I didn't want to talk about it, and I thought no one would believe me. I have come to terms with my feelings because it is so necessary to release them. I pushed them down. I see how much they guided so much in my life from that time. My anger and rebellion came out."

Lori was nine years old the very first time she was molested. The perpetrator was her fourth grade teacher and principal at St. Paul's Lutheran Church school in Kankakee. She said he molested her repeatedly over four years. Lori said she could not discuss it with her parents, and she locked the secret away for decades. The molestation shaped the course of her life. Her damaged self esteem led to a lot of bad decisions, including the choices of abusive men in her life. It is a situation faced by many women, she said.

The image of Nancy and Danny being partners in crime was another invention of the prosecution. Nancy's friends had a different story when they testified on her behalf at her trial in 1988. They say the same thing today.

"Nancy was afraid of Danny. She was trying to get away from him," Lori Brault said in 2013.

"Danny battered her and he pulled a gun on her at least once. Danny was acting crazy and doing massive quantities of cocaine. She was scared to death for Ben's life and her own life. She told me he was scaring her. He was doing strange stuff. She wanted to be self sufficient and she wanted to be away from him if possible."

This is noted in reports at the Bourbonnais Police Department. Police responded to their house on a domestic abuse call on December 24, 1986. Nancy called the police, telling them Danny's cocaine use was the cause. He damaged her property, too. But she declined to sign a complaint.

She made another domestic abuse call on May 11, 1987. Danny was throwing out her clothes. She told police she moved his car while he was drinking at the Dam Tap, and he became enraged. Nancy spent the night at a friend's house. She did not press charges.

Stories of Danny abusing Nancy, and how she was afraid of him, are supported by testimony from Nancy's friends in the chapter on the trial. It also is supported by Nancy's answers to police, in the chapter on her interrogation. In those reports, she told police the details of when Danny pulled a gun and threatened to kill her and her son.

In a written statement for Nancy's trial in 1988, Lori wrote that she went to Nancy and Danny's house on Sand Bar Road in 1986 for dinner one night. Lori said as she and Nancy were preparing dinner, "she was expressing to me how crazy Danny was getting, to the point of almost being scary. She was rather confused about exactly where their relationship stood, and she still had her apartment on Greenwood. She wasn't really completely living with him at the house on Sand Bar Road because his wife and kids were over frequently and it made the situation delicate and uncomfortable for her. Also, when I spent the night at her apartment, she still had what appeared to be all of her furnishings and belongings there."

The two young women had an emotional discussion. "She expressed to me how confused she was about Danny and whether or not she really loved him. She was just so tired of being in relationships that never turn out, and feared what it was doing to Benji. She cried because she didn't have any skills or education and couldn't ever see things really changing for her."

"She never dreamed of nice cars or furs, just stability, happiness and loving someone who could return her love for real."

"She is a very proud woman, but has low self esteem and a lack of confidence in her potential. She's not the type to make things happen, but lets life just kind of happen to her. She doesn't really view herself as having anything to offer other than her love and her beauty. She's a very loving, caring, fun and domesticated woman."

Lori said she drove home that night crying about the dire situations she and Nancy faced. "I knew that I was going to make it and that maybe she never would unless I could get her away from that nasty town and literally show her the way till she could have more confidence in herself and get up on her own two feet. I've always felt that Nancy has so much potential that she's never been able to realize because she's never had the opportunity."

"We still kept in touch regularly by phone and she was always telling me about how strange Danny had become. She hated his coke habit and felt that he was really in much too deep when he quit his job and started dealing. She was upset that he wasn't what she thought he was or would be. He slept all day and was constantly irritable to her and Benji. It was at that time that she told me she would love to leave him if only she could. There had been several bad fights with him. But she was very scared of him and what he would do to her if she left him -- if she could."

Things between Nancy and Danny were so bad in April 1987 that Nancy came and stayed with Lori near Oak Brook for a few days. It was Lori's way of trying to get Nancy a job and get her out of Kankakee. As they talked, Lori wrote, in her in October 1988 statement, that Nancy said she was "very scared at that time since Danny had been busted. She had told me about it over the phone and couldn't believe what was happening. I don't think she had been realizing exactly what all he had been involved in or how heavily. If one were able to say that Nancy Rish could have but one fault, it is only that she has always been a little too naive for her own good."

It was this type of testimony that the prosecution cut short very quickly at Nancy Rish's trial. Lori did not spend much time on the witness stand before she was pulled off. It was not the sort of thing the prosecutors wanted jurors to hear.

"I knew that with Small's name and money, Nancy didn't have a chance. There wasn't anything fair about it. It was election time at the time of Nancy's trial. Nothing was going to get past that mob of politicians."

"It could have very easily have been me or any other woman at the time."

Lori Brault retold the story in 2013 of Nancy's visit in April 1987.

"Nancy was grasping at straws to try to get away from him. He battered her. He was never a nice guy and he never had much of a conscience."

"Out of the blue she contacted me. I worked at Snelling & Snelling (employment agency) in Oak Brook. Nancy was scared of Danny Edwards. This was after he pulled a gun on her. Nancy said, 'I need some refuge and I need to talk to you.'"

"The last time I saw her, she followed me to my office in Oak Brook. We were sitting in my car talking for a long time. She was crying. I didn't know how to help her."

"I was a recruiter at an employment agency. I was trying to get Nancy a job as a recruiter, but she was still living in Kankakee. She had no money. She was completely reliant on Danny. She had a child to be responsible for. She stayed here four days. She knew she had to go back. She didn't have Benjamin with her."

"Life was hard back then for young women with children to support, and none of us was getting child support. There weren't a lot of options, just like for a lot of women."

"Self esteem played a huge role in what happened to Nancy. It was self-inflicted naivete. You just closed your eyes. You didn't want to believe it and have to change your life. Once you had somebody who loved you, you didn't want to believe it wasn't true," Lori said.

"Nancy got sucked in by Danny the vampire. He was a narcissistic control freak. He was quite the talker."

In Lori Brault's situation, she lived with a man who would tell her, "'Who do you think you would be if you weren't with me?' Like he was some kind of savior. He beat me up emotionally and physically. They don't want to lose you because you're their voo-doo doll. They say they can't live without you and they make you think you can't live without them."

It was a common situation for a lot of women, she said.

What was the attraction that Nancy felt for Danny?

Nancy was beautiful, Lori said, but Danny was a pothead, a loser and not at all good looking.

I asked Lori: So just what did Nancy see in Danny?

"It isn't what Nancy saw in Danny, it was what she couldn't see in herself."

Nancy wrote to Lori from the county jail on January 5, 1988:

"You know we both have had our share of hard times and somehow we've managed to get through them, but I tell you what, this time I just don't know if I can hang on. It's tough, Lori. I sometimes wonder how you would get through this if it were happening to you. And that kind of helps me because I feel that you would take it one day at a time and fight like hell for your innocence, right to the bitter end, cuz God didn't make us tough cookies for nothing! You give me confidence, whether you know it or not."

"Benjamin was in at X-mas to see me. He got me some Calvin Klein Obsession. The boy has good taste! I might have hinted just a bit! He's been pretty strong through all this, but the holidays were pretty tough for him. Him and I both."

In another letter on September 14, 1988, Nancy tells Lori, "My worst fear is going insane and not knowing it. Everyone has their limit before going over the deep end; the question is how do you know you've reached the limit before you lose it? I feel I've come close a few times now. It's not enough just to deal with the fact and reality of how screwed my life has become, but to have to think about and see what it's doing to Benjamin and my family and friends, that's what I can't handle. Benjamin will always have this to deal with. So Benjamin is going to Alan Shepard (school). It's going to be awful for him when this trial gets started. You know how cruel kids can be. I'm so worried about him."

"Thank God for Jesus that He lets us know of a better place to live after this trying trip is over."

And on November 8, 1988, Nancy wrote, "Dear Lori, Here I sit, waiting to be sentenced to life. Unreal, isn't it? I wish it were!"

"I was very happy to see Benjamin. He is one of a kind. He is such a strong little boy. He deserves so much better. He gives me more strength than I give him. I had kept telling myself as long as Benjamin and mom could handle it, if it came to this, then I could, too. Well, they are handling it fairly well, but I'm not! Not at all! The first three days I would have to say I was in some sort of stage of shock. It's just now really hitting me what is happening

239

to me. Lori, I am scared. I'm scared of being out in a place, a separate world from everyone else, where all the people there carry a number and time on their backs." Nancy added that she was desperate for someone to help her and she apologized for being a burden with her problems. "I talked with Benjamin on the phone last night. He had just brought home his report card that afternoon. Six A's and four B's."

Nancy Rish and Lori Brault had something else in common. They both had men who did a lot of cocaine and a lot of damage to them.

Kankakee was a drug-soaked city in the 1970s and 1980s, and it remains so today to a large extent. The Kankakee "underground" at that time was especially scary, Lori said.

"I can remember those days every time I would drive past the Homestead (restaurant), how eerie it was on certain nights. All those cars with McBroom campaign signs on top, like it was the meeting place of monsters. There was a subconscious fear that this was going on in your hometown, and anything unjust can happen to anyone. It sure did to Nancy."

Lori's ex-husband Craig Brault was a target of drug agents in the early 1980s. He left town as Operation Snow Cone was under way in 1984. There was a narcotics informant in Kankakee named Ed, and he got $300 for every name he turned in. "Ed was looking for Craig. They couldn't find Craig, so I was the next best thing." Lori was arrested at her job at Manteno State Hospital. She and Craig had been separated for a year before this happened. There was no case against her and charges were dropped.

"That was the whole reason I left my husband. I could feel the heat coming."

Nancy Rish also could feel the heat surrounding Danny Edwards, but she never conceived of the notion that he could do what he did. She never imagined the turn her life suddenly would take.

Nancy was no different from many of her contemporaries in Kankakee. She just had a lot less luck surviving the obstacle course.

"Nancy didn't get out fast enough like I did," Lori said.

"My hope for your book is that Nancy shouldn't have to die without people knowing the real Nancy. There is not one single fiber in that woman's body that could have committed that crime."

"It is a lesson for many women. She was betrayed like many women have been."

More insights into Nancy Rish are in papers she wrote for a speech class she was taking in prison through Lewis University in 1998 and 1999.

In a January 1999 essay, Nancy wrote, "When I was fifteen, I thought I found love, but instead I found myself pregnant. At 23, I thought I found love, but instead found myself on my way to prison. All in the name of love. I asked myself, how could love be so devastating? This is when I went in search of the true meaning of love. Because I knew it had to be better than this!"

"I began to realize that what I thought was love was not love at all. Realizing that I couldn't recognize love because I had never actually seen it. I had a picture in my mind of what it should be, but that picture, that image, had been broken a long time ago. If I only knew then what I know now, what a difference my life coulda been! Coulda, shoulda, woulda, it was time to move forward, not back in regret."

"Nowhere do we learn more about ourselves and life than in relationships. We do the best we can, until the day comes when we are stronger, wiser and willing to do better for ourselves. Love and being loved is a big responsibility. It means you must look at yourself as well as those you love with an expansive view, knowing that nothing stays the same. Love and being loved also means that you must always look for the good! The good qualities, the good potential, the good that has been done with you and for you."

"It means you must look with merciful and forgiving eyes, trusting and truthful eyes, gentle and kind eyes, that always see beyond the behavior to the core, the essence, the soul. You may not always want to do this. It's not always easy. The key is to always affirm that love is your guiding force. Once you have accepted this degree of responsibility for yourself by forgiving yourself for what you have created, it will be easy to love those who played a role in your creation."

"Love should never require us to give up our dignity, self worth, careers or our good common sense."

"Don't be so quick to take all the credit for your growth and evolution. Give God the credit because it was God who never, not even for a second, gave up on you! There are also angels watching over you at all times."

It is her faith that has sustained her in prison, she said.

Nancy has always had a strong faith, but like many young people, she didn't let it get in the way of her youthful pursuits. It was in 2000 that she turned her life to Jesus.

There was no large incident that caused her faith to blossom. It was the Holy Spirit coming into her life. It means accepting Jesus Christ as her savior, she said.

"I accept Jesus. Even as a teen I did, but I was not living it. When it became real, I rededicated myself. And I have grown since then."

"My faith is strong. If I didn't believe, I wouldn't have agreed to this interview. I have grown as a person, as a Christian."

"I was brought up in a Catholic setting. My mother was in Bible study. She was born-again. Since 2000, I really began to open myself up with having a relationship with the Lord. It is real. If I didn't have my faith, I don't know how I would do it from day to day. It gives me a reason, a purpose.

"There is a bigger picture, and more than what is here right now."

"It means opening your eyes and reading more. It's like someone turning on a light and everything is so much clearer. I even feel different from just a year ago. He reveals more. You have to want to know."

"I went through what I did. Maybe God wanted to get my attention. Drinking and doing drugs at a young age brings negative choices and bad people. Nothing good can come from drugs and alcohol."

The shock of going from an average morning to an evening of being booked for kidnapping and murder was a mind-numbing experience.

"At the time of my arrest, days and months following, my mind could not, did not, wrap around all of what was happening," Nancy said in 2014. "Not only with myself but with my family, including my own son. It was just too much for me to grasp. Something inside of me shut down. I was on auto-pilot, going through the motions. It was very surreal sometimes, almost a feeling of being outside of myself, especially during my trial, looking on as a spectator, as if it were happening to someone else. Very, very difficult to explain."

"I would not be able to do this if I did not have my faith. I would be an angry, bitter woman if not for my faith in God. I would have lost all hope. I would have just given up. I do see a future. I do hold on to hope. I've learned to forgive. It goes back years, holding in guilt, it goes back to my dad."

"I was wanting to find what I lacked at home. I never wanted wealth. If I had that someone I was in love with, and had a family, it was what I wanted. I wanted that fairy tale situation."

"I'm seeing it clearer. It's about accepting your circumstances and making the most of it. (Faith) definitely changed my way of thinking and feeling and dealing with things. I don't have a chip on my shoulder."

Kelly Klein is another person with an insight into Nancy Rish. She isn't family or a childhood friend. She is a recent friend.

Kelly Klein met Nancy in prison. Klein was convicted of aggravated battery of a child in 2012 and was sentenced to six years in prison. A seven-month-old boy was injured in Klein's home day care business in Wilmington. She said the boy bumped his head while reaching for a toy. He had other injuries, and it was not determined if these were previous injuries. He was hospitalized and he recovered. The facts of the case are not clear cut and are in dispute, but Klein was found guilty in a bench trial. Her appeal is being handled by a law firm experienced in wrongful convictions.

Klein said Reva Small, Stephen's mother, told her she believed Nancy Rish is innocent.

"I met Mrs. Small in 2004. She was a resident of a senior living community called Westwood Estates. I was the marketing coordinator who assisted her in preparing her move, along with items for her new home."

Klein helped Mrs. Small in choosing carpet samples, tile and other things for her new living quarters.

"When my son was born in 2005, Mrs. Small invited me to her home to have lunch and to meet my new baby."

When Kelly Klein visited Reva Small in June 2005, Mrs. Small showed her a picture of her son.

"During my visit, Mrs. Small shared with me that her son Stephen was kidnapped and buried alive. When she told me this, I couldn't believe what I was hearing. She then told me the man and woman were serving a life sentence. While still in shock of what I was hearing, Mrs. Small told me that she forgave the woman and felt she had nothing to do with this crime."

"Years later, in 2007, I ended up with my case. In 2011, I was found guilty and knew I would be going to prison. I decided to look up Stephen Small's case and find the woman in this case. I felt I needed to share my conversation. I wasn't sure how I was going to meet Nancy, but God had a hand in that. Being innocent myself, I felt I needed to help her. I just couldn't believe someone could get life for something they never played a part in."

"I arrived in Dwight in January 2013, and received visits every Sunday. One given Sunday, Nancy happened to be walking as I was headed to my visit. It was at that moment I asked her if she was Nancy Rish. She said yes, and I proceeded to share with her what Reva Small told me eight years prior. Of course, she was shocked, a stranger coming out of nowhere."

"That was the start of our friendship. I have since grown to know this amazing, strong woman, mother, grandmother and friend. There is no way she would have ever done such a crime."

Kelly Klein signed a sworn affidavit to her meeting with Mrs. Small. She told me, "Nancy needs to go home, to enjoy her son and grandchildren, watch them grow up, to find the love of her life and live in peace and joy. I'm blessed to have Nancy in my life. I look at her as if she were my family."

Nancy Rish said in 2014 that she had no idea what lay ahead for her after her divorce.

"Who knew but God? My mother thought her and my father's problems were her own business. It was never open for discussion. But in reality, their problems became our problems, my sisters and mine, and formed our personalities, which became a huge influence on how we dealt with life."

"I can clearly see my mistakes now, looking back all throughout my life. It's not about placing blame on either my mother or father. It's about getting some clarity, understanding and forgiveness. We don't choose our family or our life as children. But as adults, having lived through a life of mistakes, we can choose to learn how to cope differently. Today, I'm learning to deal more openly with my feeling, being true to myself and working on building self confidence and self worth. I thank God my epiphany came better late than never."

While in Dwight prison, Nancy Rish earned her GED high school (equivalency) diploma and a two-year AA (Associate) college degree. She earned a degree in cosmetology, and a license in sanitation which qualifies her as an assistant manager in culinary arts.

She also has been a certified dog groomer for more than 10 years. Nancy has worked in the prison's Helping Paws program. The program trains dogs to be service dogs for the blind and for other people with handicaps.

Dwight was the only facility with this program. The program was moved to Logan Correctional Center after Governor Pat Quinn closed Dwight prison in March 2013. Nancy continues working in the Helping Paws program at Logan, grooming and assisting in training the dogs.

And she still has hope.

"I want nothing for myself, if I got out," she said in 2013. "I just want to take care of my mother in her last years and my boys (grandsons)."

"And I would like people to know that I did not do this crime."

Chapter 17
Clemency for Death Row

"There's just one word to describe life on Death Row."
Danny Edwards, August 8, 2013

Danny Edwards spent nearly 15 years on Death Row in the Illinois penitentiary at Pontiac. His life was spared when Governor George Ryan issued an edict in 2003 that commuted the sentences of everyone on Death Row.

A total of 167 murderers had their sentences commuted to life in prison. Danny Edwards was one of them.

Also reprieved from Death Row was Eric Lee, who murdered Kankakee Patrolman Anthony Samfey in cold blood in 1996. Seven other cop killers were reprieved. Also getting a pass off Death Row was Timothy Buss of Kankakee, who murdered five-year-old Tara Sue Huffman in 1981, was paroled in 1993, and murdered nine-year-old Christopher Meyer in 1995.

The commutations happened three days before Ryan left the governor's mansion, as Ryan was under investigation for a variety of crimes and corrupt practices.

Some people have speculated that Governor Ryan's moratorium on the death penalty, and his commutations for everyone on Death Row, was just a ploy to gain sympathy and admiration in order to stave off his own prosecution and to pander to those who held his fate in their hands.

Other people believe Ryan had a genuine concern about the fairness of the death penalty. Ryan received praise from the Pope, Nelson Mandela, Bishop Desmond Tutu and a variety of other world leaders and show-biz celebrities.

As a state legislator, George Ryan was a supporter of the death penalty and he helped reinstate it in Illinois in 1977. His career ended in disgrace when he was convicted in 2006 on 22 counts of racketeering, fraud, tax evasion and other crimes, and was sent to a federal prison.

George Ryan knew the Edwards family. Danny Edwards' parents were friends of Stephen Small's parents. The mothers of Danny and Stephen were good friends who played golf and tennis together in Kankakee. Danny's brother David went to school with Stephen and they were friends. Tom Ryan and Duke Edwards were business partners.

Stephen Small and George Ryan were next door neighbors. Only a narrow alley separated the back doors of their houses, with Small on Cobb Boulevard and Ryan on Greenwood Avenue. Stephen Small mowed the lawn and shoveled snow at Ryan's house, and he babysat Ryan's children.

In a lengthy speech in January 2003, explaining his decision to commute all death sentences, Governor Ryan talked about his friendship with Stephen Small and the Edwards family. He intended his words to show he understood both the victim and the killer. However, Stephen Small's family condemned Ryan, a feeling shared by many family members of other murder victims. Nancy Small told the *Washington Post* that George Ryan betrayed her family for political gain. Mrs. Small said, "I can't believe that our family friend and neighbor from years ago, who saw our grief first-hand, could do this. I really feel he has used our family."

She told the *New York Times,* "He used our family. It was very convenient for him that he personally knew one of the victims and had watched our suffering. I would like George to personally hand-write a letter to each of my three boys telling them why he decided to have their father's murderer taken off Death Row."

Even George Ryan's wife, Lura Lynn, said she was "angry and disappointed" at her husband's act.

Danny Edwards told the *New York Times* he didn't want his sentence commuted. He had his own cell on Death Row and did not want a cell mate. "I'm not looking forward to group showers."

It is ironic that Governor Ryan, who projected a heart bleeding for the murderers on Death Row, including Danny Edwards, was so harsh in condemning Nancy Rish following the 1993 *Chicago Tribune* stories.

Poetic justice happens sometimes, even if only for a short time. During part of the years from 2007 to 2013, George Ryan and Danny Edwards both sat behind prison walls.

Danny Edwards' opinion about clemency was the same in 2013 as it had been a decade earlier when Governor Ryan issued his decree.

I asked, What was life like on Death Row?

"There's just one word to describe it -- sweet."

"I had my own cell. I took law classes, Bible studies, art classes, I exercised in the yard, I had showers every day. A one-man cell is a biggie. I wasn't upset about being on Death Row because I didn't care if I was executed."

How did you feel about clemency?

"I was mad. People think I should have been relieved. I knew different. I didn't want to shower with 40 to 50 people. I had a single shower on Death Row. There are a variety of reasons why Death Row is better -- except for the conclusion, when the state might kill you some day. But that didn't bother me."

After more than a decade on Death Row in Pontiac, Edwards was sent to Stateville penitentiary near Joliet for a year and a half. He went back to Pontiac, into the general prison population. Stateville and Pontiac, he said, are like night and day. The conditions are much worse at Stateville, and so are the guards.

"Here (Pontiac) they treat you like you treat them. If you act like a fool, they treat you like a fool. If you act like you have brains and have respect, they treat you that way."

Edwards works six hours a day in the prison kitchen, from noon to 6 p.m. He gets to exercise in the yard on Wednesdays and Saturdays.

"I prepare meals for those in segregation. Those are prisoners out of the general population. They're in orange jump suits. They have no TV or radio, they take meals in their cells, they spend 24 hours a day in their cells. They get there if they are in fights, if they assault an officer or have contraband. I prepare the meals and load the trucks. It's a really good job. I don't have to spend a lot of money in the commissary (because of working in the kitchen). I earn $30 a month. The kitchen job is the only work assignment I want. I earned it because of good behavior."

"The food here in Pontiac is the best in the state prison system," he said. He appears well fed. Because of his heart condition, he is in a quieter building. "When I'm done with work, I go home, take a shower and watch TV."

There is no air conditioning in the prison, but he does have a fan in the summer. The prison is heated in the winter. He gets to spend time alone because his cell mate works as a mechanic from 8 a.m. to 2:30 p.m.

"I came here (to Pontiac) on June 1, 1988. I've been here 25 years. I have no tickets, no write-ups, I cause no trouble, I don't curse. Some inmates always gripe and are in a bad mood. I'm at peace. That's how you know you've made it."

The really bad guys do not give him trouble. "The Bible says the weeds and the grain will grow together in the same field. If you mind your own business, you don't have anything to worry about. You get in fights only if you said something to somebody, or if you owe somebody money for drugs or for gambling."

Danny Edwards is easy going and compliant at Pontiac prison. He is friendly to others and he gets in no trouble. His fellow prisoners like him. The guards like him and they treat him well.

Danny said going to prison saved his soul. It also saved his life. The drugs or someone would have killed him. His days in prison are structured, his food, clothing, medical care and everything else is provided for him.

Chapter 18
Black Cowboys, Rumors, and Odd Circumstances

"I don't know where people come up with this."
Danny Edwards, December 20, 2013

There is more to the Stephen Small case than what has been made known. There are background details, information in the police files that was not made public, conflicting statements, and rumors that "everybody" knows.

There is a lot more, and not all of it is true, even though some people believe they know better.

Let's start with those mysterious black cowboys.

Were they accomplices with Danny Edwards in the plot to kidnap and bury Stephen Small? Were they the enforcers for drug dealers up north who were forcing Danny Edwards to kidnap Mr. Small? Were they just hired hands for Edwards?

Or were the black cowboys something that Danny Edwards invented as an excuse to shift the blame from himself?

There certainly are black cowboys in Pembroke Township. The Pembroke Rodeo is one of the few black rodeos in the nation. It was started in 1975 by Thyrl Latting, an African-American rodeo rider who also spent more than two decades as a Chicago vocational school teacher. He started producing rodeos in 1964. It remains a very big annual event.

There are horse ranches there, notably Boots & Saddles Ranch.

Danny Edwards told the police a lot of wild stories when he was arrested. He implicated Kent Allain, Mitch Levitt and unnamed black cowboys as part of the plot. Edwards was adamant in his insistence, but he must not have been very convincing. The police didn't believe him.

The trouble with Edwards' stories was that none of them matched the others, and they did not make sense. In one account, Edwards said Levitt was threatening his life for trying to set him up. In another account, Edwards said he was expecting a big sum of money from Levitt as a reward for tipping him off about the set up. In yet another story, he said Levitt was forcing him to kidnap someone to make up for the money lost in the drug raid. Then he said Allain and unnamed black men were forcing him to kidnap a rich man for money (why they would insist that an unimportant druggie was essential to their scheme was not explained); and he said black cowboys were guarding the grave site (a connection between black city thugs and black rural cowboys also was not explained). Of course, this plot was so crazy that it is doubtful anyone else could have imagined it or willingly participated in it. Drug cartel bosses in Chicago never would have picked (and insisted) that Edwards be a part of this, and they certainly wouldn't have had him be the main figure to carry it out. They never would have had their victim buried alive and they never would have known about these remote sand hills.

When Danny Edwards finally decided to talk on September 5, 1987, he gave the police a lengthy statement before his lawyer told him to keep quiet. It would be 26 years before Danny Edwards would talk about the crime again, and it was in interviews for this book.

His statements in 1987 were totally self-serving. It was along the same lines as those two letters he had someone else send while he was in the county jail. It all was nothing more than an attempt to shift the blame.

Edwards clung to his story, of being forced to kidnap Mr. Small, through many years of appeals in the courts. Today, he admits it all was a lie.

In the lengthy story he told police in 1987, he said he met Kent Allain at Fat Rats bar on North Fifth Avenue in June and they went to the Party House tavern and met two black men who said they wanted help in kidnapping a rich man. Edwards said he told them no. Then they showed him pictures of his wife and kids and threatened to kill his family if he didn't cooperate. They told him he would get $100,000 from the ransom money. They told him they would not get caught "because they had it planned to the T." Edwards said he was told by Allain on July 4 to build a box big enough for a body, so he bought the wood at Security Lumber on the next day. Edwards said he, Allain and a black man met at Fat Rats late on Tuesday, September 1. Edwards said he made the phone call, waited for Mr. Small to come out and then took him at gunpoint to rural Pembroke Township, where they buried him in the box. He said black cowboys with shotguns guarded the site. There was a lot more to this tale, but it is not necessary to complicate things by recounting all the false details here. This is the story that Edwards told to police. They did not believe him. There was no evidence to support it. But once told, true or not, a story gets legs of its own. That is why there are people today who believe this or parts of it.

Edwards told his story of conspiracy to anyone who would listen.

The rumors about black cowboys took hold and grew from other sources. The Kankakee police file has a report from Detective Sgt. Maurice Meitzner and Detective Kevin McGovern about a meeting with a confidential informant on September 8 at the B-Back Inn in Bradley. The man told police about a party at Tom Kinkin's house in Manteno on Labor Day weekend, where there was talk about the crime. The police interviewed three people who were at the party. They told police rumors about Allain and two drug dealers from Pembroke having something to do with the crime, and rumors that Danny owned Mitch a large sum of money from the drug bust.

Kankakee Police Lt. John Gerard's report from the burial site noted fresh horse tracks and motorcycle tracks. The state police file has crime scene photos, taken the day after Small's body was found, and a few pictures show hoof prints in the sandy ground. It is off the beaten path. But that was an area where people rode horses and dirt bikes.

Add that to Nancy Rish's statements to police on September 8 about dropping Edwards at a horse ranch in Pembroke Township on September 3, where she saw two black men, one wearing a cowboy hat. When she said this to police, she did not know anything of the claims Danny Edwards made about black cowboys.

Not all the talk is idle gossip. Some of the talk about black cowboys is serious. One man who prefers not to be identified insists there is a black man known as Cowboy who helped locate a place for some men to bury something. He said Cowboy was hired to watch the spot, along with other black men on horseback. The man said he knows Cowboy. But, he said that even today, more than 25 years after the crime, Cowboy is unwilling to talk because he still fears for his life.

As Danny Edwards explained in a previous chapter, there was no need for black cowboys or anyone to guard the site. Mr. Small was buried in a remote area that no one could have found, and there was no way Mr. Small was going anywhere with all that sand on him. If anyone else was involved in the kidnapping, they could have watched Mr. Small above ground. And there was no one to watch Mr. Small because Danny Edwards acted alone. There is no evidence or proof to the contrary. But that doesn't stop the rumors.

A lot of people cannot believe that Edwards acted alone. Someone had to help him with this scheme and help him with this box. But that argument makes no sense. If anyone else was involved, they would have told Danny Edwards it was crazy and it would not have happened.

There is a lot more to the Stephen Small case. And there is a lot less. No grand conspiracy, no black cowboys, no drug kingpins, no scheming girlfriend. Just Danny Edwards. Alone.

That brings us to the biggest oddity in this case. It is disturbing, but it seems that "everyone knows" the "real story" of the Stephen Small case that is not being told.

From crazy conspiracy theories involving the assassinations of John F. Kennedy and Martin Luther King Jr., all the way to theories about space aliens from other planets visiting here or Elvis being alive, people like to believe in a dark side that is being hidden from them by the authorities. In America, it seems the crazier the theory, the more widespread it becomes.

The rumors in this case are crazy, but they have to be addressed here or they will continue to circulate.

The most common rumor in this case revolves around theories that

Stephen Small and Danny Edwards knew each other and that Mr. Small was a cocaine customer. Many people who say they have knowledge of this case or the people involved, including a half dozen or so ex-cops who spoke to me, claim they "know" it. A number of people expand the rumor to the point that Mr. Small was the mastermind of the plot in order to extort money from his family. Some say it is because Stephen Small went out too easily that night and he had no marks of being forced into the box.

It does not need to be explained why this is wrong in so many ways.

These ideas are bizarre and defy logic. But ultimately, there are only two people who know if this is true: Stephen Small and Danny Edwards.

"I don't know where people come up with this," a perplexed Danny Edwards told me.

Edwards said he did not know Stephen Small. He said he did not sell drugs to Stephen Small. The only time he ran into him was when they both happened to be in a boat store at the same time.

And most importantly, Danny Edwards undoubtedly would have used this as a defense when he was on trial for his life, if it was true. With all the crazy stories he told to try to shift the blame, this one was too crazy even for Danny Edwards to dream up.

The autopsy report in the police file shows no trace of cocaine in Stephen Small at the time of his death.

That should be the final word to all the conspiracy theorists.

Perhaps this idea got its start from remarks Sheldon Reagan made to the jury.

On the tape, Stephen Small said he first thought the kidnapping was a joke. Reagan wondered if perhaps Mr. Small was in on this joke.

"Remember the tape of Mr. Small. You heard it twice and you read a transcript of it. Remember Mr. Small saying on the tape, 'God, I thought this was a joke or something, but it is no joke. This is not some party at Yurgine's.' Now, if a gun was used, ladies and gentlemen, would Mr. Small say, 'God, I thought this was a joke?' Is it a reasonable inference to draw that Mr. Small would think it was a joke if someone had a gun pointed at him?"

Reagan continued, "This raises another question I would like you to think about. Why would Mr. Small say he thought it was a joke? Did he know his kidnappers? What could possibly lead him to believe that this was a joke? And if he didn't believe it was a joke, why would he say it? Is it a reasonable inference, ladies and gentlemen, that Mr. Small did know his kidnappers? Yes, I think so. And I think the evidence shows this for two reasons. There is no physical evidence, or evidence of physical abuse to Mr. Small by the kidnappers, and by the tapes of Mr. Small's voice saying that he thought it was a joke."

The rumors could have stemmed from these remarks. They certainly grew. Even Danny Edwards cannot un-do what he started.

Rick Gilbert, one of the primary detectives on the case, said he heard the tape that Mr. Small was forced to make. He told me, "If you listen to that tape, it was clear he knew he was going to die."

There are people who tell me they saw Stephen Small and Danny Edwards together. Two people said they saw Small's red Ferrari Testarossa at Edwards' house on different occasions. However, Edwards had a red Pontiac Fiero GT, which was designed to look like a Testarossa. It was the car that was repossessed after his drug arrest.

So much for the rumors about those Ferrari sightings.

There even are numerous people who said Governor Ryan commuted the death sentences of all 167 prisoners on Death Row just to save Danny Edwards' life.

That is another idea so crazy that it need not be discussed.

How does one explain so many unrelated people across such a wide area "knowing" these same theories? This started in an era when there was no social media, no electronic bulletin boards on which to spread gossip. But on the other hand, gossip has always moved fast in a small town, internet or not.

The theory that Stephen Small and Danny Edwards "had to know each other" carries no more weight than the theory that Nancy Rish "had to know" what Danny Edwards was up to when he was building a plywood box in their garage.

The rumors and unanswered questions in this case started with false statements by some and suppositions by others. There weren't many facts coming out in the beginning to correct these rumors. Nature abhors a vacuum, so the rumors filled the space where the truth was supposed to be. No one was interested in finding the truth -- they were more interested in finding enough to get a conviction -- so the rumors stuck.

These rumors are untrue, no matter how many people "know" it. The only reason they are mentioned here is because they still are so widespread in Kankakee. If they were ignored, readers would think the author missed the real story, the story they all "know," and they would continue to believe it.

I have spent more than a year working on this story full time, researching police files, court transcripts, and everything possible, as well as talking to everyone possible. You would not believe how many people are convinced that Stephen Small knew Danny Edwards, that black cowboys are involved, that Tracy Storm was somehow involved, that Mitch Levitt or other drug lords up north put Danny Edwards up to this. It is so deeply ingrained that I am not sure anything I write will change a lot of minds.

I can find no truth to the rumors about Mr. Small, the black cowboys, or other rumors and suppositions that are unsupported by facts.

But it is disturbing that they are so widely believed, even after all these years.

There are more odd circumstances in this case. There were witnesses who did not testify, evidence that was not made known, and just plain baffling situations.

And Nancy Rish wasn't the only one with a conflicting story. Several police and lawyers had stories that did not match. Some stories were differing accounts of the same incident. Some were omissions. Some were facts deliberately withheld from the defense.

And some were just plain lies.

Lawyer (and future judge) Scott Swaim said that when he arrived at the Bourbonnais Police Department on September 4, he was told by FBI Special Agent Elizabeth Lamanna, "We (police) don't feel Nancy is involved in the kidnapping of Stephen Small. All we need is a statement and she will be free to go."

At Rish's trial on October 3, 1988, Swaim testified, "Miss Rish was very concerned about her son, about the activities of that morning, with all the officers in the house, with guns drawn and what was going on. She was very emotional. Officer Lamanna turned to her and tapped her on the arm or knee and said, 'Calm down. After you give your statement, you'll be out of here.'"

Swaim said Lamanna may or may not have said, "Calm down, Honey."

Lamanna testified she made no such statement or promise to Nancy Rish or to Scott Swaim. She also denied touching Nancy or calling her "Honey."

Investigator George Clodfelter interviewed Scott Swaim on August 1, 1988. In his report, Swaim said Lamanna told Rish, "Don't worry, Honey, you will be out of here in a little while."

Scott Swaim and State's Attorney William Herzog also were far apart in their versions of their conversations.

After Rish was taken to the county jail at 7 p.m., on September 4, Swaim said he called Herzog and protested that she was being booked, saying it was his understanding she would not be arrested because she was cooperating. Swaim testified, "I called Small's house and asked for Bill Herzog. I said, we were told, Miss Rish and I, that if she gave a statement and cooperated, which I believe she had done, that she would be allowed to go home. And he said -- and I can't quote verbatim, it's been a year -- 'Scott, if she tells us where Steve is, we will give her the million dollars.' My reply was, 'She has not indicated she has any knowledge of that.' And he said, 'She's not going anywhere. She's going to spend the night (in jail).'"

Herzog testified that Swaim told him Nancy Rish was not involved and that Swaim believed her.

"I said, 'Scott, she's lying to you,'" Herzog said. "'She's in it all the way, based on the information I've received on the search warrants. She was present at least at one of the ransom calls. She's lying to you. You should

253

really go back and have her tell you the truth.'"

Herzog said Swaim was surprised to hear Rish was present at the ransom call. "He (Swaim) said, 'I'll talk to her and I'll get back to you.'"

"I talked to Swaim that evening on the phone," Herzog testified. "He said Nancy Rish said she was present when one or more calls were made, and she did it because she was afraid of Danny Edwards. Swaim said there was no basis to charge or hold her. I said 'Scott, she's still lying to you. She's in it all the way. She lives with the guy. They have been at the house all day. It's important we find out where Steve is, if he is still alive. Please go back and ask her, she's got to tell the truth. Tell her she's got to tell the truth.'"

Herzog said Swaim asked, "Does this mean she's not going home tonight?" Herzog said he replied, "She's not going nowhere."

"He became furious at me," Herzog said. "He threatened to sue me, he threatened to sue the county, the state police, all the officers involved there. I said, 'Scott, we all got to do what we got to do.'" That ended the conversation.

Herzog said he typed the search warrants and showed them to Willis and Gerard. They asked if there would be enough evidence there to arrest the pair. Herzog said yes.

Swaim and Herzog couldn't even agree on where the call was placed. Herzog said Swaim called him at his house, not Mrs. Small's house.

As for promising the million dollars to Rish for the safe return of Stephen Small, Herzog said Swaim's testimony in court was the first time he heard of that. "It's news to me," he told the court.

Swaim went back on the stand. He reiterated that Herzog did make the statement about the million dollars. Did Herzog say she's in it all the way, she's lying? No, Swaim said.

"I didn't threaten to sue him. I said he was violating her constitutional rights and could be subject to a lawsuit for doing such."

Donald Eckels could have been a key witness on behalf of Nancy Rish. But he was never called to the witness stand.

Eckels was a Kankakee County sheriff's deputy who had been the head of internal investigations. He got a lateral demotion when Bernie Thompson was elected sheriff, the sort of political shifting common in Kankakee. Part of his duty in 1987 was to fly his private airplane over certain areas, looking for stolen or abandoned cars. The remote badlands of Pembroke Township is one such spot.

Eckels said he flew his plane over that area one afternoon in late August 1987, a few days before the kidnapping. Eckels said he saw five men there, and a white van with a box sticking out of the back. Three men were white, two men were black. Another white man with light colored hair was sitting in the passenger side of the van.

He mentioned this to Sgt. William Willis, just after it was learned that Mr. Small's body was found there. Willis told him to write a report and give it to Sgt. Ed Jackson.

Eckels was one of the officers who guarded the crime scene on the night Small was found, while Small's body was left in the ground overnight. Eckels said he mentioned his sighting from the air to other officers.

Eckels said he typed up his report and turned it in.

However, Eckels said he was asked not to testify because he was told his information "was of no value to the investigation."

Nancy Rish's lawyers didn't learn about this until long after her trial. They contacted Eckels about this during the appeals process. Eckels was retired when he swore to his sighting in an affidavit dated October 23, 1993.

"In late August 1987, I was flying with Deputy John Ruch over Pembroke. I observed a white van parked on Cable Line Road. A wooden box was sticking out of the back end of the van. A white man was standing in the box, and two black men were standing on the ground behind the box. There was at least one other white man who ran around the van when I flew over. A white male was sitting in the right front seat of the van," Eckels swore in his affidavit. "After hearing of the kidnapping, I told Ed Jackson of the sheriff's department. He had me tell Willis, who told me to write a report and give it to Jackson. I did, and gave it to Jackson."

Eckels said Jackson told him the sighting had nothing to do with the investigation.

Eckels was fired in 1991 after being caught up in the Operation Backdraft investigation of arson for hire in Kankakee County. He left his keys in his car, which then was taken and burned by someone he knew. Eckels turned in an insurance claim. He later paid it back. He lost his job, was fined $4,670 and was given three years probation. There is reason to believe Eckels was set up by the local powers for some reason. But that is another Kankakee story.

Joshua Sachs, Rish's appeal lawyer, subpoenaed Eckels' police report on February 10, 1994. Kankakee Police Sgt. Robert Anderson, complying with the subpoena, replied to Judge Michela on March 7, 1994.

Anderson said there was no such document in the city police department's case file with name of Eckels. Kankakee County Sheriff Tim Bukowski wrote to Sachs on March 11, 1994, saying there was no such report in the county's records.

If the report existed, Sachs never got it.

Whether Eckels' story is credible or not, whether he saw Edwards' van or someone else's vehicle, his testimony could have been helpful at Nancy Rish's trial -- if her lawyers had known about it.

Eckels' account is similar to two other witnesses, James Witvoet Jr. and Thad Wells. Witvoet, manager of J&B Vegetables farm, testified at Rish's trial about seeing a van, with white men and black men and a blond-haired person, coming out of those woods a day or two before the kidnapping. Thad Wells, a driver for J&B Vegetables, also testified about seeing a white van at that spot, with two white men and one black man. Wells previously received police training, spending two terms at the police academy, and he worked as an auxiliary policeman. He said he was trained in observing unusual circumstances, such as the men and the van in a place they did not belong.

What was not known at the time of Nancy Rish's trial was that Witvoet had been charged with "operation of an unlicensed migrant labor camp." The charges were brought by Kankakee County State's Attorney William Herzog on behalf of the Illinois Department of Public Health. The state declared Witvoet's farm camp to be unkempt, unsanitary, overcrowded, infested with insects "and it presents a serious health hazard to the occupants." The criminal complaint, filed on July 26, 1988, claimed Witvoet had no state license between June 16 and July 26.

The trial was set for January 17, 1989, with Larry Beaumont appearing for the state and Chris Bohlen appearing for Witvoet. The case was dismissed that day.

Between the time the complaint was filed and the time it was dismissed was when Nancy Rish's trial occurred.

It wasn't until five years after the trial and conviction that Rish's defense lawyers found out that Witvoet was facing these charges when he testified at Rish's trial. The information was in a *Chicago Tribune* story on Nov. 30, 1993, by William Gaines and Paul Weingarten.

The state Department of Public Health was not notified that the charges were dropped. Bernard Turnock, the department's director, learned about it two months after the fact. He wrote to Herzog for an explanation. He got no reply. He wrote again three months later and again got no reply.

Patrick Metz, a health department inspector, told the *Chicago Tribune* that it was "unreal" that action wasn't taken in the Witvoet matter because the state "had a strong case."

Witvoet told the *Tribune* he did not trade his testimony against Nancy Rish for an agreement to have the charges dropped. Herzog refused to give a comment to the *Tribune,* but he did tell *The Daily Journal* that the charges were a misdemeanor, the charges against Witvoet did not affect his credibility, and they were dropped because they were made against the wrong man -- the charges should have been against James Witvoet Sr., who owned the farm, not Witvoet Jr.

Sherri Carr told the *Tribune* that Witvoet was the "linchpin" of the case against her client in 1988. It was Witvoet who said he saw a blond-haired passenger in Edwards' van at the scene of the crime, even though phone records showed Nancy Rish was 17 miles away at that time. Carr said she would have challenged Witvoet's credibility if she had known about these charges. She told the *Tribune* that withholding of information was deliberate on the part of prosecutors.

Did Witvoet and Wells see Edwards' van, or was this another van? There is another fact that was not mentioned. Detective C. Mathis and Sgt. Maurice Meitzner filed a report, noting that they talked to a man named Don Montalta, who said he saw a white van going by his farm near Aroma Park five or six times, and the people in the van looked like Mexicans. The report is in the police file, but it was not used in court. Could it be that the people who said they saw Danny Edwards and others in a white van really were seeing farm workers?

And why did Eckels' report disappear, and why was he not called to court? Could it be his sighting of several men in a white van did not fit the prosecution's case of Danny Edwards and Nancy Rish alone?

Eckels said he did not know the exact day when he saw this van, but it wasn't a weekend because he didn't work weekends at that time. Danny Edwards said he buried the box there on a Sunday, and he did it alone, with no other men helping him. Edwards said he doesn't know what Eckels saw. Maybe Sgt. Jackson was right, it had no relevance.

One of the biggest mistakes of Paulauskis and Carr was focusing too much on Tracy Storm. The defense tried to show Tracy Storm was guilty, instead of concentrating on proving Nancy Rish was innocent. When they couldn't do this, it blew up in their face and undermined their credibility.

The defense tried to get the jury to believe that Tracy Storm was the blond who was seen with Danny Edwards in the van in Small's neighborhood and in the woods. They argued it was a case of mistaken identity, it was a blond man who was the real accomplice.

It turns out there was no blond or blonde accomplice.

There was as much circumstantial evidence against Tracy Storm as there was against Nancy Rish. But Tracy Storm was not on trial. The prosecution decided to go after Nancy Rish, not Tracy Storm. The defense failed to realize that whether or not Tracy Storm was the blond seen in the van at any time with Danny Edwards, it was not relevant to their case. The relevant issues were Nancy Rish being in the car when the ransom calls were made, the box being built in her garage, the confusion in her interrogation -- and whether or not she knew what Danny Edwards was planning. Proving that there may be another possible accomplice did not clear her.

In her opening remarks to the jury, Sherri Carr indicated that Storm would be a prime focus.

"Who done it? Believe it or not, this is a murder mystery. They would like you to believe the mystery is solved. The mystery focuses around who helped Danny Edwards. I believe you will realize during this trial that the mystery is why this young woman is sitting here before you today, and that there is a blond person walking the streets. Who is this person? They don't want to tell you. We will tell you."

But there was no more case against Tracy Storm than there was against Nancy Rish. Both had been seen often with Danny Edwards in the weeks before the kidnapping, but so what? Rish's fingerprints and hair sample did not match evidence at the scene. Neither did Storm's prints or hair.

Tracy Storm showed up at Nancy Rish's trial. Michael Ficaro had Sgt. Robert Anderson point out Storm, and then Ficaro asked Storm to stand up. Here was a witness, in essence, giving testimony without being sworn and without having to be cross examined. The surprise here was that Storm's long blond hair was cut short and dyed a dark shade. This prearranged act undercut the defense contention about a man with long blond feathered hair.

It would be interesting to observe Michael Ficaro if his job was prosecuting Tracy Storm instead of defending him.

There were a lot of foul-ups by the police.

FBI agents recorded ransom phone calls to Nancy Small's house. After recording the 11:28 p.m. call, they rewound the tape and were playing it back. Edwards made another call 18 minutes later. The FBI could not record this conversation because there was no tape in the recorder. To record this call, they would have had to put the cassette tape back in the machine and record it over the previous call. The 11:46 p.m. call was not recorded because the FBI owned only one cassette tape.

The FBI knew that Stephen Small told his wife on the phone that he was being put in a box "under a couple of feet of sand" and he mentioned Joe Yurgine's name. Yurgine lived near Aroma Park, which is near the only sandy soil in the area. That information did not immediately register in the minds of the police. They didn't even ask themselves the question, "Who's Yurgine?" It was later when Sgt. Bill Willis recognized the name that he thought the name might be a clue.

And just how did trained FBI agents following a drug-addled man manage to lose their prey in the streets of a small subdivision? How did a coke-head manage to lose an FBI tail in broad daylight? Instead of alerting local police to be on the lookout for the white van, the perplexed FBI agents went back to Edwards' house and waited for him to come home. He was gone 90 minutes. They never learned where he went.

Local, state and federal police were staking out the phone booths in Aroma Park, trying to look inconspicuous, after tracing a ransom call there. Danny Edwards spotted the surveillance cars immediately. He saw one FBI agent staring at him as he drove past him. Edwards also saw the cops outside his house and in a nearby park. The police were staking out his house waiting for him to come out and lead them to the victim. These trained officers did not go unnoticed.

258

The FBI log for Thursday, September 3, shows surveillance was discontinued at 2:15 p.m. and resumed at 4 p.m. The agent reported "lights out" at the residence at 10:21 p.m. Surveillance was discontinued at 11:50 p.m.

If Danny had left the house, either to check on his victim or to escape, he could have done it.

He did.

He did leave the house, without anyone there to see him, and he did go back to Aroma Park early Thursday morning to check on Mr. Small after losing the FBI. To this day, the police and FBI do not know this.

How dumb is someone to be outsmarted at that time by Danny Edwards?

The police made a decision not to arrest Danny Edwards when they first had him on Wednesday night. They hoped they could follow him to where Stephen Small was being held. This was in hopes of saving Stephen Small's life.

And with Stephen Small's life in the balance, they went home for the night.

FBI agents brought a tape recording to Nancy Small's house on September 8, 1987, only days after she heard the ransom calls from the kidnapper. This tape contained a conversation between Danny Edwards and Mitch Levitt, recorded on January 28, 1987, just after Danny Edwards was busted for cocaine. Mrs. Small listened to the tape and said she "could not rule out" the possibility the voice of the 3:30 a.m. ransom call was Levitt. But she couldn't make a positive identification.

Despite the question of the voice on the tape, and even though the police knew Levitt supplied Edwards with cocaine, and despite Edwards' insistence that Levitt forced him to kidnap Stephen Small, Levitt was never questioned by police.

Was this because Levitt, like Eckels' information, did not fit the Danny-and-Nancy case the state prepared?

Another inexplicable foul-up was that police left the townhouse on Stratford Drive East unsecured. They had not completed searching the place or examining it for further possible evidence. And yet, on Saturday, September 5, the day after the raid, Tracy Storm was able to enter the residence and take a motorcycle from the garage. The house was unlocked. No police were guarding it. After the police found Storm when he came back a second time, the only security they placed was a yellow police tape line.

And there are the contradictory statements among the top officials. Swaim claimed Herzog said Rish could have the million dollars if she told where Small was; Herzog denied he said it; and Lamanna telling Rish she could go home after making a statement and then denying it.

Lamanna testified that she saw the car in Aroma Park after the ransom call, and Nancy was in the passenger's side of the car. Every other police officer, as well as Nancy and Danny, said that Nancy was driving. Lamanna testified, "The passenger turned and looked at me and she had a look on her face of, it was either like fright or panic because I just looked back at her and it startled me. And then right after she did that she turned around and completely turned around to look out the back window of the car." But how reliable is her testimony about Nancy Rish's demeanor if she was wrong about something as simple as which side of the car she was sitting?

The police and prosecutors never addressed the dilemma raised by the findings of Lauren Wicevic, the FBI's fingerprint expert. Wicevic testified that there were 15 latent fingerprints collected from the wooden box, the light, a flashlight and other items at the crime scene that remained unidentified. That is a startling fact. Danny Edwards and 15 other people left fingerprints at the crime scene, but Nancy Rish was not one of them. So why was Nancy Rish prosecuted? And who are these other 15 people?

Perhaps the biggest foul-up was the deal the Kankakee County state's attorney made with Danny Edwards in March 1987. Edwards, facing 30 years for possession of cocaine, was promised probation if he set up another drug dealer. It didn't happen, but Edwards still got probation. Steve Small might be alive today if the state had sent Danny Edwards away for his drug bust in early 1987.

There are a number of coincidences in this case, but that is not unusual in a small town. Some are small coincidences, some are eerie.

Stephen and Nancy Small's wedding rehearsal dinner in 1969 was at Yesteryear restaurant, the building Stephen bought in 1986.

One of Nancy Small's seven prenuptial bridal showers was a tea hosted by Marie and Darlene Woodrich. They were cousins of Nancy (Woodrich) Rish.

Nancy Small's maid of honor was Nina Lorand. Nancy Small was a bridesmaid for Nina a year later when Nina married dentist Steven Epstein in the Gold Room of the Hotel Kankakee. Nina Epstein was elected the first woman mayor of Kankakee in 2009, and she was reelected in 2013.

Stephen Small's body is interred in the mausoleum wall at Mound Grove Cemetery, about eight feet off the ground. Ironically, the only time Stephen Small was buried underground was when he was buried alive.

Nancy Rish's parents, Paul and Genevieve Woodrich, met in the 1940s when Genevieve was working at LeCour's women's store. Paul's sister worked with her. His sister was Genevieve Westerhoff, whose son Jeff helped Danny Edwards buy the wood for Stephen Small's box.

After Nancy Rish's father was beaten to death in 1986, Noble Smith was charged with murder but was found not guilty by reason of insanity. The judge was Fred Carr, the father of Nancy's defense lawyer.

Danny Edwards was best man at the wedding of his friend Bill Mohler. Mohler was best man at the wedding of Danny and Peggy Edwards in 1976, and he was best man at the wedding of Terry and Nancy Rish in 1978. His brother, Tom, married Peggy Edwards' sister, Carol McKenna.

Nancy's son, Benjamin, faced a number of judges for traffic and other violations over the years, including Scott Swaim, Michael Kick, Sheldon Reagan, Gordon Lustfeldt and Fred Carr.

Kent Allain, who was briefly implicated in the kidnapping, at first denied any connection to Stephen Small, and then admitted they had a traffic accident. It happened at 3:47 p.m. on March 7, 1987. Stephen Small was towing a boat and he accidentally backed into Allain's car, which was parked at 151 E. Station Street. Stephen's sons Ramsey, Barrett and Christopher were in the car. The left front fender, bumper and lower panel door of Allain's car were damaged. Small was ticketed for improper backing. Kankakee Patrolman Walter Sykes wrote the ticket. He was not on the police force very long after that, and later became a police officer in Mississippi.

How ironic and odd that the brother of Governor Ryan went into business with the brother of the man who murdered the great-grandson of Governor Small? Former mayor Tom Ryan and Duke Edwards were part of a group of connected local people who started Comguard, a company that manufactured ankle bracelets for convicts. This was in 1988, only months after Stephen Small was murdered by Danny Edwards. The devices never really worked, but the company got hundreds of thousands of dollars in state contracts and local loans before defaulting.

Ed Benson owned Security Lumber, where Danny Edwards bought the plywood for the box. He was Sherri Carr's step-grandfather. Sherri's grandmother, Connie Benson, was very upset with her for agreeing to defend Nancy Rish. The Bensons were close friends with the Smalls. Ed Benson's son was Judge Roger Benson, who presided at the arraignment of Nancy Rish and Danny Edwards. Benson went back into private practice and was one of the lawyers who had an office in the former Yesteryear/Bradley House.

The trial of Danny Edwards was costly for the taxpayers of Kankakee and Illinois. County auditor Richard Winkel put the bill at $137,466. This included $100,144 for Edwards' defense lawyers. It did not include any part of the annual salary of $59,016 Michael Ficaro earned as an assistant attorney general, or the state salaries of the other prosecutors. It doesn't include the salary of the judge, the court clerks and others. The figure also didn't include 15 years of legal fees for appeals paid by the taxpayers, to which Danny Edwards was entitled because he was on Death Row. For his work defending Nancy Rish, Vincent Paulauskis was paid $55,536 plus $5,064 to reimburse expenses; Sherri Carr was paid $32,591. Thousands of dollars more was spent on legal costs, meals and lodging for jurors for both trials, and more. It could be that the total cost for both trials approached the million dollars that Danny Edwards was looking for.

These are just a few of the odd facts related to this case.

Danny Edwards said the mug shots of him and Nancy that went on the news wires across America were not their original mug shots.

"We were showered and groomed that morning when we were arrested," he said in 2013. "We looked too good. The picture (in the newspaper) wasn't our booking photo. Bill Willis woke us up at 4:30 a.m. (three days later) and took us in for a picture. He said it was for the FBI, but it was for the Kankakee paper, and it was in every newspaper in the country. It was because we didn't look guilty enough before."

The purpose of the pictures, Edwards said, was to "horrify the public. They wanted to monster-ize us."

The uncropped color photos shows the date of September 7, three days after Edwards and Rish were arrested and booked. Edwards appears bushy haired, unshaven, sleepy-eyed and defiant. Rish's eyes are swollen and red. "She had been crying for three days," Edwards said.

Edwards said his mug shot was taken first on September 4 and again on September 7. Rish remembered that her mug shot was taken when she was booked on September 4 because the person who took her fingerprints was really rough with her, and that sticks in her mind.

The September 7 mug shots are the only ones in the police files.

Kankakee County Chief Deputy Ken McCabe said he checked his files, and the pictures from September 7 were the only mug shots taken. He told me Edwards and Rish were booked on September 4, but their mug shots were not taken until September 7.

Edwards insists otherwise. "I can prove it. Our original September 4, 12:35 a.m. booking photos are in the Brady (appeals) material in the police reports and witness statements. It is in the court house. I know it's there because I picked it out of the volume it was in to show my parents the booking pictures they could have used. The name of the person who booked and fingerprinted and took the booking photos (September 4) was Sgt. Daniel."

The September 7 booking photo shows that Officer Ervin took that mug shot of Edwards, and Officer K. Jones took the mug shot of Rish. The "7" on the date of Rish's picture clearly is written over the number "4."

A statement in the police file by Sgt. Ronald Daniel on September 4, 1987, noted that he booked Danny Edwards and put him in a holding cell at 7 p.m. The Illinois State Police files notes that Danny Edwards, Nancy Rish and Kent Allain were fingerprinted on Saturday, September 5.

If there were pictures taken on September 4, they cannot be found in the sheriff's files or in the courthouse files.

The kidnapping of Stephen Small was not the first deadly threat to the family. While campaigning for governor in 1920, Len Small received a "Black Hand" letter threatening death to him and his family unless he paid $40,000. The "Black Hand" was a shadow group of Sicilians whose extortion racket became outmoded when Prohibition allowed the Mafia to become a more organized and more profitable operation.

The extortion letter was full of misspellings and poor grammar, perhaps to make authorities believe it was written by ignorant immigrants. It turned out that the extortionists were not Sicilian. They were farm hands from Manteno, Byron Caudell and Neucomb Palmer. And they were not too smart. Their boss, farmer William Allers, saw the letter on Caudell's dresser and heard Caudell talking on the phone to Palmer about it. Allers went to Small's bank and told him.

Len Small and his son Leslie went to Chicago to see Mayor "Big Bill" Thompson to get experienced police detectives to track down Caudell and Palmer.

The Chicago and Kankakee police didn't need to work too hard. They staked out the road near Momence where the extortionists told Small to drop the money. Since Caudell had stolen Allers' car, both the vehicle and Caudell were tracked down in Spring Valley. Police picked up Palmer at his house.

Caudell pleaded guilty to stealing the car and was sentenced to 1-to-20 years in the penitentiary. Palmer was not charged.

And here is another odd and eerie fact: Danny was not the first Edwards to judge a Small. The judge at the 1922 trial of Governor Small was Claire Edwards.

Also, Judge Edwards' brother put up the bail money for gangster Eddie Kaufman when Kaufman was arrested for his involvement in Governor Small's jury bribing. Claire Edwards left the bench and went back into private law practice. One client was mobster George "Bugs" Moran, who years earlier bought a parole from Governor Small, and then got his gang back together, resulting in the St. Valentine's Day massacre.

When Governor Len Small was indicted in 1921 for embezzling two million dollars from the state, his lawyers argued that the governor was above the law. The court rejected this argument, so Governor Small found another way to beat the rap -- he had Al Capone's hoodlums bribe the jury. When the state had no case against Nancy Rish, it used "guilt by association" with the evidence it had against Danny Edwards. That was Small justice then, that is Small justice today, both in Kankakee and in Illinois. That is the Small justice that Nancy Rish received as punishment simply for living with the wrong man.

Danny Edwards was just 11 years old when Barbara Jane Mackle's story made national headlines.

The 20-year-old daughter of a millionaire real estate developer from Florida was with her mother in a motel in Georgia on December 17, 1968. Steven Krist knocked on the door and identified himself as a police officer, telling the girl that a close friend had been hurt in a traffic accident. Krist and his accomplice, Ruth Eisemann-Schier, went in the room and chloroformed Barbara's mother and tied her up. They forced Barbara into a car.

They took Barbara to a remote area and buried her alive in a box.

This box, however, had a pump with two plastic pipes that provided air from the outside. It also had a battery powered lamp that worked, and water and food.

The kidnappers demanded $500,000 from Barbara's father. He paid the ransom, and Krist sent police directions to the burial site. Barbara was rescued after more than three days buried in the box.

The kidnappers left a lot of clues. They were caught, convicted and sent to jail. Eisemann-Schier was sentenced to seven years, but was paroled after four years. She later was deported back to Honduras. Krist was arrested off the coast of Florida in a speedboat he bought with some of the ransom money. He was sentenced to life in prison, but was paroled after 10 years. He was given a pardon so he could attend medical school. Krist's medical license was revoked in 2003, and he later was arrested for smuggling cocaine and illegal aliens.

Barbara Jane Mackle wrote a book in 1971 about her ordeal, *83 Hours 'Till Dawn*. It was condensed in a *Reader's Digest* article and was made into two TV movies, *The Longest Night* in 1972 and *83 Hours 'Till Dawn* in 1990.

Danny Edwards said in 2013 that he never heard of that case, but he knew that the police searched the records of several local libraries to see if he or Nancy checked out any books about burying someone alive. The police files show that neither Edwards nor Rish checked out any books at any library.

Pot smoking or the passage of time may have affected Danny's memory.

Randy Irps, his best friend from high school, clearly remembered an instance which he recounted in an interview with me in November 2013.

"We were watching a movie on TV in the basement of his parent's house on Eagle Street one night," Randy said. "It would have been about 1972 or 1973. I remember, I was sitting in the recliner and Danny was sitting on the couch. It was about a girl who was kidnapped and buried alive."

"Danny thought a bit and then said, 'A person could get away with that.'"

There are three more odd Kankakee-related stories that can be mentioned here: Wiley Morris, Diana Oughton and Sam Sheppard.

There as just one legal execution in Kankakee County history. Wiley J. Morris was hanged inside the lobby of the Kankakee County courthouse in 1861. He was a black man who was accused of murdering a white woman near Pontiac. Despite reasonable doubt and his own protestations, he was convicted and sentenced to death.

Morris had a reasonable explanation for the evidence against him, but no one was willing to listen to him.

In that era, when slavery was still legal in the United States, and when black people were blamed for the approaching Civil War, Morris didn't have a chance. It would be another 17 years before the real murderer confessed on his deathbed. The scales of justice aren't always perfect, but in Kankakee County, there is a long history of a very fat thumb on one end on the scales.

And that history continues today. Robert Agostinelli, Rish's appellate public defender, told the *Chicago Tribune*, "Nancy Rish was convicted by circumstances that could easily be explained." Unfortunately, no one in Kankakee was interested in listening to explanations in 1987 any more than they were in 1861.

Nancy Rish was 25 years old with a nine-year-old son when she went to prison. She is now a grandmother in her 50s, having spent more than half her life in prison. There are a lot of people in Kankakee who still believe in Nancy Rish's innocence. But no one in power seems to be willing to do anything about it.

Danny Edwards took Stephen Small's life.

He also took Nancy Rish's life.

Danny Edwards acted alone when he took Stephen Small's life.

But he had a whole lot of help in robbing Nancy Rish of her life.

The Smalls were friends with the Oughton family of Dwight. The Oughtons had almost as much money as the Smalls.

Diana Oughton's great-grandfather was W.D. Boyce of Ottawa, Illinois, who was the founder of the Boy Scouts of America. Another great-grandfather, John R. Oughton, founded the Keely Institute for alcoholics in Dwight. Diana's father, James Oughton, owned a bank, thousands of acres of profitable farmland and a lot more. The 20-room Oughton mansion in Dwight is one of the most beautiful houses in the Midwest.

Diana turned against her family and her country and became a radical in the 1960s, joining the terrorist Students for a Democratic Society (SDS) and Weathermen group. Her live-in boyfriend was Bill Ayers, who later became a close ally of fellow Chicago "community organizer" Barack Obama. Ayers was the ghost writer of Obama's autobiography, *Dreams Of My Father.*

265

Ayers modeled Obama's unnamed former girlfriend in the book after Diana Oughton. Bill Ayers was another spoiled, petulant rich boy who turned against his family and his country. He said his only regret was that he didn't kill enough people, particularly policemen and soldiers.

Her family disapproved of her actions, but Diana lived off daddy's credit card and her personal corporate dividends. Diana Oughton was killed on March 6, 1970, in a Greenwich Village townhouse in New York City. She and others were building bombs to set at a dance at Fort Dix, when a bomb went off in her hands. Two other terrorists also died. It took four days for her remains to be found under the rubble, and another week before she was identified. That is because her head, hands and one foot were blown off in the blast. Not much was left but the tip of a finger, which was matched to fingerprints from a previous arrest.

Police found 57 sticks of dynamite, four pipe bombs and 30 blasting caps in the rubble of the Greenwich Village townhouse. *The Daily Journal* ran two very favorable obituary stories for Oughton at the time. She was motivated by "compassion and concern for the world," and there was "openness and warmth in her," and she had "goodness and care and thoughtfulness in her heart," according to the stories. She was "always concerned about other people and wanting to improve conditions of poverty." It said she previously taught at a private school operated by Ayers.

Later in 1970, Jean Alice Small commissioned a fairly sympathetic series about Diana Oughton to show she was not all bad. However, Oughton was so radical that she and fellow Weatherman Kathy Boudin called themselves "The Fork" after their "war council's" three-finger salute, a reference to the fork that Manson cultists used to murder Sharon Tate and her unborn child in 1969. That bit of information was not in the series authorized by the Smalls. The series won a Pulitzer Prize for national reporting. When the prize was awarded, Mrs. Small said she was happy that the writers "never lost a sense of compassion for Diana and her family."

The Smalls had much kinder words for murderer and terrorist Diana Oughton than they had for Nancy Rish.

In 1966, when Scott Swaim was attending college in Wooster, Ohio, he spent a weekend at a friend's house in Cleveland. His friend's parents, Mr. and Mrs. Charles T. Hall, bought the house from Dr. Sam Sheppard just after Sheppard was convicted of murder. It was in this house in 1954 that Sheppard's wife was slain.

Sheppard was convicted in "the trial of the century," even though he said he saw a "bushy-haired man" running from the crime scene. The circumstances were copied a decade later for the TV series, *The Fugitive.*

Dr. Sheppard's conviction was overturned in 1966. He got a second trial and was acquitted. Richard Ebeling, who died in 1998 in an Ohio prison while serving a sentence for killing another woman, is believed to be the murderer of Marilyn Sheppard.

Contributing to Dr. Sheppard's conviction was public outrage that he was having an affair with his nurse. The affair was seen as a motive for murder. And on top of that, Sheppard lied about the affair on the witness stand. (In another strange coincidence, that nurse, Susan Hayes, went to high school in Bradley, Illinois, part of the greater Kankakee-Bradley-Bourbonnais community).

Concerning Dr. Sheppard, one newspaper reporter wrote in 1954, "He was tried for murder and convicted of adultery." A similar statement could be said about Swaim's client, Nancy Rish, who was tried for murder and was found guilty by association.

Steve Small was the smartest kid in his class at Longfellow Grade School. Everyone in the school knew it. His parents were devoted to education in Kankakee, and all the children appreciated the support and the treats they provided at school events. Burrell and Reva Small would present slide shows of their trips around the world to classes at Longfellow. Steve was not athletic, but he was exceptionally brainy.

A few of the brightest kids were assigned to write short plays for a special evening assembly of students and parents. It was for Mrs. Dunbar's sixth grade class in 1958.

"Steve's play was the last one presented that evening," said Fred Morrissette, one of Steve's closest friends during grade school. "The play included bringing a large coffin on stage. At the end, he got in the coffin and was carried off in it."

The Edwards family lived at 440 S. Alma Avenue. The boys went to Longfellow and they were in the audience that night, Morrissette said.

"I thought about that when Steve was killed, and I thought how eerie it suddenly became," Morrissette said in 2013.

Chapter 19
Perspectives Today

*"We knew this guy (Ficaro) was out for blood,
and he was going to do anything to get it."
Sherri Carr, November 2, 2013*

A number of people connected to this case gave their perspectives in interviews for this book.

This was Sherri Carr's first big case out of law school. It also is where she met Vincent Paulauskis. They were married a year and a half later.

Sherri said there were several instances of deception at the trial.

"Danny Edwards bought something at Englewood Electric. The receipt had both names, Danny Edwards and Nancy Rish. But the receipt was a copy. I knew someone at Englewood, and they pulled the original receipt. Nancy's name was not on it."

Another deception concerned the appearance of Tracy Storm.

"Tracy Storm had long blond hair, shoulder length, like Nancy's. He also had a white van. When Tracy was on the stand, his hair was cut and it was dyed dark. It undercut the description of him that was given."

And there was no way Nancy could have helped Danny with the box, Sherri said. It was not just a matter of strength. Nancy was fastidious about her appearance and she did not like to get her hands dirty.

Sherri Carr said she wanted Danny Edwards to testify at Nancy's trial. "I went to Pontiac to talk to him. He was willing to testify, but his lawyers wouldn't let him because of the appeals."

"There was certain pressure, given who he (Stephen Small) was. I was surprised how fair the coverage was in *The Daily Journal,*" she said, adding that it could afford to be fair, knowing a conviction was certain and the jury did not read the newspaper.

"Nancy said a big deputy made the statement about the electric chair and she said it was Erickson. Erickson guarded her after she testified about that. You can't tell me that wasn't premeditated."

"Nancy Rish naming Erickson was simply a misidentification. It was Willis who said it. And this was before she knew what they were investigating. She didn't know what Danny had done."

"Nancy made so many statements to the police. They talked to her over days. She was not volunteering information, just answering their questions. She was petrified. She told a few lies, but her lies were not material. What she thinks will make her look bad did not."

And while Nancy Rish took the stand in her own defense, she was barred from testifying to what she was told by Danny Edwards. It was considered hearsay, even though all Nancy knew was what Danny had told her.

When Danny Edwards was supposed to be doing confidential informant work with the police, he gave Nancy the idea that some of the things he was doing just before the kidnapping was part of this work.

Sherri said Nancy did not come across very well on the witness stand. "Nancy did not seem likeable on the surface. She was beautiful, but they tainted her as a gold digger, and she did not seem sympathetic."

Sherri also said Swaim allowed Nancy Rish to talk, effectively without counsel. His intention was to find Stephen Small, but there were local and state police and FBI agents looking for Small. Swaim should have let them do their job and his client should have been his first priority.

"Ficaro was such a bully in that prosecution," Sherri said. "Whether that was just his way or because of political pressure, I don't know."

"Ficaro was such a bully that he scared the shit out of every witness he interviewed. And he intimidated witnesses for Nancy. He'd ask, 'Do you like your job?' Some of them worked for the state. It sounds innocuous on the surface. It would be lost on the jury, but the witnesses knew what he was getting at. It was psychology, threatening them with losing their jobs."

"We knew this guy (Ficaro) was out for blood and he was going to do anything to get it. He was vicious. And when he made his comment, 'the spider to the fly,' like Nancy was calling him (Mr. Small) out for a tête-à-tête, that was ridiculous. Stephen Small was going to leave his bed for a sweet talking woman he doesn't know in the middle of the night?"

At Danny's trial, Ficaro said Danny made the call, and at Nancy's trial he said she made the call. "One way or another, he lied," Sherri said.

Ficaro would not respond to a request for an interview for this book.

The "spider to the fly" comment was where Ficaro said Nancy Rish made the phone call that got Stephen Small out of his house. Paulauskis and Carr did not make an objection.

There were several factors why the lawyers did not object.

"We were so stunned, we couldn't believe he just said that," Sherri said. "We didn't object because of shock and just flat out exhaustion. We were working six days a week. We'd get done at 6 or 7 at night and then burn the midnight oil for the next day. Vince had an abscessed tooth and went to a dentist the night before his closing argument. He was in the hospital three days after the trial. All that was factored in."

Sherri Carr has high praise for Judge Michela. "He is a phenomenal legal scholar. He had that practical sense, not just book smart. He was a tremendous mentor."

Sherri Carr said she does not believe Danny intended for Stephen Small to die. She said she also believes Nancy Rish was told she could make a statement and go home. It might have ended that way except for the political pressure to drag Nancy down with Danny. The pressure continues today. Sherri cited several cases, including notorious murderer Monroe Lampkin, who killed two policemen and a civilian in a 1979 shootout on Interstate 57, and who was convicted in two trials in Kankakee County. His cases were sent back on appeal, and yet Nancy Rish's appeals have been denied again and again. That, she said, is unbelievable.

At Lampkin's trial, John Michela was the judge, Vincent Paulauskis was the defense counsel, and State Police Sgt. William Willis was the arresting officer.

If there was any pressure about this case, Judge John Michela said he did not feel any.

"No. I felt none," Judge Michela said in 2013. "I wasn't surprised that I felt none. I wouldn't have been surprised if others put pressure, but there wasn't any, and never by the Smalls."

Michela said he did not know Stephen Small. He said he never belonged to the country club or ran in those circles.

Michela said some lawyers were reluctant to represent either Edwards or Rish. When he was looking to appoint lawyers to the case, he contacted several lawyers. "I didn't want to embarrass them, so I said if you are interested, I will consider you." A few lawyers avoided him because they didn't want to come to his attention.

Michela said he picked Rockford for jury selection because it was far enough away that people did not know about the murder. He said he thought of places like Ottawa or Rock Island, but eliminated them because the Smalls own newspapers there.

As for Nancy Rish's guilt, Michela said, "My impression was that there was no way, given her relationship with Danny Edwards, there was no way she could not have been aware. There is no doubt she made the call to Mr. Small. There was no one else who could have done it. The circumstances indicated her guilt."

What about Ramsey Small saying it was a man who made the call?

Michela was not sure about that. "It was a husky voice. He may have said it was a man's voice. My recollection is that he said it was a 'husky' voice, whether it was him (Ramsey Small) or the prosecution who said it."

As for Rish's demeanor while testifying, Michela said, "My recollection of her testifying (giving an impression of guilt or innocence) is not overwhelming one way or another."

"She was being as straightforward as possible in her answers. I accepted her at face value (what she said) in the courtroom."

"Judge Victor Cardosi told me, 'Women don't lie. By the time they get to the witness stand, they believe what they say.' I told him that could be true for any witness. He said yes."

Nancy Rish "seemed believable, but that doesn't mean she was telling the truth."

"I was convinced (of her guilt) by the evidence in the Edwards case. I already believed she was guilty before her trial. I had no doubt by the time her trial started that the state was justified in bringing the charges, and I was not surprised by the jury finding her guilty."

It was a jury, not the judge, which decided on the guilty verdict.

"If she asked for a bench trial, I would have said get another judge. I knew by then. I would have walked away."

Michela agreed that the Rish trial basically was a replay of the Edwards trial.

Judge Michela said, "I was always surprised Danny Edwards didn't testify at her trial. He could have taken the stand and at least attempted to save her."

"Danny Edwards' case was always cut and dried, even on appeal. Only a huge error by me would have been cause for reversal. Nothing in his case cried out for reversal."

Of Rish's trial, Michela said, "The jury had no such knowledge of the Edwards case" because it was a different jury.

Was Ficaro over the line in his courtroom behavior?

"He was at the extreme end of being a prosecutor. He was within bounds, but at the extreme end," Michela said.

"One of Ficaro's assistants said Ficaro had gone to acting school. He learned that part of the business before going into law. He was very dramatic."

According to a biographical sketch by Olivia Clarke in *Leading Lawyers Network* in 2012, Ficaro was a speech and drama major at DePaul University. He later went to DePaul University College of Law.

When Vincent Paulauskis filed post-trial motions on December 19, 1988, he noted, "Whatever case Mr. Ficaro is on, you can bet it will be the worst defendant he's ever seen and the worst crime he's ever seen."

"Danny Edwards' conversion to Christianity is not uncommon in prison," Michela said in 2013." I think it helps keep you sane. I can't imagine anything worse than being in prison."

Is it possible Nancy Rish is telling the truth and is innocent?

"Yes, it is possible. But probable, no."

"I have a problem. I have always been a believer in the jury system. My thinking was, I didn't listen to the evidence in a jury trial. I listen to witnesses. They will do anything to try to save themselves. That's human nature. If what she told wasn't the truth, that was the jury's take. I wasn't listening to every word."

Is it unusual for a defendant to testify in their own behalf? He wasn't sure, but "lawyers keep them from testifying. Prosecutors are pretty good in breaking them in cross examination."

Benjamin Rish lost his mother to prison when he was nine and his father to a heart attack when he was 16. Benjamin is 35 now and is trying to get his life on track after a devastating start.

Benjamin was an A and B student and was involved in sports before his mother was arrested. His life changed dramatically. A quarter of a century later, it is still extremely difficult for him to talk about the hell he went through in those years, from the treatment from other children at school to the police and other adults in the community.

"My life was on TV and in the newspapers all the time," he said when we sat down in December 2013. "People were talking about my life over the dinner table every night. It's still that way because of my name. My kids have that name. When I got arrested (in later years), the newspaper made a big deal of it. People know me by my mother."

Putting it into words was difficult enough. Getting through the emotional pain to say the words was even harder. He understandably choked up trying to come up with the words. "It wasn't good," he managed to say. "It molded me into a different person."

"I wasn't looking to go to college. I chose to do what was in, what was happening, what was cool. I rode motorcycles, drag racing, the fast life."

His rebellion is shown in the files in the Kankakee circuit court. There are 81 citations up until 2013, mostly for traffic violations. It was as if the cops were following him, he said.

"Then I had these two boys and it switched me back," he said. "I didn't want this for them."

His son Vance was born on April 24, 2007, and Benjamin Jr. was born on April 12, 2008. Benjamin said he has been raising the boys while working part time jobs for a little money. His girlfriend Christina moved out in July 2013, and she took weekday custody after Benjamin started a full time job with long hours.

Benjamin said he is working at being a good father. But he continues to struggle with the tremendous burden he has carried all these years. He has dabbled in drugs in the past. He knows what a descent into darkness can do to a life, and he is fighting that. "There are no retired drug dealers. They're in the ground or in the penitentiary."

Mitch Levitt is now living in Florida. He told me in 2013 that his involvement with Danny Edwards was minimal. A minor Kankakee drug seller introduced him to Edwards. "At first, he sounded like a good customer."

Actually, he said Edwards was his biggest customer. Edwards bought a half kilo of cocaine for $17,000, perhaps three times. Levitt's other customers bought one to four ounces.

Edwards' attempt to set up Levitt was detected the moment they met in the Snuggery Lounge in February 1987 for the deal. Edwards had a cut on his nose. Levitt thought he got it in a drug arrest, and he sensed a set up.

The deal did not go down. But the police were on to Levitt. A month later, Levitt was busted for cocaine possession in Wheeling.

"A federal agent named Noble made the arrest saying, 'Greetings from Danny Edwards.' It was so weird."

Levitt got four years probation. "I was just about off my probation when I got busted in 1992 in Illinois. A childhood friend set me up. I did nine months in a federal prison in Minnesota, and four months in a halfway house in Illinois."

Levitt saw the TV show *Top Cops* when it aired in 1990. In the last segment, Bill Willis mentioned something about a drug dealer from Chicago, and Levitt knew he was talking about him. But he really panicked two years later when he was in the Minnesota prison and he read an article about the Small kidnapping and it mentioned Edwards' claim that a Chicago cocaine dealer named Mitch Levitt forced him to do it.

"I freaked out. I was so worried, I thought I was going to be involved. I contacted my lawyer at the time and he put me at ease, saying it was just the desperate storytelling of a mental case killer trying to avoid the death penalty."

"I was appropriately shocked and scared at the same time, being diminished and vulnerable from the prison experience. Clearly, though, I had nothing to do with it. However, you never know in life. We've all seen innocent people wrongly convicted."

Astoundingly, Levitt was never interviewed or even contacted by the police after the kidnapping and murder of Stephen Small. Despite Edwards' insistence that Levitt put him up to it, the police did not talk to him.

Levitt said he started selling cocaine in about 1982 when he was a student at Northern Illinois University in DeKalb. He moved to Schaumburg and continued selling there.

Did you stop after your bust in 1992?

"You would think that, but I kept at it."

After serving prison time in 1993, he went back to selling cocaine. He was arrested again in 1997, but the charges were thrown out of court because of illegal search and seizure by the police.

"I have always been a money motivated person. I was never a bad guy. But you have to realize, the 1980s, everybody and his brother were doing cocaine."

Levitt and his girlfriend had a son in 1999. That was a life changing event. "The day I had my son, I never did it (sold drugs) again."

His son is the biggest thing in his life, and he is active in his son's life, even though he lives in Daytona and the boy lives with his mother in

Jacksonville. Levitt now works for a high end used car business that deals in Mercedes, Porsches, Land Rovers and other expensive vehicles.

"I have a wonderful life. I have a condo on the beach in Daytona with a spectacular ocean view. And he (Danny) is eating baloney sandwiches and not getting laid."

"Now I look back on those times and all sorts of thoughts and feelings are stirred up, some real good, some not so much."

Levitt changed his named to Mike a few years ago, saying he never really liked the name Mitch.

"Now I'm 49 with a good job, a great oceanfront condo, a car and motorcycle and a super 13-year-old son. Life is good. Taking shortcuts never works out in the long run."

Levitt asked, "Is Danny Edwards still alive? What an idiot! He built a box and buried a man in it. What a freak!"

I asked if he knew Nancy Rish. He said he never met Nancy, but he thinks he knew Danny had a girlfriend named Nancy. He was surprised to learn Nancy was convicted and is serving life. After researching her online, he said, "I have read about her case. My heart goes out to her."

— **Jeff Westerhoff** gave Danny a job as an assistant on construction work. Jeff was Nancy's cousin and he felt sorry for Danny. He said in 2014 that Danny didn't work for him more than a dozen times between February and July 1987, and he didn't do much more than hand him tools.

In February 1987, Danny said, "I got a question for you, Jeff. I need to build a box for my brother. I need your help."

Danny said it was for pool chemicals for his brother.

"He wanted me to build the box for him. I went and bought the wood on account. I got the wood myself. I got the sheets of plywood and stored them in my parents' garage. They sat there two weeks. He called and said, 'I can't wait any longer. I gotta build this box.'"

Danny came to Jeff's house and got the wood around the Fourth of July. "He lit a big firecracker, a bomb, at his place and it shattered some neighbor's windows."

"I saw the box he built. He was really proud that he did a good job. He was not a carpenter. It wasn't that good, but it was the best he could do. I held my breath and said, 'That's good.'"

The police questioned Jeff. "They came to my work site and picked me up and took me for a ride to my parents' house. We got the receipt, and they also took the round piece of wood that came from the hole saw. I told them everything I knew, that I was in the dark about what he was doing."

Why was Nancy prosecuted? "They thought she was too close to everything to not be involved. They thought she had to know, she was with him. I think Nancy was railroaded. She was brought down by association."

Illinois State Police Sgt. **William Willis** gave his perspective on the case in 1990 in interviews with producers of a CBS-TV program *Top Cops*. Willis said he was notified of the kidnapping early on September 2.

"At that time, they did not request Illinois State Police assistance. But by 9 o'clock in the morning, they called back. Decided they were over heir heads, the FBI was," according to Willis' 1990 transcript.

There was no doubt that Willis made it clear in this interview that he was running the show, coordinating FBI, state and local police. Other police said Willis inflated his own importance.

Willis said he considered the various options and he planned strategy. And, he said, his job was to keep Nancy Small cool and to keep his officers, who wanted to "make arrests and bust heads," cool.

"My job at the command center was to kind of coordinate the whole investigation. And make sure that information was getting out to everybody. Like a staff officer in Army command. Keeps the generals advised. I'm not trying to blow my own horn here. I'm just trying to tell you the way it really happened. That's what is so damn important about the case. All the other police commanders took out, and I was the only one who kept his head and stayed there."

And he talked about the pressure he was under.

"I knew the eyes of the world were on me. Director of the Illinois State Police called me direct. Lieutenant governor of Illinois. Everybody was giving me advice. I was not a lieutenant at that time. I was a master sergeant, and working in a position about two ranks above my rank. I've got to really soft-shoe it around the chiefs of police. FBI guys are very heavyweight."

"I'm worried about the family and getting this guy back alive. If I make a mistake here, I get this guy killed. I've got life and death here. That weighed on me heavily."

"I had confidence in my guys. But I knew if I made a wrong decision or suggest the wrong thing, I'm gonna eat this thing. Number two is the dance with the local police administration and the FBI. Put in a helluva position. Talk about a pressure cooker. Feds can be a f…ing pain in the ass."

Willis said he was the one who recognized that the reference to Joe Yurgine on Stephen Small's tape was a clue to Nancy Small.

"He's trying to tell her something when he made the tape recording at the time. She barely mentioned it at the first interview, and no one caught it. When they relayed it to me verbally, it rang like a bell. Yurgine is a local attorney, a reputable defense attorney He's also a former FBI agent. I know him quite well." Willis knew Yurgine lived in Aroma Park, and when the first ransom call was traced to Aroma Park, he knew it was a strong lead.

"I suggested to the crew, hey, listen, let's get our asses out to Aroma Park. I've got 16 agents in this room doing nothing. We might as well put them out there some place."

"It was a long and tense wait for the agents between the 5:03 p.m. call, which they identified as coming from Aroma Park, and the next call at 11:28 p.m. The police and FBI agents kicked around all sorts of scenarios and options. They kept reminding themselves that their main objective was to get the victim back alive."

Willis said he kept getting calls from Lt. Governor George Ryan and other important people. He said when Edwards first demanded a lawyer, he called for Joe Yurgine. It was ironic, Willis said, because Yurgine's name was mentioned by Stephen Small on the tape. "Edwards calls Yurgine. I can't tell Yurgine what I know. Yurgine is being ethical, after all, he's not playing under handed. He comes back and says my client doesn't know anything. He wants his client to cooperate. He said Danny Edwards doesn't know anything. I told him you're in for a surprise. Won't quote what I said." (*Note:* Edwards was not Yurgine's client).

There are more interesting details from Willis' 1990 TV transcript.

"The main thing was trying to get Steve back alive. Tried every trick in the trade to get him (Edwards) to cooperate. Plus we gave them open carte blanche. State's attorney would let them go, but they've got to bring Stephen alive. That was told to both Danny's lawyer and Nancy's lawyer by Ficaro."

Willis remained at headquarters while the police went with Edwards to get Mr. Small. "Danny leads them right to the grave site. There were no black cowboys on horseback. He told us there were black cowboys on horseback carrying shotguns to protect the area. Black couple in the area, nothing to do with this crime. Trying to lay stuff off on other suspects. Always ends up being lies."

"It was dark. One of the state cops on the tactical team stumbles and accidentally discharges a weapon that night. Still pitch dark. Make it real. Scared the shit out of everybody."

"Danny takes them to the grave. We didn't know it was a grave at that time. We didn't send anybody with shovels. Danny tells them where two shovels are at, about 20 feet from the guy. We've got 10 guys out there at the grave site. This box is 6-foot by 3-foot. It was about 3-foot tall. Coffin. Got a battery and a light."

"Gerard radios back. 'We're on the spot.' They start digging. They've got to uncover enough sand to lift this lid. And one and a half minutes later, they had it open. Coppers are digging with their bare hands, like dogs digging out a pit. They bloodied their hands scratching the earth. Got to the box and uncovered it. Everybody is hanging on it. Gerard says, 'We're at the location. We're digging.'"

"Silence. One minute and thirty seconds later, I'm timing this, taking notes. Everything at the command post is tense. You can imagine. Everybody shuts up. Twenty people inside there. You can hear a mouse fart. All you hear is Gerard: 'Too late.'"

"That's when the adrenaline leaves you. Jesus Christ. We lost him. The whole mission was to get this guy back alive. Tried it by the book and we f..... up. That was the opinion of everybody."

"There was tears in the officers' eyes. Twenty-five-year veterans, not rookie cops. Gerard is an ex-Marine. Tough ass cops. Real macho bastards. And g-ddamn, what a kick in the ass. We lost him."

Willis had a few harsh words for a few colleagues.

"The reason I'm the head of the unit is because I replaced a former director of the unit because he gave Edwards a deal to get off. He should have gone to the pen on a cocaine case, and because it was mishandled by the prosecution and the police, the bastard had the opportunity to kill Stephen Small."

"Damn, don't burn me with that one. If you're going to do this, make sure you say it was the former director that gave him the deal. In fact, one of the former directors of the unit lived right across the street from Small. We asked to use his house. Single person. He would not let the agents come in his house to set up video equipment. That's why he's not commander no more. I burned his ass with that one. Perfect surveillance, looking right out the living room window. Can't use his home? I'd turn the whole house over. Won't read that in the police reports either, buddy."

There are several interesting things about the *Top Cops* episode. The show opens with an on-camera introduction by the real Bill Willis. Then the dramatization begins. Stephen Small answers the phone call from the Kankakee police about a burglary -- the caller is a woman's voice! The FBI calls Willis and says they can't function without him. Willis takes control. The cops get a call from Lt. Governor George Ryan, and Willis tells the top brass to tell Ryan to back off. Willis threatens Edwards with the death penalty. Willis narrates: the more Edwards keeps quiet, the more I think it's a one man operation. In the next scene, Willis is in Nancy Rish's cell. He tells her the next seat could be the electric chair, girl. Willis is portrayed at the site when Mr. Small is dug up (something Willis admitted was wrong; he was at headquarters). In the TV dramatization, Willis opens the lid, gets in the box and pronounces Small dead. Willis has to be restrained as he goes after Edwards to try to kill him. The show was filmed in Canada with low production values.

Rick Gilbert and Ralph McClellan were the Kankakee officers who questioned Nancy Rish during those first four days. Gilbert said he still believes Nancy Rish is guilty. "It was her presentation," during the interrogation, he said. "There was a lot of hesitation, like she was trying to buy some time to come up with an answer." He said she saw the box being built in her garage and he wonders "how could she not know?" Gilbert said Scott Swaim did almost nothing for Rish during the questioning.

McClellan also remains convinced of Nancy Rish's guilt. "She lied from the first interview, from the beginning to the end. She changed her story so many times. It was hard to believe anything she said. Why wouldn't she tell the truth if she wasn't involved?

I asked, Did she lie because she wanted to hide her guilt, or because it was what Danny told her to say, or because she wanted to make a statement and go home? "I think it was a little bit of all of those," he replied.

She also was afraid and scared, McClellan said. "She was crying. Once we had to leave the room for a few minutes."

Did Scott Swaim speak up in her behalf at all, or tell her not to answer? "No, he didn't. I was surprised, pleasantly surprised (as a police interviewer)."

"In my 28 years, it was the only time I got to interview a suspect more than once. If there is a lawyer present, sometimes not at all."

Pat Hickey wrote this on his blog on March 10, 2011: "A few months before the murder, my wife Mary and I sat on a picnic table with Danny Edwards, who happened to be a cousin of the people throwing a Fourth of July picnic in the Kankakee Riverview neighborhood. Danny was a celebrated pot-head and loser, whose parents happened to be very nice and good people. Danny imagined himself, and projected the image of, a drug kingpin. He was a snotty, simpering and obnoxious jerk. I thought two of his cousins were going to pound him into atoms. Danny departed the party, to which he brought nothing but his stoned-to-the-bone assininities. He had an electrician's card, but his real game was dope, or so he proclaimed. Mary and I had met the weasel on a few occasions. Every family seems to have one."

A few people provided comments on Facebook and in emails in 2013 and 2014. Sherry Parbs-Offermann Lockwood wrote, "I was in St. Louis at the time for the weekend. I got up that morning, and my husband (Barry Offermann) was up feeding our infant son. He was watching it on the news. My husband said, 'I know where he is buried.' He went on to tell me how he and Danny, who he lived by while they were growing up, and some friends and relatives used to go snowmobiling in Wichert, and how secluded it was out there! And that is the area where Mr. Small was found. Creepy, too close for comfort, knowing someone who could do that." She added it wasn't any information her husband had, just his instinct.

R. Craig Nafziger wrote, "Steve was a friend of mine when we were in our teens. His murder was horrific and lingers on as a tragic end to a friend's life. If you haven't been told, Steve was a very mild mannered and kind man. I never heard him speak disparagingly about anyone. This is at a time when some teens like to pick on others due to their own insecurities. He left a wife and children. Steve would not have ever hurt anyone, either with word or deed. He will be missed."

Virginia Shields Koger wrote, "Steve Small was a good guy. He wore his heart on his sleeve. Outspoken. When he used to see my dad, they would strike up a conversation and it always leads to fishing. We still talk about him today. He was one of the good guys of Kankakee."

Mike Dyson wrote, "The late Mr. Small I remember as always being very kind, as well as all the Smalls I met or knew." Felice Anderson-Wilson wrote, "Steve Small was a friend of my parents. He was such a good man. He was very involved in the community and in ways to help bring Kankakee back to life. What happened is so horrible, and made even worse by George Ryan commuting the death sentence to life, especially since he was a next-door neighbor of the Smalls and their kids were friends." Pam Bruso wrote, "I used to live on South Greenwood Avenue and was sleeping on the front porch the night all this happened. I noticed a dark colored van parked on Greenwood Avenue and wondered who it belonged to. This neighborhood was a family neighborhood and we all looked out for each other."

Pamela Kay Tutt Sinclair: "I followed the case and regularly attend ed Nancy's trial. The political uproar of this high profile case led me to believe that Nancy never stood a chance. I knew Nancy from school, friend's get-togethers, I had been to her home, met her boy and we worked at Alden's. Nancy and I were not extremely close, but I can tell you she had a 'heart of gold,' very compassionate about animals and children. While she was a smart girl, I think she was somewhat gullible and trusted too much, especially getting mixed-up with Danny. Danny was a fool and unstable, in my opinion. This was a speedy trial, in regards to Nancy. What I saw in court was a weak defense and a very aggressive prosecution. It was heartbreaking when the verdict came in. I rushed to the courthouse, I saw Nancy get off the elevator, we met eyes, she smiled warmly at me, and I gave her the thumbs up and smiled back. Before the jury was called in, the judge warned the courtroom that there were to be NO emotions shown during the reading of the verdict until the jury was dismissed. To see Nancy from about 15 feet away in the courtroom, and how her body just sunk, was just awful, but she followed the judge's request and maintained dignity and grace. After the jury was dismissed, she fell to tears and terror. I just felt so bad for her, and the speedy process in which she never had a chance, given it was the Smalls."

Maxine Shores wrote that after Nancy Rish's trial, "my life went on, but I never stopped thinking about her. Most everyone who really knew her believed her to be innocent. I am a strong Christian woman and wanted to do for others, so I started to visit nursing homes. I visited two here in town. We talked mostly about their lives. They just wanted someone to listen to them. They didn't want to be forgotten. I did this for four years. I also started going to the prison to visit Nancy. I wanted to encourage her. I was amazed how great her walk with God was. She has spent 27 years in prison for a crime she didn't commit."

Chapter 20
Nancy Rish Is Innocent

What did she do, how did she help him? "We don't know how she helped.
She didn't do anything, I guess. She was just charged
with abetting him, of being with him."
William Gaines' interview with Rish jurors in 1993.

Danny Edwards and Nancy Rish have spent more than a quarter
of a century in prison after being convicted of kidnapping and murder.

There is no doubt about Danny Edwards' guilt.

But there is plenty of doubt concerning the verdict for Nancy Rish.

A jury said she is guilty. Was this justice? Or was it blind vengeance
from a jury that was sickened by the horrible details of the murder, and
swayed by a prosecutor's dramatics and false assertions?

The prosecutor's opening statements to the jury admitted that the
state's case against Nancy Rish was circumstantial. However, the prosecutor's closing statements to the jury were just the opposite. The prosecutors
made false statements to the jury about Nancy Rish's involvement that
already had been refuted by testimony and evidence. These impassioned
statements, presented as facts, were the last words the jury heard.

Circumstantial information and false statements, spun by zealous
prosecutors, convinced a jury to accept conjecture over facts.

The heat of the moment is over.

It is time to look at the facts objectively.

Nancy Rish is innocent.

Nancy Rish said, from the first day, she did not aid in the kidnapping and that she had no knowledge of it.

Danny Edwards also said, from the first day, that Nancy had nothing to do with the kidnapping and she had no knowledge of it.

Both Danny Edwards and Nancy Rish have not changed their
claims in all the years since.

The state put on a case against Nancy Rish that really was just a
replay of its case against Danny Edwards. The evidence and the witnesses
were the same.

Nancy Rish almost was an incidental character at her own trial.
Most of her trial focused on Danny Edwards.

It had to be focused on Edwards. There was no forensic evidence
to link Nancy Rish to the crime. Her fingerprints were not on the box, the pipe

or anything else. Her shoes did not have any sandy soil from the burial site. The hair samples from the scene did not match her hair.

She did not help build the box. She did not dig the hole for the box. She did not help obtain any of the materials for the box, or items that went in the box. She did not make any of the ransom phone calls. She did not take Stephen Small from his home at gunpoint, or drive him to Pembroke Township, or force him to make the tapes, or force him into the box, or shovel the sand over the box.

The evidence positively proves that Danny Edwards did every one of those acts.

All the evidence positively proves Nancy Rish did none of those things.

And yet, Nancy Rish was found guilty by the evidence that established Danny Edwards' guilt, not by any evidence tied to her.

There was no evidence to show that anyone helped Danny Edwards. And yet, a jury decided that Nancy Rish knowingly helped in the kidnapping, and a judge decided she must pay with her life.

The prosecutor said she was liable if she aided the kidnapper, with the knowledge about it before it happened. The prosecution never proved this in court. They didn't need to prove it. All they had to do was to say it in a manner that convinced the jury of their contention.

Consider the evidence that was instrumental in convicting her.

The three main points by the state were that Nancy was with Danny when he made the ransom calls, the wooden box was built in their garage, and she lied to the police several times.

First, Nancy was there when Danny made some of the ransom calls, but she was sitting in the car at least eight feet from the phones. These were outdoor drive-up pay phones, designed for a person to make a call while sitting in the car. Danny deliberately had her park at a distance while he got out. He had his back toward her while he spoke. He did this so she couldn't hear what he was saying. A man witnessed one of the calls and the police witnessed another call, and they all said a white male was standing at the outdoor phone while a white female sat in a car several feet away.

Second, Nancy Rish saw Danny Edwards building the box. She asked him what it was for and he said it was a box for pool supplies. She knew only what he told her. Every woman has known a man who has deceived her. Danny was a drug dealer, a womanizer, a liar, a thug.

Third, Nancy Rish told police a few lies when she was first questioned. She admitted some of what she said was untrue because she was scared and confused and she was telling a story Danny told her to tell. After the first day of interrogation, she told the truth and she admitted to the lies she told. But the damage was done. Prosecutors used it to argue that she was a liar who could not be believed, even though none of the lies she told

281

had anything to do with any involvement in the crime.

Nancy Rish's statements to the police prove she is someone who makes very poor choices, and who lies when she is scared, but it does not prove murder.

Michael Ficaro told jurors that, if nothing else, they should convict Rish only on her naming of the officer who made the remark about the electric chair. But that was a misidentification, not a lie. She gained no benefit in naming the wrong officer. It makes no difference if she identified the man who said it, or if the remark was said at all. The remark had nothing to do with the kidnapping, murder, or any involvement. Wasn't the prosecutor's argument an attempt to confuse the jury? Wasn't it a bigger lie to tell a jury that, because a frightened young woman gave the wrong name of an officer in an irrelevant statement, it made her a murderer?

The prosecutors told the jury that Nancy Rish lived with a drug dealer, so they said she must be guilty of murder. She saw Danny Edwards building a plywood box, so she must be guilty of murder. She drove him to make phone calls, so she must be guilty of murder. She lied to police about her whereabouts on the night of the kidnapping, so she must be guilty of murder.

Consider the testimony of the key witnesses.

Caroline Mortell said she thought she saw a white van in Small's neighborhood on Wednesday morning, hours after the kidnapping. She said the driver was a female blonde. She couldn't positively identify Rish or the van. Mortell got away with testimony speculating that the driver appeared to be casing the neighborhood. Mortell said she saw it twice more that day. But she admitted she could not identify the driver, she admitted she couldn't tell if the driver was a man or woman because she didn't get a close look at the face, she was not sure it was the same van the next time she saw it, she wasn't sure she did see it a third time that same day. The time she gave for the second sighting was 1 p.m. Wednesday, the same time Rish was 15 miles away at the dog groomer.

This was the witness whose testimony placed Nancy Rish in Stephen Small's neighborhood on the morning of the kidnapping.

But assuming Mortell did see a van, what if it was a different van and was there by chance, totally unrelated to the kidnapping? Jerry Bergeron told the FBI he saw a Chevrolet van, dark brown with silver mag wheels, a chrome visor over the front window, and chrome fittings, in the neighborhood on the same morning. The prosecutors did not share that information with defense lawyers, as they should have done. Was this the van Mortell saw?

And assuming Mortell really did see a white van going through her neighborhood that day, why didn't any police or FBI agents in the neighborhood report seeing this van? At that time, the police did not know about Danny Edwards or his white van, but they certainly would have been observing the neighborhood and noting any vehicles, just as they later did in Aroma

Park. So why did no one -- not any neighbors, and not even any trained police or FBI agents -- report seeing this white custom GMC van?

Karen Thacker testified she saw a van going down the alley behind Small's house eight to ten times between late June and late August. A man was driving and a blonde woman was next to him. Thacker did not identify Danny Edwards as the driver. She did identify the woman as Nancy Rish, but not until two months after Rish was arrested and her picture was on TV and in the newspapers. But it makes no sense. As Danny Edwards said, that was his neighborhood and he did not need to scout it. No other neighbor (not even Caroline Mortell) reported seeing the van that allegedly was in the alley so many times that summer. And Edwards certainly was not driving down that alley all those times, with all those neighbors outside during that summer, with a plan to grab Mr. Small in broad daylight, on a chance that Mr. Small would just happen to be in the alley when he drove by.

Danny Edwards did not need to risk himself and his custom van being spotted so many times behind Small's house. He said he didn't drive his van to Pembroke later on the day of the kidnapping to look for the bolt cutters because his van was distinctive and he didn't want it to be noticed. If Edwards was afraid of his unique van being spotted in the remote Pembroke area, he certainly would have been worried about it being seen in the busy Riverview neighborhood. No one in the neighborhood or in the woods noted anything distinctive in describing the van they saw. They saw white people, black people, blond people, but nothing special about the van.

James Witvoet said he saw a white van near the grave site before the kidnapping. A person with blond hair was in it. He said he couldn't positively identify the van or determine if the blond was a man or a woman. The time Witvoet gave was the same time phone records showed Rish was making a phone call to her hairdresser from her Bourbonnais home, 15 miles away. What wasn't introduced at the trial was a police report where local farmer Don Montalta said he saw white van going by his farm near Aroma Park several times, and the people in the van looked like Mexican farm workers. That certainly would have countered Witvoet's testimony, if it had been known to the defense team.

Don Eckels was the pilot who said he saw a van, with several men, in that area before the kidnapping. Danny Edwards said he went to the grave site alone. He said he saw no small plane flying overhead when he took the box there. Eckels was unsure of what day he saw the van from his plane, but he knew it wasn't on a weekend because he didn't work those days. Edwards said he buried the box on a Sunday. When Edwards said that, he did not know Eckels ruled out a weekend for his sighting.

The manager and the clerk of the hardware store had conflicting stories about a couple they could not identify. Both testified at Edwards' trial. At Rish's trial, the prosecution used only the clerk's testimony, since the man-

283

ager's account put the time he saw the couple after the box was buried. Even so, this couple was looking at PVC pipe, but they didn't buy any.

A grocery store clerk testified that Edwards came in to buy bottled water and candy bars. She said Nancy Rish was not with him. None of the clerks at the hardware store or the grocery store identified Rish as being in their stores buying water or candy bars, but prosecutors told the jury in their closing statement that they did.

The water in the box was tap water in an old milk jug. Neither the water nor the jug was introduced as evidence.

And yet, prosecutors put pictures of PVC pipe and distilled water bottles on a large map, as if Rish was purchasing water bottles all over Kankakee County. It was a dramatic visual effect for the jury.

Nancy Rish came across badly on the witness stand, due to fright and anti-anxiety medication. And there was so much irrelevant information in the trial. She lived with a drug dealer. She saw him building a box in their garage. She misidentified the policeman who made the remark about the electric chair. And then there was the gruesome videotape of the body in the box in the woods. The trouble was, none of it tied her to the crime.

A reading of the transcripts shows her trial was a farce.

Ficaro told the jury Nancy Rish was with Danny Edwards when he bought the materials he used in the kidnapping. That was untrue.

Ficaro flat out told the jury that Nancy Rish made the phone call that lured Stephen Small from his house. That was not true. Ramsey Small answered the phone and he said it was a man's voice.

Ficaro told the jury Rish was at the grave site from 11 a.m. to 1:30 p.m. on September 1. Phone records showed that on that date, Nancy Rish called her hairdresser at 12:49 p.m., from her home in Bourbonnais, 15 miles away, and evidence from her shoes proved she never was at the site.

Prosecutors said Nancy's greed was behind Danny's quest for money. That was yet another assertion that not only was not supported by testimony, it was refuted by testimony. Everyone who testified said Nancy was not concerned about money. No one testified to the contrary.

At Edwards' trial, Ficaro said, "Don't ever lose sight of why Danny Edwards did this. It wasn't a moment of passion. It wasn't in an instant of excitement. It wasn't the result of jealousy. It was cold. It was callous. And it was inhumane. Danny Edwards prepared this box like he prepared his plan. He got the materials. He got the handcuffs. He got the pipe. He got the gun. He got it all ready. Danny's greed, his lust for the big score, formed that plan, drove those nails into the box, dug that grave and buried Stephen Small alive."

Danny got the pipe, he got the gun, he got the materials. Ficaro and Nowicki made elaborate statements about Danny Edwards' greed. But that was at Danny Edwards' trial. All this changed for Nancy Rish's trial. Suddenly, Nancy was the one who got those items. Suddenly, it was all due to her greed. Suddenly, she was the cold, callous one planning the crime.

Judge Michela admitted Nancy's trial was a repeat of Danny's trial and that is why he had his mind made up that Nancy was guilty before her trial started. However, Danny's trial makes a better argument for Nancy's innocence than it does for her guilt. She was exonerated in his trial. Edwards' trial proved he did it all; the evidence at his trial tied her to nothing.

Danny Edwards' trial proved that Danny Edwards was guilty. Nancy Rish's trial proved that Danny Edwards was guilty. The state didn't have to lie about Danny Edwards at his trial. But without the false assertions at Nancy Rish's trial, the state never would have gotten a conviction.

Because of the tremendous local political power connected with this case, Kankakee County State's Attorney William Herzog went all the way to the top, turning a local murder case over to Illinois Attorney General Neil Hartigan. Herzog specifically asked for assistant attorney general Michael Ficaro and Frank Nowicki. He got them. Ficaro and Nowicki were on the case on the morning of September 3, the day before the suspects were arrested, before the body was found, before there was a murder, before the police had interviewed the suspects, before the police had built a case. Bill Willis said Ficaro was approving deals with Danny Edwards on September 4, while the police were still looking for Mr. Small.

In what other case is the top prosecutor in the state called to a small town before anything is known except that a rich man had been kidnapped?

The local powers also brought Cook County Medical Examiner Dr. Robert Stein from Chicago to do the autopsy on Mr. Small, and they paid him to testify at the trial of Danny Edwards. In what other case is the top medical examiner in the nation called for a small town murder case, to do an autopsy that any doctor could have done?

This is an indication of the power of the Smalls, the Ryans and others in the Kankakee political organization.

Herzog stepped aside as prosecutor, citing a conflict because he was a friend of the victim. It is understandable why acting as the attorney for the defendant is a conflict if the attorney was a friend of the victim, but how is it a conflict for the prosecutor?

The only reason the local state's attorney stepped aside for the top prosecutors in the state to come in was because they wanted to convict Edwards' girlfriend, too. Anyone who had no more legal training that watching a few episodes of *Perry Mason* could have won a conviction of Danny Edwards. But the case against Nancy Rish was flimsy. The state put on an extensive case against Edwards so they could use it all again against Rish.

Nancy Rish had a hard time finding a lawyer. A lot of local lawyers were friends of the Smalls and they had no desire to go up against the powerful forces in town. Vincent Paulauskis was a modest lawyer from Bourbonnais, and his assistant, Sherri Carr, was just out of law school. Ficaro and Nowicki, however, were experienced and accomplished prosecutors, and they had heavyweight reputations. Ficaro is listed as a "Super Lawyer" by his peers and was described by the *Chicago Tribune* as "abrasive, known for his theatrical style," and for his "scorched earth closing arguments."

Nancy Rish testified in her own defense at her trial. That is something guilty people do not do. That is something almost no defendant does because their lawyer knows the dangers of cross examination. She talked openly on the witness stand for the same reason she talked openly to the police for four days when she was arrested more than a year earlier. She knew she did nothing wrong and she was willing to try and explain herself.

When Nancy Rish was arrested and brought in for questioning, she was promised that she could go home after she made a statement. So who was behind the decision to go after Nancy Rish? Was it the Small family? George Ryan? Attorney General Neil Hartigan? State's Attorney William Herzog? The Powers That Be that need no direct marching orders?

There are two things that stump a lot of people. The first is the belief that Danny Edwards could not have acted alone, that had to have had help. The second is the belief that Nancy Rish "had to know" what Danny Edwards was up to.

A better question is, how could Danny Edwards have had any help? This is crazy enough for the mind of a desperate coke head. Is it reasonable that two people could think this was a good idea? He had to have acted alone. If Danny Edwards had help of any kind, if he had asked anyone else to join him, that other person certainly would have broached the simple question: "Are you crazy???"

The main reason for Nancy Rish's conviction was the belief that "she had to know" what Danny Edwards was up to. A better question would be, "how could she know?"

Her boyfriend is building a box in the garage and on the driveway, in plain view of the whole world. It looks nothing like a coffin. It's too big. It looks more like a shipping crate. He says it's for pool supplies for his brother. That sounds right. How could she know what it was really for?

She and her boyfriend are taking the dog to the groomer. He says pull over, I gotta make a call. He makes a call at a pay phone, gets back in the car, and they go home. How could she know who he was calling or why?

His strange behavior is getting stranger. He won't tell her where he is going or what he is doing. She knows better than to ask. He could be selling drugs or he could be setting up a drug dealer for the cops. Don't ask. He doesn't tell. How could she know he was planning an insane scheme to bury

286

a man alive?

The trouble with this case is that the wrong questions were asked. Instead of looking for the truth to prove guilt or innocence, the authorities were looking only for a way to convict Nancy Rish. They missed half the case and they missed the entire truth.

The idea that Nancy Rish "had to know" the purpose of the box is ridiculous. Benjamin Rish told me in 2013 that he remembers seeing Danny Edwards build the box in their garage. He said Edwards told him it was for his brother in Florida for pool supplies. That is the same thing Danny told Nancy at the time. Using the state's reasoning, should nine-year-old Benjamin have been sent to prison for life because he saw the box being built in his garage, so he "had to know" what it really was for? Of course not. Jeff Westerhoff bought the wood and he saw Danny building the box in the garage. Does that mean Jeff should have been sent to prison for life? Of course not. It is terrible reasoning, it is not logical and it certainly is not proof.

Would George Ryan agree that his wife Lura Lynn should have been prosecuted and sent to prison with him because "she had to know" where her incredible wealth was coming from? Not likely.

There was just too much that was questionable in the trial of Nancy Rish to justify a guilty verdict, much less a very quick guilty verdict.

Three people -- a farmer and two neighbors -- testified they saw a blond in a van at three different times, when phone records proved Nancy Rish was 15 miles away each time. There were store clerks who said they saw a couple they could not identify asking for something that was not used in the crime. There was the importance placed on a threat from a misidentified policeman. There were false assertions to the jury that went unchallenged. All this was crucial in convicting Nancy Rish.

The jury appeared to be paying more attention to Michael Ficaro's words than to the witnesses or to the evidence.

Frank Nowicki told the jury Nancy Rish was a "pathological liar." He said that, based on a few lies she told at the beginning of her police interrogation; it was not based on any psychiatric evaluation by a doctor. Nowicki said, "Nancy Rish never admitted anything during the course of her statement unless the police already knew it or she was confronted with facts she couldn't deny." That also was untrue.

Ficaro told the jury, "We have her in the electrical store in the afternoon buying electrical straps." Vincent Paulauskis objected, saying there was no evidence to support that statement. Ficaro continued, "Let me rephrase that. We have her with Danny Edwards, sitting in the van with Danny here." That was a huge change in his contention, but the damage was done.

The state continuously lied about Nancy Rish in court, at the same time it was condemning her as a "pathological liar."

287

While giving Nancy Rish the maximum sentence, Judge Michela said, "This defendant was involved in every major phase of this event." That was not true. Michela said the box was built in her garage and it was transported in the van of Danny Edwards. Was there any proof she helped transport it? No. Michela said, "Evidence would indicate that the defendant had been up and down the alley of the Stephen Small residence earlier in the year, casing the locality." That was not true. Michela said, "An inference was drawn from the testimony of Ramsey Small that this person made the phone call that lured Stephen Small from his home. That was an inference that the state was allowed to make, it was for the jury to debate whether or not that occurred. Even if that did not occur, this defendant was a part and parcel of this offense." That was not true, and yet the judge told the jury it didn't matter if it was true or not.

Michela told the jury, "She was there at the phone booths, whether 30 feet away or five feet away. She was there when the calls were made to the Small residence. She was there as the evidence was being thrown out the window of the car." None of that proves her involvement. Showing she may or may not have unwittingly aided Edwards does not prove she knew what he was doing or that she knowingly helped in a criminal act.

What is especially strange about the words Judge Michela spoke at Rish's sentencing is that they are almost the exact words Michael Ficaro spoke in his closing argument. The difference is that Ficaro was not paid to be objective, he was paid to attack. And although a jury may have found her guilty, the judge should not have given the maximum sentence based on the questionable testimony at this trial.

During the interrogation, the authorities were angry at Nancy Rish because she would not tell them where Stephen Small was being held. They were angry because she would not tell them details that would help them convict her and Danny Edwards. They were angry with her because she showed no remorse. They never once considered that she had no information or remorse because she was innocent.

Testimony from friends and family showed that Nancy Rish was not the cold blooded person as portrayed. She worked three jobs to support herself and her son. She was trying to get away from Danny Edwards and his drug dealing. Even her ex-husband said Nancy did not place a big importance on money and she was incapable of committing such an act.

And yet, so many things were put in place against Nancy Rish. Everything was set up to railroad this woman into prison. She did not get a fair trial. She did not stand a chance in a Kankakee County courtroom.

A memo in the Illinois State police files to Detective Robert Anderson dated September 22, 1987 reads, "Mike Ficaro indicated physical evidence to link Nancy Rish to the crime or crime scene was needed for grand jury on Thursday, September, 24, 1987."

No evidence ever was produced. There was none.

"It was her entanglement with Edwards and her knowledge of his drug dealing that ultimately sunk Nancy Rish," Robert Agostinelli told the *Chicago Tribune* in 1993.

"Please understand this," Danny wrote in April 2014. "Nancy had no job, her son was enrolled in the Bourbonnais school district, and she was dependent on me. I dominated our relationship and took advantage of her situation. She was trapped, and I used her as a tool, the same way I used Bill Mohler for his battery charger or Jeff Drury for his gun. Did Bill Mohler know what I was using his battery charger for? No. Did Jeff Drury know what I was using his gun for? No. Did Nancy Rish know what I was using her for? No."

When Nancy Rish finally found a lawyer who would represent her, she could not have had worse luck.

Scott Swaim was a friend of the Small family. When he got to the police station on that first day, he talked to Nancy Rish for less than 10 minutes before her police interrogation continued. He did not get her story. He did not have the information to guide her during the interviews. He heard what she had to say the same time the police heard it. During four days of interrogation, Swaim did not advise her or object to the questions or to the tactics of the police. Swaim told Rish she had a right to remain silent, but he did not tell her to remain silent during all those hours. He didn't even know she was sitting in the car when Danny Edwards made a ransom call. Swaim heard about that later from Bill Herzog.

When Rish went to court a few days later for her arraignment, Swaim left her on the courthouse steps, and she faced the judge alone. She had to nod her head to answer questions because she was so frightened and traumatized that she could not speak.

Swaim gave sworn testimony later, in appeals court proceedings, that he didn't represent her. He said he came to the police station only to be present during questioning.

"Now, when you arrived at the police station, it was your understanding, was it not, that Miss Rish had exercised her right to consult with a lawyer, is that correct?"

Swaim: "No, that's not correct. It was my understanding that Miss Rish had asked that I be present while she gave a statement. Now, whether that's an exercise of her right, I don't know what had gone on prior to my being there."

Rish believed Swaim was there to protect her rights and represent her. Swaim did not consider himself as representing her, but he did not tell her this. Swaim's unpreparedness in conferring with his client, and his actions as a spectator rather than a lawyer, shows that Nancy Rish was not adequately represented.

One of the first phone calls Nancy Small made upon learning of the kidnapping was to Ed Mortell. Swaim told police that Edwin Mortell said to him, "You are either with us or you are not." That veiled threat may have been the reason why Swaim quickly dropped Nancy Rish as his client. And it could explain why public defenders and local lawyers did not want to touch her.

From the moment she was arrested, Nancy Rish cooperated with the police. Rish said she was willing to talk to the police, and she did. That is not something guilty people do. She was grilled over the next four days. The police report for Sunday noted the interview was "at her request because she had more to say."

Her willingness to talk was noted by the lead interrogator, Sgt. Ralph McClellan. He told me in 2014, "In my 28 years, it was the only time I got to interview a suspect more than once. If there is a lawyer present, some-times not at all."

I asked McClellan, Did Scott Swaim speak up in her behalf at all, or tell her not to answer? "No, he didn't. I was surprised, pleasantly surprised (as a police interviewer)."

Nancy testified at her own trial, something defendants rarely do, and something guilty people never do. Danny did not testify at his trial.

Nancy Rish agreed to go on a ride with police officers over the route she took on the night of the ransom calls. A guilty person would not do that.

Police were able to question Jeff Drury on September 9 about the gun used in the kidnapping, only because Rish told them about it the previ-ous day. A guilty person wouldn't give up such evidence against themselves.

It is important to remember that no one ever accused Nancy Rish of participating in the kidnapping or knowing about it -- no one except The Powers That Be and the high-powered prosecutors they hired. No family, no friends, no witnesses at the trial said it. The Powers decided she was guilty on Day One, before the facts were known, before she was questioned, before Mr. Small's fate was known.

There is the matter of Danny and Nancy's behavior in the week of the kidnapping. Danny was frantic, panicky and even crazier than usual. That's because he was planning a kidnapping. Nancy, on the other hand, acted normal and happy. She made a hair appointment, she made an appointment for the dog, she took her son to football practice, she visited her sister, she helped a friend wallpaper her house. Everyone who saw Nancy that week testified that she acted normal and she was happy.

The prosecutor tried to paint this behavior as the actions of a cold, calculated criminal mastermind.

About that box and those phone calls. Could someone build a box in your garage and tell you it's for pool supplies, and you believe him? Could someone tell you to pull the car over so he could make a call from a pay phone, and you not know who he was calling or why?

Certainly. Especially if the man is a convicted drug dealer and has lied to you consistently.

Nancy saw Danny building a large plywood box in their garage. He told her it was for pool supplies for his brother. She believed him. Why would she not believe him? That is the question that should have been asked. At about the same time Danny Edwards was building a large wooden box in his garage, I was building a large wooden box in my garage. I told my wife it was a toy box for our daughters. She believed me. The difference here is not in the women, but in the men. Danny Edwards was building his as a coffin. I was building mine as a toy box.

William Gaines and Paul Weingarten wrote two lengthy stories about the Rish trial for the *Chicago Tribune* that were published on October 19 and 20, 1993.

The *Tribune* stories were headlined, *Justice Also A Victim In Small Murder Case,* and *Small Murder Prosecution A Crime In Itself.* The focus was on the fairness of Nancy Rish's trial and the questionable methods that got the conviction.

The *Chicago Tribune* stories asserted Nancy Rish was innocent and she was railroaded to prison.

Gaines, who won Pulitzer Prizes in 1976 and 1988 for investigative reporting at the *Chicago Tribune,* wrote that some of the testimony at the Rish trial was not accurate, and that prosecutors misrepresented facts and withheld evidence from defense lawyers.

Gaines and Weingarten wrote, "Prosecutors, eager for a conviction, took full advantage of the emotional atmosphere surrounding the crime. They wove facts, half-truths, sketchy witness accounts and sheer conjecture into a compelling but deeply flawed portrait of Rish as a ruthless 'gold digger.' They ignored contradictory evidence that could have affected a jury's decision, and they glossed over important distinctions in the law."

And, they added, "Rish faced not only skilled prosecutors. There also was the rage and revulsion of a small town confronting a monstrous crime against one of its leading citizens, and the vast, subtle influence of its most powerful family."

The Smalls fanned the flames in the local newspaper. *The Daily Journal's* extensive coverage turned this story into the Kennedy assassination, Lindbergh kidnapping, Pearl Harbor and 9/11, all in one. The murder of a black man in the ghetto might get a few paragraphs, but the murder of this particular rich white man was the biggest story in Kankakee history.

Being buried alive is a gruesome story. But is it any more gruesome than when Edward Baptist murdered his girlfriend in Kankakee in 1982, cut off her head and displayed it on the front porch of her mother's house? Was it more gruesome than Bernon Howery, a Kankakee County Board member, who was angry at a former lover so he set her house on fire in 1989, killing their four children? How about Ophelia Williams, who was raped, stabbed, doused with gasoline and burned to death in 1995 by Todd Saxon, the day after the girl's thirteenth birthday? Baptist, Howery and Saxon and their victims are black. Did that make their stories less important?

Gaines said some witnesses who wanted to remain anonymous were questioned by the police in *Daily Journal* offices. He also noted that Small newspapers in Kankakee and Ottawa, where the trial and appellate courts are located, endorsed the judges for those seats. The Kankakee newspaper endorsed Judge John Michela.

Gaines visited Nancy Rish in Dwight prison and Danny Edwards in Pontiac prison in 1993. But there were conditions. Nancy's interview was supervised by her lawyer, Joshua Sachs, and Gaines was limited to asking her only about what happened before she met Danny Edwards. And Danny was still telling lies at that time. Edwards told Gaines he took police to the grave site in order to save Small's life, and he said others were involved in the kidnapping. Gaines was not buying Edwards' story. He knew most of it already had been proven untrue. "Sounds like a one person job. A stupid person," Gaines wrote in his notes at the time.

William Gaines revisited the issue in a *Tribune* story on October 6, 1996, as Nancy Rish's lawyers were preparing another appeal.

"At her trial, Rish was portrayed as ruthless and money-hungry," Gaines wrote. "Prosecutors had no fingerprints, hair samples or eyewitnesses to link her to the crime, so they crafted an intricate scenario of her complicity, based on circumstantial evidence. Huge gaps in the scenario were filled in by shaky conjecture."

"And nothing was shakier than the chilling closing argument of prosecutor Michael Ficaro," Gaines wrote. Ficaro's closing statement told the jurors that Rish placed the phone call to get Stephen Small out of his house. "Right there on the phone, sweet-talking Nancy, the spider to the fly, come on out, my million's waiting for me," is what Ficaro said.

This was in spite of testimony that showed a man, not a woman, made that phone call, Gaines wrote.

Gaines noted that Rish's attorneys, Paulauskis and Carr, failed to object to Ficaro's statement.

What jurors heard at the trial was not accurately portrayed by a prosecution team that was much more skilled and much more aggressive than the defense team.

Rish's 1996 petition for a new trial cited ineffective counsel, based on their failure to object to Ficaro's statement that Nancy Rish made the initial call to the Small house. In an unheard of move, Rish's own trial attorneys admitted their fault.

Paulauskis and Carr signed an affidavit on April 29, 1994, for an appeal filed by another lawyer acknowledging, "I was aware that no evidence had been adduced at trial to support this argument, yet I failed to object."

Paulauskis said in "Ficaro's rebuttal summation to the jury, he said Nancy Rish made the call to Stephen Small to lure him out. There was no evidence at the trial to support this. I was made aware, yet I failed to object to the court. I also failed to make a motion for a mistrial, nor did I ask the judge to instruct the jury to disregard."

Paulauskis added that he was not informed by the state about Deputy Don Eckels seeing a white van at the site from his airplane or that it was Sgt. Willis who threatened Nancy Rish with the electric chair.

The state also did not tell the defense about charges against James Witvoet at the time of Rish's trial, which were dismissed after the trial. This wasn't known until the *Chicago Tribune* story in 1993. Sherri Carr told the *Chicago Tribune* that Witvoet was the "linchpin" of the case against her client. It was Witvoet alone who said he saw a blond-haired passenger in Edwards' van at the scene of the crime, even though phone records showed Nancy Rish was 15 miles away at that time.

"It is extremely rare for obvious reasons," John T. Theis, past chairman of the criminal justice committee of the Illinois State Bar Association, told the *Chicago Tribune* when the hearing was scheduled in October 1996. He said lawyers can open themselves to malpractice claims by admitting they did a bad job. "Ineffective assistance of counsel is a serious criticism. It dramatizes how strongly Rish's lawyers feel."

"It was her entanglement with Edwards and her knowledge of his drug dealing, that ultimately sunk Nancy Rish," Robert Agostinelli, Rish's appellate public defender, told the *Chicago Tribune* in 1993.

"Nancy Rish was convicted by circumstances that could easily be explained," he told the newspaper.

Agostinelli added, "I've been in this office for 20 years, and I'm not an easy touch for people who say they are innocent. But I would not hesitate to say I believe she was not involved."

"I look back now and I see that it was stupid to involve her," Danny Edwards told Gaines and Weingarten for their *Chicago Tribune* stories in 1993. "She didn't know about it. She didn't do any of it. The state fabricated evidence. They sent an innocent woman to prison for life."

The investigation and new information in the *Tribune* "contradicts almost every element of the prosecution's case," Gaines wrote. He concluded, "It shows that there was no hard evidence to prove that Rish knew Edwards was planning and carrying out a murder."

The *Chicago Tribune* stories ran more than 20 years ago and nothing has been done. It still bothers William Gaines.

Gaines is 80 today, retired and in poor health. But he still gets worked up when the Nancy Rish case is mentioned.

"A wrong has been done here that has never been corrected. There is no question about it," he said. "Anyone familiar with the facts knows she is innocent."

Gaines said he did get negative pressure after the series ran. So did the *Tribune*. There were more stories by Gaines that the *Tribune* did not run. "One of the things the Small family said was that the story was rehashed and they claimed the *Tribune* was just trying to expand its circulation area and it assigned me to do this. That was crazy."

Gaines interviewed several jurors in 1993. He told me in 2014 that he found them to be "shockingly dumb."

"They just accepted everything the prosecution said. All the jurors were extremely impressed with Ficaro. He was the big show. Ficaro was such a theatrical person. The jurors accepted it because it came from him."

"One guy said he thought Nancy was guilty because she was with him all the time, when he bought the tie straps, the water bottle, and so on. None of it was true."

His unpublished notes from 1993 include interviews with jurors. One was Howard Hendershot.

"He remembered the box and the pipe system and his stay in Kankakee, but when I asked him about Rish, he was a little confused. What did she do, how did she help him, I asked. 'We don't know how she helped,' Hendershot said. 'She didn't do anything, I guess. She was just charged with abetting him, of being with him.'"

Gaines asked Hendershot, Didn't Rish have to do something to be charged? "I don't know," Hendershot replied. "It's a big mystery about the whole thing. I know that the lawyer against this girl was very good. One of the jurors said afterward that if she had had the other lawyer, she would probably have gotten off. Sometimes you wonder about those things."

Juror Anthony Delmont told Gaines, "There was no question that she was guilty, but I thought that it was too severe a penalty. I believed that she was in his control and I think that the defense should have shown that, but they didn't. I mentioned that idea to the other jury members, but they wouldn't have any of it."

Delmont told Gaines, "She assisted him in all his movements, selecting the tools and equipment. She was a nice looking woman, but it was as if she didn't have a mind of her own. I don't think they meant to murder him. It was a botched job."

"One of the jurors brought up the part about her lying," Delmont said. "She did a lot of lying, and lied on the stand." (Gaines asked what did

294

Rish lie about; "Delmont said he didn't remember what about, even though I asked if it was about the policeman threatening her.")

How did the prosecutor catch her lying? "Oh, he would ask her about things and then show that they weren't true."

Delmont especially remembered the tie straps. "He was an electrician. The guy was ingenious. He used these electric straps to bind him."

What did Nancy Rish do? "She was going around with him, getting all those things. She was there when he fabricated the box," Delmont said.

"After the verdict, the Small family came over and shook our hands," Delmont said.

Juror David Anderson told Gaines, "Ficaro was quite a showman. He gives classes for other attorneys on how to do closing arguments. They were saying that the box was too heavy for him (Edwards) and a woman to carry out of the van and drag it, I don't know how far, to the place it was buried, and then he (Ficaro) took it with one arm and dragged it across the floor."

Gaines asked, "Did Rish know what Edwards was doing?"

"She had to," Anderson said. "They were lovers. They lived together. He was into drugs. He was definitely a slick operator, but I don't think anyone could have been that naive not to know."

Anderson told Gaines he didn't remember Rish lying about anything, but he said, "Everything the defense brought up just didn't fit in."

It was not true that Rish helped Edwards in all his movements, selecting tools and equipment. She was not with him when he obtained any of the items for the box. The tie straps were not used on the victim, and they were ruled out by the judge and not admitted as exhibits. The jurors would have known that if they had been paying attention to the testimony and the evidence instead of to Ficaro.

These were the jurors who took away a woman's life: She was with him all the time. How did she help him? We don't know how she helped him. She didn't do anything, I guess. Didn't she have to do something to be charged? I don't know. It's a big mystery about the whole thing. She selected the tools and the equipment. She did a lot of lying, I don't remember about what.

The verdict came from a jury where at least one member thought Danny Edwards was ingenious.

It has been argued that the trial was fair because the jurors were from Rockford, not Kankakee. But they still heard the details of a gruesome and cold blooded crime, they saw the box, viewed the grisly video of the body in the grave, and they heard the prosecutor make false assertions. None of it proved Nancy Rish's guilt.

These people never should have served on a jury where a person's life was at stake. This was the jury the state wanted.

Ficaro called upon his training as an actor to work himself into a frenzy during his presentations. He was so good, he also managed to work the jurors into a frenzy.

It took a jury one hour and three minutes to decide Danny Edwards was guilty. Given the overwhelming evidence, they really only needed the three minutes. Nancy Rish's jury took about 20 minutes longer than Edwards' jury to find her guilty. Less than 90 minutes is a very short time for any jury to reach a conclusion, given the discussion and the reviewing of evidence they should be doing.

By contrast, the jury that convicted John Wayne Gacy took two hours to reach its verdict. And they had the bodies of 33 murder victims excavated from the crawl space beneath Gacy's house! Even with all that evidence, Gacy's jury took the time to review everything and deliberate before reaching a conclusion.

With no evidence and only sketchy circumstantial information, the Rish jury should have acquitted her or they should have been out for days before reaching a verdict.

George Ryan felt the need to inject his opinion and assert his pressure after the *Chicago Tribune's* stories were published in 1993.

In a letter to the editor, published in the *Chicago Tribune* on November 30, 1993, Ryan wrote that the articles "so disturbed me that I am compelled to respond."

Ryan's response was nothing more than a rehashing of what was said in court, and not all of it was true. For instance, Ryan wrote that Rish was seen in Small's neighborhood and she accompanied Edwards to buy the materials for the crime.

Ryan, who was Illinois secretary of state at the time, wrote that the *Tribune's* stories "misled the reader" by its suggestion that the prominence of the Small family had an influence on the jury. Ryan used the flawed argument that the jury was not prejudiced since the jurors were selected from Winnebago County. However, they were influenced by the false statements they heard from the prosecutors.

Ryan wrote that "equally disturbing was the suggestion that prosecutors twisted testimony, glossed over facts and ignored contradictory evidence to build a case against Nancy Rish."

The *Tribune's* "greatest tragedy here is to overshadow the fact that Stephen Small, a fine man, a father, husband, son, brother, friend and a pillar of his community, was murdered because of the greed of Nancy Rish," Ryan wrote.

The verdict, and its affirmation by the Appellate and Supreme courts, was good enough for him, Ryan wrote. As it was pointed out, the higher courts were restricted by the evidence at trial. There was no new evidence introduced at appeal.

William Gaines told me in 2014, "Somehow, George Ryan didn't understand the law. The letter mentioned the appeals court ruling. The appeals court set out the same erroneous facts used at the trial."

In making his speech on January 11, 2003, about emptying Death Row, Governor Ryan showed more sympathy for murderer Danny Edwards than he had shown for Nancy Rish in his letter a decade earlier.

There was a mad irony in George Ryan's words in his 1993 letter to the *Chicago Tribune*.

While Danny Edwards was killing Stephen Small, George Ryan was selling driver's licenses to unqualified drivers who would kill dozens of people on our nation's highways.

George Ryan was the undisputed boss of the corrupt political machine in Kankakee and in the state of Illinois. He ran party politics and state business like an Organized Crime family, and he eventually went to a federal prison on convictions for racketeering, fraud, tax evasion and more.

Nancy Rish is innocent of the two crimes for which she was convicted. George Ryan is guilty of the 22 counts on which he was convicted, and he is guilty of a whole lot of other crimes for which he was never charged.

George Ryan wrote about Nancy Rish's greed. People who have known George Ryan for his entire career know that "greed" is the one word that suits him best.

"Six children were innocent victims resulting from a political scheme to raise campaign money," said Scott and Janet Willis at George Ryan's sentencing hearing. It was their six children who were killed in a traffic accident caused by an unqualified truck driver who bought his license through bribery at George Ryan's office.

It was ironic that George Ryan introduced a "Truck Safety Program" in 1991 while selling driver's licenses to unqualified truckers. It was as ironic as calling someone else greedy.

Nancy Rish was portrayed as a greedy "gold digger, a girl that will do anything for money." It was an image the prosecution had to sell to make their whole package fit.

"The million dollar jackpot," Ficaro said at Nancy's trial. "That ticket to life on easy street. Life in the fast lane."

Nancy Rish never lived on easy street. She grew up in a very small, modest house on the east end of Kankakee. She later had her own apartment, working two or three jobs while struggling to support herself and her son. For a while, she lived with Danny Edwards in a shack on Sand Bar Road and in a small duplex in Bourbonnais. Even after Nancy moved into Danny's house on Sandbar Road, she didn't give up her own apartment on the corner of Eagle and Greenwood streets.

Nancy's family and friends all said Nancy only wanted a family and a home, and she was not out for money. They described Nancy as "friendly, sensitive, out going, trusting." Even Terry Rish told police Nancy "is incapable of hurting anybody or being involved in any criminal activities... and could not be involved in anything like this because it does not fit her character." He said she made no complaints to him during their three-year marriage about their lack of money. How often does someone testify so favorably for an ex?

Anthony Turro was not called to testify at Nancy's trial. He was interviewed by police just after the kidnapping because he dated Nancy in 1982 and 1983, when he worked at Leo's tavern and she worked in the supermarket deli. After they broke up, Turro said he saw her out with Danny, but she did not introduce him because she knew he wouldn't like Danny. "I told Danny he just better never hurt Nancy or Benjamin. Danny said nothing. He just walked away." Turro told police he and Nancy never had much money when they were together, but Nancy never complained. That wasn't helpful to the state's case against Nancy, so it wasn't used in court.

The idea that Nancy Rish was a gold digger started in testimony from Tracy Storm, who did not like her. He was Danny Edwards' best friend at the time. His testimony in a hearing was aided by leading questions from Frank Nowicki.

Nowicki asked if Rish had been romantically involved with other men. Storm said he didn't know. Nowicki then led Storm where he wanted him to go.

Nowicki: "And would it be fair to say as Nancy would become dependent upon them financially, is that your understanding, is that what you had told me?"

Storm: "I believe so, yes."

Nowicki: "I believe your words were that she would like to do, then, is quit whatever job she had and live off whoever she was with, and she liked to be provided for by them, is that correct?"

Storm: "That sounds good, yes."

Nowicki: "And that way, I believe you indicated to me, she was very concerned, very interested in money and the lifestyle that goes hand in hand with having money, is that right?"

Storm: "I would imagine. I can't say that she's ever said that to me."

Nowicki: "But that is your understanding, based on people that know her and people that you, and your dealings with her, is that right?"

Storm: "Yeah. You know, I guess I feel that way, yeah."

The exchange was amazing. Nancy Rish could not testify about what Danny Edwards told her because that would be hearsay, but Tracy Storm was allowed to give hearsay that was much farther removed from a source than what Nancy had.

Michael Ficaro claimed Nancy Rish wanted to get back her fancy lifestyle, which included fancy cars and big boats. This was not true.

Danny didn't have a lot of money or a fancy car or boat when he moved Nancy and her son into a small house on Sandbar Road. There never was a "good life" at any stage of their relationship.

Danny didn't buy a new car until after Nancy had been with him for quite awhile. He bought a new Pontiac Fiero from Robert Geekie at Midwest Auto Sales for $10,500 on November 28, 1986. He paid $4,000 down. The car was repossessed when Danny defaulted on his car payments and it was resold on May 20, 1987.

Danny never had a big boat. He had a 14-year-old Marlin, which was not much different from what so many other average boaters had in this river town. The boat was "kind of beat up, and every once in a while he would need parts to fix it," according to testimony from David Denton, manager of the boat store in Momence.

Denton said it was Danny who made the remark about desiring a car like Mr. Small's Ferrari. It wasn't Nancy who said it.

Denton said Danny was in his boat store all the time, but Nancy was with him only twice. Nancy today says she doesn't remember ever being in the boat store. It must have been that unimportant.

David Denton said Danny Edwards was always looking for bigger boats. He made a down payment on an expensive boat, but he did not get it. He always hoped he could buy a bigger boat when he became a bigger drug kingpin. But Nancy did not care.

So this was the greedy gold digger who wanted the cars and the boats?

Danny Edwards said it was he who was hungry to get back the big money he was making, the big money that he made for such a short time. He even burned his arm with a lit cigar, on a bet, to get a twenty dollar bill.

"We took a trip to the Virgin Islands and paid cash, we went out and had nice meals, jewelry, paid cash on a speed boat. I got used to all this money. Then I didn't have it any more," Danny said.

The relationship between Danny Edwards and Nancy Rish was over even before their trip to the Virgin Islands in December 1986. The trip was a disaster. That was part of the reason why Nancy Rish and her son moved from Aroma Park to Bourbonnais in December 1986.

Nancy was living in a small duplex with her son. She took Danny in three months later when he had no place else to go. He had no money, no fast car, no boat. They slept separately.

To think that she would be a partner with him in a scheme to kidnap a man and bury him alive, after the crazy behavior and physical abuse Edwards had shown her throughout that year, is ridiculous.

And on top of it all, there was no testimony from anyone about greed on Nancy Rish's part. Think about that. The jury heard this barrage about

Nancy Rish being a greedy gold digger, a spider who wanted the million dollar jackpot on easy street. And it was entirely the product of the imagination of Michael Ficaro and Frank Nowicki, and no one else.

Nancy Rish was driving a four year old car, living with an unemployed man who had a nine year old van.

Where was all this gold she was digging?

Danny Edwards always said Nancy Rish had no part in this. And he made some important statements in 2013 that he never said before.

First, he said he chose to bury his victim because he didn't know where else to put him.

"It was supposed to be a holding place for the man. Nancy had nothing to do with it, so I couldn't bring him back to the house. And I couldn't sit in a hotel room with him for three days. I was restricted by what I could do."

And, "If anyone else had been involved, there would be no need to put Stephen Small in a box. We would have put him in a hotel room and sat with him. I was working alone."

If there were black cowboys in Pembroke helping him, they could have guarded Mr. Small in a tent in the woods, Edwards said. Edwards thought burial was his only option because he had no one else to guard his victim.

As for Nancy, he said, "It would have been a lot easier if she was helping me."

Second, he said his unusually erratic behavior during the week preceding the kidnapping was because he was trying to do two difficult things at the same time -- plan a kidnapping, and keep it from Nancy.

He said he did not tell Nancy because he knew she never would have gone along with it.

"It was a Danny operation, and no one else was involved."

When Danny and Nancy were arrested, Danny spent the day denying he had anything to do with the kidnapping. When he finally talked, it was because he knew the body was about to be found. And even then, he told stories about others to build an excuse, and he tried to make a deal with prosecutors. Nancy, on the other hand, spoke freely. That is not something a guilty person does. Danny did not take the stand at his own trial. He did not want to be cross-examined because he was guilty. Nancy took the stand in her own defense because she knew she was innocent.

If Nancy Rish was the mastermind, as was the argument of the prosecutors, why would she have Danny Edwards build the box in an open garage in plain view of the Bourbonnais police station and in plain view of so many friends, neighbors, mailmen and everyone else who saw it? It doesn't make sense. The same goes for sitting in the car while Edwards got out to make a ransom call. Why would she want to be at the scene of the crime?

She sat there, she did nothing, so why did she go? If it was to make sure he made the call and got it right, why was she out of earshot? Why would she have Edwards go back to the same telephone to make the next call? This is not the plan of a mastermind; it is the plan of a man with cocaine for brains. Even today, cocaine-free for more than 26 years, Danny Edwards cannot explain why he did what he did.

Nancy had a hair appointment at two o'clock on Tuesday at her hairdresser in Aroma Park. What woman makes a hair appointment just a few hours before kidnapping someone at gunpoint and burying him alive? The prosecutor's assertion that keeping the hair appointment shows she is cold and calculating is preposterous.

Aiding and abetting a murderer, even if the person did not participate in the act but knew about it beforehand, is called "murder by accountability." However, simply knowing someone, without knowing what that person is planning, is called "guilt by association." Nancy Rish certainly is not the first person to be so convicted.

Nancy got a letter from John Lucas in June 2006. Lucas had been on Death Row with Danny Edwards for a few years until his case was overturned and he was released. Lucas told Nancy he was writing to her because he read about her case, and he remembered that Danny told him and other inmates in the late 1980s that she did not have anything to do with his crime.

Lucas and the other prisoners asked Edwards why he didn't do anything to clear Nancy, and Lucas said that Edwards told them that his lawyer said it would hurt his appeal.

"We laughed at him and told him that he was screwed anyway because his case was highly politically motivated, and that he should go ahead and do what he could to get you out of there." Edwards did nothing.

There is another piece of new evidence, never told before now. We know from the record that Nancy and Danny went to Aroma Park to pick up the dog on Wednesday afternoon. Danny had Nancy pull over so he could make his 5:03 p.m. ransom call. When they got home, Danny told Nancy to get a babysitter for Benjamin, so Nancy took her son to his Grandmother Rish's house. After that, Danny and Nancy took the bicycle to Jack's place. That is when Danny stopped for his 11:28 p.m. ransom call.

But where was Nancy Rish between 5 and 11:30 p.m. on Wednesday? It was never mentioned.

Nancy was at the house of Maxine Shores in Kankakee. Maxine had been doing shows for Mary Kay cosmetics for 10 years. Nancy sold the cosmetics, but she needed to attend three shows before she could be authorized to do her own shows. Nancy came at 7 p.m. She told Maxine she had to leave by 8:30 because her mother-in-law needed to babysit Benjamin.

Nancy left Maxine's house at about 8:30 p.m.

Maxine was shocked when she learned of Nancy's arrest two days later. She said Nancy was "not upset, nervous or anxious" on that Wednesday evening, and it did not make sense "why Nancy would be selling cosmetics if she expected a million dollars that week." Maxine called the state's attorney's office to offer to be "a character witness for Nancy." The state's attorney's office called back and said they didn't want her testimony.

"I was upset about that. I thought I was doing right by going to the authorities." (I told Maxine they were only interested in convicting Nancy, they weren't interested in the truth or justice. "I found that out," she replied.)

Anita Hamilton told the police Nancy was at Maxine's house, and Anita advised them to talk to Maxine. They never did.

If Nancy Rish knew what Danny Edwards had done earlier that same day -- kidnapped a man and buried him alive -- does it make sense that she would go to a Mary Kay cosmetics demonstration (between ransom calls) and act perfectly normal? Of course not. Of course she did not know.

You won't find the Mary Kay story in the police files or in the transcripts of the police interrogation or in the trial transcripts. Why didn't Nancy didn't mention this to the police? For the same reason she didn't mention a lot of things at first, such as the bolt cutters, the dog groomer or a phone call: because she didn't think such a detail was relevant, and because she wasn't asked about it. The police would call that a lie, as they did about other things they called "inconsistencies." But we know better now.

Mr. Ficaro chose not to reply to requests for an interview.

I wanted to ask him: Who made the phone call that got Mr. Small to leave his house that night?

Without an answer from him, let's see what the evidence says.

Ramsey Small took that phone call at 12:30 a.m., and the next call at 3:30 a.m. He said it was a man's voice on both calls. Nancy Small said the 3:30 and later ransom calls were made by a man, the same man.

The Illinois Supreme Court had this to say in its decision on Edwards' direct appeal in 1991: "Small received a telephone call at his home from an individual who identified himself as a member of the Kankakee police force." Himself.

The Supreme Court on January 29, 2001, in denying another appeal for Danny Edwards, said it again. The issue concerned the taped telephone recordings made to the Small home (referred to as "the house tape") and the tape recording of Mr. Small's voice, which was played over the phone and later was found along a country road (referred to as "the road tape"). The justices wrote, "With respect to the road tape, the court cited Mrs. Small's testimony that the voice that can be heard speaking to her husband on that tape was the same voice that she spoke with on all four ransom calls."

302

The Seventh Circuit's ruling in 1994 on Edwards' appeal said, "On September 2, 1987, at approximately 12:30 a.m., Mr. Small received a telephone call at his home from a man who identified himself as a member of the Kankakee police force." The judges acknowledged the call came "from a man" who identified "himself."

On the tape from the burial site, Stephen Small said, "There's somebody and I've got handcuffs on and I'm inside some, I guess, a box." Mr. Small didn't say there were people there. He said there was somebody, singular. Just one. And it wasn't Nancy Rish by herself.

And finally, there is one fact in particular I just cannot get past. Nancy's bicycle.

When Danny Edwards went out that Wednesday night to make a ransom call, he put Nancy's bicycle in the trunk of the car.

Why on earth would a kidnapper put a bicycle in the trunk of his car at that time?

The bicycle did not fit inside the trunk. It stuck out. He had to tie down the trunk lid, and he drove from Bourbonnais to Aroma Park and back with the bike sticking out.

Any reasonable police officer on patrol might see it and conclude it was a stolen bicycle. Who drives late at night with a bicycle sticking out of the trunk unless it was just stolen? A cop would stop the car and ask questions.

The FBI agents staking out the pay phones saw it sticking out of the trunk. The police staking out the apartment saw it when the car returned home. The fact was noted at the Rish trial, but just barely.

That bicycle didn't fit in the trunk and it doesn't fit in the story.

It only makes sense if Danny Edwards was in it alone. If Nancy Rish was part of the kidnapping plot, that bicycle makes no sense.

Remember the TV show *Columbo?* There always was that one bit of evidence, that one act, that one circumstance that didn't make sense to Lt. Columbo, and he just could not get past it. Everyone else missed it except Columbo. It was a turning point in the case for him. It was a key element of the show.

Columbo would be scratching his head about Nancy's bicycle in the trunk of the car as they went out to make a ransom call.

Danny told Nancy they were taking the bike to be repaired. That was a ruse to fool Nancy.

If Nancy was part of the plot, they wouldn't take a bicycle to be repaired when they went out to make a ransom call. There would be no reason.

Danny needed the bicycle as an excuse because he was hiding the real reason from her, the ransom call.

And if she didn't know about the ransom call, then she wasn't a part of the plot. That means she had no knowledge of the kidnapping and she is innocent.

The same goes for the dog's appointment. It was Danny Edwards who told Nancy Rish to make the appointment with the dog groomer near Aroma Park for that time, so he could make the 5:03 p.m. ransom call on the way -- just as he told her he was taking the bicycle so he could make the 11:28 p.m. ransom call on the way.

He had to make up a lie both times, not to fool the police but to fool Nancy.

And the reason for that is because she didn't know what he was up to. And that means she is innocent.

Two kidnappers in league with one another would not put a bicycle in the trunk while going out to make a ransom call. It would make no sense.

Nancy was smarter than to drive around with a bicycle sticking out of the trunk if she knew they were going out to make a ransom call. Danny also should have been smarter than that, although I have not met anyone from that era who gave him credit for having any brains. Danny today admits he did not do much straight thinking in those days.

Apparently, Danny thought it was more important to fool Nancy than it was to be inconspicuous that night, and that certainly is consistent with Danny Edwards' thinking at the time.

Danny Edwards' defense lawyer was right when he said Danny committed "the most stupid and bungle-able crime imaginable." And no one else but Danny Edwards alone could have dreamed up and carried out such a crazy scheme.

The bicycle in the trunk was something that jumped out at me the first time I read it in the police files, early in my investigation, long before Danny told me it was a lie. It is unfortunate that the police and Nancy Rish's lawyers missed this point entirely.

What is the remedy for Nancy Rish, who has spent more than a quarter of a century behind bars for a crime she did not commit? A new trial? Another untold number of years in prison before the case comes to court again?

There are powerful forces in Kankakee and in the state of Illinois. These people do not want the embarrassment of being exposed for having sent an innocent woman to prison for all these years. They do not want it known that it was a deliberate effort on their part, not just a mistake. Their pride and their reputations are important. They still wield a lot of power. The present mayor of Kankakee is one of Nancy Small's best friends and was maid of honor at the wedding of Stephen and Nancy Small. George Ryan, who claims he was wrongfully convicted, does not afford the same charity toward Nancy Rish, and he remains unbowed since he was released from his own term in prison. There is still clout for the Ryans; George Junior was convicted of drunk driving in 2013, but he got off with probation.

Look at the viciousness George Ryan showed in 1993 when the *Chicago Tribune* raised questions about Nancy Rish's verdict. Ficaro also had nasty comments for *The Daily Journal* in response to the *Tribune's* stories. The same can be expected from the other prosecutors and the powerful politicians if a new trial should be considered for Nancy Rish. The prosecutors, in defending their reputations, and the powers in Kankakee, in defending their sweeping vengeance, would put up one hell of a fight. The state has endless financial resources. It would be a mismatch of power, as was her first trial.

A courageous governor could end the injustice with a pardon for Nancy Rish, or a commutation to time served. It might be controversial, but it would be just.

A lot of people in Kankakee believe Nancy Rish is innocent. Two courageous Chicago lawyers also believe in her innocence.

Steven Becker and Margaret Byrne recently came to Nancy's case independently while representing other clients who took time from their own plight to point out the injustice done to Nancy Rish.

Becker has had success representing people who have been wrongfully convicted or who have pleaded guilty after being tortured into making a confession.

Byrne has been affiliated with the Illinois Clemency Project for Battered Women. Since the late 1980s, her efforts have resulted in the release of 15 women who were wrongfully convicted or who had been convicted after being cruelly abused by their victim.

"Regarding Nancy Rish's case, the word 'travesty' does not even begin to describe it," Byrne said.

Becker has reviewed the documents and he said he has found "substantiating gross prosecutorial misconduct, pervasive political influence, police misconduct, the introduction at trial of erroneous witness testimony and ineffective assistance of counsel, both with respect to the statements elicited from Ms. Rish during four days of police interrogation and to the conduct of her trial. I have come to the abiding conclusion that Ms. Rish is wholly innocent of the crimes alleged against her. It is for this reason that I have decided to take her case *pro bono*. In addition, the salient fact that any romantic relationship between Danny Edwards and Nancy Rish had ended long prior to the kidnapping of Stephen Small, coupled with the physical threats made by Danny Edwards to Ms. Rish and her son prior to the abduction, just further confirms my personal conclusion."

"It is not a crime to have chosen a bad partner in a relationship. Guilt by association is not a permissible basis for assigning criminal culpability. Moreover, it is well established that mere presence at the scene of a crime

305

does not equate with criminal liability."

Becker added, "There is no physical evidence whatsoever linking Nancy Rish to the abduction or burial of Stephen Small. Ms. Rish was convicted not because the State proved beyond a reasonable doubt that she 'knowingly' aided and abetted Danny Edwards in his ill-fated ransom scheme; instead, Ms. Rish was convicted because prosecutors misstated critical facts to the jury, withheld exculpatory evidence from the defense, and through theatrics and innuendo, successfully painted the attractive and vulnerable Ms. Rish as a scheming *femme fatale* in a sensational, high-profile murder case. It is time for Ms. Rish to come home. Her nightmare has lasted long enough."

He is absolutely right.

Mr. Becker is preparing court action. Ms. Byrne is preparing to file a petition for clemency. Readers of this book can help the clemency effort by writing letters of support to the governor.

In one of the letters to Governor Quinn, former inmate Jacalyn Wojtowicz wrote (in April 2014) of Nancy, "I was feeling down due to my sentence, but she encouraged me by telling me that 'God wouldn't give you more than you could handle.' I thought, wow, she's doing life and still she encourages others to be strong and have faith, rather than be down on her own circumstances."

Wojtowicz happened to meet Danny Edwards in 2006 when both were prisoner/patients in a Chicago hospital. She said Edwards told her Nancy was in prison for his crime, and he was the one who got Nancy involved with drugs. He told her Nancy was "completely unaware of what he was planning or doing before or at the time of the kidnapping." He also said that he told Nancy the box was for his brother, and he "never intended for Mr. Small to die, but it was just a plot to get money to support his drug habit."

"I ask you, sir," Wojtowicz wrote to the governor, "why would a complete stranger ask me about her, and then divulge that she 'had nothing to do with his kidnapping scheme' if it were not true? He even asked me to get a message to her and say how sorry he was that he got her implicated in his case when 'she had nothing to do with it.'" Wojtowicz added, "Now I see a woman who has spent nearly 27 years of her life for something that she was too naive to even comprehend at the time. Is this truly justice?"

Wojtowicz said she and Nancy weren't close friends, "but I always held the upmost respect for her while I was incarcerated because she gave me the first kind words to make it through my time. As the years went on, she always inspired me, no matter what the circumstances."

They worked together on the Helping Paws Program, "and she is positively the most caring, encouraging woman I have ever met in my life." Paroled in 2009, Wojtowicz owns her own business today, "and I am what Nancy always thought I would be: Successful. Sir, I know in my heart that if Nancy were to receive clemency, she too will make a success of her life."

Nancy Rish was convicted on the lame supposition that "she had to know" what Danny Edwards was doing, just because she lived with him. The prosecution expanded that to mean she had to know what the box was for, what the phone calls were for, what the items in the box were for, she had to know everything he was doing, even though he told her nothing except to not ask any questions. A jury bought the argument, without any testimony or evidence to prove it. But it was nothing more than just an argument.

This shouldn't be a matter of sympathy for Nancy Rish. It should be a matter of justice. If she had nothing to do with this crime, she should not be in prison.

It also shouldn't be about rehabilitation, although Nancy Rish has a record of good behavior, higher education and training for the outside world that she acquired in prison. It isn't rehabilitation if she didn't commit the crime.

Nancy's story about making bad choices because of an unhappy childhood and the lack of a father is a familiar theme today. But it is irrelevant if she didn't commit the crime.

The only way the prosecution could get a conviction of Nancy Rish was to tie her, not to the evidence, but to Danny Edwards. They tried to portray Danny and Nancy as being partners in crime. It was their way to connect the two so they could use the evidence against Danny against Nancy.

The truth is, Danny and Nancy were not partners at all. Danny used Nancy and treated her badly. They were not partners in love, they were not partners in crime.

They were not partners in business or in anything else. Nancy sold Mary Kay cosmetics. Danny sold cocaine.

Murderers, rapists and assorted fiends have been sentenced to less time. Some eventually receive a parole. Nancy Rish is serving a life sentence with no possibility of a parole. In this case, it is a shameful blot on our justice system because she is innocent.

People, including a governor who has the power to pardon or to commute a sentence, should not be ruled by a personal anger about a truly horrible crime, or by the influence of rich and powerful people.

The governor cannot give Stephen Small his life back. But he can give Nancy Rish her life back. He can right at least one wrong.

Ultimately, this should be about justice, not blind vengeance.

Chapter 21

Epilogue

"I would like to reach out to them (the Small family) but they wouldn't want to hear it. They hate me. I don't blame them."
Danny Edwards, August 6, 2013

"It's funny how one person's life can do so much damage to so many other lives," Danny Edwards said as he sat in a small room in the penitentiary at Pontiac, Illinois, on a warm August day in 2013.

It was a tragic murder that had a tragic aftermath for many, many people.

"Stephen Small's three boys grew up without a father. My two kids grew up without a father. Nancy Rish's son grew up without his mother. The entire Small family and my entire family had their lives ruined. And it was all because of me."

"It weighs very heavy on my heart."

Danny Edwards' plot to get rich ended with Stephen Small's death, untold misery for everyone touched by the act, and life sentences for him and Nancy Rish, who is in prison simply for living with Edwards at the time.

The crime ruined Danny Edwards' life. But, he said, it put him on a path that saved his soul. It was in prison that he found God, as well as forgiveness and redemption, he said.

"The world can't forgive me, but God does."

None of Danny Edwards' family will have anything to do with him. He said they do not call or write to him. When I visited him in prison in August 2013, he told me that I was his first visitor in eight years.

"I come from a good family," he said. "I can't blame them for disowning me. I kidnapped a man and buried him alive."

This was the only point in our interviews where he briefly started crying. He pulled a rough brown paper towel from his pocket to wipe his eyes and blow his nose.

Danny said he was truly sorry for what he did and for hurting so many people. He has never approached the Small family to apologize because he does not think they want to hear from him and he does not think they would accept any apology.

"I would like to reach out to them, but they wouldn't want to hear it. They hate me. I don't blame them."

And he is very sorry that Nancy Rish is being punished for something she did not do.

"I have a lot of apologizing and making up to do to that woman

(Nancy Rish) and it might take an eternity. I hope I see Stephen Small in heaven. I want to give him a big hug and tell him I am so sorry."

"Life would have been different if I wouldn't have been such an idiot in my younger days. My father bought a store in Aroma Park. He bought it for me because he knew I wasn't going to be an electrician. That store could have been mine when I was 28."

Nancy Rish and Danny Edwards have remained behind bars since they were arrested on September 4, 1987. Nancy is in Logan Correctional Center in downstate Lincoln. Danny is in Pontiac Correctional Center. But what happened to the rest of the people in this story?

Terry Rish, Nancy's ex-husband, married Jane Goodman on October 9, 1987, a month after the kidnapping. Terry and Jane had a son, Andrew, and a daughter, Abigail. Terry Rish worked as a carpenter, and for Weather Seal Nu-Sash. He died of a heart attack on July 31, 1994, at the age of 35. Benjamin Rish was 16 when his father died, and he was sent to live with his paternal grandparents.

Terry was working as a carpenter at Jimmy Keene's house. When Terry didn't show up one day, Keene went to Terry's house to check on him. Benjamin found his father on the floor and called the ambulance. Keene arrived and turned Terry's body over to check him. As Keene heard the sirens approach, he fled the scene, telling Benjamin, "I was never here. You didn't see me." Keene, a drug dealer in Kankakee and Chicago, was afraid Rish had died of an overdose of drugs supplied by him.

Keene recently has been trying to sell a movie idea about Danny and Nancy, which he claims is based on his personal knowledge. Danny Edwards and Nancy Rish told me they do not know Jimmy Keene.

Benjamin Rish has had a troubled life since his life became a living hell when he was just nine. He presently is working and is trying to be a good father to his two young sons, but life continues to be a struggle.

Genevieve Woodrich, Nancy Rish's mother, is 85 years old now in 2014. She still lives in Kankakee and is a faithful member of Life Christian Fellowship in Gilman. She visited Nancy often when Nancy was in the near-by Dwight prison. But it has been harder since Dwight closed and the women were sent to Lincoln, because of the great distance and because of health problems at her age. Mrs. Woodrich remembers, as a young child, her mother talking about Governor Small taking state money and not paying all the interest to the state. She also remembers cutting rhubarb on Small's farm when she was a young girl. She believes in her daughter's innocence. She said Nancy was acting completely normal the week before the kidnapping, calling her for recipes and other things. Mrs. Woodrich believes the political pressure of Kankakee and the prominence of the victim's family was the reason Nancy was prosecuted along with Danny Edwards.

Margaret "Peggy" McKenna Edwards became a surgical nurse in Kankakee. She moved to Overland Park, Kansas, after her ex-husband's arrest. She later worked for a home health care business. She did not remarry. Danny's children also live in Kansas. Brandon Edwards works for a computer company. His wife, Joanne, is the daughter of Hall Of Fame pro golfer Tom Watson; they have a daughter. Gina Edwards Spencer is divorced and has three daughters. No one in his family has contacted Danny for years except for a few brief notes from his daughter. None of the Edwards family wanted to talk for this book.

Nancy Small Frederick lives in South Carolina. Susanne Small Bergeron lives in Colorado. Ramsey, Barrett and Christopher Small live in Florida. Leslie Small lives in Arizona.

William Herzog was state's attorney from 1984 to 1997. He served 15 months in Vietnam as a Marine artillery officer. He retired as a lieutenant colonel from the Marine Corps Reserve in 1990. After leaving the state's attorney office, Herzog became a member of the Foreign Service Office, serving for seven years in Australia, India and Mexico. He retired in 2009.

Kent Allain has been in court 83 times in the last 20 years and has served a few terms in prison. Charges include aggravated battery against a peace officer, obstructing justice and destroying evidence, drugs offenses, battery, passing bad checks, theft and various traffic offenses.

Tracy Storm today owns a carpentry-millwork business in Kankakee.

Jeff Westerhoff owns a construction company in the Seattle area. He has a wife and a 24-year-old daughter. He is a born again Christian. He visited Danny in prison in the early years, and is one of them men credited with turning Danny Edwards to Jesus.

Michael Ficaro has had a distinguished legal career, both in the attorney general's office and in private practice. He has had success as a prosecutor, as a defense lawyer and in gaming law. He was designated a "Super Lawyer" by *Chicago* magazine. An AVVO internet rating site in 2013 gave Ficaro its highest rating and said no professional misconduct was found in his 41 years of practicing law. He now is a partner in the Chicago law firm of Ungaretti & Harris.

Frank Nowicki left the attorney general office to join Johnson & Bell law firm in Chicago. Timothy Reynolds started his law career in 1987 in the attorney general's office, assisting in Danny Edwards' prosecution. He retired from practicing law in 1995 to work for Family Video, a chain of stores owned by his wife's family.

Sheldon Reagan, who defended Danny Edwards at trial, had a distinguished legal career in Kankakee. He was named a Kankakee County circuit court judge in 1989, a year after Danny Edwards' trial. He is now retired in Missoula, Montana.

J. Scott Swaim practiced law with his father George in Kankakee for a few years. Swaim's grandfather, George Swaim Sr., was appointed county farm advisor by former governor Len Small in 1933.

Scott Swaim ran for a seat on the Kankakee school board in April 1974. He lost by one vote. However, a month later it was revealed that one fourth of the votes in one precinct were cast by ineligible voters. It was a precinct that totaled one third of all the votes. The matter went to court and four months later a judge threw out all the votes from the disputed precinct because of fraud, and Swaim was awarded his seat on the school board. However, the Appellate Court reversed the circuit court decision in January 1976 and Swaim was out.

Scott Swaim became a circuit court judge in Kankakee after the Rish trial. He died on February 22, 2009, at the age of 62.

A number of other public defenders and local lawyers who would not represent Edwards and Rish became judges. William O. Schmidt was a public defender for 20 years until he became an associate judge in July 2001. He resigned in January 2010 and moved to Colorado. Ken Leschen became a judge in 2009 to replace Swaim, after Swaim's death.

Michael Kick ran against William Herzog for the Republican nomination state's attorney in 1988. He lost. However, Kick was elected state's attorney in 1994, serving until becoming a judge in 2000. Kick was named chief judge in 2012.

Public defender Allan Kuester died on June 2, 2008, at age 61. Kuester became a public defender in January 1975, after all three lawyers in the office (William Eaken, Joseph Yurgine and Jerry Lucas) resigned, citing low pay and heavy caseloads. Before that, Kuester was an assistant state's attorney. Public defenders Greg Morgan and Edward Glazer are law partners with Gus Regas. Glazer still takes public defender cases.

Vincent Paulauskis and Sherri Carr met and fell in love when they got together as Nancy Rish's defense lawyers. Vincent divorced his wife after the trial, and he and Sherri were married on February 24, 1990. He was 43, she was 24. Vincent and Sherri had three children, Anthony, Joseph and Veronica. Vincent died on June 28, 2013, at the age of 67.

Sherri Carr became a public defender in Kankakee County in February 1989. The family moved to Virginia Beach, Virginia, in 2002. She has been the public defender in Norfolk, Virginia, since May 2006. Sherri's father, Fred Carr, served in the U.S. Marine Corps from 1955 until he retired as a lieutenant colonel in 1976. He served two tours in Vietnam and earned two Bronze Stars for valor. He was named a judge in Kankakee County in 1993. Fred Carr was widely praised as a good judge when he retired in 2002. He died in 2011, at the age of 74.

John Michela was appointed a magistrate in Kankakee in 1965. He became an associate judge in Kankakee in 1973 and a circuit court judge in

1976. He and his wife Janet had three children. He also had a distinguished and colorful career. Michela is now retired in Melbourne Beach, Florida.

Gordon Lustfeldt, who denied Nancy Rish's appeals for a new trial, is still a judge in the Kankakee-Iroquois circuit.

Joseph Yurgine continues to practice law in Kankakee and is a columnist for *The Daily Journal*. He has had a distinguished career in law, and he was an FBI agent before practicing law in Kankakee.

Ralph McClellan retired from the Illinois State Police in 2008 after 28 years, with the rank of captain. He lives in Bourbonnais and in Phoenix, Arizona. Rick Gilbert became chief of police of the village of Herscher, in western Kankakee County, in 2007. He lives in Bourbonnais.

Jeffrey Oetter today has his own construction business in Bourbonnais. He accepted Jesus Christ as his lord and savior. "I accepted Jesus on June 12, 1998. It was my 40th birthday, and I figured I had wandered in the desert for 40 years." It was the Holy Spirit leading him to verses in the books of John and James that humbled him. Before that, he had done several terms in prison for drugs, burglary, forgery and more. He said that life ended when he accepted Christ and became a new man.

Just as Danny kept his crimes from Nancy, Jeffrey said he kept his cocaine selling from his wife Sherry. And he said he took Nancy Rish to her first concert when she was 14. The band was ZZ Top and he said he could tell the wild atmosphere "was a different world for her." He also had a later contact with Danny Edwards, when they both were in prison. It was Jeffrey's job to bring meals to Danny on Death Row.

The Witvoets were arrested perhaps 200 times between 1965 and 1975 for selling produce in Chicago's Randolph Street Market without a sales tax certificate. Witvoet Sr. claimed he had the right to sell his farm goods, and he went to court numerous times, acting as his own lawyer. Some rulings were in his favor, some were not.

Thad Wells, the driver for J&B Vegetables who testified about seeing a white van near the Small burial site, was found murdered in his Pembroke Township home on July 28, 2013. He was killed by a shotgun blast through a closed door from outside his house. Two 15-year-old boys, intent on burglary, were arrested and charged. Wells had been dead at least a week before his badly decomposed body was found.

Elizabeth Lamanna received her law degree in 1981 and worked as an assistant district attorney in Pittsburgh, Pennsylvania, before becoming an FBI special agent in 1986. She became ill in 1992 at the age of 37, but her fybromyalgia and chronic fatigue condition were not properly diagnosed. She went on disability in 1996. She received benefits until 2004, when the FBI determined she could return to work. This FBI agent has been fighting the government -- the FBI, the Special Agents Mutual Benefits Association, and the Social Security Administration -- to regain her disability benefits.

Mitch Levitt is living the good life in Florida, with an oceanfront condo and a 13-year-old son. He has a good job leasing cars.

David Pinski, a customer of Edwards who testified in exchange for immunity, is the son of a prominent Kankakee doctor. His brother, Michael Pinski, is a local developer who pleaded guilty in August 2011 to violating the Clean Air Act for dumping hazardous waste in Pembroke Township. He was sentenced in January 2013 to six months in federal prison and six months of home detention. Matthew Mullady, another Edwards customer, is the son of legendary local outdoors writer Ed Mullady. Matt today is a fishing guide on the Kankakee River and is a Kankakee Valley Park District commissioner.

Thyrl Latting, the African-American rodeo rider and school teacher who started the Pembroke Rodeo in 1964, died on January 5, 2013, at the age of 80. His acclaimed Pembroke Rodeo continues.

William Willis was a state police officer from 1969 to 1993. He retired as a captain. He was paid for the CBS-TV program *Top Cops* in 1990, and he had a part in the show at the beginning and at the end. An actor portrayed him in the dramatization.

George Clodfelter, the investigator for Nancy Rish's defense lawyers, died in Fredericksburg, Virginia, on July 2, 2013, at the age of 60.

William Gaines, a reporter for the *Chicago Tribune* from 1963 to 2001, won two Pulitzer Prizes while at the *Tribune*. He also taught journalism at the University of Illinois and at Columbia College. He is now retired in Munster, Indiana.

Governor George Ryan, convicted on 22 counts of corruption in 2006 and sentenced to 6-1/2 years in prison, was released in 2013.

Danny Edwards' parents died in 2006: his mother, Gertrude Edwards, died on January 1; his father, George Edwards Jr., died on November 5.

Burrell Small, Stephen's father, died on February 22, 1981, at the age of 62. Reva Small, Stephen's mother, died on November 2, 2008, at the age of 89. Len H. Small was killed in an auto accident near Kankakee on March 10, 1980, at the age of 65. Jean Alice Small died on September 13, 2002, at the age of 88.

Michael Ficaro, Nancy Small Frederick, Susanne Small Bergeron, Joseph Yurgine, Peggy Edwards and Brandon Edwards declined to be interviewed for this book. I wrote to Nancy Small Frederick and Susanne Small Bergeron only once. I did not write to them again because I did not want to appear to be harrassing them. They got the message. I did not write to the sons of Stephen Small, although I did contact the son of Nancy Rish and the son of Danny Edwards.

There is speculation about intentions or motivations for telling this story. The issue was raised in the Kankakee newspaper, so let's address it.

My motivation as a writer has always been truth and justice.

The Stephen Small story was intended to be a few pages in my *Kankakee Confidential* book. However, I found a long time ago that the story always goes where my research and information takes me. The story about Governor Small was intended to be a few pages in my *Wild Kankakee* book. With both Governor Small and Stephen Small, I soon saw the story was too detailed and too important to be just a chapter. The story made the decision for me. Both subjects became books instead of just chapters, with the publication of the initial books delayed. It is only by coincidence, and the fact that my field of local history is Kankakee County, that the subjects of both of these books are the Smalls.

I wrote to Danny Edwards and Nancy Rish in 2012. Nancy politely declined to be interviewed, writing that she did "not look forward to having this case published in a book." Danny did not write back at all. I persisted and wrote back several more times before I convinced them to talk to me.

Danny never wanted to talk to anyone. But when he started talking to me, he talked at length and he told everything.

Danny freely admitted his guilt, and said Nancy had nothing to do with the crime. He had said it from the beginning, but no one wanted to listen to him. No one wanted to listen to Nancy's pleas that she was innocent.

One might ask, why should we believe the words of people who have been convicted of murder?

Danny Edwards was a murderer in 1987. He is a different man today. He said he can confess the truth of what happened and his sorrow for causing so much pain because he is a born again Christian. And it doesn't matter to him who believes it.

One also might ask, why should we believe Danny Edwards now, when he has lied so consistently over the years?

Well, the police didn't believe him in 1987 about Kent Allain, Mitch Levitt or the black cowboys, no matter how insistent he was. His story now is at least consistent with what the police have believed all along. In the absence of any evidence that black cowboys or anyone else was involved, it would appear Danny Edwards is now telling the truth. It also appears that Danny Edwards is not trying to fool anyone. There is no one left to fool.

There are some who may be cynical about his jailhouse conversion. This is not a casual transformation. It started when he was in the county jail and it remains strong, a decade after being taken off Death Row. He has studied the Bible intensely. There are people who are a Christian only on Sunday morning, and then there are people who are a Christian every minute. Danny Edwards is the real thing in that regard. Even the cynics need only to read his Bible essays to know that he has spent a lot of time, research and thought on them, and he has been doing it for many years before he was approached by anyone who wanted to write about him. You don't have to agree with his writing to know that he is sincere.

And there will be some people who think that anyone who could kidnap a man and bury him alive has a heart so black that it cannot be redeemed. But the Bible teaches us better than that. Jesus said He did not come to call the righteous, but sinners.

The rumors about others being involved have some people speculating that Danny Edwards is hiding something in order to protect his family. Hiding what, and from whom, and why, after all these years? It makes no sense. And there is no evidence to support it.

The explanations Edwards gives today make sense, unlike the stories he told after his arrest. If Nancy Rish or anyone else was helping him, he wouldn't have had to put his victim in a box. If only he did have someone else with him at the time, this horrible act never would have happened!

There are those at the Kankakee newspaper who say Danny Edwards is trying to save his girlfriend now. But he didn't try to save her when she needed it the most, at her trial in 1988. Clinging to an impossible appeal was more important than telling the truth to help Nancy. Edwards has never made any effort to speak out since that time.

Nancy Rish ceased being his girlfriend long before that day in September 1987, when the police raided their house.

Danny Edwards went on the record for the first time when he signed an affidavit on September 25, 2013, swearing that Nancy had nothing to do with the kidnapping and she had no knowledge of it. The affidavit was not his idea. He was hesitant to sign it because he believes it will not do any good against this powerful system. His interviews came only at the prodding of this writer. The affidavit was at the request of Nancy's new lawyer, Steven Becker. The interviews and the affidavit were agreed with reluctance. Nothing was initiated by Danny Edwards.

Danny also didn't think any positive portrayal of his Christianity will soften his family's hearts towards him. I said the Holy Spirit can turn anyone's heart, as it did for him. He said he did not think that would happen.

"This book isn't going to do me a lot of good," Danny said at our last interview. "I kidnapped a man and buried him alive. All this is going to do is get a big weight off my shoulders."

In what way? He replied, "For years, I could give you a big lie about Mitch Levitt and others and give you evidence -- calls to the Small house from Chicago, Mrs. Small not sure about the voice on the tape, Eckels seeing a van, two shovels at the crime scene when one man needed only one shovel, the police lies on the search warrant. Now I can tell the truth."

Motivation. Danny Edwards has nothing to gain and nothing to lose by telling what he knows. There is no motivation to talk at all. He knows he never will walk out of that prison. He also knows that swearing to God in a lie brings more fearful repercussions than any here on earth.

Joseph Yurgine, in the only comment he would make about this book, wrote in *The Daily Journal* that he thought a possible motivation for my book is perhaps I was being used. Without money to file appeals, he wrote, people in prison "need attention...they need publicity. Without money, their only recourse at times is to latch on to a writer to do research on the case, who can then maybe call attention to some mistake made during the course of the proceedings." This especially applies to Danny Edwards, he added, who lost his free legal counsel when Governor Ryan took him off Death Row. "At that point, all an inmate may have left to escape the slammer is the work and attention of a murder mystery writer," Yurgine wrote.

I have known Joe Yurgine for years and I respect him. There probably isn't anyone in Kankakee who doesn't respect him. However, Nancy Rish and Danny Edwards did not try to attract my attention. Danny Edwards is not pushing this story; Nancy Rish is not pushing this story; I am the one pushing this story. Danny Edwards and Nancy Rish did not volunteer to talk to me or even want to talk to me at first.

I spent more than a year talking to numerous individuals, going through boxes of trial transcripts and appeals briefs, stacks of local police and state police files and a lot more. I looked diligently for that smoking gun that would prove Nancy Rish is guilty. I did not find it. On the contrary, every bit of evidence showed she has been telling truth about being innocent. And I was surprised to find so many people who believe in Nancy's innocence and who believe she was wrongfully convicted.

I believe Nancy Rish is innocent. I believe she was railroaded into prison. I believe she did not get a fair trial.

However, Nancy Rish did not know this book would take that position when she agreed to talk to me. She gave me several interviews in prison and had no idea at that time what I would write, whether it would be helpful or harmful to her.

I also did not know at that time. I went to Dwight prison in early 2013 to ask her the details of the kidnapping, for a small chapter in another book. I was surprised at what I found. It became the beginning of my investigation, not the end. I needed to work and to wait to find which way the investigation would take me.

Danny Edwards is guilty and belongs in prison. He knows he belongs there and he knows he is there for life. Nancy Rish does not belong in prison because she is innocent. She hopes for her freedom because she knows she did not commit this horrible crime.

This book does not make a hero of Danny Edwards -- after all, he killed a man by burying him alive! There may be some people who will find inspiration in the story of an evil man who found salvation for his soul and

316

who is leading men in prison to the Lord. He spent the first 30 years of his life doing evil; he has spent the last 30 years of his life trying to do good. But he is not a hero, and he does not think he is a hero.

William Gaines, who wrote about Nancy's Rish innocence and her preposterous trial in the *Chicago Tribune* more than 20 years ago, expresses the same motivation: truth and justice.

So does attorney Steven Becker. So does attorney Margaret Byrne. What other motivation can there be?

My motivation never was to try to spring a guilty person from prison. I write facts, not murder mystery fiction. This book is a true crime history. I did not intend to write this book like a murder mystery or a thriller. I am sure I write more like a newspaper reporter than a mystery writer. I probably included too many details and facts that some people might think get in the way.

There are a lot of stories in this world about bad men in prison and in society. There also are stories of bad men finding redemption. No one is advocating that they be released from prison. They are in prison on this earth for what they did on this earth. They will remain in prison. Their sins may be forgiven, but their crimes are not. Their release will come in another world.

Danny Edwards is in that category

There also are stories in this world of innocent people in prison, wrongfully convicted, and there are stories of innocent people being vindicated and released.

Nancy Rish belongs in that category.

Some people say that everyone in prison claims they're innocent. Not everyone. However, there definitely are innocent people in prison, and Illinois is well known for it. Jon Burge, the infamous Chicago police commander, ordered his officers to torture more than 200 suspects between 1972 and 1991 in order to force them into confessions. This was "business as usual" in Chicago. Burge was acquitted of brutality charges, but he was convicted of felony obstruction of justice and perjury and was sent to a federal prison. Dozens of people who went to prison based on confessions obtained through torture got new trials, acquittals, commutations or pardons, and the city has paid $500 million in legal fees and in settlements to victims.

Burge's reign of terror was part of the reason given by Governor Ryan for commuting all death sentences in 2003. A study showed 13 people on Death Row in Illinois had been wrongfully convicted. Ryan said "the system is broken." It isn't just the system regarding capital punishment; it is the entire justice system in Illinois. There is plenty of proof that there are innocent people in prison who got there by accidental or by deliberate means.

I wanted some personal background information to show that Danny Edwards is a human being who started out like anyone else before the root of all evil ruined his life. I did the same for Nancy Rish and my other subjects, finding information to humanize them, to make them more than one-dimensional characters. I tried to show that Stephen Small was more that a one-dimensional victim; he was a husband, a father, a friend, someone who contributed to the community. But none of the Small family or close friends agreed to speak to me. That is unfortunate. Those people who did give a brief comment said that Stephen Small was a fine man.

My book on Governor Small, *Len Small: Governor & Gangsters,* did not make me popular with the family or with "The Powers That Be" in Kankakee. Portraying Danny Edwards and Nancy Rish as human beings rather than as movie monsters also will not please them. Publishing a few of Danny Edwards' Bible studies, particularly his *Ahab and Stephen Small Factor,* no doubt will infuriate the Small family for giving light to what they will consider to be crazy. However, every bit of information, every detail of the lives and thoughts of Danny Edwards and anyone else connected to this case illuminates the entire story. Knowing what Danny Edwards believes about his reason for this tragedy is important. You don't have to like it.

In any event, I do not expect this book will get me an invitation to join the Kankakee Country Club. I do not expect to be invited to a party at Yurgine's.

I have never fit in with that crowd. My motivation is truth and justice, not a country club membership. That is how the story of Governor Small and the story of Stephen Small went from a few pages to an entire book that tells the whole story that no one else wanted to tell.

The purpose of this book is not to make Danny Edwards look good. The purpose of this book is not to make Nancy Rish look good. The purpose of this book is not to make Danny Edwards, Nancy Rish, Michael Ficaro, John Michela, Mitch Levitt, Scott Swaim or anyone else look bad. The purpose is to tell the story of this case, and to tell it as factually as I can ascertain from the record and from interviews.

Danny Edwards committed an unspeakable, despicable act. Randy Irps said the Danny Edwards he knew in high school was not the same Danny Edwards who committed this crime. The Danny Edwards I interviewed in 2013 and 2014 is not the same Danny Edwards who committed this crime. The difference is marijuana and cocaine, and what drugs does to a person. In a way, Danny Edwards, now known to the state of Illinois as N82122, is not in the penitentiary because of murder. The reason for a life sentence is drugs. It was marijuana and cocaine and the love of money that led to the murder. That is something for everyone who is using drugs to think about. That is something for everyone who thinks marijuana is harmless to think about.

Few people know any more about this case other than a wealthy man was kidnapped and buried alive, and a man and a woman are serving life sentences for this crime. There also are rumors without foundation. A lot of people know the rumors, but not the whole truth. Until now, no one was interested in finding the truth.

They believed the prosecution's argument that Nancy Rish "had to know." The truth is, the only thing she knew was to not ask questions. "You don't want to know" was the answer she got when she did ask. And after Danny pulled a gun and threatened to kill her and her son, she did not ask again.

Did the jury realize that all the forensic evidence -- fingerprints, hair, shoes and more -- exonerated Nancy Rish? Did this jury pay more attention to the dramatics and the allegations of the prosecutor than it did to the evidence and the testimony? The speed in which the jury returned indicates they did not deliberate or consider the testimony or the exhibits at all.

If the powers in Kankakee had used any sense of truth and justice, they would have used Nancy Rish as a witness in Danny Edwards' trial instead of putting her on trial for his crimes. They substituted vengeance for brains

The family and the powerful people in Kankakee can feel satisfaction that the guilty person, Danny Edwards, will spend the rest of his life in prison. That is settled. But the lynch mob mentality of some people for Nancy Rish is the kind you see in old Westerns.

It is one thing to feel good about winning a conviction when the defendant is obviously guilty.

It is something else to win a conviction when the defendant is not guilty, and to stick with it because one's pride and reputation is more important than another person's life.

The facts prove that Nancy Rish should be pardoned for a crime she did not commit. The only thing that can stop it is the political pressure from the powerful people in Kankakee and in the state.

It remains to be seen if money has more influence than truth.

It remains to be seen whether or not real justice will be done.

Not Kankakee justice and not Small justice.

Small justice is no justice.

INDEX

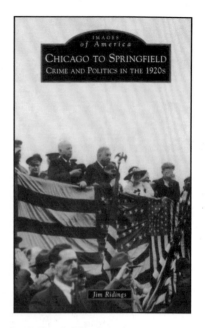

Further Suggested Reading

Len Small: Governors and Gangsters, by Jim Ridings (2009)

Chicago To Springfield: Crime and Politics in the 1920s, by Jim Ridings (2010)

Wild Kankakee, by Jim Ridings (2012)

Kankakee County Confidential, by Jim Ridings (coming in 2015)

One Hundred Percent Guilty: How an Insider Links the Death of Six Children to the Politics of Convicted Illinois Governor George Ryan, by Ed Hammer (2010)

The Man Who Emptied Death Row: Governor George Ryan and the Politics of Crime, by James L. Merriner (2008)

The Case of Frank L. Smith: A Study in Representative Government, by Carroll H. Wooddy, University of Chicago Press (1931)

Big Bill of Chicago, by Lloyd Wendt and Herman Kogan (1953)

The Dry and Lawless Years, by Judge John H. Lyle (1960)

Al Capone: Biography of a Self-Made Man, by Fred Pasley (1930)

Mr. Capone: The Real & Complete Story of Al Capone, by Robert J. Schoenberg (1992)

Capone, The Man and the Era, by Laurence Bergreen (1994)

Capone: The Life and World of Al Capone, by John Kobler (1971)

People of the State of Illinois vs. Len Small, 190-page book, a collection of seven attorneys' closing arguments to the jury (1922)